The Aurora Project

Counselling
People with Developmental Disabilities Who
Have Been Sexually Abused

By
Sheila Mansell & Dick Sobsey

Abuse and Disability Project
J.P Das Developmental Disabilities Centre
University of Alberta
Edmonton, Alberta
Canada

Developed with support from
The Joseph P. Kennedy, Jr. Foundation
&
Health Canada

D1712859

Library of Congress Number: 2001 130288

ISBN: 1-57256-016-9

1st Printing 2001

Printed in the United States of America

TABLE OF CONTENTS

Acknowledgments   7
Preface   9
Overview   11

Part 1: Introduction

---

1   Understanding the Challenges Associated with   15
     Sexual Abuse of People with Developmental
     Disabilities
     Definitions   15
     Definition of the problem   30
     Barriers to acknowledging abuse and developing
     therapy   35
     Adapting Therapy   40

Part 2: Patterns and Effects

---

2   Sexual Abuse Patterns and Heightened   69
     Risk for Sexual Abuse
     Research on patterns of sexual abuse   69

3   The Effects of Sexual Abuse on People   93
     with Developmental Disabilities
     Sexual abuse effects   93
     The trouble with coping   113
     Sexual Abuse Sequelae study   119

TABLE OF CONTENTS (cont)

Part 3: Individualizing Therapy

4	Individualizing Therapy: Client evaluation	133
	Distinctive therapy characteristics	133
	Evaluating the client	134
	The appropriateness of the Diagnostic and Statistical Manual	136
5	Individualizing Therapy: Communication issues	153
	The use of an interpreter	155
	Communication in adults with mild or moderate mental retardation	158
	Communication in people with severe or profound mental retardation	163
6	Individualizing Therapy: Modifications for Therapies	173
	Less verbally oriented therapies	174
	Specific therapy components	176

Part 4: Therapy Modalities

7	Family Systems, Disability Issues, and Therapy	197
	Lorraine Wilgosh & Sheila Mansell	
	Family systems conceptual framework	198
	Parent and sibling issues associated with disability	201

TABLE OF CONTENTS (cont)

8   Play Therapy with People who have   225
    Developmental Disabilities
    Claire Millar, Tansel Erdem, and Sheila Mansell
    Play   226
    The development of psychoanalytic
    play therapy   226
    The debate about the nature of play   229
    Growing interest in play therapy   233
    Play therapy for children with developmental
    disabilities   235

9   Assessment and Treatment of Individuals with   257
    Developmental Disabilities Who Have Been
    Sexually Victimized and Who Victimize Others:
    Rights in Treatment
    Dave Hingsburger
    The denial of sexuality   257
    Developing a hypothesis   260
    Developing a treatment plan   266
    Summary   274

References   275

ACKNOWLEDGMENTS

The authors of this book would like to thank the Joseph P. Kennedy, Jr. Foundation, Health and Welfare Canada, and the Social Sciences Humanities Research Council for their generous financial support for the Aurora Project. The Joseph P. Kennedy, Jr. Foundation provided major funding for this project. Health Canada provided additional support for the video production. The Social Sciences and Research Council of Canada has provided the University of Alberta Abuse and Disability Project with funding for our basic research on sexual abuse and disability that provided a foundation for the development of these materials. The opinions expressed in these materials are those of the authors and not necessarily those of the funding agencies.

We would also like to thank the many people who worked, wrote, and contributed their ideas to this project. Our appreciation and thanks go to Dr. Lorraine Wilgosh of the University of Alberta, Dave Hingsburger of I Contact Consultants, Dr. Tansel Erdem of the University of Alberta, and Claire Millar and Dr. Yona Lunsky of the Surrey Place Centre in Toronto for their significant contributions to this book. Our thanks also go to Dr. Madhavan Thuppal of the State University of New York at Stoney Brook, Dr. Nora Baladerian of the Abuse and Personal Rights Project in Culver City, California, Linda Page of the D.E.A.F. Connect Society in Edmonton, Debbie Reid of the Calgary S.C.O.P.E. Society, Calgary, Alberta, Bill Angus of the Community Inclusion Support Team in Calgary, and Cathy Marcotte of Community Behavioral Services, Edmonton, Alberta for their ideas, input, and feedback throughout the development of this book. Thanks to Dr. Ann Poindexter for her support of this project. Thanks also to Dr. Rosemary Moskal for the use of her dissertation data and Don Wells for his prompt, professional editorial work. Also, we would like to thank our spouses and families for their patience and support during the development and writing of this book and the making of the video.

Many ideas and practices presented in this book are drawn from the work of the pioneers in the field who challenged traditional biases in therapy and believed that people with developmental disabilities were suffering from the effects of sexual abuse and could both participate and benefit from therapy that was appropriately adapted. Their labors represent a significant contribution and impetus for this book.

This book is dedicated to people with developmental disabilities who have been sexually abused and the very patient group of clients who continue to teach us about therapy and themselves.

PREFACE

The Aurora Project was conceived and developed because of the growing body of research that demonstrates that people with developmental disabilities are at greater risk for sexual abuse and that appropriately adapted therapy services for people with developmental disabilities who have been sexually abused are rarely available. The Aurora Project training materials consist of two parts: (1) this book and (2) Alone in a Crowd, an introductory videotape for counselors of people with developmental disabilities who have been sexually abused. These materials may be used independently or in combination. The videotape is intended to introduce some of the basic issues and approaches to counseling people with developmental disabilities who have been abused.

This book is intended as a text and resource material to assist counselors to work with sexual abuse victims with disabilities. It is based on an integration of recent research and formal and informal input from practicing counselors. Their input was provided through a survey of counselors working with people with developmental disabilities who have been sexually abused, feedback from pilot training sessions, and evaluations of draft materials. This book is designed for professionals with counseling training or disability-related training who are interested in providing therapy to people with developmental disabilities who have been sexually abused. It does not attempt to provide basic training in counseling. Those requiring that training should obtain it and supervision from appropriately qualified sources. In addition, this book primarily deals with issues in counseling clients with a developmental disabilities who have been sexually abused. It does not focus on the investigation of sexual abuse of people with developmental disabilities. Readers interested in investigative aspects of sexual abuse of people with disabilities should consult some of the excellent sources on that subject (e.g., Baladerian, 1985, 1992; Glasgow, 1993; Valenti-Hein & Schwartz, 1994).

In compiling this book, we have attempted to be eclectic, drawing on a wide range of counselling approaches and techniques. An eclectic approach was selected for two reasons. First, counselors individual-izing their approaches to specific clients need the broadest possible array of strategies and techniques to draw on. Second, most counse-lors currently working with people with developmental disabilities who have been sexually abused indicated that they found an eclectic approach to be useful. Finally, by aiming this book toward counse-lors using a broad spectrum of approaches, we hope that those choos-ing a specific approach (e.g., behavioral, feminist, psychoanalytic, systems theory) will find at least some of the material in this book useful in their work.

This book contains information from current research on patterns of sexual abuse of people with developmental disabilities and the ef-fects that sexual abuse has on them. In preparing this material, we have reviewed the literature on various therapy approaches, effects of sexual abuse, therapy accommodations for people with develop-mental disabilities, and related psychological issues. We have out-lined the relevant issues involved in providing therapy that is appro-priately adapted to meet clients' varied communicative, cognitive, psychological, and developmental needs, and suggest how to indi-vidualize treatment to address clients' specific treatment goals. Nev-ertheless, since counselling people with developmental disabilities is a relatively new field and there has been little systematic evalua-tion of therapy adaptations for people with developmental disabili-ties, the contents and recommendations of the Aurora Project Train-ing materials should be considered provisional. We hope that research and clinical experience will help to validate some of the content of these materials and to guide us to new and better materials in the future.

Overview of this Book

The book is divided into four parts and further subdivided into nine chapters: Part 1 includes the first Chapter and provides background on professionals' denial of and misconceptions about the sexual abuse of people with developmental disabilities. In addition, Chapter 1 includes results from a survey of professionals involved in this practice and discussions pertaining to adapted therapy, various therapist issues, and associated implications for therapy practice.

Part 2 covers the patterns and effects of sexual abuse as experienced by people with developmental disabilities using results drawn from research conducted by the University of Alberta Abuse and Disability Project. Chapter 2, the sexual abuse patterns chapter, uses a developmental perspective to examine the social and cultural circumstances that contribute to heightened vulnerability to abuse experienced by people with developmental disabilities and associated disability related psychological issues. Chapter 3, the sexual abuse effects chapter, provides a brief review of sexual abuse sequelae research. It presents recent research dealing with the sexual abuse sequelae noted in people with developmental disabilities and integrates this research with psychosocial issues associated with having a developmental disability.

Part 3 includes Chapters 4, 5, and 6 and primarily focuses on examining the process of individualizing treatment for clients with developmental disabilities and outlines the distinctive components of therapy that are used to address the effects of sexual abuse. Distinctive components of therapy include working and consulting with the client's sometimes extensive network of caregivers and evaluating the client's developmental level and communication and comprehension abilities. Additional distinctions may include psychoeducational components dealing with sexuality and social skills, sexual abuse, self-protection, affective vocabulary, and some behaviorally oriented approaches for secondary behavior problems. Part 3 also presents examples of adapted therapy for people with developmental disabilities who have been sexually abused.

Part 4 includes Chapters 7, 8, and 9 and covers therapy modalities that include family, play, and specialized therapy and assessment for the treatment of sexualized behaviors.

Part I
Introduction

•• **1**

Understanding the Challenges Associated with the Sexual Abuse of People with Developmental Disabilities

In this first chapter before proceeding with a discussion of the problem of sexual abuse of people with developmental disabilities, treatment considerations, and the results of an international survey of professionals engaged in this work, it will be helpful to clarify some terms used in this book. The definitions presented here are not the only, or necessarily the best, definitions of these terms, but they reflect the authors' use of terms throughout this book and represent a useful set of concepts for addressing the content of this book. It is important for readers to remember that there is considerable variability in the definitions used by researchers and clinicians. Without knowing the definitions used in a particular situation, it may be difficult to interpret the information presented and particularly problematic to compare that information with information from other sources that may be using different definitions. For example, there are many different clinical, legal, and research definitions of child sexual abuse. Estimates of the incidence of child sexual abuse vary widely, and much of the variability is related to how child sexual abuse is defined.

DEFINITIONS

The definitions used in this book are intended for use in counseling rather than research or law enforcement. The definitions emphasize the subjective effects on the individuals who are abused rather than the objective criteria of the experiences. Subjective effects often are more relevant to counseling because it is the subjective effects that are most often the focus of treatment. However, it is important for counselors to remember that they may need to consider and adopt other definitions if they become involved in the research or law enforcement aspects of abuse.

Sexual abuse

Although sexual abuse is a common topic of conversation in contemporary society and there seems to be a general consensus on what we mean by sexual abuse, there appears to be no precise definition that is shared by those who address this topic.

In this book and related training materials, *sexual abuse* includes: (1) child sexual abuse or (2) sexual assault. Each of these terms is defined below.

Sexual abuse includes any sexual interaction that results in harm or is likely to result in harm to an individual. It typically involves the use of physical force, authority, coercion, misrepresentation, or a combination of these factors. Frequently, sexual abuse is associated with other forms of abuse (i.e., physical abuse and/or psychological abuse), and when this situation occurs, the effects of sexual abuse cannot be meaningfully assessed unless the effects of these other forms of abuse are also assessed.

Child sexual abuse

According to Browne and Finkelhor (1986), child sexual abuse includes two types of interactions: forced or coerced sexual behavior imposed on a child and sexual activity between a child and a much older person, whether or not there is obvious coercion. Child sexual abuse covers a wide a range of acts: incest, sexual assault, fondling of genital areas, exposure to indecent acts, sexual rituals, or involvement in pornography. Researchers and law enforcement agencies often require highly structured definitions to objectively determine which cases to include or exclude for their particular study. Sobsey (1994) defines child sexual abuse as any sexual interaction between an adult and a child age 12 years or younger or any sexual interaction involving an adolescent between the ages of 13 and 17 years in which there is a clear indication of harm, coercion, or the exploitation of a relationship of authority or trust.

Some definitions include nudity within the family or the use of sexually explicit language. Other definitions do not. Who is right? The answer depends on a great number of interpersonal and contextual factors. What may be more important, however, is that if an individual experiences the behavior as threatening, intrusive, or traumatic that individual may need support and counseling. Similarly, under the law in some places, a 12-year-old child may give consent to sex with a 15-year-old, but a 14-year-old may not consent to sex with a 16-year-old. As a result, the former situation would not be automatically considered to be sexual abuse, while the latter situation would be considered sexual abuse.

For the purpose of these training materials, precise and objective criteria are not necessary. For the counselor, the effect on the individual and the systems in which they live are typically much more important than the actual event.

In this book and related training materials, *child sexual abuse* includes: (1) all sexual interaction between children and adults or much older children; (2) sexual interaction between children when a child's participation is secured through physical force, coercion, authority, or misrepresentation rather than mutual consent; (3) sexual interactions involving children or adolescents that result in psychological or physical trauma.

Sexual assault
Like child sexual abuse, the most significant aspect of sexual assault for counselors is the subjective effect on the person who has been assaulted rather than any objective definition.

In this book and related materials, *sexual assault* includes any sexual interaction that lacks voluntary consent of both (or all) parties involved.

Therapy
As used here, *therapy* is not intended in its medical sense, that is, a "cure" for some pathological condition. Not all abuse victims de-

velop pathological conditions. Pathologizing victimization risks increasing the harm done and encourages individuals to assume a passive role and adopt negative expectations regarding their own resources for coping. The conceptualization of abused people as "sick" may also add to the stigma associated with victimization and threaten the individual's self-esteem. Therapy should normally be done *with* a client and not *to* a client. This distinction may be particularly critical in treatment.

As used in this book and related training materials, *therapy* refers to counseling, education, support, and a variety of other interventions intended to enhance the individual's sense of well-being and address any specific problems associated with previous experiences of abuse.

Nevertheless, people with developmental disabilities appear to have a heightened risk for the full range of psychopathologies (Borthwick-Duffy, 1994). Consequently, therapists need to appreciate that there can be a wide range of biological, social, and psychological consequences that can be addressed with the assistance of different disciplines using differing interventions including counseling and pharmacotherapy.

Terminology and Disability

This section provides considerable discussion of terminology commonly used to describe people with developmental disabilities. This discussion is provided for several purposes. The first purpose is to explain the terms that we use. The second purpose is to identify some current issues related to the use of terminology. The third purpose is to make some suggestions about how counselors use these terms. In making these suggestions, we recognize that there is no single standard that can be applied. Each individual must determine her or his unique style. In presenting this discussion, we do not wish to overemphasize the importance of terminology or to contribute to an atmosphere of "political correctness." Nevertheless, the way that words are used is an essential aspect of counseling and issues surrounding the use of terminology and developmental disabilities are important ones.

The terminology used to describe various types and degrees of mental disabilities has always been subject to change (Sandieson, 1998). Earlier terminology used to describe mental retardation is often considered to have been denigrating by today's standards. In more recent years, there have been rapid changes in terminology. Increasingly, current parlance in the disability field has attempted to reflect a more respectful, person- and ability-centered perspective.

Terminology also varies across geographic boundaries. For example, in North America, the terms developmental disability, intellectual or cognitive disability, and mental retardation sometimes refer to the same condition that in the United Kingdom is referred as mental handicap, learning difficulty, and learning disability (Fernald, 1995). Occasionally, there is confusion between professionals from different nations when they use the same terms with different meanings. In North America, the term learning disabilities refers to specific learning problems in areas such as reading, writing, or math that are not associated with general deficits in intellectual ability. By contrast, in the United Kingdom, learning disabilities clearly refer to with general deficits in intellectual ability. In this book, the authors use North American terminology.

The use of labels and categories to describe disabilities is a controversial topic (Hastings, 1994). In spite of this controversy, language is an important consideration for anyone who is counseling or providing other services to people with disabilities. Counselors need to use language that is respectful, precise, and responsive to the preference of clients and other professionals. In addition, counselors should avoid jargon and unnecessarily complex language. Finally, counselors must be careful in interpreting labels and categories. Labels and categories can provide useful information, but they can also be misleading. It is sometimes difficult to meet all five of these criteria at the same time, but it is essential to consider them at all times.

Several problems have been noted with the use of *mental retardation* as a descriptor and with the use of categories such as mild, moderate, severe, and profound. The term *mental retardation* has been associated with a history of discrimination and stigmatization. For example, the eugenics movement that dominated much of the first half of the twentieth century and continued as a significant force in the second half of that century characterized "the mentally retarded" as a dangerous, socially destructive class that must be eliminated. The term *retard* continues to be used as a general slur in North America. As a result of this history, many people, often including individuals with developmental disabilities and their advocates, object to the use of the term *mental retardation.* In some places, the term has been abandoned completely in favor of other terms considered to be less stigmatizing. In the United Kingdom, for example, terms such as *learning disabilities, learning difficulties,* and *intellectual disabilities* are used to refer to the condition that would be called mental retardation in the United States. Using the term mental retardation in the United Kingdom is typically considered both anachronistic and rude, much as using terms like *idiot, moron,* or *imbecile* would be in the United States.

Some people suggest, however, that it is not the term but the attitude associated with it that is stigmatizing. These individuals argue that continuing to change terminology to avoid stigmatization only adds to the problem by spreading the stigma to new terms. Jokes about such euphemisms as *mentally challenged* seem to support this view. Those supporting this view suggest that rather than abandoning stigmatized terms that we demand that they be used respectfully.

Adding to this controversy is the issue of person-first language. Person-first language refers to the practice of using disability descriptors after rather than before words used to designate the person. For example, in person-first language, we say *a woman with a disability or a boy with mental retardation.* We would not say *a disabled woman or a mentally retarded boy.* The goal of person-first language is to take away the emphasis of the descriptor and place it on the whole person. Person-first language, however, has also been criticized. For example, one woman was furious when an editor changed her description of herself from a *disabled woman* to a *woman with a disability.* She indicated that she is proud of being a disabled woman, being a disabled woman was a very important part of her identity, and being a disabled woman was relevant to the reason that she was writing. She did not want it trivialized. In her view, de-emphasizing it was equivalent to saying that there was something wrong with it.

This point of view needs to be recognized for two reasons. First, people can and should be encouraged to take pride in all aspects of their identity. People can be proud and choose to emphasize their gender, race, religious background; why not their disability status? Second, as stated above, our use of language needs to be responsive to the people to whom and about whom we are speaking or writing. If someone chooses to use or avoid particular language for talking about himself or herself, why should we deny them that choice? As a counselor, it may be possible to imagine a situation in which a client might use language in a self-destructive way perpetuating a damaged identity and a counselor would likely intervene to change that self-image.

In addition, the relevancy of the disability descriptor is important to consider in our language. One of the problems that person-first language was intended to overcome was excessive focus on the individuals disability. There was often a tendency to include descriptors like *retarded,* when they were irrelevant to the topic being discussed. The woman who asserted her right to being called a disabled woman did so in the context of an article that she had written dealing with disability issues. If she had written an article about gardening or Shakespeare, her disability status might have been irrelevant.

Finally, the use of complex euphemisms to take the place of terms that we are trying to avoid sometimes reveals an underlying discomfort with the subject. They also complicate our language and this is an important consideration when working with clients who have difficulty with complex language.

We recommend the use of person-first language as a general rule in formal reports and professional writing because it is typically accepted as a respectful way of writing about people with disabilities. When conversing with clients, their families, and other professionals, we recommend using whatever language conveys respect and reflects their choices or comfort zone (Hastings, 1994).

"Persons with disabilities" or "persons with mental retardation" are phrases that have been frequently used in professional literature. This looks like a grammatical error, since normally the plural of *person* is *people*. In most cases, the use of *persons* is simply professional jargon and the word *people* should be used. When emphasizing the unique nature of each person in the group, the term *individuals* may be a good choice. For example, one might say, "*individuals* with disabilities have a right to make their own decisions." The use of *persons* is correct only when referring to special definitions of person used in law or ethics. The status of person is associated with the rights and responsibilities under the law. At some times and in some governments, various groups including slaves, women, and people with disabilities have not been treated as persons under the law. Personhood confers rights and responsibilities. In legal and ethical discussions about the legal status of individuals with disabilities, it is appropriate and relevant to refer to them as persons, alluding to the fact that they have or should have the full rights of citizenship. Outside of such discussions, however, the use of persons simply reflects inappropriate generalization of legal terminology into professional jargon.

An even more complex variation on person-first language is to refer to people "who are labeled as…" or "people diagnosed as mentally retarded." These expressions generally derive from the concern over whether the condition is biologically determined or socially constructed. Social construction theory suggests that people are "mentally retarded" largely because we have constructed a view of the world that sees them that way (Allen & Allen, 1995). While such a notion may seem radical, there is considerable empirical support for this view when one considers that definitions and prevalence of mental retardation vary across cultures. Furthermore, significant numbers of children in our own culture are not viewed as mentally retarded before or after their school years, but are considered to be so in the school setting (Smith, 1997). Our current definition of mental retardation reflects a compromise between biological determinism and social construction.

We recommend avoiding such complex phrases as "who is labeled as mentally retarded" unless there is a particular reason for emphasizing the labeling process. For example, it may be important to focus on the diagnostic process if that process is being called into question. For example, "Mary, who was diagnosed as mildly mentally retarded after being given an IQ test in grade three, functions normally at home, work, and the community as an adult."

Another trend in contemporary language has been to simply avoid using disability terminology. Terms like *resident, client,* or *consumer* focus on the individual's relationship to the service system rather than disability status. This use of language is helpful when used appropriately, but problematic when it is generalized beyond the appropriate context. For example, some agencies use the word *consumer* to refer to any individual with a developmental disability in any situation. When discussing services that the agency renders to *consumers* of those services, this term is appropriate. When discussing anything else, the term is inappropriate and might be seen as disrespectful. All of us are consumers of various goods and services, but we are much more than that. Most of us also would like to be respected for what we contribute to society, not simply what we consume. It is ironic that in the 1930s when the Nazi's took power, the term that they used to vilify people with disabilities can be translated as *consumers* or *eaters* (Burleigh, 1994). They used this to justify the mass extermination of people with developmental disabilities, who were portrayed as consuming goods and services but not contributing to society. We suggest using these terms when appropriate to the context, but not generalizing them beyond those contexts.

The use of generic terms has often been used to avoid disability labels. Identifying people as *facing challenges or having special needs* avoids the use of stigmatizing terminology, but creates ambiguity. For example, if we refer to some of our counseling clients as having special needs, our meaning is unclear. In the broadest sense, all clients have special needs because all people have special needs. Certainly, some individuals may have greater counseling needs than others and some have more specialized or individual needs than others do. Those with greater or more specialized needs, however, are not necessarily those who have disabilities. Therefore, when referring to anyone who has special needs or who faces challenges, these terms are appropriate. If these terms are being used simply as a way of avoiding more direct disability labels, they are simply euphemisms to be avoided.

A number of terms have been used been used to describe the severity of mental retardation. These terms are described below and are also controversial. On the positive side of the argument, some disabilities are more severe than others, and the severity of mental retardation does have some implications for the appropriateness of various approaches to counseling. On the negative side, the use of categories, especially those based solely on IQ scores, may give a false impression of precision and often have provided a rationale for withholding services that might have proven useful. Since severity categories are generally unidimensional, a measure of severity that does not consider sensory or physical disabilities can be very misleading. For example, an individual with moderate mental retardation who is also blind and has cerebral palsy is affected by the interaction of all these conditions.

Because these categories of severity are commonly used, we have included them here. They can be useful in getting a rough picture of what to expect from a new client, however, counselors must be careful not to be blinded by those expectations. Some of the general patterns associated with various levels of severity can be useful in forming hypotheses about individuals' lives and experiences, however, such hypotheses are not always correct and should be considered in light of other information. Counselors must be cautious not to misinterpret or over-interpret what they read or hear and should also guard against others misinterpreting what they say or hear. Two strategies for doing this are providing adequate explanation and asking those who read or hear them how they interpret the message.

Before providing a more specific discussion of developmental disability terminology, it may be useful to review six general principles for the use of language and terminology. In summary, each counselor must determine his or her own preferences in use of language. The counselor should consider six principles in use of terminology:

1. Be respectful.
2. Be precise.
3. Consider the preferences of the people who you are talking to and talking about.
4. Avoid jargon and unnecessary complexity.
5. Be careful not to be misled by labels and categories that have limited value.
6. Be cognizant of how others might interpret (or misinterpret) what you write or say.

Developmental disabilities and mental retardation

Developmental disability refers to a group of neurological deficits that cause impaired functioning in areas such as intelligence, motor abilities, and personal-social interaction and are frequently attributed to mental retardation, autism, cerebral palsy, epilepsy, and other conditions. Mental retardation, as defined by the American Association of Mental Retardation (Luckasson, Coulter, Polloway, Reiss, Schalock, Snell, Spitalnik, & Stark, 1992), refers to a substantial limitation in present functioning. Mental retardation manifests itself before age 22, and it is characterized by significantly subaverage intellectual functioning (IQ < average, -2 standard deviations), existing concurrently with related limitations in two or more of the following adaptive skill areas: communication, self-care, home living, social skills, community use, self-direction, health and safety, functional academics, leisure, and work. The 1983 AAMR definition (Grossman, 1983) included categories indicating severity (i.e., Mild, Moderate, Severe, and Profound) listed in Table 1.1. This most recent AAMR definition (Luckasson et al., 1992), however, does not include the various levels of severity of mental retardation from the 1983 definition; instead, it refers to assessing strengths and weakness, levels of assistance required, and community support. The definition of mental retardation adopted by the American Psychiatric Association's Diagnostic and Statistical Manual of Mental Disorders - Fourth Edition (DSM-IV) (1994) shares the 1983 AAMR definition's use of categories indicating level of severity.

Table 1.1 1983 Categories (Grossman, 1983)

Category	IQ Range	Description
Borderline	around 70-85	The person may have minor difficulties in school or work.
Mild Mental Retardation	around 54-69	The person uses language reasonably well, has poor school performance, and may master skills required for independent living.
Moderate Mental Retardation	around 36-53	The person has limited use of language skills. Self-care skills may be limited, and the person often needs support or supervision into adulthood but can learn skills necessary for independent living and may perform many of these skills with little assistance.
Severe Mental Retardation	around 20-35	The person generally develops only a minimal use of language and typically requires ongoing assistance in self-care skills.
Profound Mental Retardation	around 0-19	The person may acquire little or no language and usually requires supervision and assistance with all essential functions.

The milder that mental retardation is the greater the prevalence, but larger than expected numbers appear in the severe and profound categories, suggesting a bimodal population (i.e., an approximately normal distribution of intelligence with a second, smaller superimposed distribution in the severe and profound range of children with disabilities caused by injury or illness). While the categories were commonly used in an earlier AAMR definition of mental retardation (Grossman, 1983) and are still part of the definition used by the American Psychiatric Association (1994) they represent types and rarely fit real cases, which are highly individualized. This terminology describing varying degrees of mental retardation, however, is still widely used in many settings. Mental retardation refers to an extremely heterogeneous group of people whose abilities and limitations vary widely (Gorman-Smith & Matson, 1992). A person's designation as either mild, moderate, severe, or profound suggests a wide continuum of functioning in communication, social adaptation, and cognitive skills that present important considerations in the provision of therapy.

Mild mental retardation
People who are functioning in the mild range of mental retardation learn at a slower rate than exhibited by children who are in the normal range of functioning, but in the mild range, there is a wide diversity in academic and behavioral performance. Children in preschool evidence small delays but are often not identified until after school entry following academic problems or behavioral problems (Mulick & Jacobson, 1996). Usually, people in this range of functioning will demonstrate low academic skills that will limit their vocational opportunities, however, they can develop and employ adequate social, personal, and communication skills. As adults, they can function well in a variety of contexts and may attain varying degrees of self-sufficiency and independence in the community (Drew, Logan, & Hardman, 1992; Mulick & Jacobson, 1996).

Moderate mental retardation
Comparatively, people functioning in the moderate range of mental retardation have more limited intellectual abilities, greater difficulties working with abstract ideas, and more problems generalizing learning to unfamiliar situations than people who function in the mild range. Individuals have notable delays with early developmental milestones, are likely to be identified during preschool years, and will demonstrate more noticeable delays in their language, motor, self-care, and social development (Mulick & Jacobson, 1996). Often, people functioning in the moderate range are not ready for much academic work until they reach their early teens and may exhibit clear deficits in adaptive behavior, problems with interpersonal relation-

ships, and have difficulties with social concepts, functional language, and communication. As adults, they may function in a variety of unskilled type vocational settings, however, lifestyle supports and more support and supervision are typically required in these vocational settings.

Severe mental retardation

People who are functioning within the severe and profound ranges of mental retardation often have severe physical, motor, and sensory handicaps that can include impaired vision, hearing, speech, and motor coordination (Switzky, Haywood, & Rotatori, 1982). Some people may have difficulty with maintaining an upright posture, interacting with the environment, and feeding and toileting skills. People in the severe range of mental retardation are typically identified during infancy because of substantial developmental delays and the heightened tendency to evidence biological anomalies. Key milestones such as standing, walking, toilet training may be markedly delayed by several years and there may be heightened risk for motor disorders and epilepsy (Mulick & Jacobson, 1996). People may have additional disabilities that may compound their developmental disability. As the severity of mental retardation increases, the prevalence of these additional disabilities increases. People in the severe range may also have behavioral disorders and inadequate social skills. Adults may have limited academic skills but may be able to learn important self-help skills with appropriate supervision. They may function well in more sheltered environments and require additional support in daily living.

Profound mental retardation

Similar to individuals whose functioning falls within the severe range people functioning in the profound range of mental retardation have the tendency to display marked development impairment along with biological anomalies. Children may have a greater mortality rate than those in the severe range and have additional disabilities that further compound the considerable difficulties they experience with their developmental disability. Individuals functioning within the profound range have a higher incidence of delayed puberty, institutionaliza-

tion, seizure disorders, enuresis and encopresis, poor communication, pica and rumination, self-injurious behavior, and lack of socialization skills (Switsky, Haywood, & Rotatori, 1982). Also, individuals who are functioning within this range will have variable abilities
and may be viewed as more or less high functioning depending on
the degree to which a person possess some ambulation, communication, and self-help skills and the degree to which a person has more
significant difficulties with adaptive behavior or tends to be medi-
cally fragile (Switsky, Haywood, & Rotatori, 1982). Individuals functioning in profound range do not typically develop functional vocational, social, or community use skills, however, some activities may
be performed with ongoing supervision and social responsiveness to
stimulation varies widely (Mulick & Jacobson, 1996).

Dual diagnosis

As mentioned, it is not the authors' intention to pathologize the psychological effects of victimization. Yet it is important to consider
that other psychological problems may be present. These psychological problems may or may not be a direct consequence of the sexual
abuse but will, nevertheless, need to be taken into consideration when
providing therapy. Dual diagnosis refers to the co-occurrence of mental
disorders with mental retardation. This term is used to describe people
with mild, moderate, severe, and profound mental retardation who
have a wide range of diverse psychiatric conditions (Reiss, 1993).
Mental disorders are defined by the DSM-IV as clinically significant
behavioral or psychological syndromes or patterns that occur in an
individual and are associated with present distress (e.g., a painful
symptom), disability (i.e., impairment in one or more important areas of functioning), or with a significantly increased risk of suffering, death, pain, disability, or an important loss of freedom (American Psychiatric Association, 1994, p. xxi).

Since the fairly recent professional acknowledgment of dual diagnosis, several different studies have been conducted to estimate the
prevalence of mental disorders in people with mental retardation.
For example, Rutter, Tizard, Yule, Graham, and Whitmore (1976)
found that psychiatric disturbances were 3 to 4 times more prevalent

in children with mental retardation than in children without mental retardation. Koller, Richardson, Katz, and McLaren (1982) found psychiatric disturbances were 4 to 5 times more prevalent in children with mental retardation than in children without mental retardation, and moderate to severe psychiatric disturbances were 7 times more prevalent in persons with mental retardation. These varying estimates are not easily reconciled as studies are frequently not comparable, and the wide variability in estimates may be due to the characteristics of the studies, for example, differing diagnoses and definitions, sample selection, age, level of mental retardation, type of psychiatric disorder, and evaluation method (Borthwick-Duffy, 1994; MacLean, 1993). (See Borthwick-Duffy [1994] for a discussion of prevalence studies). Despite the differences in estimates, these studies show that people with developmental disabilities are more likely to suffer from emotional disturbances than members of the general population (Matson & Barrett, 1982). In addition, people with mental retardation are likely to experience the same range of psychopathology found in the general population (Eaton & Menolascino, 1982).

Therapy accommodations or adaptations
People with developmental disabilities encompass an extremely heterogeneous group with a wide range of abilities. As when working with any client, a therapist needs to recognize and work with the unique qualities of the person with a developmental disability. This process occurs primarily through individualizing therapy so that it is appropriately adapted to fit the person's circumstances and special needs. Accommodations or adaptations refer to any changes that a therapist might make to ensure that the therapy is appropriate for the client's developmental level and his or her communication, comprehension, and language abilities.

DEFINITION OF THE PROBLEM
Acknowledgment of sexual assault and child sexual abuse
Research that addressed the sexual abuse of children and sexual assault of women began during the late 1970s when the feminist movement drew the attention of both public and professional groups to the social problems of sexual assault and child sexual abuse. This height-

ened awareness in the professional community resulted in a proliferation of research. Over the years, considerable knowledge has been acquired through research that examined the incidence of child sexual abuse (Briere, 1989; Russell, 1983), effects or sequelae (Browne & Finkelhor, 1986; Herman, Russell, & Trocki, 1986), and therapy or treatment strategies for adults, children, and their families (Briere, 1992; Courtois, 1989; Everstine & Everstine, 1989; Friedrich, 1990; Gil, 1991, 1988; James, 1989; Sgroi, 1982; Simonds, 1994; Trepper & Barrett, 1989). Increasingly, new aspects of the sexual abuse experience are being uncovered, and new groups of sexually abused victims, whose experience has previously been unexamined by researchers, are coming forward. People with disabilities constitute one such group whose experiences of child sexual abuse and sexual assault have recently become an area of study.

Historically, the mental health needs of people with mental retardation have been neglected and misunderstood by professionals. In more recent years, in part due to the deinstitutionalization movement in both North America and Europe, the mental health needs of people with mental retardation have become a subject of considerable interest. This growing interest is evident in the growing number of professional organizations that deal with the mental health needs of people with mental retardation. These include: the National Association for the Dually Diagnosed in the United States, the Mental Retardation/ Developmental Disability Division of the American Psychological Association, the Mental Health Services (SIG) of the American Association for Mental Retardation (AAMR), and community-based advocacy groups in North America and Europe.

This interest is also evident in the increase in research that deals with the prevalence of mental disorders in this population and the number of publications that address diagnostic and treatment issues. Much of this activity began in the early 1980s and coincided with the growing research literature concerning the development of treatments for child sexual abuse. These events set the stage for subsequent research concerning the sexual abuse of people with mental retardation.

People with developmental disabilities

There is a long history of abuse and neglect for people with developmental disabilities (Sobsey, 1994), and in the past few decades, there has been a growth in research conducted to examine this problem (Sobsey, Gray, Wells, Pyper, & Reimer-Heck, 1991; Sobsey, Wells, Lucardie, & Mansell, 1995). A considerable amount of research suggests that both adults and children with developmental disabilities have a heightened risk for sexual abuse (Ammerman, Van Hasselt, Hersen, McGonigle, & Lubetsky, 1989; Crosse, Kaye, & Ratnofsky, 1993; Garbarino, Brookhouser, & Authier, 1987; Senn, 1988; Stimpson & Best, 1991; Turk & Brown, 1992). An incidence study based on nationally representative samples conducted in the United States indicates that children with disabilities have a risk for maltreatment that is 1.7 times higher and a risk for sexual abuse that is 1.8 times higher than for children without disabilities (Crosse et al., 1993). Sullivan and Knutson (1994) reported mental retardation in 6.2% of their sample of 2845 abused children, but only in 1.3% of their control group of 880 nonabused children. Thus, abused children were 4.8 times as likely to be mentally retarded. Of all disabilities present in their sample, only "behavior disorders" exceeded mental retardation in the strength of association with sexual abuse. Mental retardation was the most frequent disability associated with neglect and the third most frequent disability associated with physical abuse. These findings raise concerns among both professionals and family members about the vulnerability of people with disabilities to sexual abuse. Related concerns involve the emotional and behavioral effects of sexual abuse, the availability and appropriateness of therapy to address these effects, and the development of potential strategies to help prevent or reduce this risk.

At this time, research describing sexual abuse as it affects people with developmental disabilities is relatively rare (Cruz, Price-Williams, & Andron, 1988; Hyman, 1993; Ryan, 1992; Sinason, 1986; Tharinger, Horton, & Millea, 1990; Westcott, 1993), and little is known about the specific effects of sexual abuse in people with developmental disabilities. Some researchers suggest that sexual abuse sequelae are similar to these documented in the general population, and the effects may include dissociative states, emotional withdrawal, and Post Traumatic Stress Disorder (Ryan, 1992). Other researchers suggest that the abuse sequelae are complicated by additional coping difficulties and disability related issues (Burke & Bedard, 1994, 1995; Cruz, et al., 1988). Other researchers suggest that trauma may exacerbate physical and cognitive disabilities (Bowers Andrews & Veronen, 1993) or may produce greater behavioral difficulties (Dunne & Power, 1990). The effects range from minor to very severe and appear to have the same variability found in the general population (Gorman-Smith & Matson, 1992). Despite the heightened risk for sexual abuse and the presence of sexual abuse sequelae, therapy is often inaccessible, unavailable, or inappropriately adapted to meet the special needs of people with developmental disabilities (Mansell, Sobsey, & Calder, 1992).

A variety of attitudinal and professional barriers prevented the acknowledgment of the sexual abuse of people with developmental disabilities and the development of appropriate treatment. The mental health needs of people with mental retardation frequently have been misunderstood. It is also notable that mental retardation may cause psychological disturbances to present in atypical ways. Sovner (1986) noted four pathoplastic factors including *intellectual distortion, cognitive disintegration, psychosocial masking,* and *baseline exaggeration,* which can distort the presentation of mental disorders and significantly complicate diagnosis. Often, behavioral disturbances have been attributed to either the impaired development associated with mental retardation, behavioral or learning problems, or have been viewed as inherent qualities of mental retardation. Attributing behavioral disturbances or psychological problems to mental retardation is exemplified by diagnostic overshadowing, a form of clinical bias in which professionals are less likely to diagnose psychopathology or provide a diagnosis of lesser severity when people are identified as having mental retardation (Levitan & Reiss, 1983; Reiss, 1994a). Behavioral overshadowing refers to the tendency to identify psychopathology as learned behavior while failing to recognize it as an indication of mental illness (Lowry, 1997). In diagnostic overshadowing the clinician assumes that the person's intellectual disability is the root of the problem whereas in behavioral overshadowing the clinician assumes that the psychopathology is shaped and maintained by the person's environment regardless of the person's intellectual capacity (Lowry, 1997). Also, the belief that people with mental retardation are immune to mental disorders has contributed to the neglect of their mental health needs. Some professionals believe that people with developmental disabilities do not possess an inner psychological life and, therefore, are devoid of emotional difficulties and unable to participate in or benefit from therapy. It may be helpful at this point to present some of the more commonly held misconceptions about sexual abuse, developmental disability, and therapy.

Table 1.2 Common Misconceptions about Sexual Abuse, Developmental Disability, and Therapy

- People with developmental disabilities are asexual and unattractive and, therefore, cannot be sexually abused.
- If a person with a developmental disability exhibits acting out behaviors or emotional problems, these are a product of the disability and cannot be treated with conventional therapy.
- People with developmental disabilities are sexually deviant, and they cannot control their inappropriate sexual behaviors.
- A person with a developmental disability cannot learn or achieve insight and, therefore, is a poor candidate for therapy. Also, they cannot learn to protect themselves against sexual abuse.
- People with developmental disabilities are eternal children who are child-like and do not require sexuality education.
- People with developmental disabilities are insensitive to pain, and since they do not understand what has happened to them, they do not suffer emotionally.
- People with developmental disabilities are ill-equipped to deal with interpersonal stresses and have difficulty controlling or delaying emotional expression or recognizing the causes and consequences of their behavior. They are too fragile to participate in therapy.

BARRIERS TO ACKNOWLEDGMENT OF ABUSE AND THE DEVELOPMENT OF THERAPY

Considerable research has been done to address both the short- and long-term effects of child sexual abuse and sexual assault, and for several years, a variety of sexual abuse treatment approaches have been available for the general population. For people with developmental disabilities, however, there has been a prolonged denial of their sexual abuse, inadequate access to treatment services, and a paucity of appropriately trained professionals. Similarly, the development of appropriate treatment approaches has been a low priority in both research and program funding. Providing accessible, available treatment and developing appropriate treatment approaches for people with developmental disabilities are clearly important goals in view of their heightened risk for abuse and neglect and the fact that they appear to suffer from similar psychological and behavioral effects. Nevertheless, there have been a number of attitudinal and professional barriers that have prevented the acknowledgment of sexual abuse of people with developmental disabilities and the development of adapted treatment services.

Denial

Many myths portray people with disabilities as helpless, damaged, inhuman, asexual, and insensitive to pain (Sobsey & Mansell, 1990). Myths and negative attitudes about disability have desensitized the general population to the plight of people with disabilities. Unfortunately, professionals are not immune to these devaluing attitudes and myths about disability, and the fact that professionals have misunderstood disability has had negative implications for people with developmental disabilities.

Infantilization and asexuality

Misconceptions about the "asexuality" of people with developmental disabilities have been particularly damaging to the development of therapy approaches. The infantilization of people with developmental disabilities and the resulting denial of their sexuality clearly overlook the inherent sexuality of all people. Nevertheless, this myth has justified denying both sexuality education and sexual expression to people with developmental disabilities (Abramson, Parker, & Weisberg, 1988). Denying people with developmental disabilities access to sexuality education increases their vulnerability to possible pregnancy, venereal diseases, and abuse by persons exploiting their inadequate sexuality knowledge (Shaman, 1986). Notions about asexuality probably prevented many caregivers from acknowledging the risk of potential sexual abuse and delayed implementing abuse prevention strategies such as staff education in sexual abuse detection. Myths about the asexuality of people with disabilities often combine with myths about the sexual motives in child sexual abuse and sexual assault and implicitly deny the possibility that people with disabilities can be sexually abused. These erroneous beliefs about disabilities and sexual abuse may have hindered the professional acknowledgment of the sexual abuse of people with developmental disabilities.

Deviancy

Misconceptions about the sexuality of people with developmental disabilities have also taken the form of an expectation of sexually deviant behavior. For example, when a person with a developmental disability behaves in a manner that is regarded as sexually and socially inappropriate (e.g., public masturbation), the behavior is often attributed to the mental retardation. The behavior is sometimes viewed as either understandable or inevitable because the person has a developmental disability. Unfortunately, viewing inappropriate sexual behavior as an inherent outcome associated with mental retardation overlooks the inadequate state of sexuality education, repressive policies and strategies regarding opportunities for sexual expression, and the possibility that inappropriate sexual behavior may be indicative of sexual abuse. These beliefs also contribute to the implicit acceptance of applying different standards of social/sexual behavior to people with mental retardation. This double standard ultimately puts people with developmental disabilities at significant risk for possible exploitation and offending behavior, and it puts them at a considerable disadvantage when they enter the community, often resulting in conflicts with the law.

Pain insensitivity and the absence of an inner psychological life
Myths that promote the idea that people with developmental disabilities do not feel pain imply that because a person does not understand what has happened to them they do not suffer (Sobsey & Mansell, 1990). Related beliefs suggest that people with developmental disabilities do not have an inner psychological or emotional life (Sarason, 1985; Sinason, 1992) and that they do not suffer emotional pain. The internal psychological states of people with developmental disabilities have either been ignored or considered a hallmark of their intellectual deficiency, and it was assumed that they could not respond to therapy (Sarason, 1985). These beliefs about insensitivity to pain have probably influenced professionals and hindered the development of appropriate therapies for people with developmental disabilities.

Professional pessimism
Professional pessimism about the ability of people with developmental disabilities to participate in therapy typically appears to be a product of negative, devaluing attitudes, and/or ignorance about disability (Cushna, Szymanski, & Tanguay, 1980; Spackman, Grigel, & MacFarlane, 1990). Theoretical assumptions that are not the result of any systematic research regarding therapy efficacy may also contribute to pessimism (Hurley, 1989; Sarason, 1985). The development and appropriate evaluation of therapy approaches for this group has been a low priority in research (Prout & Nowak, 1999).

Many proponents of the early psychotherapeutic approaches suggested that people with developmental disability were unsuitable candidates for traditional insight oriented therapies because their limited language and abstract-conceptual abilities would prevent them from achieving insight (Monfils & Menolascino, 1984). Level of intelligence was considered an important determinant of success in and suitability for insight oriented therapies. The emphasis on intelligence may have been an influential barrier hindering the development of more appropriate treatment approaches for persons with developmental disability. The individual's poor ability to deal with interpersonal stresses, inability to control or delay emotional expression, or inability to recognize causes and consequences of behavior were all considered barriers to successful therapy. The belief that behavioral or emotional problems are a function of disability often contributed to unrealistic therapy goals. Not surprisingly, few therapists are appropriately trained to provide therapy for people with developmental disabilities.

Insufficient experience, training, and knowledge about the abilities, special needs, and limitations of people with developmental disabilities are apparent in many professionals (Tanguay & Szymanski, 1980). The lack of appropriate treatment resources persists because of the inadequate training and experience of many therapists in the area of developmental disability (Mansell & Sobsey, 1993). Many of the difficulties associated with professional pessimism about therapy are relevant to the provision of therapy for people with developmental disabilities who have been sexually abused. Many professionals have negative perceptions of the effectiveness of adapted therapy. This perception might be a product of their own unrealistic therapy goals and might prevent more widespread use of adapted techniques. Also, many studies of therapeutic adaptations have methodological problems, for example, varying diagnoses, no control groups, no standardized treatment techniques, and inadequate measures of outcome; and these inconsistent research results have contributed to the negative attitudes held by therapists. The area continues to be dominated by case studies and more subjective reports (Prout & Nowak, 1999) and there are still few studies of the effectiveness of psychotherapy. Better evaluative research is required to determine the efficacy of therapy.

Access, availability, and appropriateness of therapy

Therapy provisions for sexual abuse sequelae experienced by people with developmental disabilities are often inaccessible, unavailable, and inappropriately adapted to meet their needs (Mansell et al., 1992). Treatment access may be problematic because there is a lack of sufficient accommodations in the basics, such as physical accessibility and resource materials. For example, not all sexual assault centers have ramps or elevators for physical access, and many centers do not possess alternative telephone devices, translation services, or nonprint reading materials. Treatment availability and the use of appropriate accommodations will continue to be problematic as long as therapists in the sexual abuse field are isolated from people with developmental disabilities in their professional training and practice. A lack of confidence appears to prevent many therapists from providing sexual abuse treatment services to this high-risk population.

Providing therapists with experience and training may give them the necessary confidence, knowledge, and skills to treat people with disabilities and increase the availability of sexual abuse treatment for people with disabilities. Also, experience and training may improve professional attitudes toward people with disabilities and heighten professional awareness of the treatment concerns of people with disabilities.

Adapted therapy
A few researchers and practitioners have challenged the importance of intelligence in determining suitability for therapy by adapting existing therapeutic techniques and using more relevant indicators of a person's ability to participate in counseling. Therapy techniques adapted for people with developmental disabilities are similar to conventional approaches used with people who do not have disabilities. Assessing developmental level, ability to form relationships, social adaptability, and family or social living circumstances provides more relevant information about suitability for therapy than intelligence alone, and these factors may help practitioners choose and adapt suitable therapeutic techniques. Researchers have reported success in adapting a variety of existing therapies for people with developmental disabilities: for example, individual counseling and psychotherapy (Blotzer & Ruth, 1995; Spackman et al., 1990; Strohmer & Prout, 1994; Szymanski, 1980; Vernikoff & Dunayer, 1992), client-centered training (Corcoran, 1982), group therapy (Brown, 1994; Duffy, 1992; Laterza, 1979; Monfils, 1985; Monfils & Menolascino, 1984; Tomasulo, 1990), art therapy (Anderson, 1992; Caprio-Orsini, 1996), play (Baum, 1994; Svec, 1992a), and family therapy (Cobb & Gunn, 1994; Gapen & Knoll, 1992; Goldenberg, 1985; Hollins, 1995; Teodoru, 1992; Turner, 1980).

There are diverse individual psychotherapy and counseling techniques that can be adapted for people with developmental disabilities. Spackman et al. (1990) suggest there is a wide variety of individually tailored therapeutic adaptations that are useful for practitioners who are willing to learn and use a client's receptive language, symbolic communications, visual imagery, and tactile and kinesthetic interactions in therapy.

Increasingly, as the need for services became more evident, a few practitioners and researchers designed a variety of sexual abuse treatments for children (Perlman & Sinclair, 1992; Sinason, 1992; Sullivan, Scanlon, Knutson, Brookhouser, & Schulte, 1992) and adults with developmental disabilities (Cruz et al., 1988; Fresco, Philbin, & Peters, 1992; Hindle, 1994; Hyman, 1993; Morris, 1993; Ryan, 1992; Sinason, 1992) using conventional sexual abuse treatment approaches. A persistent problem identified in sexual abuse therapy research concerns the lack of standardized treatments (Beutler & Hill, 1992). Practitioners require considerable knowledge about disability and sensitivity to disability and sexual abuse issues, however, to provide adapted sexual abuse therapy. They need to consider the combined impact of a client's developmental disability and sexual abuse (Cruz et al., 1988).

ADAPTING THERAPY
There are several crucial issues that therapists must consider when providing therapy to clients with developmental disabilities: the therapist's expertise (e.g., a therapist needs to have expertise in therapy practice, disability related issues, and psychology of disability), the therapist's attitudes toward developmental disability and sexual abuse, and professional self-care. It is crucial that the therapist possess the professional requirements and competence to provide therapy that ethically meets the needs of clients with developmental disabilities.

CONSIDERATIONS FOR THERAPISTS
Required expertise
The therapist's knowledge and skills are not enough to adapt sexual abuse therapy for use with clients who have developmental disabilities. Therapists also need to understand disability and should be flex-

ible enough to integrate disability and sexual abuse related issues into their repertoire of therapeutic skills. Generally, therapists require considerable knowledge about developmental and other forms of disabilities and knowledge about the psychology of handicapping conditions in order to adapt sexual abuse therapy for use with clients who have developmental disabilities (Sullivan & Scanlan, 1987). It is also necessary for the therapist to be sensitive to disability related issues and to understand how different levels of cognitive functioning will affect the therapeutic process (Prout & Cale, 1994). In addition, it is important for therapists to have experience with sexual abuse issues, familiarity with a variety of sexual abuse therapy techniques and approaches, and a willingness to work with the client's various systems.

Therapist's attitudes

Stereotypes and misconceptions about the needs and abilities of people with developmental disabilities can be insidious and may seriously impair the therapeutic relationship and process. Therapists need to be aware of the influence of their own attitudes when providing therapy to people with developmental disabilities who have been sexually abused. For example, practitioners need to examine their attitudes toward disability and be aware of both their prejudices about working with people with developmental disability and their attitudes toward sexuality, sexual expression, sexual abuse, and power relationships (Brown, 1992). Positive attitudes toward mental retardation that promote personal rights and emphasize acceptance and potential for continued learning are critical for successful therapy. The therapist's perceptions of the client can influence their expectations, and the level of energy and commitment they invest in the therapeutic process (Prout & Cale, 1994). Also important are positive attitudes toward the sexuality and sexual expression of people with developmental disabilities.

It is also important for the therapist to avoid projecting unrealistic responses onto clients (e.g., the expectation that the client be more verbal or successful) (Vernikoff & Dunayer, 1992). Counter-transference may be complicated by the presence of the disability and may take several forms: the therapist acting like a parent to the client, having rescue wishes, overprotection, and fears about setting limits with the client. Therapists may also experience frustration and discouragement about the permanence and impact of the client's disability. In order to avoid these pitfalls in the therapeutic process, therapists must develop realistic expectations and therapy goals for the client and carefully consider any assumptions they may have about the client's capacity to feel and understand. Therapists need to believe that clients with mental retardation experience the full breadth of human emotion with the same intensity as anyone else in order to be open not only to exploring the full range of emotions with clients, but also to generate new emotional responses (Prout & Cale, 1994). Similarly, it is essential for therapists to have patience with the client's rate of progress in therapy and with the client's communication abilities. Therapists who usually measure success in therapy through heightened client independence need to recognize that smaller steps of achievement will be seen (Vernikoff & Dunayer, 1992) and that therapy tends to have a slower pace and progress occurs more slowly with clients with developmental disabilities (Bates, 1992). A therapist needs to believe in the value of his or her efforts and appreciate the potential for growth and challenges evident in therapy work that requires the self-examination of both personal views and behaviors in order to find ways to meet the client in his or her world (Prout & Cale, 1994).

Professional self-care

Frequently, books for therapists that cover treatment for child sexual abuse feature a section on therapist self-care. Most often, this section tends to be placed toward the end of the text as an afterthought. The concept of professional self-care is presented in the introduction of this book to highlight its importance to both the work of therapy and to the life of the therapist.

Providing therapy to people with developmental disabilities can be both extremely challenging and extremely rewarding. The therapist's personal reactions to sexual abuse can be one of the most challenging aspects of therapy with people with developmental disabilities who have been sexually abused. Personal emotional reactions to sexual abuse are normal, and it is sometimes difficult to remain neutral or dispassionate. Feelings may range from anger, distress, and despair to sympathy and may have an intensity and quality that is uncomfortable. Emotional burnout is a very significant risk for therapists; nevertheless, there is a clear need to acknowledge these difficulties and to prevent these emotions from impairing professional judgment (Faller, 1993). Burnout can be caused by frustration, rage, emotional exhaustion, or a sense of helplessness and can result in a professional behaving insensitively toward his or her clients. To avoid this emotionally difficult and sometimes compromising situation for both therapist and client, self-care for the therapist is crucial. Self-care ensures that the therapist maintains a reasonable and ethical standard of care for his or her clients, and it helps the therapist maintain a healthy psychological balance. Many therapists find that they are overworked and have difficulty fitting self-care activities into their busy schedules; consequently, self-care needs to be a priority that is both promoted and modeled in professional training. A culture of support needs to be both developed and maintained.

A heightened sense of self, personal reactions, and clinical dynamics is vital to the psychological health of the therapist. Cox-Lindenbaum (1992) suggests the importance of having a structured, supportive, consistent process that can provide ongoing clinical support to the therapist providing therapy for survivors of sexual abuse who have developmental disabilities. Godschalx (1983) recommends the use of regular peer supervision, changing therapists after a period of one year and the use of cotherapists when providing therapy to a client with a developmental disability. Recognizing and reflecting upon personal issues and drawing on other professionals for support and supervision may help the therapist cope with the stress.

The impact of working in the area of sexual abuse may be exacerbated by a professional's own experience of victimization. Faller (1993) suggests that there are a number of warning signs that may impede clinical performance: feeling overwhelmed by fear, anxiety, disgust, or anger; intrusive thoughts; and flashbacks. Therapists who have not resolved their own abuse issues may face three impediments to conducting therapy: over identification, projection, and boundary confusion (Briere, 1992). For therapists who may be having abuse-related countertransference, additional therapy for the therapist will be necessary to ensure that a reasonable standard of care is provided to the client.

Clinical supervision may support professionals by providing feedback, guidance, and opportunities to explore their feelings. Collaboration with other professionals, never working in isolation, consultation with other professionals who are more experienced, and interdisciplinary teamwork can help the therapist avoid emotional burnout. Working collaboratively may be particularly relevant in view of the fact that many professionals will have training in either disability or providing therapy but are unlikely to possess expertise in both areas. Clinical supervision may help the therapist address some of these sometimes subtle issues. Therapists also need to assess their own comfort level with a therapeutic role that includes having considerable contact with other professionals and may involve acting as an advocate for the client.

WORKING WITH THE CLIENT'S SYSTEMS
Family and other caregivers
People with developmental disabilities frequently depend, in varying degrees, on a number of different people for help in various areas of their lives. The people with whom they are often most intimately connected may include family members and various other paid and unpaid caregivers and professionals. Approaching therapy from a systemic perspective provides the therapist with opportunities to learn about the individuals and interactions comprising the client's social system. It is crucial that the therapist understand the impact of this system on the client and the client's impact on the system. Ignoring highly influential systems may deprive the therapist of essential information about the social dynamics, resources, and influences in the client's life and may make therapy a futile exercise.

Since there are a number of people involved in the client's life, it is important for the therapist to find out who is involved, determine the various roles these individuals play, and determine their views about the client's needs. It is important to assess how supportive or resistant particular members of the client's social system (e.g., family members, group home staff, or other closely affiliated professionals) are to the client's therapy. Often, the individuals in this system have multiple and conflicting perspectives and agendas about therapy and it is vital to be both aware of and responsive to these (McBrien & Candy, 1998).

It is important for the therapist to consider what support may or may not exist in the client's social system for promoting his or her independence and healing. Some people in the client's life may claim they support increasing the client's independence and assertiveness through therapy, but they may develop a significant resistance to any actual changes in the client. This resistance can be damaging to both the client and the therapeutic process and needs to be addressed carefully. Securing and maintaining these individuals' involvement in and support for the client's therapy is a critical component to its success. The therapist will need to consider the use of specific interventions that ensure that the members of this social system can be supportive of the client's therapy.

Although the literature emphasizes the need to consult with other professionals in order to understand the full impact of the developmental disability of a client, it is also crucial for the therapist to teach these professionals about sexual abuse and its effects. Many professionals may believe that some of the client's abuse-related behavioral problems are a product of the disability and cannot be treated. Their understanding of abuse and its effects and their cooperation will be necessary for providing additional support for the client outside therapy. The other professionals in a client's life play a crucial role in the therapeutic process: for example, dealing with behavioral problems that might result from the abuse and providing additional support as the client copes with his or her feelings. In order to supply this support, staff may need training to develop greater sensitivity to abuse (McCartney, 1992), power, and sexuality issues (Brown, 1992). In addition, staff may need to adjust the client's medications, identify and treat medical problems, and institute habilitative changes that might be necessary to control any dissociative triggers that might be present in the client's environment (Ryan, 1992).

Ongoing contact with professionals may also provide valuable feedback about how the client is progressing in therapy. This feedback can provide information about whether or not a particular approach is effective, if therapy goals are being achieved, if there are barriers to therapy, and if specific changes need to be implemented. Communication and consultation with members of the client's social systems, although clearly important and informative, should always be secondary to the therapist-client relationship. The therapist needs to exercise caution in these external interactions and be conscious of potential role conflicts. Identifying their allegiances and being clear with the various parties involved about constraints and limitations to consultations can be helpful (Prout & Strohmer, 1994a). Failure to do so can complicate treatment and potentially damage the client's trust in both the therapist and the therapy (Hurley, 1989). With extensive contact with other professionals, it becomes especially important that the confidentiality of the client-therapist relationship be treated with respect. The degree to which a therapist becomes an advocate for the client also needs to be considered. For example, if a therapist takes on considerable direct advocacy involvement in the client's environment, the therapist may be placing him or herself in a dual role that may confuse the client (Hurley, 1989) and others.

Client evaluation

The client evaluation is an important ongoing process that occurs throughout therapy, and it needs to be conducted with care in order to assess the client's needs for treatment. The evaluation process provides critical information about adaptations that might be required in order to provide appropriate treatment and specific issues that might concern the client.

Although the range of effects associated with sexual abuse may be similar for people with and without disabilities (Gorman-Smith & Matson, 1992), during therapy, a variety of different issues will emerge for the client. The therapist needs to recognize the importance of the various personal and professional relationships in the client's life and appreciate the impact of disability related issues for the client. In addition, therapists must also recognize their own limitations and be willing to consult with other professionals who are more knowledgeable when a client's needs exceed the therapist's expertise. Hurley (1989) recommends the use of a directive approach for setting goals for therapy with people who have developmental disabilities; nevertheless, it remains very important to consult with the client about her or his goals for the therapy. Prout and Strohmer (1994a) suggest the importance of restricting therapy goals to those that are inelegant or focus on resolving specific problems. Identifying specific treatment issues and developing a treatment plan that includes achievable goals and objectives and input from the client are essential for successful therapy.

Therapy goals
Some goals of therapy are very similar to the goals of abuse prevention programs. Counselors can help empower clients to make more effective decisions, have greater control over their lives, and reduce the risk of further victimization. Khemka and Hickson (2000) describe an abuse prevention program for adults that is based around teaching them to make their own decisions and empowering them to control their own lives. Most of the principles behind this prevention program and many of the intervention strategies could be applied equally well to a treatment program.

People with developmental disabilities may have very little experience with making decisions. Frequently, their decisions are made for them, and they are not asked about what they want or provided with any choices. Building decision-making opportunities into therapy and providing choices for the client may act as part of greater strategies to promote a client's personal power and reduce his or her risk for sexual abuse (Sobsey & Mansell, 1990). Clients need to have opportunities to make choices, be heard, take risks, and to have their needs and wants taken seriously.

For many clients with developmental disabilities who have been socialized to be obedient and highly dependent on others, the experience of having choices and making decisions might be foreign and also very threatening. In these cases, therapists will need to provide additional support for these strategies and be sensitive to the possibility that clients have been strongly socialized and rewarded for compliant behavior. When the therapist provides additional supports that are mindful of these compliant behaviors, the therapeutic environment can provide a safe place for practicing new skills that promote independence and assertiveness; however, it is necessary to pay more than lip-service to these strategies. Therapists need to provide opportunities and encouragement for decision making and honor the decisions made by their clients.

Individualizing therapy

Individualizing or tailoring therapy to meet a client's needs is crucial to all therapists. Individualizing therapy for clients with developmental disabilities, however, requires some special considerations and knowledge. Therapists require considerable knowledge about disability and should be sensitive to the combined impact of sexual abuse and developmental disability. Although the issues associated with developmental disability are emphasized here, this is somewhat misleading, as developmental disability is not a homogenous condition. It is highly variable and includes a wide range of abilities. Also, it may be accompanied by other disabilities, such hearing, speech, vision, or mobility impairments, each of which introduces different considerations for communication alternatives and personal issues.

One of the greatest challenges for therapists lies in how to appropriately individualize therapy. Hurley (1989) offers six recommendations for individualizing therapy for people with mental retardation: (1) adapt a standard therapy technique to the client's cognitive level, (2) be directive by setting structure and limits in order to maintain focus, (3) be flexible, (4) engage significant others in the therapy because the client is dependent on others, (5) address transference and countertransference issues, and (6) consider disability as an issue.

The individualizing process requires that the therapist conduct a careful assessment of the client's special needs and abilities and potential resources and sources of support. Therapists need to carefully consider the client's communication and comprehension abilities and become familiar with the various communication alternatives and nonverbal therapies. It is important for therapists to develop additional strategies to determine client comprehension and to be sensitive to the possibility that clients may sometimes, due to an extensive history of failure and socialization emphasizing compliance and obedience, work very hard to please and feign understanding. The therapist needs to be diligent in determining what the client means by his or her language and whether the client understands the language that the therapist uses (Prout & Strohmer, 1994a). Also, the therapist needs to be aware of his or her own communication style and be willing to alter this style to match the client's communication ability. Individualizing therapy is a dynamic process and therapy must be responsive to the individual's needs, recognizing areas of difficulty, resourcefulness, and strength. It is important for the therapist to explore and build on the client's resiliency and adaptive coping strategies that support the client in his or her healing.

Validating and supporting the client's experience, strength, and ability to both heal and continue to grow are crucial to successful therapy. The therapist also must have and communicate a fundamental respect for the client's humanity and provide a curative relationship that creates a safe place in which a client can explore his or her pain. The therapist must be respectful, empathic, caring, and establish a strong therapeutic alliance with the client. The therapist must be able to communicate strength and comfort with intense affect and carefully manage both transference and countertransference issues, gain access to clinical supervision, and engage in self-care as required to prevent burnout and maintain a high standard of ethical client care. Therapy will be most effective when the therapist remains flexible and creative with his or her practice. Consequently, therapy approaches should be eclectic and multimodal in nature, drawing from a variety of existing approaches and, when necessary, combining individual, group, and/or family therapy modalities.

Therapy setting

Many people with developmental disabilities experience sexual abuse in the disability service system and develop effects such as Post Traumatic Stress Disorder (Ryan, 1992). Careful selection of the therapy setting and recognition of a client's limitations in terms of attention span and other considerations can go a long way to both reduce the likelihood of retraumatizing a client and making therapy a more productive and healing experience. For example, therapy should not be conducted in a setting associated with the abuse, whether that is an institution, group home, or family home; even so, this is an important detail that is sometimes overlooked. As evaluation of the client's treatment issues and the therapy progresses, the therapist will learn more about the specific settings or circumstances associated with the abuse. Once this information is obtained, it may be necessary to take steps to alter aspects of the therapy environment (Ryan, 1992). Also, advocacy may help to alter aspects of the client's other environments in order to reduce the presence of possible triggers that may retraumatize a client.

Therapy rooms need to be of an appropriate size but should not be too large. The environment should not be overly stimulating or distracting. The therapy setting needs to be accessible. Enhancing accessibility refers to both physical accessibility and the availability of resource materials (i.e., ramps, elevators, alternative telephone devices, translation services, and nonprint alternatives to reading materials). The therapist may want to have various nonverbal materials available for therapy. Therapy should be conducted in a particular setting on a consistent basis to contribute to a client's sense of safety through predictability of environment. Instead of the traditional 50-minute therapy hour, shorter therapy sessions may be preferable for some clients (Stavrakaki & Klein, 1986).

While therapy for clients with developmental disabilities is quite similar to therapy for people without developmental disabilities, there are a few important differences. Therapists need to be more flexible in order to meet the needs of clients and to accommodate their network of caregivers (Teodoru, 1992. Therapists also need to be aware that a client's communication skills can be strongly influenced by his or her setting.

There are numerous considerations in adapting therapy, and professionals indicate that adaptation often presents challenges. Westcott's (1992) survey of child abuse professionals working with children with developmental disabilities outlined some of these difficulties. They included problems with interagency cooperation, a sense that no one wanted to take responsibility for the children, antagonistic responses from family, families' refusal to recognize the child's disability, and problems obtaining adequate resources and specialist advice. Professionals also reported therapy accommodation-related difficulties such as trying to find the right level at which to work with the child, attempting to assess how much a child could understand, and making allowances for the child's reduced attention span (Westcott, 1992). A number of considerations and issues involved in providing therapy to clients with developmental disabilities have been presented. This chapter concludes with the results of an international survey of professionals engaged in providing therapy services to this population that was conducted through the J.P. Das Developmental Disabilities Centre at the University of Alberta.

Therapist's Accommodations Survey
Survey development
Although there has been growing interest in this area, there have been few descriptive studies of professionals' specific therapy practices, the problems they encounter, or what factors may influence their use of particular accommodations or treatment components with clients who have developmental disabilities. In this study, the literature covering therapists' accommodations, components used to treat sexual-abuse-related issues, and professionals' reported difficulties providing these services, were consulted and informed the development of the survey. This study used a survey method to obtain descriptive information about (1) professionals' training and experience, and the specific therapy devices, techniques, accommodations, and components used, (2) the characteristics of people with differing degrees

and varieties of disabilities who receive therapy services, and (3) the problems encountered by these professionals.

Method
Potential participants were targeted and selected for inclusion because they were known to 1) possess expertise in this area (e.g., published or presented relevant papers), 2) have considerable experience providing therapy to people with developmental disabilities, or 3) have professional affiliations that might promote appropriate survey distribution. Participants were selected from membership listings of the National Association for Prevention of Sexual Abuse of Children and Adults with Learning Disabilities (NAPSAC) in the United Kingdom, the National Coalition on Abuse and Disability (NCAD), and the National Association of the Dually Diagnosed (NADD) in the United States, the Sexual Abuse and Young People with Disabilities Project (SAYPD) in Canada, and the University Affiliated Programs (UAP) in the United States, among other sources.

Participants were contacted by mail, sent a cover letter describing the study, a survey, and a self-addressed, stamped envelope. All survey responses were confidential and respondents were asked to preserve their clients' confidentiality by avoiding the use of any names or identifying information. Over 300 surveys were sent out, and 105 surveys with usable data were returned within a three-month period. Some surveys were returned due to address problems and some respondents indicated they could not respond due to lack of the expertise and informed the researcher that the surveys had been distributed to others they felt were better qualified to respond. Therefore, it is difficult to determine either the exact response rate or the representativeness of the respondents. The responses of a self-selecting, non-random sample may not be representative of professionals providing this service, who either chose not to respond or were not targeted or reached as potential participants.

The Survey
The first part of the survey requested information about professional training, highest level of education, professional title, country of prac-

tice, specialized communication training, amount of experience, and the therapeutic approaches that best describe their practice. Respondents also were asked to describe the clientele with whom they most typically conduct therapy (i.e., age, gender, level and type(s) of disability). Survey respondents were asked to describe difficulties that they encounter and the therapeutic accommodations and the specific therapy techniques or components they use to treat sexual abuse related issues. This study is primarily exploratory and descriptive. Therefore, no restrictions were placed on the number of categories respondents could use. Most variables are described using multiple categories; therefore, there is considerable overlap. Additional spaces were provided for respondents' comments and, where possible, this supplemental information is summarized.

Sample
Specialization, educational level, and experience
Many respondents reported that they practiced in the UK (39%) and the US (35%). Nineteen percent reported practicing in Canada and a substantially smaller proportion reported practicing in Australia (4%), and other countries (2%). There was considerable diversity in respondents' professional disciplines and training, level of education, and amount of experience. There was representation from the medical, mental health, and mental disability disciplines (e.g., respondents included psychiatrists, psychologists, social workers, professors, art and behavior therapists, nurses, occupational therapists, etc.). The largest proportions of respondents reported that their training was in psychology (55%), social work (27%), and special education (19%). Fewer respondents reported training in disciplines such as nursing (11%), other specializations (e.g., sexuality educator, psychotherapist, behavioral or art therapist) (10%), rehabilitation (9%), and psychiatry (6%). Close to seventy-five percent of respondents reported having graduate level training (e.g., Masters [48%], Doctoral [25%], or Post-Doctoral degrees [1%]). Twenty percent of respondents had Bachelors degrees and five percent had diplomas. Respondents' experience ranged from less than a year to 37 years, with a mean of 11.5 years and a standard deviation of 7.6 years. Most respondents had considerable professional training and experience in their cho-

sen disciplines, and many respondents were trained in more than one discipline, which suggests the presence of a possible multidisciplinary orientation in this sample.

Therapeutic approaches

Respondents identified the therapeutic approaches that most represented their therapy work. A large majority of respondents identified their therapeutic approach as cognitive behavioral (62%). Fifty-six, fifty-four, and forty-nine percent of the respondents identified their therapeutic approach as behavioral (e.g., using social skills training, discrete trial training, functional analysis, functional communication training, gentle teaching, etc.), eclectic, and client-centered, respectively. Thirty-five, thirty-one, twenty-six, and twenty-one percent identified their approach as psychoeducational (e.g., human development and sexuality, abuse risk reduction), family systems, psychodynamic, and "other" approaches (e.g., attachment based analytic, gestalt, integrated sex therapy, narrative, solution focused, systems, biopsychosocial, hypnotherapy, psychodrama, etc.), respectively. Less than fifteen percent identified using feminist, object relations, and self-psychology approaches. Almost all respondents identified using more than one therapeutic approach, and many respondents reported using a variety of therapy modalities.

Frequently used modalities included individual and group therapies. Less frequently used modalities included family (e.g., family, couple, and systems), educational (e.g., development of social relationships), and expressive (e.g., play, sand, and movement therapies). The diversity in the therapy approaches and the modalities used by this sample may reflect the general trends in both mental health and disability related services, toward increasing flexibility and reduced likelihood of strict adherence to one approach. These findings may also reflect the mutual influences between the diverse disciplines providing these services. The findings appear consistent with the recommendations from the literature that professionals must be flexible, responsive, and draw from diverse therapeutic approaches and disciplines as needed to meet client's needs. A description of the clients receiving services from these respondents and professionals' use of therapy accommodations and treatment components follows.

Characteristics of clients

Respondents described the characteristics of the clients with whom they had the most experience. Over ninety percent of respondents served both males and females, however, small but equal proportions (4%) reported that they served either males or females exclusively. The majority of respondents reported that their clients were: young adults, between 20-30 years (71%), middle age adults, between 30-50 years (64%), and middle to late adolescents, between 15-20 years (41%). Smaller proportions of respondents reported that their clients were: in the middle childhood years, between 5-10 years (29%), in early adolescence, between 10-15 years (29%), and in later middle age, between 50-60 years (22%). Clients who were either in their early childhood years, between 0-5 years (16%), or in their later adulthood years, being 60 years and older (13%), were the two least likely age groups to receive therapy services from this sample of professionals.

Level of intellectual ability and additional disabilities

Respondents also described their clients' level of cognitive functioning and any other disabilities. Seventy-four and seventy-one percent respectively, indicated that their clients' cognitive functioning fell within the mild or moderate range of developmental disability. Four percent and two percent of respondents, respectively, indicated that their clients' cognitive functioning fell within the severe or profound ranges. The most frequent client disabilities included mental/intellectual (85%), psychiatric/psychological (70%), and communication disabilities (60%). Less frequently identified disabilities included motor (52%), multiple (53%), and sensory (39%) disabilities. The research literature provides more documentation of therapy conducted with clients functioning within the mild and moderate range than for clients within either the severe or profound ranges of developmental disability. The proportions of clients who were reported to be served by this sample were consistent with this documentation and the general reported frequencies of these levels of disability (i.e., mild and moderate levels of developmental disability occur with far greater frequency than either the severe or profound levels of developmental disability). These findings may also reflect the possibility that people with more severe and potentially multiple impairments may be less likely to either be referred for or receive treatment. Also it may be that some of the previously mentioned perceptions concerning mental health issues and people with greater degrees of impairment may reduce the likelihood of therapy referral.

Results
Specialized communication training

Respondents were asked if they had any specialized communication training. Nearly forty percent reported they had no specialized communications training. Thirty-one, twenty-nine, twenty-five, and twenty-four percent of respondents indicated that they were trained in the use of alternative symbol systems, sign language, electronic devices, and non-electronic devices, respectively. Nine percent of respondents had other training (e.g., Somerset total communication system, facilitated communication, and Derbyshire language scheme training).

There was some variation in the types of communication training professionals had and the clients with whom they reported to have the most experience. In some cases, however, there did not appear to be any differences between the professionals with and without communications training in terms of the clients they served. The various specialized communication-training categories are summarized in terms of the percentages of clients with varying disabilities that respondents reported serving. There were no notable differences in the percentages of clients with mild and moderate intellectual disabilities who were served by respondents with specialized communication training. Comparatively, the proportion of clients with severe and profound intellectual disabilities was higher and more variable than for those who served clients in the mild or moderate ranges. Overall, there were no notable differences in the percentages for respondents who served clients with mental/intellectual disabilities, motor, communication, psychiatric/psychological, and multiple disabilities. The largest percentages and variations were noted for respondents serving clients with sensory disabilities.

Also, of the respondents who indicated they did not have any specialized communication training, approximately forty percent reported that they served clients with mild and moderate intellectual disabilities. Twenty-six and twelve percent reported serving clients with severe and profound intellectual disabilities, respectively. The percentages for respondents who served clients with mental/intellectual disabilities, motor, communication, and psychiatric/psychological disabilities ranged from the low to high thirties. Overall, professionals without specialized communication training appear less likely to typically provide therapy services to clients who have either severe or profound intellectual or sensory disabilities. Alternately, professionals who reported the largest percentages across all of the specialized communication training categories were more likely to report providing services to clients with severe intellectual disabilities, sensory disabilities, and profound intellectual disabilities. Specialized communication training appeared less likely to influence whether or not these professionals served clients with either mild or moderate intellectual disabilities, or with mental/intellectual, motor, communication, psychiatric/psychological or multiple disabilities.

Therapy accommodations and disability
Respondents reported the therapy accommodations they use to enhance client and therapist communication and comprehension, and therapy appropriateness. The accommodations are separated into categories that include (1) devices or techniques and (2) accommodations. These are examined in relation to the type and level of intellectual disability of the clients served.

Specific devices or techniques
Devices or techniques included the use of electronic assistive communication devices (e.g., computers), non-electronic assistive communication devices (e.g., communication boards), projective techniques, special symbol systems (e.g., Bliss, PIC, Makaton), sign language (e.g., ASL, BSL), speech/lip reading, and a translator or inter-

preter who is familiar with client's communication style. Sign language was used more frequently for clients described as having profound intellectual disabilities (39%) and sensory disabilities (35%). Both projective techniques and special symbol systems were used in approximately equal proportions by respondents for all the client disability groups (i.e., ranging between mid-teens to mid-twenties). Sign language was used in similar proportions by respondents for all the client disability groups (i.e., percentages ranged between high teens to mid-twenties). Speech/lip-reading was the least frequently used technique. This technique was used by less than ten percent of respondents for all of the categories of clients with disabilities who were served.

Electronic devices were used in approximately equal proportions (i.e., percentages ranged between mid-twenties to low thirties) by respondents for all the client disability groups Respondents who reported serving clients described as having either motor (40%) or sensory disabilities (37%) used electronic devices more frequently. Non-electronic devices were used in similar proportions by respondents for all the client disability groups (i.e., percentages ranged between the middle to high thirties). The most frequent use of non-electronic devices, however, was reported by respondents serving clients described as having communication (43%), severe intellectual disabilities (48%), sensory (49%), and multiple disabilities (50%).

The use of a translator or interpreter who is familiar with client's communication style was the most frequently reported technique used by respondents across all client groups (i.e., percentages ranged between mid-thirties to mid-forties). This technique was used in approximately equal proportions of respondents serving clients described as having mental/intellectual disabilities; mild, moderate, and profound intellectual disabilities; or psychiatric/psychological impairments (i.e., percentages ranging from the middle to high thirties). Slightly larger proportions, however, were reported for clients described as having communication disabilities; severe intellectual disabilities; multiple, motor, and sensory disabilities (i.e., percentages ranged from low forties to mid-forties).

Specific accommodations

The specific accommodations included the use of concrete language, plain English, less verbally oriented therapies (e.g., play, art, sand, dolls), providing additional time for the client to respond, learning the client's non-verbal communication style (e.g., use of non-verbal [body] language, idiosyncrasies, and gestures), learning the client's verbal communication style (e.g., use of intonation, articulation, speech patterns, idiosyncrasies), and "other" accommodations. The latter accommodations included use of music, movement, concrete materials and models, pictures, video demonstration and feedback, using shorter, more structured and goal focused sessions, environmental accommodation, on-site visits, behavioral incentives, facilitated communication, inclusive practices, behavior practice and role play, repetition, and providing support to staff who work with the client, among others. Tables 1.3 and 1.4 provide descriptions of the percentages of respondents who reported serving clients with differing levels and types of disabilities using the various accommodations. The "other" accommodations were the least frequently used by respondents across all categories of clients' disabilities. The use of less verbally oriented therapies was the least frequently used accommodation reported by respondents who served clients with moderate intellectual disability (58%), but the most frequently used accommodation by those respondents who were serving clients with psychiatric/psychological disabilities (70%).

Accommodations that include learning the client's verbal communication style, providing additional time for the client to respond, learning the client's non-verbal communication style, the use of concrete language, and plain English were used by a substantial proportion of respondents. Learning the client's verbal communication style was the least frequently used accommodation by respondents serving clients with profound (69%) and moderate (68%) intellectual disability but the most frequently used accommodation reported by respondents serving clients with multiple disabilities (86%). Although a substantial proportion of the respondents reported learning client's non-verbal communication style, this was the least frequently used accommodation reported by respondents serving clients with mild

(80%) and moderate (81%) intellectual disability and mental/intellectual disability (84%). It was the most frequently used accommodation reported by respondents serving clients with motor and multiple disabilities (i.e., both percentages exceeded 90%). Providing additional time for the client to respond was the least frequently used accommodation reported by respondents serving clients with severe (86%) and profound intellectual disabilities (81%) and the most frequently used accommodation reported by those who served clients with multiple (93%), sensory (93%), and motor disabilities (98%). The use of concrete language and plain English were the most frequently used accommodations reported by respondents across all categories of clients' disabilities.

Therapy techniques and components

Respondents were asked to provide information about therapy techniques and components that they use. The different techniques and components include those used to enhance the effectiveness of therapy, reduce the client's vulnerability to sexual abuse, and address sexual abuse related effects. Many respondents indicated they used components to enhance the efficacy of the therapy. A large proportion of respondents reported that they worked systemically and enlisted parents, guardians, and staff for support when appropriate (77%), used pre-therapy preparation or relationship-building techniques (66%), and psycho-educational techniques and repetition to teach specific concepts (60%). Approximately half of respondents reported using more directive approaches to maintain focus and structure in therapy and using psychoeducational approaches to teach clients an affective vocabulary. Many respondents also indicated that they used therapy components to help reduce vulnerability to sexual abuse. Over sixty percent reported using social skills/sexuality education, sexual abuse risk reduction education, and assertiveness training, respectively. Forty-nine and forty-one percent of respondents reported using components to enhance communication skills and *in vivo* training to promote concept generalization, respectively.

Many respondents indicated that they used differing therapy components to address their clients' sexual abuse related effects. Eighty-six, seventy-one, and sixty-one percent of respondents indicated that they treated poor self-esteem, developmental disability issues, and used behavioral approaches for secondary behavior problems (e.g., inappropriate sexual or aggressive behavior), respectively. Twenty-seven, twenty-one percent, and seventeen percent of respondents reported using empathy training, gentle teaching, and teaching about boundaries, educating staff and others about confidentiality, problem solving, self-advocacy, and independence training, respectively. Clearly clients' specific treatment issues would influence the use of these different treatment components.

Problems encountered
Problems encountered by over fifty percent of respondents included adapting communication style in therapy, inadequate professional and financial support for therapy programs, and eliciting cooperation from staff or family members for therapy. Thirty-seven and thirty-three percent of respondents reported difficulties adapting the therapist's communication style to meet client's communication and comprehension needs for assessment purposes and matching therapy techniques flexibly and creatively, respectively. Approximately one-fifth of respondents reported having difficulties obtaining adequate psychoeducational or resource materials for use in therapy, access to communication alternatives for therapy, and "other" problems. The "other" problems identified reflect concerns with actually adapting therapy, securing appropriate sexuality educational and testing materials, receiving collegial validation, specialized communication training, and supervision. Problems included overcoming professional, attitudinal, and financial barriers (e.g., lack of time and money required for providing treatment or interpreters, lack of collegial support, and building accessibility), working with the legal system, and securing cooperation for treatment from the client's system and maintaining confidentiality. Concerns noted by professionals in this study appear to correspond to and expand on some of the issues noted in Westcott's study (1992).

Discussion
The results of this preliminary study suggest that many respondents providing these services had considerable professional training and experience in their chosen disciplines and that there was a strong

multidisciplinary orientation in this sample. In addition, there was enormous diversity in the therapy approaches, modalities, and sexual abuse related treatment components that they reported to use with their clients with developmental disabilities. Emphasis on multidisciplinary training and the use of diverse approaches in this sample of professionals is consistent with recommendations from the literature that professionals draw from different sources of disciplinary knowledge and underscores the importance of professionals' flexibility. There also are variable relationships between the types of specialized communication training that professionals report that they either have or do not have, their reported use of specific devices or techniques or accommodations, and the types of clients with varying types and levels of disabilities for whom these professionals provide therapy services.

There were some variations in the types of communication training that professionals had and the clients to whom they provided therapy services. For example, professionals who reported not having specialized communication training appeared to be less likely to provide therapy services to clients with either severe or profound intellectual or sensory disabilities. Alternately, professionals, who reported the largest percentages across all of the specialized communication training categories, were more likely to report providing services to clients with severe and profound intellectual disabilities and sensory disabilities.

There were also variable relationships between the kinds of devices or techniques and accommodations that respondents used and the clients they reported to serve. For example, devices that were used with relatively low frequency (i.e., speech/lip-reading, projective techniques, and symbol systems) were consistent across all the categories of disability. People who provide intervention to individuals with severe or profound disabilities use communication aids (e.g., sign language, electronic and non-electronic devices) more frequently. They also use translators or interpreters who are familiar with a specific client's communication more frequently as do those working with clients with sensory, communication, multiple, and motor disabilities. A substantially higher proportion of respondents reported using therapy accommodations, and devices or techniques that were used far less frequently. This finding appears to be consistent with a pattern of use that would be expected in view of the clients who were reported to be receiving these therapy services.

Table 1.3. Therapy accommodations used by therapists working with clients with developmental disabilities

Therapy accommodations	Clients with developmental disabilities			
	Mild	Moderate	Severe	Profound
Concrete language	89%	85%	88%	85%
Plain English	95%	93%	94%	92%
Less verbally oriented therapies	64%	58%	66%	69%
Learn client's verbal communication	71%	68%	76%	69%
Learn client's non-verbal communication	80%	81%	86%	85%
Additional time	90%	91%	86%	81%
Other	27%	23%	24%	12%

Table 1.4. Therapy accommodations used by therapists working with clients with various disabilities

Therapy accommodations	Clients with other disabilities					
	Sensory	Motor	Mental	Multiple	Communication	Psychiatric
Concrete language	93%	95%	88%	92%	89%	85%
Plain English	88%	95%	93%	96%	95%	93%
Less verbally oriented therapies	66%	69%	63%	68%	68%	70%
Learn client's verbal communication	73%	78%	71%	86%	73%	71%
Learn client's non-verbal communication	88%	91%	84%	95%	87%	84%
Provide additional time	93%	98%	89%	93%	92%	88%
Other	29%	27%	25%	34%	27%	27%

Accommodations that were reported by over 80% of respondents across all categories of client disability included the use of concrete language, plain English, learning clients' non-verbal communication, and providing clients with additional time. Also, professionals in this sample reported a range of difficulties that included actually adapting therapy and overcoming various educational, collegial, financial, and systemic obstacles (e.g., obtaining varying levels and types of support, receiving collegial validation, specialized communication training, and supervision). Although some of these issues are not unique, some identified problems are distinct to people with developmental disabilities. Also some problems appear to be related to the devalued status attached both to people with developmental disabilities and the frequently segregated, disability-based services that are created for them. Greater study and advocacy efforts are needed to consider the sources of these distinct difficulties and to produce alternatives that ensure that people with developmental disabilities receive the treatment from professionals who are adequately trained and supported in these endeavors.

Conclusion

This chapter has examined disability terminology issues as these pertain to therapists. Issues relevant to understanding the problem of sexual abuse at it affects people with developmental disabilities, treatment considerations, and the results of an international survey of professionals engaged in this work have been presented.

'Although some preliminary descriptive patterns have been presented from this survey, these results should be interpreted cautiously. These results neither suggest a cause and effect relationship between client types and level of disability and professionals' use of specific techniques or accommodations nor do they imply that these results will generalize to other professionals engaged in this work. In some patterns, large proportions of respondents reported using particular accommodations and reported working with clients with specific disability characteristics, however, there are a numerous ways of interpreting these findings. For example, it could be that these accommodations are effective, commonly used, or deemed necessary with clients with specific levels of disabilities or specific deficits such as sensory or communication impairments. It could also be that professionals working with some clients may require additional specialized training to provide appropriate therapy services, especially as this pertains to the use of specific communication devices. It must also be considered that respondents used multiple categories to describe their use of devices, techniques, or accommodations, and that this study did not use methods to determine professionals' rankings about frequency of use, or perceived efficacy as these pertain to clients with particular types or patterns of disabilities. Similarly, respondents could also use multiple categories to describe their typical client's disabilities; however, there is considerable heterogeneity both within and across categories of disability, and some definitions vary across continents (as noted in the terminology section of this chapter). Therefore, these descriptions provide an initial sketch of the accommodations that respondents report to use and the general characteristics of the clients they typically serve. These do not necessarily provide specific, detailed information about what factors influence a therapist to use particular accommodations with clients who have variable patterns of disabilities and strengths.

Further research will be necessary to examine what accommodations professionals consider to be the most effective for addressing some of the more common difficulties in therapy. Subsequent research should include examination of therapy process and communication patterns to help determine the knowledge and skills required for professionals to appropriately accommodate therapy, the specific therapist-client factors that influence their use in therapy, and therapy outcome. Professionals' consideration of the impact of their clients' disabilities underscores the importance of professionals obtaining specialized disability-related training, supervision, and consultation. Also, encouraging new mental health professionals to expand their expertise into traditionally neglected areas such as developmental disability is critical for the continued development and refinement of these services. Promoting development and collaboration in these disciplines may help alleviate the current inadequacy of treatment services and encourage the provision of more integrated mental health services for people with developmental disabilities.

The remaining chapters of this book are devoted to examining in greater detail the patterns of sexual abuse noted in this population, the therapy research literature, and the exploration of issues pertaining to therapists who are involved in adapting different therapy modalities for people with developmental disabilities who have been sexually abused.

Part 2
Patterns
&
Effects

• 68

•• 2

Sexual Abuse Patterns and Heightened Risk or Sexual Abuse

Part Two of this book includes two chapters covering the literature on the patterns and effects of sexual abuse. This chapter presents a brief overview of the literature on the patterns of sexual abuse in people with disabilities. This review begins with a discussion about a study that examined patterns of sexual abuse in people with disabilities conducted by the Abuse and Disability Project at the University of Alberta (Sobsey, 1994; Sobsey & Doe, 1991). Following this discussion, an integration of the major findings of several later studies will be presented and discussed. This chapter examines some of the reasons for the heightened risk for sexual abuse in this population, and presents disability related psychological issues using a developmental framework. This chapter also considers the implications for counselors addressing sexual abuse in people with developmental disabilities.

RESEARCH ON PATTERNS OF SEXUAL ABUSE: UNIVERSITY OF ALBERTA ABUSE AND DISABILITY PROJECT STUDY

In 1987, the University of Alberta Abuse and Disability Project began to develop a practical model to describe how disability relates to abuse. Although this project addresses physical abuse, neglect, medical discrimination, violations of civil rights, psychological maltreatment, inappropriately applied aversive treatments, and other related issues, much of the work of the project has focused on the sexual abuse of children with disabilities and the sexual assault of adults with disabilities.

The Abuse and Disability Project at the University of Alberta surveyed 215 victims of sexual abuse or sexual assault and victims' advocates regarding the circumstances of the offenses. Information was collected on the nature of the offenses, the offenders, the victims, the outcomes, and treatment. The study included both children and adults. The sample was self-selected: Forms were distributed through disability advocacy and sexual assault victims' service groups, and whoever chose to return the surveys was included in the study. The sample included people from Canada, the United States, and New Zealand. (More information on the method employed in the study and the sample is provided in Sobsey and Doe (1991) and Sobsey (1994)). The results suggest that although sexual offenses committed against people with disabilities appear to be different in some respects from offenses against victims without disabilities they are not entirely unique.

OFFENDERS AND VICTIMS
In most respects, the dynamics of sex crimes perpetrated against people with disabilities are similar to sex crimes perpetuated against the general population. The majority of victims were women (80.1%), and most offenders were men (91.2%), although male victims (19.9%) and female offenders (8.8%) were reported in smaller but significant numbers. As found in the general population, female victims were less predominant among younger victims.

In slightly more than half (53.4%) of the cases, abusers had a relationship to the victim that resembled those commonly found among victims without disabilities. These abusers included were acquaintances such as family friends and neighbors (17.0%) natural family members (16.1%), and generic service providers such as babysitters (7.6%). Another 6.8% were strangers, 3.4% were dates, and 2.5% of the abusers were stepfamily members.

In slightly less than half (46.6%) of the cases, abusers had a relationship with the victim that appeared to be specifically related to the victim's disability. Disability service providers (e.g., personal care attendants, psychiatrists, residential care staff) comprised 26.3% of the abusers, specialized foster parents comprised 6% of the abusers, and specialized transportation providers comprised 5.1% of the abusers. Another 9.3% of the abusers were other individuals with disabilities who were clustered with the victim in a specialized service program.

CHRONICITY

For the participants of this study, the offenses tended to be severe and often were chronic in nature. Single offenses were reported in about one fifth (22.4%) of the cases. Another 18.4% of reports described two to 10 incidents of abuse. The largest group (48%) disclosed abuse on "many" (greater than 10) occasions, and although they did not specify enough information for further categorization, the remaining 11.2% described abuse as repeated.

SEQUELAE

About half (50.8%) of the reports revealed physical harm, which ranged from minor bruising to death. Minor injuries not requiring treatment were reported in 21.4% of cases, and more severe injuries requiring treatment were reported in 20.3% of cases. A small number of pregnancies (2.1%) and sexually transmitted diseases (7%) were also reported, although this information was not specifically requested on the survey and may be an underestimate.

Emotional and behavioral consequences appeared to be experienced by most of the victims (97.9%). Although 2.1% of the reports indicated that no emotional harm was apparent, these opinions were third party reports of victims with severe communication deficits. This finding suggests the possibility that these cases reflect either the inability to communicate distress or that difficulties may have been present but not recognized rather than an absence of actual harm. Uncategorized emotional distress was expressed in varying degrees by 47.7% of the victims. In addition, withdrawal was reported among 21.6% of the victims. Another 20.5% exhibited aggression, noncompliance, inappropriate sexual behavior, and other "behavior disorders." Victims with intellectual disabilities were less likely to be reported as exhibiting withdrawal. The lower rate of withdrawal among victims with intellectual disabilities might reflect a difference in response, but it could also reflect the caregivers' inability to recognize withdrawal in this group, since the surveys included many third party reports. Also, withdrawal may have been masked by a communication impairment.

TREATMENT

The most frequent service sought for the victims was counseling (44.6%). Medical services (16.3%) and various services or support from current caregivers (12.9%) were also frequently sought. Protective (7.9%) and legal services (7.5%) were sought in a smaller number of cases, while abuse prevention education was sought in a very small number of cases (2.9%). In many cases, the victims and/or their caregivers attempted to access more than one service, but in 11.5% of cases, no attempt was made to secure any treatment or support for the victim.

Many victims (43.8%) had difficulty obtaining required treatment services, and even when these services were successfully located, they often failed to meet the victim's needs. In fact, 51.5% of these treatment services failed to accommodate the special needs of people with disabilities, and another 22.8% of these treatment services did not adequately accommodate the special needs of victims with disabilities. Nevertheless, about one fifth (20.4%) of the services obtained did adequately accommodate the victim's special needs, and the generic services provided to other victims were considered appropriate in 5.4% of cases. According to the surveys, none of the treatment services made any special modifications for the victims.

The patterns evident in this early study suggest that nearly half of the offenders were caregivers, working in rehabilitation service environments, although slightly more than half fit the pattern of abuse found in the general population. Severe, negative emotional or behavioral effects were almost universal for the victims. Treatment services for victims with disabilities were often difficult to access, and when these were found, the necessary accommodations were often inadequate and failed to meet the individual needs of people with disabilities.

OTHER RESEARCH FINDINGS

Since the time of this early study, international research has been contributing to an emerging picture of the sexual abuse of people with developmental disabilities. While it is important to remember that emerging information often requires revisions, a number of conclusions now appear to be adequately demonstrated to merit at least provisional acceptance. The following section represents an integration of results from a number of these more recent studies and data from the Abuse and Disability Project at the University of Alberta. While this review will not include a complete description of all these studies, it may be useful to briefly describe a second patterns study that was undertaken at the University of Alberta. The previously discussed study and this second study form the basis of much of the following review.

ABUSE AND DISABILITY PROJECT'S SEXUAL ABUSE SEQUELAE STUDY

The Abuse and Disability Project's Sexual Abuse Sequelae study included 102 individuals with disabilities and 350 children without disabilities who were referred to a child sexual abuse treatment center in Western Canada over a period of two consecutive years. The data collected in the second study are similar to the data collected in the first study conducted by the Abuse and Disability Project at the University of Alberta; however, additional information was collected on the victim's family background and the sequelae of abuse. The second study differed from the first study in three major ways. First, it was a controlled sample rather than self-selected one. Second, because children without disabilities were included, it allowed for the testing of specific hypotheses about how children with disabilities who have been sexually abused may be similar to or different from children without disabilities who have been sexually abused. and third, this sample was limited to the area of child sexual abuse and only included individuals who had entered treatment. The complete results from this study have been published elsewhere (Moskal, 1995). (A comparison of the sequelae in children with and without developmental disabilities from the second study is presented in Chapter 3.)

SEXUAL ABUSE AND DISABILITY STUDIES

Other studies contribute information that provides important comparisons and contrasts with the University of Alberta Abuse and Disability Project studies. Crosse, Kaye, and Ratnofsky (1993) provide valuable data from their prospective study of a nationally representative sample of American child protection agencies that compared children with and without disabilities. This extensive report is based on 1, 249 cases of child abuse involving 1, 834 children.

Sullivan and Knutson's (in press) study of a cohort of more than 50,000 children in the Omaha schools probably represents the most ambitious and informative study to date. They because they used data from police and foster care review files in addition to child protection services data, their study probably provides a much better view of extrafamilial abuse than previous studies that used only one source of data.

Sullivan, Scanlan, Knutson, Brookhouser, and Schulte (1992) and Turk and Brown (1992) also present analyses of patterns of abuse that demonstrate interesting points that both contrast and confirm the findings of the Abuse and Disability Project's studies. Sullivan and colleagues studied children in the United States, while Turk and Brown studied adults in the United Kingdom. Turk and Brown's sample was restricted to adults with developmental disabilities, while Sullivan and colleagues studied children with a variety of disabilities. Furey (1994), like Turk and Brown, examined adults with developmental disabilities. Westcott's (1993) study used qualitative methods to provide a rich description of the experiences of a group of adults with disabilities abused as children and compared these experiences with the experiences of a group of adults without disabilities who were abused as children.

GENERAL RESEARCH FINDINGS
Heightened Risk

It has now been established that people with developmental disabilities (and other disabilities) are more likely to be abused than people without disabilities of the same age and gender are. The amount of increased risk depends on sampling methods, definitions of abuse, age, and the gender distributions of the sample. As a result, some studies suggest only mild increases in victimization of people with disabilities, while other studies report rates that are 10 times greater than those found in the general population. Older samples and samples including more males typically demonstrate more risk associated with disability. Factors contributing to this heightened risk will be discussed later in this chapter.

Doucette (1986) conducted a survey of Canadian women with and without disabilities and found that women with disabilities were 1.36 times more likely to have been sexually abused or assaulted than women without disabilities are. A subsequent study of Canadian women with disabilities (Stimpson & Best, 1991) found that more than 70% of these women had experienced sexual violence.

Carmody (1990) reports on the prevalence of intellectual disabilities among a group of adults referred to the Sexual Assault Services in New South Wales. Of the 855 adults who were referred, 55 of them had intellectual disabilities, about twice the number that would be expected in a random sample. Carmody also found that 12 out of 14 adults entering a sex education program in New South Wales reported previous sexual abuse or sexual assault experiences.

Crosse and colleagues (1993) report that children with disabilities are 1.67 times as likely as other children to be abused. The relative incidence for children with disabilities was 2.77 times greater for emotional neglect, 2.2 times greater for educational neglect, 2.09 times greater for physical abuse, 1.75 times greater for sexual abuse, 1.6 times greater for physical neglect, and 1.21 times greater for emotional abuse than for children without disabilities. In the Crosse and colleagues study, of all the children who were sexually abused, 15.2% of them had disabilities.

An increased incidence sexual abuse of children with disabilities of 1.75 times the rate in the nondisabled population is alarming, but the authors of the report warned that their findings were likely to underestimate the actual risk to children with disabilities. They pointed out that their methods led to probable underidentification of disabilities among children in their sample, failed to adequately sample children living outside their natural homes, and probably underestimated extrafamilal abuse. Nevertheless, the findings were consistent with earlier estimates. For example, synthesizing the findings of a number of different studies, Sobsey and Varnhagen (1989) estimated that the rate was at least 1.5 times the rate in the general population. They also suggested that because of methodological limitations the estimate was likely to be a low one.

One surprising finding of the study by Crosse and colleagues was that when relative incidence was determined for specific disabilities, they found that mental retardation was not associated with increased risk. A reanalysis of their original dataset produced a significantly different result. Sobsey and Mansell's (1997) reanalysis of the data found that the incidence among children with mental retardation had been seriously underestimated. The original study used expected rates of mental retardation based on school-aged children but the sample included large numbers of preschool children and the diagnosed rate is much lower in this group. In addition, the original study had reported many sexually abused preschoolers with disabilities diagnosed as having motor delays and language delays, but these children were not included as mentally retarded in their data analysis. Similarly, children with a primary diagnosis of fetal alcohol syndrome had been excluded from the data on mental retardation. Grouping all these children with the original group diagnosed as mentally retarded into a category called developmental disability and using an appropriate comparison rate, they found children with developmental disabilities were more than three times as likely to be sexually abused as other children.

Wilson and Brewer (1992) conducted a study of crime victimization among adults with intellectual disabilities in Australia. They found that the overall personal crime victimization rate for adults with intellectual disabilities was 2.6 times the rate for the adults without disabilities. The rate of sexual assault among women with intellectual disabilities was 10.7 times the rate found among people with developmental disabilities.

McCabe and Cummins (1993) conducted another Australian study of 30 people with mild mental retardation and 50 people without disabilities. The results indicate that people with mild mental retardation were more likely to be victims of sexual assault. They were 3.6 times more likely to have been raped, 2.4 times more likely to have had unwanted sexual contact on more than one occasion, and 1.8 times more likely to have had sexual contact with a relative than people without disabilities. They were also much more likely to lack sex education and other critical personal safety information. While the relative rates reported in this study are lower than those reported by Wilson and Brewer, they are extremely high. It should be pointed out that there has been much less research done regarding violence against adults with disabilities than done on violence against adults without disabilities.

The most compelling evidence for heightened risk among children with disabilities to date comes from a study conducted by Sullivan and Knutson (in press). They studied more than 50,000 children registered in a school district in the Midwestern United States during the 1994-1995 school year. By comparing school records with records from child protection, foster care review, and law enforcement records, abuse histories were identified for 9% of the children without disabilities and 31% of the children with disabilities. Children with disabilities as a group were 3.44 times as likely to be abused as children without disabilities. They found that children with mental retardation were at even greater risk. They were 3.7 times as likely to be neglected, 3.8 times as likely to be physically abused, 3.8 times as likely to be emotionally abused, and 4.0 times as likely to be sexually abused than children without disabilities were. Not only were they more likely to be sexually abused than children without disabilities were, they were also more likely to be sexually abused than children with physical, sensory, or health-related disabilities or specific learning disabilities were. This study also showed that children with behavior problems were at even greater risk of abuse. This suggests that children who are dually diagnosed with developmental disabilities and behavior problems may experience even greater risk for abuse.

Considering the findings of all of these studies, several conclusions can be drawn. We can say with great certainty that children with disabilities are much more likely to be sexually abused than other children. The exact level of relative risk differs across studies but is typically about three times the rate found in other children. Part of the variability in reported rates is due to limitations in sampling and methods of various studies. Another part is due to differences in the exact nature of the goals and questions addressed by the study. For example, studies that look at incidence will not produce the same risk ratios as prevalence studies, and studies that define sexual abuse broadly will produce different results than those that restrict sexual abuse to the most serious offenses.

Although there have been fewer studies of sex crimes against adults with disabilities and the studies that have been completed are typically less well-controlled, we can say with a similar level of certainty that adults with developmental disabilities are much more likely to be sexually assaulted that adults without disabilities. The exact ratio of increased risk remains uncertain, but it is likely to be higher than the relative risk for children with disabilities.

These studies report an association between abuse and disability, but they cannot tell us whether having a disability increased the chances of being victimized or whether the abuse resulted in a disability. This is an important area for future research. Current research clearly tells us that physical abuse, chronic sexual abuse, and severe neglect cause some disabilities. This accounts for some part of the relationship between abuse and disability. Could it account for all of it? This is extremely unlikely for two reasons. First, since developmental disabilities must have their inception in childhood, the high rates of victimization of adults with developmental disabilities can not be explained simply by violence-induced disabilities. Second, although research to date has not addressed the relationship of etiology of developmental disability to increased risk, many individual victims appear to have developmental disabilities (e.g., Down syndrome, Williams syndrome) that can not be easily explained as resulting from maltreatment.

Nature of Abuse

The abuse experienced by people with developmental disabilities tends to be more chronic and more severe than abuse experienced by people without disabilities. In the first study conducted by the University of Alberta Abuse and Disability Project, greater severity of developmental disabilities was associated with more chronic abuse. In the second study, there was a strong relationship between disability and the intrusiveness of abuse (Moskal, 1995) (see Table 2.1). In the second study, although the average number of offenders was greater for children with disabilities (2.58%) than for children without disabilities (2.18%), this difference was not statistically significant (Moskal, 1995).

Table 2.1. Intrusiveness of Abuse

Intrusiveness of Abuse	Disabled	Nondisabled
Very Intrusive	94 (56.0%)	236 (49.6%)
Intrusive	55 (32.7%)	208 (43.7%)
Less Intrusive	15 (8.9%)	13 (2.7%)
Least Intrusive	4 (2.4%)	19 (3.9%)
Unknown	14 (excluded)	39 (excluded)

Age Differences

Abused children with disabilities appear to be significantly older than abused children without disabilities. Crosse and colleagues (1993) found a mean age of 8.6 years for children with disabilities who had experienced substantiated abuse and a mean age of 7.7 years for other children who had experienced substantiated abuse. About 24% of the abused children with disabilities were 14 to 17 years old, while only 13.2% of the group without disabilities were in that age range. These findings suggest that risk does not appear to decline with age.

Gender Differences

Crosse and colleagues (1993) found that 21% of the male victims of child abuse had disabilities compared to only 7.7% of the female victims. While this difference could be partially explained by the fact that more children with disabilities are boys (about 55%) than are girls (about 45%), it also lends support to the findings of other researchers that males are over-represented among abuse victims with disabilities when compared to abuse victims without disabilities.

A further analysis of the same data found that among 6- to 12-year-olds, there were more boys among abuse victims with disabilities than might be expected from the proportion of boys who were abused in the non-disabled population (Sobsey, Randall, & Parrila, 1997). The same study found that among sexually abused children between the ages of six and twelve, boys with disabilities were fewer than girls but were a larger minority than might be expected from their proportion among sexually abused children without disabilities.

Sullivan and Knutson (in press) also report that males make up 60% of abused children with disabilities but only 50% of abused children without disabilities. However, their study provided an appropriate control group of children with disabilities who were not abused or neglected. Boys made up more than 60% of the control group. This helps clarify the relationship between abuse, gender, and disability. While boys make up a majority of abused children with disabilities and a larger minority of sexually abused children with disabilities than might be expected from their proportion among children without disabilities, disability appears to affect risk about the same for boys and girls. Because about twice as many boys as girls are identified as having disabilities in the general population, they also make up a similar proportion among abused children. The simple implication of this finding is that appropriate service for abused children with disabilities must be available to boys and girls. While less is known about the gender proportions among adults with disabilities, there is no reason to doubt that the same applies to adults.

Social Class and Ethnic Origins

Emerging information suggests that disability may be less of a risk factor in some cultures than in others. For example, in the Crosse and colleagues study (1993), disability was much more likely to predict victimization among White American children than among African-American children. For example, White children accounted for 60.7% of all maltreated children and 72.1% of maltreated children with disabilities. While this difference was too large to ignore, it is difficult to interpret without additional research. It is possible that White children were more likely to be identified as disabled. The effect also could be related to cultural differences in the values placed on children with disabilities or to the related concept of cultural devaluation. This latter concept would predict that since non-Whites are already stigmatized and devalued in contemporary American society, disability might make less difference. Other studies (e.g., Scott, Lefley, & Hicks, 1993) suggest that risk factors, including disability, vary greatly among ethnic and racial groups. More work needs to be done in order to determine the effect of culture on abuse and why culture may affect the risk for abuse.

Relationship to Offenders

While similar categories of perpetrators are reported in most studies, the percentage of perpetrators in various categories varies substantially. (See Table 2.2 for the various categories of offenders across studies.)

Table 2.2 Major Categories of Offenders in Five Studies

Study and Subject Group	Number	Paid Caregiver	Disabled Peer	Family	Stranger
Furey (1994) Adults with Developmental Disabilities (USA)	461	19%	42%	12%	8%
Sobsey (1994) Children & Adults 74% Developmental Disabilities, 26% Other Disabilities (Canada, USA, NZ)	215	28%	9%	24%	7%
Sullivan et al. (1992) Male Children, 15% Developmental Disabilities, 85% Other Disabilities (USA)	207	About 22%	About 27%	26%	2%
Sullivan et al. (1992) Female Children (USA)	275	About 28%	About 18%	42%	0%
Turk & Brown (1992) Adults with Developmental Disabilities (UK)	84	14%	42%	18%	5%
Westcott (1993) 53% Developmental Disabilities 47% Other Disabilities (UK)	17	33%	0%	42%	0%
Weighted Averages	1259	23%	28%	24%	5%

Although percentages in each category vary substantially, similar subjects and sampling methods appear to result in similar findings. For example, both Furey (1994) and Turk and Brown (1992) report that 42% of offenders were peers with disabilities. Although these samples came from two different countries, both sampled adults with mental retardation.

While some studies found more peers with disabilities were offenders and others found more paid caregivers were offenders, they generally include significant percentages in both groups, which suggests that extrafamilial abuse is a particular problem for people with developmental disabilities. This finding is confirmed by the Abuse and

Disability Project's second study. As shown in Table 2.3, children with disabilities are more likely to experience extrafamilial child abuse than children without disabilities (p = .007), and this appears to be consistent with other findings.

Table 2.3 Intrafamilial and Extrafamilial Abuse

Intrafamilial and Extramfamilial	Disabled	Nondisabled
Intrafamilial	71 (41.8%)	237 (47.8%)
Extrafamilial	99 (58.2%)	259 (52.2%)
Unknown	12 (excluded)	11 (excluded)

It is clear that both intrafamilal and extrafamilial abuse are significant risks for people with developmental disabilities. While it has not been the subject of formal research, a number of cases have emerged of violent perpetrators who target people with developmental disabilities. In one chilling case, a group-home employee was convicted of abducting a young woman with a developmental disability, sexually assaulting her, shooting her in the face and leaving her in a remote area to die. After he was arrested it became clear that he had worked in group homes across the United States, and wherever he worked over the last 11 years, young women with developmental disabilities disappeared (McEnroe, 1999).

In August of 1999, a diary was seized from a man alleged to have committed a violent sexual assault against a 51 year-old Salt Lake City woman who was developmentally disabled. The diary detailed similar attacks against approximately twenty other women with developmental disabilities along with details of the attack he had committed. Police had difficulty finding the victims because few if any of the violent attacks had been reported. According to news reports, the rapist's diary explains why he targeted these women, saying "They won't say no and they have lower mental capacities than I do" (Brush, 1999). These and other cases of extreme predatory offenders are disturbing and can pose a significant risk to people with developmental disabilities.

Reports, Charges, and Convictions

The sexual abuse of children without disabilities is more likely to be reported than the sexual abuse of children with disabilities. As shown in Table 2.4, only 58% of the cases involving children with disabilities were reported, while 74% of the cases involving children without disabilities were reported (p = .002) (Moskal, 1995).

Table 2.4. Reported and Unreported Abuse

Reported and Unreported Abuse	Disabled	Nondisabled
Reported	85 (58.2%)	307 (73.8%)
Unreported	61 (41.8%)	109 (26.2%)
Unknown	1 (excluded)	1 (excluded)

Disclosure

Disclosure situations differed between children with and without disabilities in the Abuse and Disability Project's second study (p = .002). Medical or physical evidence was more than twice as likely to lead to disclosure among the group with disabilities, and children with disabilities were more than twice as likely to tell a noncounseling professional about their abuse. Cases involving children with disabilities were also more likely to be disclosed by a third party, and children with disabilities were less likely to tell their parents about the abuse.

The reasons for termination of the abuse also differed between children with and without disabilities in the second study (p = .002). Intervention by child protection workers was the apparent reason for termination in twice as many cases involving children with disabilities (Moskal, 1995).

Summary

As can be seen in the growing research on the patterns of sexual abuse in children and adults with developmental disabilities, it is clear that sexual abuse and sexual assault of people with developmental disabilities is a frequent problem. The incidence appears to be two to four times as high for children with developmental disabilities as for other children; and for adolescents and adults with developmental disabilities, the risk is probably several times higher than the risk for the general population.

There appears to be some differences in the patterns of sexual abuse and assault experienced by people with developmental disabilities as compared to the patterns of other victims of sexual abuse. More controlled study is needed to better understand the unique features of sexual abuse of people with developmental disabilities. The heightened risk for sexual abuse, however, represents a fairly consistent finding and suggests the importance of developing and adapting therapy approaches for this high-risk population. This finding also suggests the importance of building in additional risk-reduction strategies into the therapy itself. (The use and integration of these additional therapy components is discussed in Chapter 4.)

Heightened vulnerability may be due to a number of interacting and contributing factors. It is necessary to consider the impact of these varied factors on a person with a developmental disability in order to understand what contributes to risk and to outline specific issues that need attention when developing therapy components to reduce risk.

Reasons for heightened vulnerability
Several factors appear to contribute to the heightened vulnerability of people with disabilities to sexual abuse. It has often been thought that people with disabilities were at a greater risk for sexual abuse because they have a disability, but the situation is more complicated. Since the early 1990s an ecological model of abuse has been frequently used to organize some of the factors that contribute to risk (Sobsey, 1994). This model has been further refined into a multifactorial model of violence against people with disabilities (Sobsey & Calder, 1999). The heightened risk for abuse probably has more to do with the atypical social circumstances in which people with disabilities often live, specific practices in the disability field, and the disempowered, devalued status of people with disabilities than with the direct effects of a person's disability.

Atypical social circumstances

People with disabilities often live in atypical social settings that are segregated, isolated, and sheltered from the general community and from the family. These settings might include specialized service oriented residences that may be institutionally or community based. It is difficult to precisely compare the relative risks for sexual abuse in institutional and community environments. The available research suggests that the risk of being sexually abused within an institutional setting is two to four times greater than the risk of being sexually abused in the community (Rindfleisch & Bean, 1988; Rindfleisch & Rabb, 1984).

In these relatively isolated settings, service consumers may have contact with several caregivers who may or may not be adequately screened and trained to ensure consumers' personal safety. Clients may have a variety of personal needs that require intimate caregiving services, and this situation may make them particularly vulnerable to abuse. In a number of cases that have come to the attention of the Abuse and Disability Project, known sex offenders have taken jobs providing personal care to people with disabilities in institutions, group homes, and private residences. Although the number of previously convicted and currently charged applicants is small, the number of victims that each will be likely to have if allowed into the system is large (sometimes 100 or more). Therefore, careful and thorough reference and police checks are essential to the screening process. Employers in the service delivery system need to be sensitive to the problems produced by sexual abuse of people with disabilities and conscientious about screening staff in order to prevent it.

Service providers need to take responsibility for contract staff. For example, many schools and other programs contract for transportation services to convey students with disabilities to specialized programs. The Abuse and Disability Project's research has found many cases in which these transportation providers sexually assaulted students with disabilities (Sobsey & Doe, 1991). Failure to adequately screen staff is one example of agency irresponsibility that heightens the risk for abuse, but there are several other examples of agency irresponsibility.

Many institutional settings cluster sexually aggressive people and vulnerable people together with little attention to the prevention of violence. Institutionalization of dangerous individuals may improve safety in the community, but without adequate safeguards to protect vulnerable people living in institutions, such residents will be at great risk for victimization. The previously reviewed studies that include estimates of other people with disabilities as offenders may reflect this clustering effect. It is also possible that these behaviors may be the result of inadequate sexuality training coupled with either a situation where a sexual abuse victim begins offending or an individual who may be witnessing abusive behavior between staff and clients begins modeling these abusive interactions. Many of these abusive individuals with disabilities have been previous victims of abuse, and some of their victims will probably become future abusers. In clustered settings where many people with disabilities are kept under crowded conditions, the victim-offender cycle and modeled aggression can develop chain reactions that make violence among residents a chronic problem. If this cycle is to be broken, effective treatment for both offenders and victims is required to reduce the chance of future victimization (e.g., Griffiths, Quinsey, & Hingsburger, 1989; Vogel, 1982). Furthermore, large clustered settings and settings that cluster dangerous offenders with vulnerable people must be eliminated or controlled to reduce the effect of these cycles.

The effects of clustering were illustrated by the brutal murder of Tammy Agee, group home resident in Richmond, Virginia. Tammy Agee was a fourteen-year-old girl with a developmental disability who had been placed in a group home after child protection workers apprehended her because of alleged child neglect. A sixteen-year-old with a history of forcible rape of a seven-year-old girl and the attempted knifepoint rape of a nurse at previous residence was placed in this same home with Tammy. When group home staff sent these two out together to a local swimming pool, Tammy was raped and murdered. Incredibly, the case remained officially unsolved for 13 years, when Tammy's former housemate, while in jail for aggravated sexual battery of a 9-year-old girl, insisted on making a voluntary confession (Stewart, 1998).

Specific practices

In institutional settings, the use of various psychotropic medications and physical restraints may reduce a person's ability to resist or protest abuse. The extensive use of psychotropic drugs for behavior control of people with developmental disabilities may increase their vulnerability to abuse. In some cases, the same people who recommend, prescribe, or administer these mood and behavior altering drugs are also the offenders who sexually abuse their drugged victims. The drug may be used deliberately to reduce the resistance of victims or to interfere with the victim's ability to make a complaint.

In other cases, the use of drugs might be used with the best intentions but may unwittingly produce very damaging effects. For example, drugs might be prescribed and administered by treatment team members who are unaware of the cause of the noncompliance or other "inappropriate" behavior. They may be unaware that the behavior that they are "treating" developed in response to abuse.

Similarly, intensive and aversive behavior management programs are sometimes used to control noncompliant, aggressive, sexually inappropriate, or other problem behavior of people with disabilities. Unfortunately, these programs are often employed with little attention to the discovery of the cause of the inappropriate behavior. In many cases, the cause of such behavior turns out to be the abuse of the individual. Suppressing this behavior through behavioral control might take away the victim's last defense against abuse and might stop the victim from disclosing the abuse. Abusers may even use such programs as a coercive tool to ensure silence from sexual abuse victims. It is essential that attempts be made to identify the real cause of "behavior problems" before caregivers attempt to eliminate them through the intrusive use of drugs or punishment procedures (Sobsey, 1990).

Various forms of restraint are sometimes used to control people with atypical behavior, and this type of control can put these people at risk for abuse and assault. The Abuse and Disability Project's studies found that "therapeutic restraint" left victims vulnerable to abuse and assault. Whether restraint is accomplished physically, chemically, or through behavioral coercion, its use can create the extreme inequality of power that often leads to abuse.

As part of their socialization and education, people with developmental disabilities have often been trained to be compliant to authority. Special education practices such as compliance training have promoted passive, unassertive behavior. This emphasis on obedience and generalized compliance to authority discourages the development of discrimination skills to help people with disabilities recognize unsafe situations. An unfortunate consequence of this approach is that students with disabilities have been trained to be victims of psychological, sexual, and physical abuse. Education needs to aim at teaching students to discriminate between appropriate times for compliance and appropriate times for asserting their personal rights. Assertiveness training, choice making, and personal rights education are essential educational content areas for people with disabilities.

In a similar manner, the various myths and concerns held by others about the sexuality and sexual expression of people with disabilities have resulted in inadequate training and knowledge about sexuality and social relationships. These inadequacies create problems because many people with developmental disabilities are socially deprived and isolated, and this may fuel a strong motivation to please and gain acceptance from others that further heightens their vulnerability to exploitation (Gorman-Smith & Matson, 1992). The development and enhanced access to appropriate social and sexual relationships can reduce vulnerability to more abusive relationships. Education should emphasize an awareness of the range of lifestyles available and help students develop the ability to choose.

Disempowered and devalued status and the perception of vulnerability

Perpetrators of sexual assault typically engage in various cognitive distortions to justify their actions. For example, offenders often engage in victim blaming, claiming that the victim provoked the assault through seductive or provocative behavior. While these views may fuel existing victim-blaming distortions, they have the added benefit of diminishing any associated guilt as victims with disabilities are portrayed as not being hurt or damaged by the abuse. Devaluing attitudes toward and myths about people with disabilities that suggest the person is less than human and insensitive to pain may be incorporated into these justifications. Offenders may see people with disabilities as being less than human and unable to feel pain or understand what has happened to them. As a result, there may be far less guilt connected with causing harm to someone who is already dehumanized (Sobsey & Mansell, 1990).

Although the influence of a disempowered and devalued status is significant, it does not diminish the importance of disability in the heightened vulnerability to abuse. Instead, the combination of devalued status and the perception of vulnerability probably work together to heighten the risk for abuse. The presence of a disability may make people with disabilities seem more easily exploitable and vulnerable to people who are searching for victims (Griffiths, 1992).

Research suggests that offenders seek victims they consider to be vulnerable and unable to seek help or report the abuse (Lang & Frenzel, 1988). Communication skill deficits may contribute to an offender's perception of victim vulnerability and to the selection of potential victims. The increased vulnerability of children with hearing impairments is clearly demonstrated by research that indicates that children with hearing impairments experience a greater incidence and risk for sexual abuse than children without hearing impairments (Sullivan, Vernon, & Scanlan, 1987). It is necessary for many individuals with disabilities to learn enhanced communication skills in order to decrease the perception of vulnerability and the risk of sexual abuse.

CONCLUSION

This chapter has been devoted to outlining the patterns of abuse and the social conditions and practices that reflect the disempowered status of people with developmental disabilities and contribute to their vulnerability. At this time, the research on patterns suggests that extrafamilial abuse represents a significant risk, abuse frequently appears to be chronic, and victims experience significant effects. Clearly, several social and cultural factors contribute to heightened risk for abuse. It is fundamental to appreciate the psychological impact of the client's devalued, disempowered status and social circumstances as these often represent significant issues in therapy. Some of these factors can be addressed through staff consultation and client advocacy, but other aspects will need to be addressed through the development of individualized therapy plans.

It is paramount to address some of the sources that heighten a client's risk for further sexual abuse. Many therapy components that can be used to address these difficulties are distinct to clients with developmental disabilities who have been sexually abused. Therapy might include additional psychoeducational components: for example, sexuality, personal rights, and sexual abuse education; social skills and risk-reduction education; teaching a feeling vocabulary; behavioral treatment for secondary behaviors resulting from the abuse (e.g., sexualized behaviors); and additional support to enhance communication and assertiveness skills.

•• 3 ========

The Effects of Sexual Abuse
on
People with Developmental Disabilities

This chapter presents a review of the literature on the effects of child sexual abuse and a discussion about the various mediating and protective factors that affect the heterogeneity of victims' responses. The discussion focuses on the specific psychological developmental issues and coping difficulties experienced by people with developmental disabilities. Sexual abuse and disability issues are integrated later in the chapter, and the psychological, behavioral, and physical indicators of sexual abuse in people with developmental disabilities are presented. There is a comparative analysis of sexual abuse sequelae of children with and without developmental disabilities from a recent study conducted by the Abuse and Disability Project at the University of Alberta. A discussion of the implications for therapy concludes this chapter.

SEXUAL ABUSE EFFECTS
INITIAL EFFECTS

Researchers have documented a wide variety of possible effects of child sexual abuse. The effects of sexual abuse are highly variable and do not form a clear constellation of symptoms: For example, some people may experience seemingly minimal effects, but others experience severe psychiatric symptoms requiring considerable long-term treatment. Researchers who have examined the effects of child sexual abuse in the general population (Briere, 1989; Browne & Finkelhor, 1986) suggest that the initial effects of child abuse, those occurring within two years of the abuse, may include: fear, anxiety, depression, anger, and inappropriate sexual behavior. Lusk and Waterman (1986) identify a range of common problems sexually abused children exhibit: for example, affective disorders; anxiety and fear; psychosomatic complaints; injury; pregnancy; sexually trans-mitted diseases; cognitive and school-related difficulties; learned helplessness; aggressive, antisocial behavior; withdrawal; self-de-structive behaviors; poor self-esteem; and relationship problems.

INTERNALIZING AND EXTERNALIZING BEHAVIORS

In childhood, behaviors may be internalized or externalized, and chil-dren can exhibit both types of behaviors. This behavioral overlap may change, and it contributes to some of the variability seen in abuse effects over time. Behaviors may be internalized when a child at-tempts to cope with the abuse alone, and these behaviors include isolation, depression, and withdrawal. Externalization occurs when a child expresses and projects his or her emotions outwardly. These behaviors may include aggression, hostility, destructiveness, violence, and sexualized behaviors. Gil (1991) and Friedrich (1990) note that when children first enter therapy to address sexual abuse issues they may start out internalizing and later, as therapy progresses, exhibit more externalizing behaviors. Friedrich (1990) also notes a gender distinction: Boys tend to exhibit externalizing behaviors, while girls tend to exhibit internalizing behaviors.

Dissociation

Dissociation is defined by the DSM-IV as a disturbance or alteration in the normally integrative functions of identity, memory, percep-tion, or consciousness (American Psychiatric Association, 1994). It may involve compartmentalizing sensations, memories, affect, and perceptions. For example, children may engage in massive denial, which fuels emotional shutdown and psychological numbing. They can experience bodily anesthesias, feelings of invisibility, and amnesias for certain periods. Sometimes children use dissociation or other types of defenses during the abuse. An excessive reliance on these initially self-protective or sometimes self-destructive behav-iors may hinder the development of more adaptive strategies and contribute to significant coping difficulties (Terr, 1991). Dissocia-tion is associated with a variety of trauma experiences. Often, these experiences are severe or chronic. Dissociation may serve a valuable protective function during severe trauma; however, following actual trauma, this defense becomes highly maladaptive. The defense against conscious awareness of pain and fear prevent the person for integrating the trauma experience into their life memories. Dissociation is a natural capacity that becomes dysfunctional when a person is unable to or is unaware of how to control these responses. It is also dysfunctional when these responses occur in inappropriate contexts or have an intensity or duration that is personally disruptive.

Post-Traumatic Stress Disorder

Post-Traumatic Stress Disorder (PTSD) is widely used to describe the effects of trauma (American Psychiatric Association, 1994). PTSD is caused by the existence of a recognizable stressor that would evoke significant symptoms in almost anyone. The symptoms of PTSD include a re-experiencing of the trauma through recurrent intrusive recollections, dreams, and sudden feelings. Additional symptoms, such as a numbed responsiveness or reduced involvement in the external world, include diminished interest in activities, feelings of estrangement from others, and constricted affect. Additional PTSD symptoms include: hyperalertness, sleep problems, survival guilt, problems with memory or concentration, avoidance of activities, and an intensification of symptoms when exposed to stimuli related to the traumatic event.

Some researchers argue that PTSD is too narrow and describes only a small group of abused children (Eth & Pynoos, 1985; Finkelhor, 1988; Friedrich, 1990). Terr (1991) suggests the use of two PTSD categories: Type I disorders, which are produced by a single traumatic event; and Type II disorders, which result from multiple, longstanding traumatic experiences. Visualization, reenactment, fear, and futurelessness are symptoms common to both PTSD types (Terr, 1991). In addition, Type II disorders may be accompanied by denial or psychic numbing, rage, and unrelenting sadness. Complex Post Traumatic Stress Disorder is a term that includes more extensive symptoms such as distortions of personality, identity, and relatedness, and heightened vulnerability to repeated abuse that pertain to survivors of prolonged, repeated trauma (Herman, 1992). A recent review of 45 studies on sexual abuse effects suggests that fears, PTSD, behavior problems, sexualized behaviors, and poor self-esteem are among the most frequently occurring sequelae of child sexual abuse, with no one particular symptom characterizing the majority of effects (Kendall-Tackett, Williams, & Finkelhor, 1993).

In recent years there has been a growing research literature that has examined the psychobiological consequences of trauma (Perry, 1994; van der Kolk, 1994). This research has demonstrated that there are basic and lasting biological alterations can occur within all components of the physiological and neurological response systems in persons who have experienced overwhelming, uncontrollable trauma (Knopp & Benson, 1996). The greatest such effects are noted to occur in childhood when both neurological and physiological systems are developing and vulnerable to alteration (Perry, 1994). Hormonal, neurochemical, and structural changes occur within the components of the stress-response system. Exposure to extreme, prolonged, repeated stress may cause changes in the catecholamine response to stress that includes the locus cereleus/norepinephrine, dopamine, and the sympathetic nervous systems. Alterations cause these systems to be hyper-reactive to the point that a person's capacity to accurately assess or interpret threat and mobilize appropriate responses to new information is compromised. A person may chronically misinterpret and overreact to neutral stimuli and have acute responses to any stimuli resembling the original trauma (van der Kolk & Fisler, 1993). The development of persistent conditioned fear responses is thought to be a result of an increase in the response magnitude to norepinephrine activation and a lowered firing threshold or sensitization within the neural circuits mediated by the locus cereleus and the amygdala. This sensitization of neural circuits occurs as a result of a process called kindling. In addition, reduction of serotonin levels appear related to hypermnesia, suicidal behavior, and intrusive thoughts of trauma (van der Kolk, 1994). Manifestations of these changes to the stress-response system are found in the symptoms of PTSD that include hyperarousal, hypermnesia (persistent uncontrollable and intrusive reexperiencing of past trauma), avoidance (restricting activities), and emotional anesthesia (Knopp & Benson, 1996).

Dissociation constitutes a defense against trauma. As in PTSD the neurological mechanisms that mediate the dissociative response can become highly sensitized and hyper-responsive so that the ability to handle even mild levels of stress becomes compromised in those exposed to extreme, uncontrollable stress (van der Kolk & Fisler, 1994). During dissociation the conscious self is often experienced as split or separated into an observing or detached self and a participating self. Physical anesthesia, emotional detachment, and cognitive and perceptual distortions can a create a sense that the trauma did not happen and can interfere with proper integration of the experience. One physiological consequence of dissociation is that the amygdala which assesses incoming experience as being of great emotional importance cannot appropriately categorize the experience into the septohippocampal system (van der Kolk, 1994).

Although psychobiological research presents compelling examinations of the possible consequences of chronic trauma, it is important to admit that at this time our knowledge in this area is in its infancy. It is also critical not to prematurely overstate the physiological impact of chronic trauma and not to frame these possible physiological consequences as immutable. It is important to remember that much of this research is based on animal studies and that these results may not generalize to the experience of traumatized children and adults living in variable social environments with highly variable personal resources and coping mechanisms. There is not only great variability in human responses to trauma but the consequences of trauma not only wax and wane over time but can improve with appropriate treatment and intervention.

Long-Term Effects

Briere (1992) notes that the long-term psychological effects of sexual abuse include post-traumatic effects, cognitive distortions, altered emotionality, dissociation, and impaired self-reference. Long-term behavioral and relationship effects may include difficulties with intimacy and trust (e.g., assumptions about aggression in relationships), altered sexuality, manipulative behavior and aggression, and various avoidance behaviors (e.g., psychoactive substance use, suicidality, and other behaviors intended to reduce tension) (Briere, 1992). Browne and Finkelhor (1986) suggest that long-term effects, those occurring two years or more after the abuse, may include: depression, self-destructive behavior, feelings of isolation and stigmatization, poor self-esteem, tendencies toward revictimization, substance abuse, sexual maladjustment, and difficulties establishing trust.

Briere (1992) conceptualizes the effects of abuse as dynamic and interactive but unfolding in three stages: (1) initial reactions, (2) accommodation to ongoing abuse, and (3) long-term elaboration and secondary accommodation. Friedrich (1990) suggests that the effects of child sexual abuse wax and wane over time and that this contributes to some of the variability seen in both the short- and long-term effects and symptoms that might be experienced by victims of child sexual abuse.

SEQUELAE FOR MALES

Most of the research documenting the effects of sexual abuse has been conducted with female victims, but in recent years, some research has been conducted to examine the effects of sexual abuse on male victims (Vander Mey, 1988). At this time, little is known about the sexual abuse sequelae for males. There are, however, some significant treatment issues that emerge for males: concerns about homosexuality and masculinity, sexual confusion, and the risk of becoming a perpetrator. For example, if the offender is also male, there may be issues about masculinity because the victim may believe he should have been able to defend himself. Concerns about sexual orientation may be present if there was a close relationship with the offender or if the victim experienced some physical pleasure during the abuse. When the offender is female, the male victim may minimize any traumatic impact (Nasjleti, 1980), or he may have difficulty having the abuse taken seriously by others, who may regard it as initiation or seduction and not sexual abuse. Long-term effects of sexual abuse for males might include emotional withdrawal, feelings of isolation, depression, feelings of masculinity loss, fears about homosexuality, and negative self-worth (Dimock, 1989; Kilgore, 1988; Nasjleti, 1980; Pierce, 1987). However, one study, using the Trauma Symptom Checklist (Briere, Evans, Runtz, & Wall, 1988), notes no significant differences in long-term sequelae between males and females.

MODEL OF TRAUMAGENIC DYNAMICS

To explain the effects of child sexual abuse, Finkelhor and Browne (1985) created a model of traumagenic dynamics that includes traumatic sexualization, betrayal, powerlessness, and stigmatization. The dynamics of traumatic sexualization, betrayal, powerlessness, and stigmatization are important for trauma assessment and the development of treatment goals.

Traumatic sexualization

The dynamics of traumatic sexualization may include: the child being rewarded for sexual behavior that is inappropriate to their developmental level, the offender teaching the child that they are to exchange sex for attention and affection, and the child learning misconceptions about sexual behavior and morality from the offender. As a result sex can be strongly conditioned with negative emotions and memories. The psychological effect of traumatic sexualization may involve a heightened importance of sexual issues and confusion about sexual identity. A child may experience confusion about sexual norms, sex and love, and caregiving relationships. There may be aversions and phobic reactions to sexual arousal or intimacy. Behavioral manifestations may include: preoccupation with and compulsive sexual behaviors, sexual dysfunctions, precocious or aggressive sexual activity, promiscuity and prostitution, arousal and orgasm difficulties, flashbacks, and the inappropriate sexualization of parenting.

Betrayal

The dynamics of betrayal may include: the exploitation of trust and a violation of the expectation that others will provide care and protection as the child's well being and protection is disregarded. The psychological effect of betrayal for the victim may include grief and depression, extreme dependency, mistrust, anger and hostility, and impaired ability to judge others' trustworthiness. The behavioral manifestations of betrayal may include clinging, vulnerability to subsequent abuse, isolation, discomfort in intimate relations, failure to protect one's children from victimization, aggressive behavior, and delinquency.

Powerlessness

The dynamics of powerlessness may include repeated physical violation and experiences of fear and an offender using force or trickery to abuse child. A child may feel unable to protect him or her self, stop the abuse, and may be unable to make others stop the abuse. Powerlessness may produce anxiety and fear, a lowered sense of efficacy, and self-perception as a victim. A child may have a strong need to control and may identify with the aggressor. Behaviors associated with powerlessness may include: nightmares, phobias, various somatic complaints, eating and sleeping disorders, depression, dissociation, running away, school problems, truancy, employment problems, potential for revictimization, aggression, delinquency, and becoming an abuser.

Stigmatization

The dynamics of stigmatization may include the offender blaming the victim, the child being pressured for secrecy and others responding with shock and disbelief. The psychological effect of stigmatization may include guilt and shame, lowered self-esteem, and a sense of differentness from others. The behavioral manifestations of stigmatization include: isolation, drug or alcohol abuse, suicide attempts, criminal involvement, and self-mutilation.

Due to the variable effects of child sexual abuse over time, it is unlikely that the existing conceptualizations capture its full complexity; even so, research and models do identify many possible treatment issues. Some of the variability in sexual abuse effects may be attributed to the combined effects of sexual, psychological, and physical abuse (Briere, 1992). The considerable variability of child sexual abuse effects also may be due, in part, to several mediating or protective factors. There are several factors that mediate the impact of abuse and it is essential that therapists consider these factors and understand the unique impact abuse may have on their clients.

MEDIATING FACTORS

The impact of abuse is mediated by a variety of circumstances surrounding the victim, the abuse, and social supports. The person's level of development during the abuse, the severity and chronicity of the abuse, the relationship to the offender, level of threats used by the offender, and the parental response to the abuse are all important factors that may influence the impact of abuse. Briere's review (1992) outlines specific characteristics of sexual abuse that may be associated with greater trauma: greater duration and frequency of abuse, multiple perpetrators, penetration or more invasive forms of sexual abuse, physical force, concurrent physical abuse, abuse at an early age, abuse with bizarre features, the victim's sense of personal responsibility for the abuse and feelings of powerlessness, and betrayal or stigma. Friedrich (1990) suggests that the coping resources and general child and family functioning, both prior to and following disclosure, and the transactional effects between parents and child all influence the impact of sexual abuse. In addition, the emotional climate of the family in areas such as attachment, boundaries, and amount of disorganization, the person's mental and emotional health, and the presence of various protective factors prior to the abuse may affect the potential impact of sexual abuse.

Chronicity and Severity of Abuse

Chronic abuse is believed to create considerable psychological damage since children may develop a long-term reliance on coping mechanisms such as dissociation to defend against trauma. Excessive reliance on these strategies may hinder the development of more adaptive means of coping. The more severe the abuse in terms of the invasive nature of the contact and the closer the relationship with the offender, the greater the potential impact of the abuse (Adams-Tucker, 1982). The level of threats used by the offender to silence the child and ensure secrecy might produce a paralyzing sense of fear, isolation, and confusion in the child that exacerbates the impact of the abuse (Finkelhor & Baron, 1986).

Family Functioning and Response to Abuse

The emotional climate of the family prior to the abuse and also following disclosure influences the impact of abuse on children: For example, Conte and Schuerman (1987) found a strong correlation between poor family functioning and the impact of abuse on children. Many abusive families are characterized by multiple problems and operate at high levels of dysfunction: for example, these families may exhibit chaos and disruption, alcohol or substance abuse, inadequate or highly permeable boundaries between members, enmeshment, and role reversal. Families who display over-reactive or unsupportive reactions to the disclosure induce greater trauma in the child. If the child is removed from the home the child may feel that he or she is being punished instead of the perpetrator, and this may exacerbate guilt feelings.

The nature of the relationship between the mother or the nonoffending parent and the child can have significant effects on the willingness of the child to disclose and on the response to the disclosure. Censoring, blaming, and disbelieving responses from the mother or the nonoffending parent can create greater guilt and shame in the child, and it may put additional stress on what potential support may be available in the relationship. A mother might have significant issues concerning her relationship with the child, the offender, guilt about failing to protect the child, and, in some cases, competition with the child for the offender's affection.

Quality of attachment
The nature of a child's relationship with caregivers is strongly influenced by the quality of attachment. A child's experiences with attachment figures will influence the manner in which a child forms internal representations of others' behavior. Children who experience inconsistent, insensitive, and abusive parenting may have difficulty forming secure attachments with others, both in childhood and adulthood. In some circumstances of extremely poor parental care children may develop Reactive Attachment disorder. The essential feature of Reactive Attachment Disorder is markedly disturbed and developmentally inappropriate social relatedness that has onset before age five years and is associated with care that is grossly pathological (American Psychiatric Association, 1994). Grossly pathological care would include a caregiver's persistent disregard of the child's basic emotional and physical needs or repeated changes of a primary caregiver that prevent the development of stable attachments. Pre-

sentation may be of the Inhibited or Disinhibited Type (American Psychiatric Association, 1994). In the *Inhibited* Type a child persistently fails to initiate and respond to most social interactions in developmentally appropriate ways (i.e., the child may appear hypervigilant, highly ambivalent, or may be resistant to comfort). In the *Disinhibited* Type a child exhibits indiscriminate sociability toward attachment figures. Reactive attachment disorder is not necessarily a consequence of sexual abuse alone, however, it may be present in children who have experienced combinations of child abuse including physical, sexual, and emotional abuse and neglect. Poor attachment and abusive experiences might result in a child's expectation that detachment or abuse is "normal" and that the world is an unsafe and unpredictable place. The representational model of self is negative and depicts the self as unworthy and unlovable. The child might view him- or herself similarly. Sexual abuse may be preceded by insecure attachment, which can exacerbate the long-term effects of sexual abuse (Alexander, 1992). In therapy, one of the primary tasks of the therapist is to create a safe environment and a curative relationship in which the client can explore the more painful aspects of his or her life. Clearly, a client's inabilities to form secure attachments with others might carry over to therapeutic relationships and impede or dramatically slow the development of a therapeutic alliance.

Child's Level of Development and Emotional Health

Younger children might have the greatest vulnerability to sexual abuse effects due to their limited coping strategies, although the developmental stages that a child must pass through during the abuse may be more relevant to impact than age per se (Friedrich, 1990). The child's mental and emotional health prior to the abuse might affect the child's response. Various protective factors associated with the child's ability to cope and be resilient despite extraordinary stress may help inoculate the child against some of the effects of sexual abuse.

Protective Factors and Resiliency to Stress

Research on protective factors against stress suggest that a variety of personal characteristics may help inhibit the development of psycho-

logical problems (Garmezy, 1983). Resilience describes a constellation of personal characteristics that protects people from developing
psychological problems: the ability to take an active stance and see a
problem as something that can be overcome, changed, or endured;
the ability to persist to improve things or return to a positive state
and develop a range of problem-solving skills in various situations;
and the ability to be flexible and to use only those strategies appropriate for a given situation. The development of resilience depends
on these abilities resulting in successful or gratifying experiences, at
least part of the time. Rutter (1981) identifies several factors that
affect resilience in children: the presence of at least one adult figure
with whom the child can have a positive relationship, an environment outside the home that is conducive to the child's development
(e.g., a well-run and supportive school), and the number of stressors
experienced by the child. The presence of any one stressor does not
necessarily lead to psychological difficulties; however, several stressors may have a multiplicative effect. Rutter (1983) notes that high
self-esteem, a sense of achievement, problem-solving skills, and high
intelligence may act as protective influences that promote resilience.
Garmezy (1983) identifies school achievement and problem solving
as protective, but also notes the importance of family environment
and peer relations.

Several factors mediate the impact of abuse: the abuse circumstances;
the victim's resiliency and emotional history; and the relational context, which includes familial attachments or social supports and their
response to abuse disclosure. A therapist working with a client with
a developmental disability also needs to consider how these factors
may help or hinder their client's progress in treatment and how these
factors could otherwise be influenced by the presence of a developmental disability. In addition, it is important to consider how the
client's sexual abuse treatment issues may interact with the psychological issues associated with developmental disability.

Psychological Impact of Developmental Disability
A person with a developmental disability has the same psychological
needs as a person without a developmental disability. Nevertheless,

there are several psychological and social challenges that may affect the adjustment of a person with a developmental disability. These challenges and issues change across the course of the person's development and are influenced by the family, social context, and coping difficulties associated with the developmental disability. It is important to consider these possible barriers to adjustment in order to determine various ways to ameliorate their effects (Hallahan & Kauffman, 1991).

The presence of a developmental disability presents several possible psychological issues that vary throughout a person's lifespan. The variability of issues will be influenced by the individual's experiences, personal resources and limitations, and developmental level. Across the lifespan, however, there are common challenges associated with particular developmental periods that have significant effects on both the person with a developmental disability and his or her family and other systems. The following discussion places emphasis on the psychosocial effects of a developmental disability. More specific family systems issues are examined in detail in Chapter 7.

Infancy and Early Childhood
During infancy and early childhood, a child with a developmental disability experiences various delays in motor development, self-care, acquisition and use of language, and acquiring knowledge of social life (Baroff, 1991). The child might be delayed in achieving a variety of developmental milestones, but the amount of delay will depend on the severity of the developmental disability, the presence of any additional disabilities, and other factors.

The birth of a child with a developmental disability creates numerous demands on caregivers' time, and these demands influence the family system's resources, role structure, emotional stability, and ability to handle stress (Blacher, 1984). Parents might be faced with the child's possible health problems and various financial and mental demands; they might experience frustration due to inadequate services for their child, isolation from others, and pressure on their coping abilities. Also, siblings may experience increased role demands, such as caretaking for the child with a disability, which can contribute to role confusion, disengagement, and frustration (Wilkins, 1992).

In the family, the child with a developmental disability will have a heightened reliance on others and reduced self-confidence. Busy family members might find it easier to do things for the child than to teach him or her, and the child with a disability may develop the expectation that others will take responsibility for tasks that he or she could learn.

Parental reactions to the child's disability

Parents can experience a variety of changing emotional responses after learning of their child's developmental disability. Parents have many dreams and hopes for their child's future that may be shattered. A great variety of emotional responses can be experienced by parents: for example, denial of the disability; projection of blame (Drew et al., 1992); grief (Huber, 1979); chronic sorrow (Wilder, Wasow, & Hatfield, 1981); guilt and self-blame; and depression, helplessness, and low self-esteem (Nixon, 1993). For some parents, feelings of failure or loss may be temporary, and yet for others, the feelings may never be successfully resolved (Drew et al., 1992).

Much of the earlier research on parental responses to the birth of a child with disabilities has been fraught with methodological problems and assumed both the subsequent development of family pathology and a homogeneity of parental response, describing these responses primarily in terms of grief and loss. The application of Kubler-Ross' stages of death and dying to parental adjustment to the news of their child's disability has been a popular conceptualization and many parents identify with feelings of loss, shock, and disbelief. Ditchfield (1992) suggests that parents' subsequent adjustment, however, is far less predictable than would be suggested by this stage model. Later researchers critiqued these grief stage models (Blacher, 1984) and provide greater recognition for the heterogeneity of parental response. Blacher (1984) outlines three main categories of response. Stage 1, initial reaction, includes shock, disbelief, denial of the diagnosis, and sometimes rejection of the child. Stage 2, emotional disorganization, refers to parental experiences of guilt, anger, sadness, or disappointment. Stage 3, emotional organization, refers to a period of adjustment and acceptance. Blacher, however, points out that parental responses are highly individual, and parents cannot be expected to move through any particular sequence of phases.

Although much emphasis has been placed on parental reactions, increasingly, research has revealed the systemic, reciprocal, and circular influences of familial relationships in their ecological context (Crnic, Friedrich, & Greenberg, 1983). More recent research has focused on stress, coping, and the adaptation processes of families, and has examined the dynamic nature of these highly variable responses and the influence of the parents' cognitive appraisal of the situation, personal coping resources, previous experience with disability, amount of social support, and other ecological factors. Adjustment of the family to the child's disability, however, is extremely important to the child's development in the social, emotional, and communication spheres. Difficulties in early adjustment have consequences for the family's development of attachment to the child.

Disruption of attachment

Parents of children with disabilities sometimes appear less attached to their children than other parents (Wasserman, Lennon, Allen, & Shilansky, 1987). The reasons for such attachment problems are poorly understood. Some children with disabilities have specific impairments that may interfere with the perception or processing of stimulation essential for the development of attachment (Andrew, 1989). For example, a child who is deaf and blind may require extra stimulation through contact and movement to develop attachment between the child and caregivers. Also some children with sensory integration difficulties such as tactile or eye gaze aversions may complicate the development of attachment and may require that parents learn about their child's particular difficulties and learn different ways to approach and connect with their child. Some parents may reject their children with disabilities because of their pre-existing attitudes toward disabilities or because similarly rejecting attitudes are expressed by others and influence parental behavior. Some parents may have internalized attitudes of rejection toward people with disabilities that they must overcome before they can accept and love their own child. Often, attitudes expressed by some professionals and other members of society continue to give parents the message that "they should not let themselves become too attached" to their child as this will only cause them grief and pain.

Stress related to the birth of a child with disabilities or the diagnosis of a child's disability might interfere with the development of attachment. This may be particularly true when the diagnosis is made shortly after birth, an important time for the development of family attachments. Also, well-intentioned professionals may encourage parents to establish a quasi-professional relationship, such as therapy assistant or behavior manager, with their child. While this practice is not necessarily harmful, these new role requirements should not interfere with the parents' caregiving role. Similarly, siblings are often relegated to caretaking roles for their sibling with a disability, and this situation can lead to frustration, resentment, and disengagement (Powell & Ogle, 1985). Although much family stress research has assumed the development of pathology, it is becoming increasingly evident that many families are resilient and do adjust well to the birth of a child with a developmental disability (Singer & Powers, 1993). Family resiliency, the ability to deal with stress and acceptance of the child are central to the development of the child's self-esteem.

Childhood and the School Years

Throughout the school-age period, the child with a developmental disability can experience difficulties with: learning ability, academic skills, knowledge, reasoning, the ability to cope with new situations, developing personal responsibility and autonomy, and establishing satisfying social relationships (Baroff, 1991). Also, communication might be a problem, and the child may experience slow language acquisition and difficulties with articulation. As the child enters school, the full extent of the child's cognitive difficulties become clearer. School can become a source of chronic frustration and difficulties for both parents and child. Parents might find themselves frustrated when attempting to gain necessary services for their child and with the child's lack of progress in school. Ongoing difficulties with learning that result in repeated experiences of failure and disappointment can fuel a child's existing sense of inadequacy and poor self-esteem. Peer relationships can be marked by rejection, exclusion, teasing, and ridicule, and it is possible that the child will experience the stigma of disability and the loneliness, pain, and isolation that often accompany disability. Friendships can be difficult to establish due to limited contacts and opportunities, inadequate social skills, and speech difficulties that might make communication or initiation of relationships difficult. This chronic frustration may result in a variety of behaviors that the child uses to manage emotions: For example, a child can be distractible, withdrawn, have a low frustration tolerance, poor self-regulation, be impulsive, and be easily aroused emotionally. The child will likely appear more immature than his or her same-age peers and the behaviors the child uses to handle his or her emotions will reflect this emotional immaturity.

Parents may become socially isolated. The reasons for this isolation are poorly understood, but it would appear that the intensive caregiving demands can result in fatigue (Singer & Irvin, 1991). Difficulty obtaining childcare can result in limited leisure time and restricted social interactions. Parents might encounter rejection as a result of the stigma associated with disability, or they might reject others who hold negative attitudes about their child. Due to the child's frequent segregation from the community, other family and community members may lack opportunities to access social networks that could provide vital support: For example, neighborhood mothers may get together to discuss the local school, but the mother of a child sent to a "special school across town" is unlikely to be included.

Adolescence
In adolescence, many of the psychological issues associated with a child's school years can become exacerbated as previous challenges will be intensified (Drew et al., 1992). Repeated experiences of failure and disappointment, stigmatization, loneliness, ridicule, and rejection by peers might further entrench a sense of personal inadequacy and poor self-esteem at a time when there is a heightened need for

social acceptance and self-efficacy. People with mild mental retardation might want to avoid the stigma associated with socializing with other people with disabilities as they may regard this peer group as inferior even though they might not be readily accepted into the social circles of people without disabilities. Difficulties associated with forming friendships in childhood can persist well into adolescence. To counter their loneliness and isolation, some people with developmental disabilities may overcompensate by calling their friends too often, talking too long on the phone, demanding attention, and not being able to give others space or room. Similarly, some people with developmental disabilities may attempt to become friends with their various professional contacts.

As with adolescents without disabilities, adolescents with developmental disabilities may experience heightened concerns with personal appearance and identity, physical changes, peer acceptance and conformity, freedom, and a growing interest in sexual matters. Although these are normal issues, teenagers with developmental disabilities will have fewer resources to deal with this stormy period and greater difficulty negotiating these issues. At this stage, people who are described as higher functioning might struggle with their disability as it pertains to their own identity. There may be a very strong desire to be perceived as normal and accepted by others and to avoid unwanted attention caused by behavior or appearance. Some individuals may come to accept their disability and understand it in terms of both their abilities and limitations, while others may be less successful in this endeavor and deny the existence of the disability entirely. As with other adolescents, there might be an increased need for freedom and autonomy, although this will likely occur somewhat later than in adolescents who do not have a developmental disability (Baroff, 1991). The increased need for autonomy can lead to considerable struggles with parents and other caregivers, and achieving autonomy might create problems due to the adolescent's dependency, coping difficulties, and emotional immaturity.

An adolescent's naturally growing interest in sexuality and the need for intimacy are likely to cause problems for parents who have children with developmental disabilities. Many parents come to regard their maturing child with a developmental disability as an eternal child who will never have any interest in sex and does not require sex education. As mentioned earlier, there is considerable discomfort surrounding sexuality and developmental disability, and many parents have significant concerns and fears about their child's blossoming sexuality. Parents often worry that their child will be exploited by others, behave indiscriminately, or get pregnant or contract a sexually transmitted disease (Hingsburger, 1993; Wilgosh, 1993). Compared to their peers without disabilities, adolescents with developmental disabilities are less informed about sex, have fewer social skills and opportunities for opposite sex interactions, have less access to potential partners, and have less privacy. Greater restrictiveness on sexual behavior combined with inadequate sexuality education, sexual frustration, unfulfilled needs for intimacy, and loneliness may contribute to inappropriate sexual behaviors that heighten the risk for any of the above mentioned parental fears. (See Chapter 7 for a discussion of parental concerns and chapter 9 for a discussion of assessing inappropriate sexual behaviors).

Young Adulthood
Prout and Strohmer (1994a) note that although there is little developmental information on adolescents and young adults with mental retardation, many of the problem-solving tasks and life issues faced by this population are similar to those faced by adolescents and young adults without disabilities. As adolescents with developmental disabilities complete their schooling and approach adulthood, they hope that their graduation will free them from the frustrations associated with school. Even so, they may encounter difficulties in the transition from school to vocational life. Throughout the school years, personal relationships with classmates, teachers, and others may be well established and provide important, consistent sources of support, comfort, and friendship. In addition, a student may have developed some security from the consistency and structure provided by school life. Sometimes a young person will have had inadequate preparation for post-school life and experience difficulty adjusting to the changes associated with entering a new social situation and the dif-

ferent requirements of being part of the workforce. Many people will enter work-study following school to receive some vocational training. Individuals in the mild range of mental retardation are frequently employable in unskilled jobs, and many people who function in the moderate range may find employment in sheltered workshops (Baroff, 1991); but in some cases, people with disabilities will have difficulty either finding or keeping a job or will not have received adequate vocational preparation, which may further complicate and frustrate his or her prospects of earning a living and becoming independent.

Sometimes a young adult with disabilities who is attempting to enter the world of work may return to live with his or her parents following his or her out-of-home placement, and this can create a difficult situation for families. The earlier dynamics of the family may suddenly return. Family members may find themselves engaged in their former roles of parent and child while dealing with their child's struggle for independence. Older parents may experience a conflict between their parental concern for and desire to protect their child and the child's desire for independence, friends, dates, and sexual and intimacy needs. These struggles may result in frustration, anger, and heightened behavior problems, and in some cases, previously acquired independent living skills may deteriorate. The young adult might desire greater independence but experience his or her previous level of dependence in the family. Parents facing advancing years and declining health might find themselves uncomfortable fulfilling parenting roles with their now adult but still dependent adult child. Additional concerns involve ensuring living arrangements for their child in the event the parents become ill or die. In some situations, caregivers attempt to shield people with developmental disabilities from the full range of emotional experiences on the basis that they cannot understand will be harmed, or will behave inappropriately. As a consequence people with developmental disabilities might have little experience dealing with emotions (Bicknell & Conboy-Hill, 1992), and often, there is little preparation for life events such as death and even less consideration given to the grief and bereavement experienced by a person with developmental disabilities (Waitman & Conboy-Hill, 1992).

THE TROUBLE WITH COPING

People with developmental disabilities experience difficulties coping for several reasons. Some of these problems are related to socialization and maturity, problem-solving difficulties, cognitive limitations, and a vulnerability to stress and a susceptibility to emotional and mental health problems.

SOCIALIZATION, ISOLATION, AND DEPENDENCY

Many people with developmental disabilities are socially deprived, lonely, and isolated, and this can fuel a strong motivation to please and gain acceptance and approval from others (Gorman-Smith & Matson, 1992). Strong socialization practices that emphasize the value of obedience may teach people with developmental disabilities that compliance is in their best interest. This socialization can cause people with developmental disabilities to become fearful or, perhaps worse, unaware of the possibility of questioning those in authority. Many people who are highly dependent on the care of others have almost no experience with choices or making decisions and no conceptualization of their personal rights. They may have an extensive history of failures, an intense desire to avoid ridicule, internalized self-hatred, and feelings of inadequacy. Poor self-esteem, a limited ability to deal with interpersonal stresses, weak communication skills, limited sexuality knowledge, and prolonged dependency may present significant difficulties.

LESS RESILIENCY TO STRESS

People with developmental disabilities are less likely to possess many of the protective factors, identified by Rutter (1983) and Garmezy (1983), that could provide some inoculation from the potential effects of stress. For example, they are unlikely to have high self-esteem, high scholastic achievement, effective problem-solving skills, strong social skills, good peer relations, and secure attachments. Reiss (1994b) suggested that it is necessary to try to imagine life through the eyes of a person with a developmental disability to appreciate the psychological risk factors. He noted that people with mental retardation are often treated as if they are objects to be avoided. They tend to be lonely and may find few friends in life and are likely to be unemployed in adulthood. In addition, they are rarely asked for their opinions as it is assumed that they are not smart enough to have any opinions (Reiss, 1994b).

SUSCEPTIBILITY TO EMOTIONAL DIFFICULTIES

People with developmental disabilities are likely to suffer more emotional disturbances than members of the general population (Matson & Barrett, 1982; Borthwick-Duffy, 1994). People with mental retardation typically have weak social coping skills, poor self-esteem, and repeated experiences of failure. People with developmental disabilities can experience difficulties with recognizing and labeling emotions in self and others, perspective taking, problem-solving skills, and impulse control. In addition, people with developmental disabilities may have difficulties perceiving social situations and conceptualizing the intentions of others accurately (Brown, 1994). Some of these difficulties may contribute to problems with anger control or aggressive behaviors (Benson, 1995). Also, severe and profound levels of mental retardation are frequently associated with various brain abnormalities. It would appear that these factors may interact and contribute to the heightened susceptibility to mental disorders. The presentation of mental disorders is also influenced by developmental level and complicate diagnosis (Charlot, 1998).

Reiss and Benson (1984) outline a variety of psychosocial risk factors that predispose people with developmental disabilities to psychological difficulties and behavioral problems. These researchers note that people with developmental disabilities often experience prolonged stigmatization and other negative social conditions: for example, labeling, rejection and social disruption, segregation, restricted opportunities, victimization, and infantilization. Some people with developmental disabilities are often very aware of the stigma associated with the label mentally retarded, become defensive about their competencies, and may take considerable pains to appear as normal as possible and deny their disability. Rejection, social disruption, and segregation exacerbate the loneliness experienced by people with developmental disabilities. Segregated living conditions that separate people with developmental disabilities from parental support may result in the person with a developmental disability blaming him- or herself for separation from the family. Restricted social and personal relationship opportunities limit access to valuable social learning experiences and opportunities for closeness and intimacy. Victimization and exploitation in various forms are common, and despite considerable life experience, adults with developmental disabilities are often treated as children. Although these are common experiences, there is great variability in coping abilities, and not all people with developmental disabilities will display all these characteristics to the same degree (Hallahan & Kauffman, 1991).

PROBLEM-SOLVING DIFFICULTIES
Baroff (1991) outlined a number of cognitive characteristics associated with people who have developmental disabilities. These characteristics may influence problem-solving and coping abilities, and they are extremely heterogeneous. Poor problem-solving abilities are likely to have a multiplicative effect for the person with a developmental disability when several stressors are present.

People with developmental disabilities may be more suggestible and easily influenced by external factors. They may have more difficulty considering more than one factor at a time; they may have a poor short-term memory; they may make more errors in logic; and they may lack an awareness that they can help themselves. They may be easily distracted and use only part of the relevant cues in the environment during problem solving or when interpreting social situations (Brown, 1994): For example, often, they do not spontaneously use strategies to aid in learning or remembering. They may experience difficulties with metacognitive processes: for example, those processes that enable a person to plan to solve a problem, monitor the use of a solution strategy, and evaluate the results (Hallahan & Kauffman, 1991). When experiencing a problem, they may lack critical judgment, using any solution and appearing careless and indifferent to inconsistencies. Most adults with mild retardation will achieve Piaget's level of concrete operations but are unlikely to achieve formal operations. Thinking is most often concrete, focusing on what is directly knowable in the here and now and what is bound to the particular. A person functioning at this level will not necessarily think abstractly, test hypotheses about their world, or understand the concept of probability (Prout & Strohmer, 1994a). In addition, a person functioning at the concrete operational level might have a strong orientation to the present and may have difficulty with the concept of time. Recall of the past may occur without a sense of order, regularity, or understanding of causal relationships between events (Prout & Cale, 1994). Therefore, a person with a developmental disability will have difficulty in generalizing or applying what has been learned and will have a limited capacity to plan ahead and consider consequences. (The impact of these cognitive characteristics as these pertain to therapy modifications is discussed in later chapters.)

THE IMPACT OF ADDITIONAL DISABILITIES
A person with a developmental disability may have additional disabilities, and specific disabilities often suggest different psychosocial issues. A comprehensive review of these issues is beyond the scope of this chapter and will not be provided here. The interested reader may refer to the research that deals with the psychosocial issues associated with various physical disabilities (Best, Carpignano, Sirvis, & Bigge, 1991) and hearing impairments or hearing loss (Hallahan & Kauffman, 1991; Moores, 1987; Savage, Evans, & Savage, 1981). It is important for the therapist to be aware of any additional disabilities and consider the potential effects of these disabilities for particular clients. The presence of multiple disabilities probably has more comprehensive, multiplicative consequences that will affect the person's total behavior than simply the additive effect of different psychological issues (Sullivan & Scanlon, 1987).

ISSUES ASSOCIATED WITH SEXUAL ABUSE AND DEVELOPMENTAL DISABILITY
Cruz et al. (1988) note that women with developmental disabilities who were sexually abused as children have several issues that should be addressed in therapy: guilt, intimacy needs, lack of self-esteem, dependency, feelings of isolation, and difficulty handling and expressing anger. Clients with developmental disabilities may be concerned and confused about their sexuality, feel they are "damaged goods," and have very strong, negative feelings associated with their mental disability (Hurley, 1989). Often, clients have received little or no sexu-

ality education. Cruz et al. (1988) found that many of the women with developmental disabilities in a group therapy program held the secret belief that they deserved the abuse because they were retarded. Specifically, many women in the group therapy program thought that all (step)fathers were allowed to molest their "retarded" daughters.

Westcott's (1993) qualitative study of survivors with and without disabilities illuminated some similarities and differences in effects experienced by survivors with developmental disabilities. Westcott notes that the effects reported across all groups who were interviewed in the study (those who are nondisabled, physically disabled, or have cognitive disabilities) appeared to be consistent with the child sexual abuse effects research. Notable differences experienced by the people with developmental disabilities include appearing to be feeling more long-term fear and vulnerability. For example, the perception of vulnerability was exhibited as an extreme fear about the repercussions specifically that there would be consequences for even having participated in the interview (Westcott, 1993). The quotes from survivors with developmental disabilities also reveal that they feel devalued and powerless to stop the abuse, and they believe that their disability contributed to their vulnerability to sexual abuse:

"I was more vulnerable because I already had a disability, and also, I probably had a bit less going for me and was easier to prey on."

"She chose me...probably because I had no one else, probably she knew I wouldn't tell anybody."

POSSIBLE INDICATORS OF SEXUAL ABUSE

There are several behaviors that may indicate that an individual with a developmental disability has been sexually abused (see Table 3.1). The presence of one of these would not necessarily prove the presence of sexual abuse; but many of these signs in combination could suggest the possibility of sexual abuse, and in such a case, further investigation is warranted. Some of the behaviors are similar to those noted in people without disabilities. A few behaviors may be more specific to people with developmental disabilities: for example, elective mutism; loss of independent living skills; compulsive sexual behavior (e.g., chronic masturbation); regression to infantile behavior; the onset of head banging, self-biting, or hair pulling; or sounds (e.g., humming, screaming, or groaning). Unfortunately, many behaviors have been ascribed only to the disability, and the possibility of sexual abuse has been overlooked.

Table 3.1 Possible indicators of sexual abuse

- presence of sexually transmitted diseases
- pregnancy
- stained, torn, or bloody underclothes
- trauma to breasts, buttocks, lower abdomen, thighs, or genital or rectal openings
- pain, itching in the genital area or throat, difficulty going to the bathroom or swallowing, gagging
- recurring physical ailments with no apparent somatic or organic base (i.e., frequent stomachaches, persistent sore throats, vomiting, etc.)
- unusual or offensive odor

- onset of nonsexualized self-destructive behavior (i.e., head banging, self-biting, hair pulling)
- role reversal or imbalances (i.e., child acting like an adult or parent or a client acting like a staff member)
- initiation of sounds (i.e., humming, screaming, groaning)
- verbalizations that suggest being threatened or silenced (i.e., "Don't tell or I'll kill you.")
- simulated sexual behavior with siblings or friends or sexual attention to pets or animals
- compulsive sexual behavior (i.e., masturbation)
- sudden change in feelings about a particular person or people (i.e., fear or anger)
- evidence of an unusually secretive "special" relationship with an older person, particularly one involving elements of bribery, trickery, or coercion
- nightmares, night terrors, sleep disturbances, sleepwalking
- regression to infantile behavior (i.e., enuresis, encopresis, smearing)
- self-destructive behavior (i.e., drug abuse, prostitution or indiscriminate sexual activity, self-mutilation, suicide attempts)
- compulsive lying
- unusual behavior, aggression, compliance, depression, withdrawal
- low self-esteem, critical of self
- persistent or inappropriate sex play for an individual's age or developmental level
- onset of sexual aggression (i.e., sex talk, grabbing or touching the body parts of others)
- onset of personal sexual behavior (i.e., masturbation, putting dangerous objects into the genitals with no indication of pain, self-fondling, self-exposure, nudity)
- onset of nonsexualized antisocial behavior(i.e., stealing, verbal aggression, running away)
- change in eating/sleeping patterns and habits
- elective mutism
- loss of independent living skills

ABUSE AND DISABILITY PROJECT'S SEXUAL ABUSE SEQUELAE STUDY

At this time, little is known about the specific effects of abuse on people with developmental disabilities (Cruz et al., 1988; Gorman-Smith & Matson, 1992; Hyman, 1993; Martorana, 1985; Perlman & Sinclair, 1992; Ryan, 1992; Sinason, 1986; Tharinger et al., 1990; Varley, 1984; Westcott, 1993). When outlining treatment, some researchers have provided some indication of the effects of sexual abuse (Bowers Andrews & Veronen, 1993; Cruz et al., 1988; Ryan, 1992; Sinason, 1986; Westcott, 1993). Ryan (1992) suggests that people with developmental disabilities who have experienced various trauma, including sexual abuse, experience dissociative states, emotional withdrawal, and PTSD. Some researchers believe the effects of child sexual abuse may include greater behavioral difficulties. Dunne and Power (1990), drawing from a sample of 13 sexually abused adults, outlined a range of behavior problems, or indicators, that they believe represent attempts to communicate distress where a person's verbal expressive skills are poor. They identify short-term effects as generalized anxiety, distress, and fearfulness. Long-term effects included greater vulnerability to revictimization, increased restrictiveness placed on their personal freedom, long-term depression and anxiety, and inappropriate sexual behavior (Dunne & Power, 1990). Other researchers suggest that trauma may exacerbate physical and cognitive disabilities. Bowers Andrews and Veronen (1993) note that trauma can magnify speech problems, and that a person with a developmental disability may have greater confusion and difficulty in understanding his or her sexual abuse. Sinason (1986, 1992) suggests that the sexual abuse trauma often worsens the existing disability by creating an opportunistic or "secondary disability" used as protection against the trauma. There are few research studies that examine the effects of sexual abuse on people with developmental disabilities, and almost all of the current literature takes the form of clinical case studies that are anecdotal and based on clinical experience. At this point, a review of this still fairly small literature suggests that the effects of sexual abuse are similar (Cruz et al., 1988) and appear to share the same range of heterogeneity that is found in the general population (Gorman-Smith & Matson, 1992).

A recent study conducted by the Abuse and Disability Project at the University of Alberta tested some of these hypotheses about the comparability of sexual abuse sequelae. Selected results from the Abuse and Disability Project's Sexual Abuse Sequelae study comparing the sexual abuse sequelae of children with and without developmental disabilities are presented, and the treatment implications of these findings for therapists are discussed. A full discussion of the construction and application of the SAIR is available elsewhere (see Moskal, 1995) and the results pertaining to sequelae are examined in greater detail in Mansell, Sobsey, and Moskal (1998).

METHOD

Recently, a study was conducted at the Victoria Child Sexual Abuse Society (VCSAS) in Victoria, British Columbia, Canada. The data consisted of client files drawn from the VCSAS using the Sexual Abuse Information Record (SAIR) developed by Moskal (1995). The SAIR was used to record data from the files of consecutive walk-in clients (n = 452) attending the treatment center from April 1991 to the end of March 1993. The SAIR has 149 items and is comprised of four parts: victim demographics, abuse in the family genogram, offender demographics, and sexual abuse sequelae. The SAIR differentiates seven categories of sexual abuse sequelae: school/academic/work activities, personal relationships, sexuality, bedtime, hygiene, behavioral/emotional, and medical. Moskal (1995) developed the items for the SAIR based primarily on the sexual abuse sequelae documented in the general population; however, a few of items did not appear to be direct reflections of the effects of child sexual abuse as much as differences that appeared related to experiences of people with developmental disabilities. Due to the enormity of the data amassed in this study and the space limitations of this chapter, only comparative data on the sexual abuse sequelae between children with and without developmental disabilities will be presented. For the sexual abuse sequelae study, consent was obtained from all the participants by VCSAS. The study received approval from the ethics committee of the University of Alberta and permission to use the data generated by VCSAS was granted to the principal investigator of the Abuse and Disability Project at the University of Alberta.

SAMPLE

The sample in this study was nonrandom since it was comprised of two years of consecutive admissions (n = 452) who were receiving counseling services at a treatment center. The nature of this sample suggests a few limitations for the study's results. The sample may not necessarily be representative of sexually abused children who do not receive treatment or those receiving treatment at other centers. This lack of representativeness, however, might be offset somewhat by the fact that the treatment program was funded by the government of British Columbia, making services more accessible to children who ordinarily may not have been able to afford services. Nevertheless, the fact that the children were entering a treatment program may have implications for the sexual abuse sequelae under consideration. Also, the sample is of a fairly small size (n=43) and was drawn from a specific region in North America, which might not be representative of other areas. Consequently, there may be some clear limitations on the generalizability of the study's results.

Children with Disabilities

The entire sample includes 452 children, and 102 of these children were identified as having various disabilities: physical disabilities, psychological disabilities, neurological disabilities, developmental disabilities (IQ below 69), autism, mobility disabilities, fetal alcohol syndrome/fetal alcohol effects, learning disabilities, attention deficit disorder (ADHD), borderline (IQ 70-89), visual and hearing impairments, and unspecified disabilities (see Table 3.2). The percentages provided for the various categories, however, do not suggest the relative risk for sexual abuse for the various disability categories due to the nonrandom sample.

Table 3.2. Children's disabilities in the sample (n = 102)

Physical	Psychological	Autism	Borderline (IQ 70-89)	Motor	Visual
21.6%	4.9%	3.9%	40.2%	3.9%	3.9%
Neurological	**Developmental (IQ below 69)**	**FAS/FAE**	**Learning**	**ADHD**	**Hearing**
2.7%	40.2%	6.9%	2.9%	9.8%	7.8%

Children with developmental disabilities

From the sample of 102 children with disabilities, 43 children with developmental disabilities were selected for this study. The children identified as having other disabilities were not included in this analysis. The sexual abuse sequelae of equal numbers of children with and without disabilities (n = 43) were matched for age and gender. In both groups, 33% of the children were males, and 67% of them were females. The mean ages for the males and females in the developmental disability group were 5.9 years and 7.2 years, respectively. The mean ages for the males and females in the group without disabilities were 5.8 years and 7.3 years, respectively. The selected data are categorical, and Chi Square tests of independence were used to analyze the frequencies and relationships among various forms of sequelae for children with and without developmental disabilities.

RESULTS

Overall, the comparative analysis of the results suggests that most of the sexual abuse sequelae tapped by the SAIR do not appear to be significantly different in children with and without developmental disabilities. Of the SAIR's numerous items on sexual abuse sequelae, only 9 items reached statistical significance (p < .05) (see Table 3.3).

Table 3.3. Findings in Children with and without Developmental Disabilities

Sexual Abuse Sequelae (SAIR) Disabilities	Developmental Disabilities	No Developmental Disabilities
Aggressive/Dominant behaviors	58%	47%
Poor self-esteem	53%	51%
Inappropriate anger	51%	35%
Poor sense of personal safety**	44% (p = .002)	14%
Nightmares	42%	37%
Little or no appropriate sexual information**	40% (p = .00001)	0%
Inappropriate sexual comments*	30% (p = .03)	9%
Regression	30%	21%
Has few friends	30%	19%
Is easily influenced	28%	12%
Withdrawal into fantasy*	26% (p = .04)	7%
Self-abuse*	26% (p = .04)	7%
Unusual comments about home/family*	26% (p = .01)	5%
Unkempt or grooms excessively**	19% (p = .009)	0%
Extreme Withdrawal at school/ work/counseling*	14% (p = .03)	0%
Unkempt*	14% (p = .03)	0%
Alcohol abuse*	0% (p = .03)	14%

Note: * indicates statistical significance (p < .05), ** indicates statistical significance (p < .01)

School, Academic, Work Activities

None of the items from the school/academic/work activities category occurred with a frequency greater than 28% in the children with developmental disabilities. Items occurring in greater than 20% include: difficulty concentrating or staying on task (28%), avoids school/work/ counseling (26%), extremely demanding or withdrawn in school (24%), and sexualized or bizarre artwork (21%). Items occurring in less than 14% of the children with developmental disabilities include: shows sudden decline in school/work/counseling (14%), extreme withdrawal in school/ work/counseling (14%), extremely demanding in school (9%), and unwilling to undress for gym (7%). Only the item indicating extreme withdrawal at school/work/counseling was statistically significant (p = .03).

Personal Relationships

A few items from the personal relationships category, such as showing inappropriate anger (51%) and aggressive/dominant behavior

(58%), occurred in more than 50% of the children with developmental disabilities. Other items occurred less frequently: has few friends (30%), is too easily led or influenced (27%), and is very shy and withdrawn (21%). No items were statistically significant. The high frequency for the anger-related items suggests that anger management might be an important approach to help clients with developmental disabilities cope with their feelings.

Sexuality Related

A few items concerning sexuality occurred in more than 30% of the children with developmental disabilities, but there are some interesting patterns that suggest a great deal about both the vulnerability to abuse and the importance of implementing psychoeducational components that address sexuality and self-protection in therapy.

Most sequelae were not statistically significant, and only a few items from the SAIR will be discussed. For example, the items indicating a poor sense of personal safety (44%) and verbalizing inappropriate sexual remarks or comments (30%) were both statistically significant at $p = .002$ and $p = .03$, respectively. The item concerning inappropriate or excessive touching of self/adults/children (33%) occurred in approximately one third of the children but was not statistically significant. Items that indicated inappropriate touching of children (19%) and initiating sexual games with children (12%) and/or adults (12%) occurred with even lower frequency and were not statistically significant; however, the item indicating little/no age appropriate sexual knowledge (40%) was statistically significant ($p = .00001$). This item probably taps into the experiences of many children with developmental disabilities; however, it is problematic for assessing sexual abuse sequelae for several reasons.

The wording of the item little/no age appropriate sexual knowledge is problematic as it may actually suggest the opposite of an expected effect of child sexual abuse. Many children who have experienced sexual abuse display sexualized behavior and sometimes exhibit a fairly sophisticated level of sexual knowledge for their developmental level and age due to their experience and/or exposure to sexual behavior. Children with developmental disabilities are frequently denied an adequate sexuality education due to myths and fears about their sexuality, and this inadequacy, in turn, heightens their vulnerability to abuse. The problematic wording of this item may be a stronger indicator of an inadequate state of sexuality education and potentially heightened vulnerability, but as it is worded, it is not an effect that is consistent with the research literature or even an expected result of sexual abuse. Notably, this item was associated with no children in the group without disabilities (0%). Some of these items may not necessarily reflect sequelae differences as much as the presence or absence of a developmental disability. This finding may reflect the fact that this population often does not receive adequate sexuality education and suggests the potential importance of early implementation of sexuality and sexual abuse risk reduction education.

Bedtime and Hygiene Sequelae

Only the item indicating problems with nightmares or recurring dreams occurred in over 40% of children with developmental disabilities (42%); however, this item was not statistically significant. Only the items concerning grooming proved to be significant, although these percentages were fairly low. The items that suggest either that the person is unkempt/dirty or grooms excessively (19%) or that the person is unkempt/dirty on a regular basis (14%) occurred in less than 20% of all children with developmental disabilities, but both items were statistically significant at p = .009 and p = .03, respectively. Notably, none of the children without developmental disabilities (0%) were reported to have these difficulties.

Behavioral and Emotional Sequelae

Behavioral and emotional sequelae occurred with a wide range in frequency (0% to 53%). A statistically significant item (p = .03) indicated that use or abuse of substances, specifically alcohol, occurred in 0% of children with developmental disabilities compared with 14% of children without developmental disabilities. Poor self-esteem (e.g., unassertive, guilt, shame, poor body image, and so forth) (53%) was highest in frequency, occurring in over 50% of the children with developmental disabilities; however, this was not a statistically significant item. Frequencies of greater than 20%, occurred with the following items: regressive behavior (e.g., thumb sucking, enuresis, encopresis, baby talk, clinging behavior, and so forth) (30%), attention seeking behavior (21%), depression on a regular basis (26%), unusually nervous or anxious (26%), and inordinate guilt and self-blame (21%). None of these items were statistically significant.

An item indicating dissociative episodes (37%) occurred in a greater percentage of children with developmental disabilities, but was not statistically significant. Although there was a considerable percentage of children with developmental disabilities with various dissociative related sequelae, the item indicating Multiple Personality Disorder (now Dissociative Identity Disorder in the DSM-IV [American Psychiatric Association, 1994]) occurred in 0% of children with developmental disabilities and only 2% of children without developmental disabilities. Dissociative Identity Disorder, however, is rarely diagnosed in people who have developmental disabilities and psychiatric disorders. Svec (1992b) suggests that the under-reporting or under-diagnosing of these psychiatric diagnoses in people with mental retardation may due to professional skepticism. Statistically significant items include: withdrawal into fantasy (26%, p = .04), self-abuse (e.g., hair pulling, head banging, and so forth) (26%, p = .04), and unusual comments about family or home life (26%, p = .01).

Medical or Physical Sequelae
Medical or physical sequelae occurred with a small range in frequency (2% to 21%). Only one item occurred in more than 20% of the children with developmental disabilities. The item indicating the presence of nervous disorders, stomachaches, and headaches (21%) occurred with the greatest frequency and was followed by the item indicating the presence of regular stomachaches (14%). The remaining items in this category, however, did not exceed 10% of the children with developmental disabilities. Findings occurring in less than 9% of the children with developmental disabilities included: pain in genitals urinary or gastrointestinal tract (9%), regular headaches (9%), STDs and/or yeast infections (7%), inappropriate behavior during medical exam (7%), vaginal and penile discharge and/or inflammation (5%), and injury to lips or genital area (5%). Very low frequency items (2%) include: bruises, scratches, bites, pregnancy, regular skin

irritations, and pain during urination. There were no statistically significant differences between the medical or physical sequelae of children with and without developmental disabilities.

DISCUSSION

The results from this study suggest that a few sexual abuse sequelae in children with and without developmental disabilities may be significantly different. These results appear to be consistent with other researchers (Gorman-Smith & Matson, 1992; Ryan, 1992) who suggest sequelae are similar to those documented in the general population. Presently, it is likely premature to suggest that there are no important differences. In particular, some of the limitations of the SAIR need to be considered in terms of whether some of the statistically significant items were actually assessing sexual abuse sequelae. A few items, particularly those pertaining to sexuality related sequelae (e.g., possesses little or inadequate sexuality knowledge for developmental level and poor sense of personal safety), actually may be tapping into effects associated with the often inadequate state of sexuality education for people with developmental disabilities. Other items (e.g., those concerning grooming, inappropriate sexual comments, or specific forms of self-abuse) might be more closely associated with developmental disability than with specific effects of sexual abuse.

Research

The study of sexual abuse sequelae in people with developmental disabilities is in its early stages, and not enough is known to determine whether there are specific similarities or differences in the sexual abuse sequelae in people with and without developmental disabilities. It is not adequate to simply draw on the existing research literature conducted with the general population in order to understand the effects of sexual abuse for people with developmental disabilities. The growing literature on dual diagnosis, however, can provide therapists and researchers with valuable information about the interactions that can occur between developmental disability and various psychological difficulties that may be associated with sexual abuse. Examining the developmental psychopathology associated with people who are dually diagnosed is a critical undertaking and addition to this research (Charlot, 1998). Research using larger controlled samples will be necessary to learn about sequelae specific to people with developmental disabilities and commonalities in their reactions to sexual abuse. Integrating findings from the dual diagnosis, developmental psychopathology, and sexual abuse trauma literature may help in the development of future checklists that assess the effects of sexual abuse and developmental disability. Also, research may help determine what resources can act as protective factors or reduce the effects of the psychosocial risk factors for people with developmental disabilities.

For most of the items in this study, although the group differences were not statistically significant, many of the items may still be relevant to clinicians. In this study, children with developmental disabilities appeared to have more sequelae than children without developmental disabilities had. Further research on the base rates of behavioral and psychological problems in people with developmental disabilities who have not been sexually abused may contribute to determining the role played by sexual abuse in modifying base rates. From a therapist's perspective, it is just as important to be aware of how developmental disability might affect the manifestation of sexual abuse sequelae as it is to be aware of how patterns of sexual abuse patterns and vulnerability to sexual abuse for persons with developmental disabilities might differ from the general population.

CONCLUSION

At this time, research on the effects of sexual abuse suggests a few implications for therapy. Based on the limited research, it is reasonable to assume that some of the items illustrate potential clinical issues that might need to be addressed in treatment. Various items suggested potential difficulties that might heighten vulnerability to abuse (e.g., being easily led or influenced, having a poor sense of personal safety, poor social and/or coping skills, and social isolation). Many of these potential difficulties might be addressed through additional therapy components that are covered in greater detail in Chapters 4, 5, and 6. Drawing from the existing sexual abuse research conducted with the general population, it is clear that there is considerable heterogeneity in response that is influenced by several factors. Therapists working with people with developmental disabilities who have been sexually abused frequently use existing therapy approaches and principles. It is crucial to consider the various factors and characteristics that may be associated with the person's developmental disability and their influence on the manifestation of psychological difficulties to ensure that therapy is appropriate (Charlot, 1998; Prout & Strohmer, 1994a). Recognizing the importance of psychosocial, emotional, cognitive, and communicative differences and additional developmental factors are crucial considerations for therapists.

Part 3
Individualizing
Therapy

•• **4**

Individualizing Therapy: Client Evaluation

Part Three of this book examines distinctive therapy features involved in evaluating a client, modifying communication and individualizing treatment to treat sexual abuse in this population. This chapter begins the discussion of some of the distinct qualities of this therapy work.

DISTINCTIVE THERAPY CHARACTERISTICS

Many aspects of therapy with sexually abused people who have developmental disabilities are similar to therapy practices with the general population; however, there are some aspects of this process that are distinct for clients with developmental disabilities. The importance of knowing a client's developmental level, communication and comprehension abilities, level of behavioral and psychological functioning are distinctive features that influence the therapist's use of specific therapy accommodations. Therapists need to actively consider the systemic influences of the client's culture and atypical social circumstances and work collaboratively with the client's network of caregivers. In addition, the therapist will need to use specific therapy components that take into account the importance of the different social realities and experiences of the person with developmental disabilities. Therapists need to recognize the psychological impact of their client's devalued, disempowered status and the impact that cognitive and communicative limitations may present for therapy. In order to identify treatment issues, the therapist must consider the combined influences of sexual abuse and developmental disability. Client evaluation or assessment is a critical, ongoing process in therapy that helps guide the therapist's decision making with determining therapy interventions, accommodations, goals, and progress.

EVALUATING THE CLIENT

As when conducting therapy with any client, the client with a developmental disability will need to be evaluated or assessed to determine his or her specific treatment needs. The amount of emphasis placed on the importance and nature of this process varies across theoretical approaches. Yet it is still important for the therapist to determine the client's particular sources of difficulty and to explore the potential sources of strength or resiliency that may help the client cope. In many respects, this process with clients who have developmental disabilities is very similar to the evaluation process conducted with clients without developmental disabilities, yet there are some important distinctions.

Developmental Level

The therapist should learn about the client's level of development and the nature of his or her disability and consider the psychological issues this may present for the client. A person with a developmental disability will have delays in intellectual, adaptive, and communicative functioning. However, delays will be highly variable across clients, even within the same ranges of intellectual and adaptive functioning. Learning about the client's developmental history and developmental disability can provide important suggestions about the potential impact of the client's developmental disability on the therapeutic process.

The client's developmental level is assessed primarily through intelligence testing. Developmental levels, mental ages, and IQ scores can provide useful information to clinicians. Many assessments of developmental level have relied on the concept of mental age, but this been heavily criticized because of the potential to do harm as a result of misuse. The potential harm arises when the results of these assessments are considered exact and inflexible measures of an individual's abilities, when they are viewed as total measures of all aspects of an individual's functions, when they create negative expectations that interfere with accurately viewing an individual's abilities, or when they are generalized to all areas of a person's life. An example of the misinterpretation and misuse of mental age is evident when a 36-year-old adult with a developmental disability is assessed as having a mental age of 8 years and is viewed as being just like a 8-year old and is treated like an 8-year old. Unfortunately, this misinterpretation suggests that mental age means that a person is exactly like a person of a particular chronological age (Baroff, 1991). Adults with a developmental disability are often treated as if they were children, despite their considerable life experiences. It is important for the therapist to acknowledge and respect the life experience of an adult with a developmental disability.

Although there are concerns about the use of intelligence test information, it can provide rough estimates of starting points for communication and reasoning skills. The information drawn from intellectual assessments, particularly verbal abilities, can have considerable influence on some therapist's use of verbal or nonverbal therapy modalities and other modifications that might be required to accommodate a client's cognitive ability, attention span, and receptive and expressive language abilities (Prout & Strohmer, 1994b). For example, most individuals whose mental age places them between 7 and 11 years will have achieved concrete but not formal operations. People who have achieved concrete operations will have a distinct present orientation, and many of the normal markers for the passage of time do not seem to be integrated into memory (Prout & Cale, 1994). Therefore, a person's ability to recall past events might lack a sense of order and regularity, and he or she might have difficulty with concepts such as time and causal relationships. This limitation has clear implications for the client's ability to provide a history. Also, once a person has achieved concrete operations, they are capable of conducting logical, concrete operations and are open to reasoning and more likely to benefit from verbal therapy (Prout & Cale, 1994).

Some researchers suggest that only people who can function at a 6- to 7-year-old cognitive level minimum or who function within the upper moderate to mild ranges of mental retardation can benefit from direct therapeutic intervention (Prout & Strohmer, 1994a). Others suggest that people with even lower cognitive functioning may benefit from psychotherapy (Sinason, 1992). Although assessing developmental level is important, it is critical to remain cognizant of the limitations of these assessments and to be aware of additional sources of information that may be more directly relevant to the purposes of therapy. Just as it is important to understand how different levels of cognitive development can affect the therapeutic process and diagnosis, it is also important to be aware of the possible psychological issues that may be associated with the developmental disability. As noted in the previous chapter a review of the sexual abuse sequelae literature suggests that the effects of sexual abuse are similar (Cruz et al., 1988) and appear to share the same range of heterogeneity that is found in the general population (Gorman-Smith & Matson, 1992). Although the results from the study presented in that chapter produce findings consistent with this literature and suggest that only a few sexual abuse sequelae in children with developmental disabilities were significantly different, it is also important that clinicians be aware of the possibility that their clients may have a heightened risk for mental disorders, and that developmental level can influence the appearance of clinical disturbances.

Dual Diagnosis

Dual diagnosis refers to the co-occurrence of mental disorders and mental retardation. This label is used with people who have mild, moderate, severe, and profound mental retardation and covers a wide range of diverse psychiatric conditions (Reiss, 1993). In dual diagnosis, the two conditions interact and tend to exacerbate each other, creating a situation that is more exponential than additive in its overall effects (Shaver, 1992). Dual diagnosis presents therapists with a variety of complicated diagnostic issues that are typically not involved with clients who do not have developmental disabilities.

THE APPROPRIATENESS OF THE DIAGNOSTIC AND STATISTICAL MANUAL OF MENTAL DISORDERS

Several authors have debated the appropriateness of the *Diagnostic and Statistical Manual of Mental Disorders* (DSM) (American Psychiatric Association, 1994) system for use with people who have mental retardation. Issues about appropriateness typically concern the interpretation of differing clinical manifestations of psychopathology, especially as these pertain to levels of severity, and various aspects of mental retardation that require clinicians to adapt their traditional interviewing and assessment approaches. For some time, people with mental retardation have been systematically excluded from studies of clinical pathology, and the DSM system is based on manifestations of mental disorders in clinical populations without mental retardation (Sovner, 1986). Charlot (1998) adds that the surface manifestations of mental health disorders may differ in people with developmental disabilities while the diagnostic classification schemes reflect "normative" phenomenology. In addition, differential diagnosis can be complicated by a range of factors associated with overlapping and differing clinical features found in people who have mental retardation. Myers (1999) illustrates that a range of disorders including major depression, autism, stereotypy, aggressive and movement disorders, temporal lobe seizures, dissociative and anxiety disorders (including obsessive compulsive disorder), fantasy and imaginary playmates, semantic and pragmatic deficit disorders and hearing loss or deafness can be misdiagnosed as psychotic disorder.

Some authors suggest that the DSM system is appropriate for people who function in the mild and upper levels of moderate mental retardation, but this system is viewed as neither adequate nor appropriate for people whose assessed level of functioning places them below an IQ level of 50 (Menolascino, Levitas, & Greiner, 1986; Reiss, 1993). In particular, people functioning in the low moderate, severe, or profound ranges may be poorly served by the DSM.

Sovner (1986) suggests that four specific factors limit the use of the DSM system with people who have mental retardation: *intellectual distortion*, which represents the influence of cognitive deficits on the client's ability to label and communicate their experiences to the interviewer; *psychosocial masking* or the impoverished social skills and life experiences that may result in the clinician's failure to detect psychopathology or to misattribute a person's nervousness or silliness as psychiatric features; *cognitive disintegration*, which refers to stress-induced disruptions in the ability to process information, which can lead clinicians to consider a diagnosis of schizophrenia; and *baseline exaggeration*, which refers to a heightened severity of pre-existing cognitive deficits and maladaptive behaviors that may cloud the diagnostic process (Sovner, 1986).

Charlot (1998) indicates that a person's developmental level impacts the presentation of clinical features. She notes that surface features are sometimes altered by developmental variables and that some symptoms may take on different meanings depending on a person's stage of development or age. She recommends drawing from the developmental psychopathology and "age effects" literatures to consider the likely impact of delayed development on clinical presentation. Lowry (1998) reports that it is important to consider what a person with a developmental disability is likely to do if he or she is experiencing such symptoms. Charlot (1998) indicates that it is likely that some people with developmental disabilities at similar stages of cognitive development to young children will display the same variation in phenomenology. In short, clinical presentation of a mental disorder may vary at least in part because of the person's level of development and that clinicians expecting a client's depression or anxiety to appear according to DSM-IV criteria may miss or may misdiagnose the person's problems altogether when these developmental considerations are not made during the diagnostic process. See Table 4.1 for a summary of Charlot's 1998 review.

Guidelines for Diagnosis

In response to the difficulties associated with using the DSM system with clients who have mental retardation, several clinicians have presented guidelines to aid the diagnostic process. Diagnosis becomes more complicated, at least in part, because of the traditional reliance on the client's ability to provide a verbal report of his or her symptoms (Price-Williams, 1989). Sovner (1986) recommends adapting the DSM system for use with people who mental retardation by reducing the categories to observable behaviors, which might minimize diagnostic inference. Some authors believe that clinicians need to rely more on signs (observed behaviors) and rely less on the symptoms (verbally reported distress or dysfunction) that characterize the various psychiatric disorders (Menolascino, Levitas, & Greiner, 1986). Lowry (1998) outlines the importance of operationally defining key symptoms and associated problem behaviors. This is particularly relevant for clients who function in the moderate, severe, and profound ranges of mental retardation or who are described as nonverbal. Diagnosis can be complicated by a client's problems with verbal communication since therapists may have difficulty discerning a client's thought processes, in particular, deciphering a client's comprehension of fantasy and reality (Price-Williams, 1989).

Reiss (1993, 1994a, 1994b) provides a series of guidelines for diagnosing psychopathology in people with developmental disabilities, noting that behavior problems alone do not provide sufficient evidence of psychopathology. Charlot (1998) notes that a person with a developmental disability may not be able to report and communicate about their subjective emotional experience and there can be heavy reliance on others' perceptions, however, care must be taken in evaluating these sources of information. Focusing on behavior changes (e.g., those that suggest a change from a premorbid state) can help a clinician decide whether a behavior problem is a manifestation of mental retardation or psychopathology. This guideline, however, does not apply to personality disorders, which by definition tend to be chronic in nature. It will be necessary to make allowances for the impact of a person's mental retardation and his or her associated social or living circumstances on the manifestation of symptoms. As noted although people with developmental disabilities who have been sexually abused may experience a range of possible sequelae commonly encountered areas of difficulty are associated with mood and anxiety.

Disorder Presentation
Lowry's (1998) analysis of prevalence data in the general population and large samples of people with developmental disabilities reveals there is a tendency to underdiagnose mood disorders and that these conditions often go untreated. Charlot (1998) notes that adults with developmental disabilities display some features that are similar to children without developmental disabilities when depressed that include higher rates of irritable mood and associated conduct problems (i.e., aggression to self and others). When evaluating for mood disor-

ders Lowry (1998) outlines the importance of operationally defining key symptoms and associated problem behaviors but to also consider what a person with a developmental disability is likely to do if he or she is experiencing such symptoms. When relying on others to provide reports of the person's behavior and symptoms there is a strong emphasis on the observable behavior, however, as Charlot (1998) notes this can result in an overemphasis on externalizing type behaviors and a failure to recognize the internalizing symptoms that are also present in the mood disorders. Charlot (1998) recommends that clinicians explore thoroughly the presence of less dramatic symptoms and to consider the likely impact of delayed development and the known age effects on presentation of the disorder.

Reiss (1996) in his review on anxiety indicated that there was as yet not a clear picture of the prevalence of anxiety disorders in people with developmental disabilities. There was evidence noted that anxiety and stress were more common in this population, however, it is not necessarily the case that this group is at greater risk for anxiety disorder (Epstein, Cullinan, & Polloway, 1986). Mayer and Poindexter (1999) report that the assessment of anxiety disorders can be complicated by communication difficulties and will require the clinician to determine whether or not anxiety exists. As when treating anxiety of any kind energy will be devoted to learning more about the anxiety and its etiology, scope, context and situations, intensity, and duration. As part of ongoing evaluation it will be important to find out whether or not it meets DSM-IV diagnostic criteria. For example, a person may be anxious in some particular circumstances, have limited problem solving skills, and cognitive rigidity or may even possess an anxiety sensitivity but would not necessarily meet the full diagnostic criteria for an anxiety disorder. As with depression there can be atypical presentation in anxiety. Some behavioral manifestations may include aggression and self-soothing behavior, clinging, and in some cases sexual acting out (Mayer & Poindexter, 1999). For example, in some circumstances people may use a range of different behaviors to draw others close to them so that they can receive reassurance and contact when they are feeling anxious but are unable to communicate either their emotional states or their needs to others.

Sometimes it is helpful to look at some behaviors in terms of what possible psychological functions these may serve for the person with a developmental disability who is having difficulty coping (e.g., reassurance, closeness, intimacy, avoidance, etc.)

Clinicians also need to admit the limitations of their knowledge and acknowledge diagnostic ambiguity when faced with a situation where it is difficult to make a confident diagnosis. Reiss recommends the use of comprehensive clinical assessments that are based on multiple sources of information: for example, case records, medical/biological tests, behavioral observations, client and staff interviews, formal measures of dual diagnosis, aberrant behavior, and personality (Reiss, 1993, 1994a, 1994b). A variety of psychometric assessment scales have been developed to assess a wide range of psychopathology in people with mental retardation. (A full discussion of these scales is beyond the scope of this chapter, and the interested reader is referred to Aman [1991] or Reiss [1994b] for a review of psychopathology psychometric instruments for people with developmental disabilities.)

Pharmacotherapy
As in the treatment of psychiatric difficulties in the general population, pharmacotherapy is also widely used with people who are dually diagnosed. The use of medications, however, may be further complicated by the increased likelihood of additional medical and health problems, especially for people in the more severe and profound ranges of functioning. The use of psychoactive medications with dually diagnosed clients has sometimes resulted in significant overprescription and oversedation. More recently, there has been increasing advocacy for ending the practice of using medication as the only or total treatment approach for clients with dual diagnosis. More balanced, careful approaches to treatment that consider the specific effects of psychoactive medications on the person with mental retardation are recommended. Menolascino (1989) regards the use of psychoactive medications as an aid during the initial phase of treatment to help reduce inappropriate behaviors and to help clients become

· 142

Table 4.1 Typical Presentations of Some Possible Sequelae of Sexual Abuse in Children and Possible Presentations in Adults with Developmental Disabilities. (Adapted from Charlot, 1998)

Category	Presentation in Children	Possible Presentation in Adults with Developmental Disabilities
Generalized Anxiety	Anticipatory anxiety	many anecdotal reports
	Restlessness	similar findings are likely
	Self-conscious, perfectionism	similar findings are sometimes reported
	Excessive need for reinforcement and approval	many reports of "attention-seeking" behaviors
	Sleep disorders (typically insomnia) and fatigue	similar findings are likely
Specific Phobias	Some fears are common in young children, (diagnosis should applied only to severe manifestations)	Fears similar to age-matched controls
	Crying	Crying
	Tantrums	Tantrums, may also be seen in other anxiety disorders
	Fear may be generalized to those who have characteristics like the offender	Similar findings are likely
	May not consider fear to be excessive	Similar findings are likely
Social Phobia	Excessive anxiety with peers and adults	May be misdiagnosed as depressive or psychotic withdrawal, or PTSD-induced withdrawn behavior
	Often takes form of school phobia	Possibly seen in persons with DD who refuse to go to day programs;
	Crying, tantrums, and "freezing" are common	may use noncompliant, aggressive, or disruptive behavior to avoid or escape social activities or programs
	may not recognize fear as atypical	Symptoms of crying, tantrums, freezing likely
		Excessive anxiety in response to changes in caretakers may be related to social phobia
PTSD	May have nightmares	Similar presentations have been described
	May re-enact traumatic in repetitive play	
	May not recognize they are reliving past somatization (e.g., headaches, stomachaches)	
Major Depression	Irritability (as opposed to sadness typical of adult depression)	May present as irritability or withdrawal
	Associated conduct problems withdrawal	May show associated aggression and self-injurious behavior (SIB)
	Somatic complaints (e.g., stomach pains)	Withdrawal
	Separation anxiety	Somatic complaints may occur in persons with mild cognitive delays
	Sleep disturbances.	Has not been investigated
		Similar presentations frequently have been described.
Sexually Inappropiate Behavior	May exhibit sexual behavior inappropriate for age or situation	Similar presentations frequently have been described.

more open to engagement in therapy. Careful monitoring of medications for iatrogenic effects, sedation effects, and contraindications is essential as people with mental retardation often have accompanying medical conditions that also require medications. Additional complications noted by Ryan (1992) suggest that neuroleptics can sometimes have iatrogenic effects, such as acting as dissociative triggers for people with developmental disabilities who have suffered trauma. Reiss and Aman (1997) note that it can be difficult to identify possible side effects as a person's functional handicap may be confused with certain symptoms, the person may be unable to report, and some features may be difficult to distinguish from movement disorders. In some cases people may be at greater risk for developing side effects. Menolascino (1989) suggests the importance of a medication phaseout period that involves careful monitoring of the slow reduction or elimination of the psychoactive medication. At this time, few sound research studies have been conducted on medications with this population, but some good reviews of this subject are available. (See Gadow & Poling [1988];Fahs [1997]; Reiss & Aman, [1998])for a review of issues concerning the use of psychotropic medications with people who have developmental disabilities.)

Recently a series of booklets have been published that can be used with clients and their families covering patients' rights and responsibilities (Aman, Benson, Campbell, & Haas, 1999a), antipsychotic medicines (Aman et al., 1999b), antidepressant medicines (Aman et al., 1999c), stimulant medicines (Aman, Benson, Campbell, & Griswold-Rhymer, 1999d), antimanic medicines (Aman et al., 1999e) antianxiety medicines (Aman et al, 1999f), and anticonvulsants (Aman et al., 2000). The use of materials that help everyone involved in treatment understand the reasons for taking medications, cost and benefits, and the signs of possible side effects or problems is critical. Therapists who are not well-versed in medications and the myriad of possible effects need to recognize the limits of their knowledge and consult with other knowledgeable professionals closely associated with the client. The importance of consultation with other professionals and caregivers in the client's social system underlines an additional distinctive characteristic of therapy with a client who has developmental disabilities. Specifically, there is considerably more contact between the therapist and the other professionals and caregivers in the client's social system.

Involvement and Contact with Caregivers and Significant Others

Much of the self-initiated referral, personal disclosure of the problem, and sharing of historical information found in clients without disabilities is frequently absent with clients who have developmental disabilities, and this process requires a third party to facilitate it (Shaver, 1992). Drawing on other sources for historical information is essential in view of the fact that it is difficult for some clients to conceptualize time or verbalize their experiences, and as a result, they may be poor historians. In addition, some clients have had such long-term exposure to both medical and psychological questioning with various professionals that they may be unwilling to disclose specific problems (Price-Williams, 1989).

The client is most likely to be referred for therapy by someone with whom they have extensive contact. Often, referrals are made by either a parent, guardian, or another professional(s) who works with the client. Frequently, clients receive services from a large network of caregivers who form part of a larger disability related or social services related system. The therapist may benefit considerably from liaison with professionals from other disciplines who are closely associated with the client. Working in an interdisciplinary, collaborative fashion may produce several benefits for the client and therapist and the various systems in which the client is embedded (McBrien & Candy, 1998). In addition, therapists will need to work closely with the client's system of caregivers in order to obtain critical sources of information that the client might not be able to provide directly.

Working collaboratively means that the therapist becomes part of a joint problem-solving effort, and he or she also becomes directly involved in the systems that have a significant impact on the client's life. Working with these systems allows the therapist to gain a greater understanding of the client's social circumstances, his or her roles in these systems, and the dynamics in these systems. Contact with other professionals can prove to be invaluable as they may know the client very well and be able to provide a thorough history and access to other salient treatment information.

History

Learning about the client's presenting problem, recent assessments (e.g., intellectual, adaptive functioning, psychological, medical), medical history, and medications (e.g., amounts, types, monitoring, possible contraindications, or overmedication) constitutes crucial information for the therapist. However, the therapist will also want to learn about the client's family history, current living situation (e.g., any changes, transitions, losses, relationships, environments, activities), coping and communication abilities, social adaptability, and overall level of functioning (Shaver, 1992). Developing a working alliance with the family can help develop a shared sense of helping and can assist working toward a common goal (Silka & Hurley, 1998). Other professionals can provide insights about the client's history of abuse, behavioral problems or any psychiatric diagnosis or treatments, specific coping strengths, and various abilities that can help the client participate in therapy. Descriptions of the problem, the person's mood, behavior, and functioning, sleeping and eating habits and information pertaining to precipitating events are all-important.

The therapist needs to know about the client's living situation or social system and how much independence the social system may or may not afford the client. The therapist needs to know the client's social and communication skills, if he or she has friends, or if he or she is lonely and socially isolated. It is also important to learn about the nature of familial and personal relationships, amount of contact, and the client's level of dependency in these relationships. Do these relationships represent sources of support, or are these relationships potentially damaging to the client? In some cases others may have a strong (but unspoken) vested interest in keeping a person dependent. Such oppressive emotional environments will affect the person's sense of agency and ability, and working to change this environment and to counter its influences can become issues in treatment. Contact with the client's other systems can also help the therapist assess how supportive family and staff members are of the client's therapy. For example, sometimes a client's behavior changes as a result of therapy (e.g., becoming more assertive), and these changes can meet with active or passive resistance from others in his or her social system. In such circumstances, the therapist needs to be aware of these possible dynamics and consider systemic interventions to overcome this resistance and help the people in this social system and the client adapt to these changes.

Learning about the sexual abuse history of the client is crucial. It is important for therapists to remember that the patterns of sexual abuse of people with developmental disabilities can differ from those found in the general population. There are several aspects of the client's abuse that the therapist should understand: For example, is the abuse an isolated event, or has it been a chronic experience? Has the client been offended against by one or multiple offenders? What was the offender's relationship to the client? Was the offender a family member, someone close to the family, a paid caregiver associated with the disability service system, or another person with a developmental disability? Was the abuse violent? Did it occur in the context of a personal, affectionate relationship or in a professional caregiving relationship? Was the abuse disclosed by the victim or someone else? Was it reported? Were charges laid? Did the case go to court, and did the client testify? Was there an important support person for the client during this time? How did the family or other systems respond to this disclosure? Was the client believed, punished, or rejected for disclosing the abuse?

Learning about the client's history through significant others can be very fruitful, suggesting a variety of issues that the client might not present directly but which may still need to be addressed in therapy: For example, it would be crucial to know if the client exhibits secondary behavior problems, received any previous treatment, and, if so, its outcome. Commonly seen secondary behavior problems may include: anger management difficulties, depression, self-injurious behavior, sexual offending behavior, a history of revictimization, or psychiatric diagnoses. Therapists need to be aware that in some circumstances referral problems may not be mental health problems so much as problems with obedience, promptness, politeness, and deference to others as defined by the client's supervisor or other caregivers (Price-Williams, 1989). These types of problems, however, are often complicated and can mask a genuine psychological difficulty (Price-Williams, 1989). Although some emphasis has been placed on learning about the client's problems, it is also important to assess the client's sources of strength and resiliency and to consider ways that these resources may be further enhanced.

Coping and Resiliency

During therapy, painful and difficult feelings will be evoked, and it is important for the therapist to assess the client's ability to cope. Often, working through different events and feelings in therapy will stimulate anxiety, fears, anger, and escalate abuse-related dreams and flashbacks in the client. If the client is having too much difficulty in these areas, therapy might be contraindicated at that time, and more intensive work will need to be done in order to help the client gain more control and improve coping skills before therapy begins. As part of providing a sense of safety for the client, he or she will need to have some sense of control over this process. Clients may have limited coping resources and strategies, and the therapist will need to consider using interventions that might help further develop these resources and strategies in the client before preceding: For example, if a client has violent outbursts of anger or terrifying nightmares, the therapist should use whatever means necessary to help the client deal with these intense situations. Benson (1995) outlines an anger management intervention program for helping adults with mental retardation that includes: identification of feelings, relaxation training, self-instructional training, and problem-solving skills training. As with most people, a person with a developmental disability benefits from contact with a supportive, safe person with whom he or she can talk or confide, receive comfort, and who can help the individual cope with his or her feelings. It will be important to have the client and others identify and practice strategies that can be used when difficulties arise. Promoting the use of the client's natural supports, available resources, and coping strategies early in the therapeutic process might help the client develop greater resiliency to deal with his or her feelings, and as a result, the therapist may have to rely less on using a crisis orientation later. Often, caregivers and family members want information about how to help the client and can benefit from additional education and support provided by the therapist. Gathering this information during evaluation can teach the therapist about a client's coping styles, potential issues for therapy, suggest available supports, and highlight possible interventions for the client's various systems.

Support Systems
It is important for the therapist to explore the client's possible support systems, level of independence, and abilities to form relationships. This information often has practical implications for therapy, which can include: the extent to which family members are involved in therapy and the extent to which a therapist can use a client's abilities to form relationships and access additional social support. The therapist may begin therapy with an individual client but will need to decide whether therapy should also include others such as the parent-client dyad or the entire family. Regardless of whether the abuse was perpetrated by a family member or not, in all likelihood, the family will experience considerable disruption. The emotional climate of the family prior to the abuse and following disclosure greatly influences the impact of the abuse. Family therapy should always be considered as a possible avenue for uncovering issues related to disability, parenting concerns, and the impact of the sexual abuse on the family. Gaining access to the observations of significant others and caregivers in the client's immediate systems may provide invaluable indicators of the client's therapy progress or potential coping difficulties. (A discussion of the various behavioral rating scales exceeds the scope of this chapter. The interested reader should refer to Reiss [1994b] for a review of some of these instruments.) Learning about the changes occurring to the client outside therapy can reveal whether additional interventions are required or whether specific coping behaviors need to be reinforced and supported by both the therapist and those in the client's systems. Although gaining access to this infor-

mation is important it is critical that as much as possible every effort be made to preserve confidentiality.

The Therapeutic Relationship

Assessing the client's social system may provide information about the client's ability to form a therapeutic relationship. The therapeutic relationship refers to the interpersonal interactions between therapist and client upon which therapeutic techniques are based, and its strength is crucial to a positive outcome (Whiston & Sexton, 1993). Although definitions of the therapeutic relationship and beliefs about its impact in therapy tend to vary across theoretical orientations, there is considerable agreement that the quality of the relationship is central to the outcome of therapy (Highlen & Hill, 1984; Horvath & Symonds, 1991; Luborsky, Crits-Cristoph, Mintz, & Auerbach, 1988).

Of the various views of the therapeutic relationship held by clients, therapists, and observers, it is the client's view that is considered to be especially predictive of therapy outcome (Luborsky et al., 1988). The strength of the therapeutic relationship is best assessed from the client's perspective by the degree to which the client: trusts the therapist and perceives him or her as warm and supportive, believes the therapist is helping, feels understood and accepted, is invested in the role of client and values the treatment process for overcoming problems, and perceives the therapist as working together with him or her toward common goals (Horvath & Greenberg, 1989; Orlinsky & Howard, 1986).

Vernikoff and Dunayer (1992), in their work with clients who have a dual diagnosis, suggest the importance of the therapist forming a therapeutic alliance with the client, but also, they illustrate the importance of considering the impact of disability related issues. It may take more time than usual to build trust with the client who has a developmental disability (Fletcher & Benson, 1994), but it is important to take the time necessary to do so as it will be crucial to the development of the therapeutic relationship (Vernikoff & Dunayer, 1992). In the therapeutic relationship, the therapist must demonstrate and communicate an acceptance of the client and appreciate the impact of his or her life circumstances. This nonjudgmental, reparative relationship must be based on a consistent and genuine interest in the client's well-being. Principles for developing a good therapeutic relationship with a client with developmental disabilities include: accepting the client for who he or she is, accepting the client's life circumstances, understanding the client's view of reality, being consistent, separating the therapeutic intervention from other aspects of the client's life, ensuring that the therapeutic relationship is devoted to the needs of the client, expressing genuine interest in the client, being real with the client, and drawing the client out (Hurley & Hurley, 1987).

Prout and Cale (1994) suggest that the therapist should engage in activities with the client outside the session that will allow him or her to participate in the client's world. These authors feel that this exercise will generate shared experiences with the client that help engender trust and establish rapport and the therapeutic relationship. They also believe that the therapist should acknowledge the value of the client's views, demonstrate a concern for the relationship, and show a willingness to listen to and learn from the client (Prout & Cale, 1994). Poor self-esteem represents a significant issue for many people with developmental disabilities, and the therapist can do much to help the client by providing opportunities for the client to experience successes in various forms and receive positive and enhancing statements, especially praise, that communicate to the client his or her strengths, abilities, and worth.

Many people with developmental disabilities have an extensive history of dependency that can contribute to an intense transference reaction with the therapist (Vernikoff & Dunayer, 1992): For example, many people with developmental disabilities have learned effective ways to accommodate caregivers in order to have their needs met, yet underneath this compliance, there may be intense rage at the therapist, who may be perceived as yet another authority figure who thwarts their independence (Vernikoff & Dunayer, 1992).

Therapists must be careful about projecting unrealistic responses onto their clients, such as an often unspoken desire for the client to be more verbal, do better, or be more successful (Vernikoff & Dunayer, 1992). The affect aroused in the therapist provides a significant form of communication for the therapist to explore. Clinical supervision can be very helpful for the therapist's perspective and can be very informative about the therapist's own issues, attitudes, and needs.

It is also important to consider that in some developmental disabilities, particularly the pervasive developmental delays (e.g., Autism or Asperger's Syndrome), there might be considerable impairment in the ability to form social relationships. The presence of these impairments clearly poses significant challenges to the development of a therapeutic relationship. Although the presence of these impairments presents considerable challenges for the establishment of the therapeutic relationship, this does not necessarily rule out the client's ability to participate in or benefit from therapy: For example, Alvarez (1992) describes her psychoanalytic psychotherapy program conducted with a boy who has autism that spanned several years.

Although other professionals involved in a client's life can be important sources of information for the therapist, some caution is required since not all the professionals associated with the client will be familiar with or knowledgeable about the client or his or her particular needs. Accepting information about a client unquestioningly can create misguided expectations about a client's abilities to communicate or participate in therapy, and these misguided expectations can do a disservice to both the therapist and the client. It is recommended that therapists carefully consider the source of any information they receive before they act on it. Additional perspectives can be obtained by working directly with the client and family members. These sources can sometimes clarify information that has been provided and help the therapist gain a clearer picture of the client's life circumstances, abilities, and therapy needs. Nevertheless, other professionals may be able to provide important information to the therapist.

Despite some of the advantages of obtaining information from sources in the client's social system, the client clearly requires opportunities to communicate his or her life experiences in the way that is most appropriate for him or her. Many people with developmental disabilities have been extensively guided, questioned, and directed. It is an important therapy goal for the client to understand that in therapy they can dictate the selection of what is talked about, be an equal partner in speech (Price-Williams, 1989), and be listened to rather than talked to (Prout & Cale, 1994). The therapeutic relationship can be enhanced if the therapist acknowledges that the client's knowledge of his or her life is an expertise that the client can teach to the therapist. Many opportunities exist to communicate positive, supportive messages about the client to both the client and his or her support systems, messages that can help build the client's sense of self-worth and promote his or her right to have a voice and be heard.

This chapter began the discussion of some of the distinctive characteristics associated with individualizing therapy for people with developmental disabilities. Knowing a client's developmental level, communication and comprehension abilities, level of behavioral and psychological functioning are distinctive features that influence the therapist's use of specific therapy accommodations. Also these qualities can also effect the presentation of mental disorders and complicate the diagnostic process. Therapists need to actively consider the systemic influences of the client's culture and atypical social circumstances and work collaboratively with the client's network of caregivers. Therapists need to recognize the psychological impact of their client's devalued, disempowered status and the impact that cognitive and communicative limitations may present for therapy. Client evaluation or assessment is a critical, ongoing process in therapy that helps guide the therapist's decision making with identifying treatment issues, determining therapy interventions, accommodations, goals, and progress. Part three of this book continues the examination of these themes and the remaining chapters examine the issues associated with modifying communication and individualizing treatment to treat sexual abuse in this population.

•• 5

Individualizing Therapy: Communication Issues

Communication is an essential element in every therapeutic relationship, yet therapists often assume that their clients have the communication skills necessary for the therapeutic process. It is the combined abilities and deficits of both communication partners that effect the outcome of therapy. Communication difficulties can present distinct challenges to the therapist working with clients who have developmental disabilities. As members of an extremely heterogeneous group, people with developmental disabilities have a great variety of linguistic and cognitive abilities. In addition, communication skills may be as strongly influenced by environment and experience as they are by inherent abilities. Although a therapist should not underestimate the client's abilities to either understand or communicate, his or her expectations should be realistic. In this chapter the unique aspects of communication strategies and considerations for clients with a range of developmental and communication disabilities in therapy are examined.

The most common language difficulty experienced by people with developmental disabilities concerns expressive language. This language difficulty might include: difficulties with articulation or speech fluency; a restricted vocabulary; and inadequate conversation skills (Brown, 1994). Receptive language ability often exceeds expressive language; therefore, many people with developmental disabilities understand a great deal more than they can express. Also, some people with developmental disabilities may use both oral and sign language to communicate. It is essential for the therapist to acknowledge and support their clients' attempts to communicate with positive feedback because this encourages their clients to continue to communicate.

The therapist may need to draw on and slightly modify his or her existing therapeutic skills for understanding nonverbal communication with a client who has a developmental disability. The therapist should be sensitive to the varied meanings attached to body language, eye contact, posture, facial expressions, gestures, vocalizations, and tone of voice since these forms of communication can provide salient information about a client's style of communication. The therapist should learn about the client's specific patterns of delays and strengths in receptive and expressive abilities, whether through assessments or from others who are familiar with the client, in order to develop a greater appreciation of the client's sometimes idiosyncratic language and nonverbal forms of communication.

Therapy must take into consideration the client's specific communication abilities and preferred modalities. The therapist needs to accept where the client is in terms of his or her communication abilities and understand the practical therapy implications: For example, the therapist needs to know how a person typically communicates. Are there specific circumstances or contexts that affect a person's ability to communicate? Does the ability to communicate change in strange and unfamiliar environments or when the client is feeling angry, upset, depressed, withdrawn, or anxious? How verbally expressive is the client, and how large are the client's receptive and expressive vocabularies? Also it can be important to know if there is a significant discrepancy between these. For example, does a client understand more than they can express verbally or do they express more than can they understand? In either case the therapist's expectations about the client's communication will be influenced. Does the client have other impairments, such as hearing, vision, or speech impairments or a combination of these impairments that might affect communication? Does the client use augmentative or alternative communication devices? If the client has a hearing impairment, does he or she typically use an interpreter? How fluent is the client in using sign in a particular language? Does the client have consistent access to an interpreter with whom he or she feels comfortable and trusts?

In order to work with a variety of communication abilities, the therapist should be well versed in various communication and therapy modalities. The therapist may benefit greatly from consulting with other professionals: For example, if the client has fairly complex communication needs, consultation with the client's speech therapist might provide crucial information about how to communicate with the client. This does not suggest that consultation will necessarily be sufficient since, when it is necessary, the therapist should be well versed in the use of sign language and the various communication alternatives.

Specific communication aids such as the use of augmentative devices and various communication boards can often be learned and used with relative ease. Consultation with a professional directly involved and well acquainted with the client's communication difficulties can be invaluable for guiding the modes of communication used in therapy. Also, these professionals can direct the therapist to any additional information and training that may be required: For example, if a therapist receives a referral for a client who is using an unfamiliar symbol language or communication board, the therapist will do well to get training, consultation, and supervision. In certain circumstances, it might be more appropriate to refer the client to someone who is more competent to provide a reasonable standard of care. Although it is not realistic to expect a therapist to be an expert in all the different modes of communication, learning additional means of communicating can be invaluable. It is preferable to relying primarily on other sources for information about how to communicate with a client who has a communication impairment.

THE USE OF AN INTERPRETER
Some clients with developmental disabilities may have hearing impairments and require the use of a qualified interpreter. The involvement of a qualified interpreter can be a source of significant concerns for therapy. Although some therapists do not believe the use of an appropriately qualified interpreter poses any problems, others do not share this view (Sullivan & Scanlan, 1987). In some cases even if the interpreter is chosen carefully (e.g., the person is not a family mem-

ber, someone close to the client, an acquaintance, or a staff member) their presence can significantly interfere with and impair the development of rapport and the therapeutic relationship. It should also be noted that in some cases the presence of an interpreter (qualified or otherwise) might compromise the client's confidentiality.

Several options exist. First, the therapist can learn to use sign language. Ideally, a therapist should be well versed in sign; however, for various reasons, therapists fluent in signing are the exception rather than the rule. Fluency in sign is not easily or rapidly achieved, and there may be considerable variability in the client's own fluency and the use of particular languages (American Sign Language, British Sign Language, and so forth) across cultures and regions. In most cases, it is unrealistic for a therapist to learn to sign to serve a single client, but it is reasonable for some therapists to become proficient signers in order to serve a significant number of signing clients.

A second option is to refer the client to a therapist who already signs. When an appropriately trained individual is available, this is typically the best option. Unfortunately, individuals with the needed sign language skills, therapy skills, and experience are often hard to find; and even when a professional is found who has the required skills, he or she might not be prepared to work with clients who have mental retardation.

A third option, available in some cases, is to use another mode of communication. For example, many signers can read lips and communicate orally, even though sign is their preferred mode of communication. Whether or not this is a good option depends on the client's proficiency in the other mode, the availability of alternatives, and, most importantly, the client's preferences.

The fourth option is using an interpreter. If the decision is made to use an interpreter, it should be understood that this presents certain compromises to therapy; however, in such a case, it is preferable that the person be certified and chosen by the client based on their own comfort level. It is also important for the therapist to feel comfortable with the interpreter.

Kang and Hingsburger (1990) outline several important issues to consider when using an interpreter in therapy with a person who has a developmental disability. It is crucial that consent is obtained from the client to use the interpreter, and a confidentiality agreement must be made with the interpreter. The therapist should interview the interpreter in order to determine his or her suitability. For example, the therapist should determine the interpreter's ability to handle the emotional content of the therapy sessions and his or her attitudes toward people with developmental disabilities. The therapist should determine if there is any past relationship between the interpreter and the client in order to avoid problems concerning client confidentiality. If the interpreter is suitable, it is also crucial that he or she can make a commitment for the duration of the therapy. An interpreter needs to be clear about his or her role in therapy sessions as the therapist depends on the interpreter to translate as exactly as possible what happens in the session. In some circumstances, the interpreter may become enmeshed in the process and want to assist with therapy. In this situation, the therapist will need to clarify the interpreter's role in therapy. Also, the therapist should be sensitive to the emotional needs of the interpreter and schedule regular debriefings to deal with any emotional issues that might result from the therapy sessions. Using an interpreter in therapy, however, can complicate the therapy process and communication can become confusing and problematic.

Kang and Hingsburger (1990) discuss various steps that a therapist can take to make any therapy process that involves an interpreter a bit smoother. The physical organization of the therapy setting requires careful consideration. In session, it is very likely that the client will tend to maintain eye contact with the interpreter; therefore, it will be important for the therapist to speak directly to and make eye contact with the client, not the interpreter. Kang and Hingsburger (1990) suggest that the interpreter should sit slightly behind therapist in order to reduce the temptation for the client to watch and communicate directly with the interpreter. When attempting to clarify something the client has communicated, it is necessary to remember the importance of eye contact and speaking directly to the client. It is always preferable to communicate directly with the client and not the interpreter, never referring to the client in the third person (e.g., asking the interpreter, "What is he or she saying?"). The therapist should use the same volume, cadence, and tone that he or she would typically use in therapy; however, it is helpful to speak more slowly and address only one concept at a time. Despite these strategies, sometimes communicating through a third person can cause confusion and frustration for both client and therapist. Kang and Hingsburger (1990) state that is important for the client to know that the therapist's frustration is not caused by the client but is a result of not understanding what has been communicated. Also, they feel that the therapist should make it clear that he or she has a great desire to understand what the client is communicating.

COMMUNICATION IN ADULTS WITH MILD OR MODERATE MENTAL RETARDATION

The ability to work in various therapy modalities is an asset when conducting therapy with people who have developmental disabilities. The training of many therapists tends to be concentrated on highly verbal techniques, and little attention is paid to nonverbal therapy techniques; yet, the integration of these techniques is essential when working with people who have developmental disabilities. Many of the verbally and nonverbally oriented therapies that are used to address the effects of child sexual abuse can be successfully adapted for clients with developmental disabilities. As with learning additional means of communication, expanding the therapist's repertoire to include less verbally dependent forms of therapy promotes greater flexibility and creativity in therapy. For the purposes of this discussion, communication impairment has been divided into two categories: (1) mild and moderate communication impairments, which involve the use of complex language (i.e., a common set of symbols and rules used to communicate), and (2) severe communication impairments, which involve the use of little formal language.

Although considerable research has been dedicated to understanding why people with developmental disabilities have communication difficulties, recent research has focussed on how children and adults communicate and what factors influence the development of their abilities to interact socially and communicate with others (Beveridge, Conti-Ramsden, & Leudar, 1989; Kernan & Sabsay, 1989; Mundy, Seibert, & Hogan, 1985). This chapter emphasizes communication in adults with developmental disabilities.

Generally, people who function in the mild range of retardation demonstrate far fewer articulatory, grammatical, and lexical deficits than are seen in people functioning in the more severe ranges (Kernan & Sabsay, 1989). Communication difficulties for adults in the milder ranges appear to be primarily associated with the ability to communicate intended meaning in discourse and the ability to engage in appropriate conduct in social interactions (Kernan & Sabsay, 1989).

An ethnographic study of adults with mild retardation found that many of the participants had a tendency to "provide information piecemeal, to omit necessary information, to include irrelevant or unnecessary details, to voice incomplete thoughts and to run unconnected thoughts together in the same utterance" (Kernan & Sabsay, 1989, p. 231). These communicative tendencies can produce considerable confusion and misunderstandings for listeners. As a result, listeners are often required to engage in a "time consuming exercise of asking questions for clarification, offering hypotheses and constructing interpretations, and occasional leaps of intuition or faith" (Kernan & Sabsay, 1989, p. 237). This study concludes that listeners require patience and need to be able to piece together the information provided based on their intimate knowledge of the speaker's life. In addition, many listeners are aware that speakers with mental retardation are sensitive about not being understood by others and that this is sometimes a source of considerable frustration. In some cases, listeners, in an attempt to prevent the speaker from experiencing embarrassment over misunderstandings will drop subjects that they think are unimportant or change the subject entirely. Although this study describes the communication problems of adults with mild mental retardation in the community, some aspects of the dynamics and dilemmas facing listeners in these interactions are also relevant to therapists.

IMPLICATIONS FOR THERAPY

The Kernan and Sabsay study of communication points out that it is important for therapists to work systemically. Drawing on several information sources from the client's support systems allows the therapist to gain access to specific information about the client's life that may help him or her piece together a client's sometimes unclear and incomplete communications.

Price-Williams (1989) notes from his work on communication with adults who have mental retardation that it is necessary for the therapist to sort out the sometimes apparent triviality of a client's descriptions of events during therapy. Therapists need to determine the important concerns that are sometimes embedded and expressed in apparently trivial events (Price-Williams, 1989). In a manner similar to the behavior of the listeners in the Kernan and Sabsay study (1989), therapists might find it tempting to dismiss seemingly trivial comments or frustrating attempts at communicating and move onto other items that they perceive as more important. Price-Williams (1989) recommends that therapists be patient and attempt to determine exactly what the client is trying to communicate through sometimes seemingly trivial discussions. As the therapist develops a greater awareness of the client's specific issues, he or she may find it helpful to de-emphasize the irrelevant dimensions of a problem and increase the perceptual salience of cues that are more relevant.

Despite some of the noted communication problems, many people with mild developmental disabilities are capable of communicating and function very well in a variety of settings. Nevertheless, therapists must be aware of how communication in people with mild developmental disabilities may differ and to consider approaches that can be used to help encourage and positively reinforce communication with their clients. A few recommendations for therapists are presented that consider the impact of communication issues as these pertain to more verbally oriented therapies.

MODIFICATIONS FOR THERAPY

Therapists who are trained in highly verbal therapies may need to engage in an active, internal translation process to make their language more concrete and their sentences simpler. For example, con-sider the scenario of a therapist asking a client about how she might "modify her behavior toward a staff member in the group home" as she responds to the therapist with silence, a lack of eye contact, and a confused look. People with developmental disabilities are rarely pro-vided with opportunities to communicate, and often, they are not asked what they think or feel about things; consequently, they may feel overwhelmed and ill equipped for the conversational nature of ver-bal psychotherapy. Nevertheless, many clients can learn the required skills with some practice (Prout & Cale, 1994). When working with a client with a developmental disability, it will be important to spend some time with the person to find out what he or she understands and how he or she communicates. It is helpful to give people with devel-opmental disabilities extra time to respond as some people will need extra time to articulate. The language technique called Plain English can be very useful (Baladerian, 1985). Plain English is the use of simple language that does not exceed a sixth grade level. It may be preferable to use short sentences that do not exceed eight words per sentence and avoid double negatives, euphemisms, idioms, slang, or the use of long or unusual words (Baladerian, 1985). Using concrete language and avoiding the use of "why" or "if" questions will reduce distress and confusion for the client. It may be more informative for the therapist and less anxiety provoking for the client to begin with simple, close-ended, yes/no type questions and expand these to fur-ther evaluate the client's communication and comprehension skills. For example, later in the therapeutic process, the use of questions that use comparisons rather than simple, close-ended, yes/no type questions might be more helpful in eliciting more specific informa-tion about a client's comprehension (Murdock & Van Ornum, 1989). Therapists may need to use a greater number of reflecting, pacing, and leading comments, and ongoing clarification of a client's state-ments may help the client communicate better and become more spe-cific in describing his or her experiences (Prout & Cale, 1994). Prosser and Bromley (1998) indicate that the use of active verbs may be more easily understood than passive verbs and the use of questions regard-ing abstract considerations of future actions or attitudes should be avoided due to the tendency of responses to be unreliable and speculative. They also recommend using anchoring events in the recent past as a means to help the client focus on the time course of events (Prosser & Bromley, 1998).

It is important to be aware that people with a developmental disability often have been conditioned to be compliant to those in authority and may exhibit strong tendencies to respond in ways that they believe will please the therapist (Price-Williams, 1989). Simple yes/no questions can sometimes encourage acquiescence (Bicknell, 1994; Prosser & Bromley, 1998). When answering questions, a client may try to read the therapist and give the answer he or she believes is desired or has been trained to give. For example, a therapist may ask a client about her anger and she promptly provides a trained response about how she should appropriately handle it. Therapists need to be aware that they might be seen as authority figures, and when a client does not understand a question, he or she will sometimes feign understanding. There can be considerable gaps between a client's expressive language, comprehension, and abstract reasoning ability (Bates, 1992). When attempting to assess if the client understands a question, an effective strategy involves asking a client to put a question in his or her own words. Bates (1992) recommends that therapists ask a question in one way to obtain an affirmative response and reframe the same question to obtain a negative response to check client comprehension. Considerable caution must be exercised, however, when asking questions in this manner as it is important to use a questioning style that assesses comprehension without "testing" or creating anxiety and distress in the client.

It may take a while to learn how to best communicate with a client who has a developmental disability. If the therapist asks a question and the client has difficulty understanding, clearly the therapist needs to modify his or her language so that it is understandable to the client. It is necessary for the therapist to take responsibility for the difficulty, making it clear that the problem has been created by the therapist's difficulty asking the question in the proper way, and that it is not the result of the client's failure to understand. Communication can sometimes be a complicated endeavor in therapy, and it is more helpful if the therapist takes a one-down position with the client and frames the communication problem as the therapist's problem. In this situation, the therapist can discuss how frustrating it can be to have difficulties with understanding. Also, the therapist can discuss communication difficulties as something that can happen when people are getting to know each other and suggest that the client will need to patiently teach the therapist how to understand.

Some aspects of therapy may involve teaching. Repetition is important (Bates, 1992; Gorman-Smith & Matson, 1992) as it takes into consideration the impact of the client's cognitive and concentration limitations: For example, it is important not to assume that the client will be able to recall information that has been presented in previous sessions. When introducing new concepts, the therapist may need to use considerable repetition, and it might be preferable to deal with one issue at a time or perhaps only a few issues in a session and to be as concrete as possible. Reviewing previously discussed issues at the beginning of a session can be a helpful prompt for clients (Gorman-Smith & Matson, 1992). Periodic reviews can provide opportunities for the therapist to review the client's progress in therapy and provide praise and positive statements for the client's work in therapy. In addition, some clients might have difficulty generalizing concepts they have learned in therapy to other settings, and the use of generalization training can be very helpful, particularly for self-protection skills (Sullivan et al., 1992). Communication in clients with severe and profound mental retardation or those who are described as nonverbal presents additional considerations for therapists.

COMMUNICATION IN PEOPLE WITH SEVERE AND PROFOUND MENTAL RETARDATION OR WHO ARE DESCRIBED AS NONVERBAL

People with severe language impairments may require more substantial accommodations in counseling. Severe language impairments can exist as a result of very severe developmental disabilities, multiple handicaps (e.g., moderate developmental disabilities with impaired motor skills in addition to hearing and vision loss), or a variety of interacting factors (e.g., environmental factors such as severe neglect can play a significant role). People with severe language impairments may use few, if any words and rarely use sentences or complex speech. However, it is important to remember that many people understand much more language than they can use. A great deal of communication can and often does take place with little or no formal language.

A great deal has been written about how people with severe and multiple disabilities communicate and use language, and this chapter presents only a tiny fraction of what is known about this topic. Those who want to learn more about this topic should consider such excellent texts as Beukelman and Mirenda (1998), Downing (1999), Reichle, York, and Sigafoos (1991), and Musselwhite and St. Louis (1988).

Most people with severe language impairments still communicate frequently and effectively through informal means. Most of them can effectively make their needs and feelings known to their communication partners. Even so, they are often limited in their abilities to communicate about abstract concepts or about events outside their current environment, and they are likely to rely on alternative modes of communication.

Communication modes are general forms of communication (e.g., speech, gestures, pictures). Normal human communication is multimodal. People with developmental disabilities should also be encouraged to combine various modes. In addition to being more normal, multimodal communication almost always results in expanded communication abilities and allows a good fit between the mode of communication being used, the communication function being expressed, and the context in which communication takes place.

Communication functions, sometimes called pragmatics, refer to the social purposes of communications rather than the form of communication or the formal message. For example, someone might say, "I'm really hungry." While the superficial message is simply to inform the listener of the speaker's state, in many situations, it might also function as a request for food. In fact, the listener who understands the meaning but fails to respond might be considered rude or insensitive. The relationship between modes and functions must be strong for communication to be effective. For example, many people with severe language impairments use communication boards, pointing to items rather than speaking words. This is a good mode for routine requests for items and events (one communication function), but it is usually a poor mode for getting the attention of a communication partner (another communication function) because the communicator must have the attention of the other individual before the other individual can be expected to see where the communicator is pointing. Therefore, vocalization is generally a better mode for getting attention.

Context also interacts with mode. For example, using the vocal mode and saying "hello" is normally a good start when meeting a friend face to face. However, greeting a friend at a distance at a loud concert would require the gestural mode (e.g., waving). Greeting the same friend from across the continent would require writing (i.e., graphic mode).

In building communication with an individual with severe disabilities, often, the first goal is to increase frequency (Orelove & Sobsey, 1996). Until frequent communication is established, it is difficult to modify or improve communication. Once frequent communication is established, every interaction provides a learning opportunity to improve the quality of communication. To build frequency, it is important for the therapist to make communication as rewarding an experience as possible. The best rewards for communication are generally functional (e.g., rewarding the communicator with the thing that he or she requested). A communication partner who is attentive, friendly, and responsive is also reinforcing for the communicator.

VOCABULARY
It may be necessary to find out if potentially critical words, gestures, or graphics have been taught and are available to the communicator. For example, many people with disabilities have never been taught a vocabulary for feelings, sexual behavior, or personal autonomy. What

may seem like reluctance on the part of a person with developmental disabilities to discuss or conceptualize his or her experience of abuse may be due in part to a lack of words or symbols. In order to reduce the risk for future sexual abuse, the therapist should work to enhance a client's communication skills and help him or her to develop a vocabulary. Some communication disorder specialists or speech or language pathologists are well-trained to work with this population, and they can make valuable contributions; consequently, consultation is desirable when setting up any aspect of therapy that contains a significant component concerned with teaching communication skills. Although a variety of communication alternatives are currently available, some communication systems are particularly controversial.

COUNSELLING IMPLICATIONS

Since most people with severe communication deficits lack elements of vocabulary and grammar, communication may be less precise. These individuals may not be able to communicate all the details of an event. Sometimes greater precision can be obtained with the use of pictures or other materials. Details of the events of their abuse, however, should not be the focus of counseling. Counseling should focus on how they feel about what happened to them. Often people with severe communication deficits are good informal communicators and find ways to let counselors know how they feel.

Context is important to all communication. People with good communication skills can create verbal context for their communication. People with significant deficits cannot do so. As a result, the physical and social environment is more important to their communication. For this reason, counselors may find that they can sometimes communicate more successfully with these clients in the environments they are familiar with and sometimes in the environment in which the events of interest took place. It may be valuable to meet some clients in these environments for some visits rather than always meeting in the counselor's office.

IDIOSYNCRATIC AND UNPROVEN COMMUNICATION SYSTEMS

The Use of FC in Sexual Abuse Disclosure

Facilitated communication is a procedure for communicating via typing, communication board, or other communication device that employs a an assistant or facilitator to help support an individual's hand or arm while they type out a message, point to symbols, or activate an electronic device. The method was developed in the 1970s by Rosemary Crossly in Australia (Beukelman & Mirenda, 1998).

In 1990, a 29-year-old woman with severe language impairment from just outside Melbourne, Australia, began to disclose severe sexual and physical abuse via facilitated communication (FC). Carla, as she came to be known, told staff at her day center that "Dad is having sex with me....He touches me inside and puts his prick in me," and mom "nestles me out of the way or tortures me in her own way by not looking when dad hits me in the mouth" (Heinrichs, 1992a, p. 9). She indicated that she had been raped by her father and brother and that her mother restrained her during the assaults. The allegations were reported to social service authorities who acted to protect Carla by removing her from her home. Carla's disclosure was the only evidence of the abuse. Her family vigorously denied the charges, and Carla resisted being taken from her family. Of course, most offenders deny their offenses, and it is quite common for abused individuals to resist separation from their abusers; however, this differed from other cases because of the unique way that Carla had disclosed. Carla was using FC. Some experts argued that Carla lacked the internal language to produce the complex statements included in the disclosure. They pointed out that Carla clearly spoke the word "no" when social services workers forcibly removed her from her home. All of Carla's spoken and nonverbal language except the FC allegations seemed to contradict the messages made through FC. Naturally, if the allegations were true, Carla was being abused and needed protection from her family. If these allegations were false and, as the experts suggested, the apparent disclosure did not originate from Carla, she was being abused by the people who were taking her away from a loving home against her will on the basis of a counterfeit disclosure.

Carla's parents went to court to demand her return. Only then was the validity of her facilitated communication tested with a double-blind test. In this test, both Carla and her facilitator wore headphones and were given a series of simple questions for Carla to answer. Sometimes, both Carla and her facilitator heard similar questions; sometimes they heard different questions. Carla did not answer any of the questions correctly when her facilitator could not hear them. Even more troubling, Carla answered several questions correctly that only the facilitator had heard. The results showed clearly that at least some and possibly all of the communication originated from the facilitator and not from Carla. With no corroborating evidence and considerable reason to doubt the validity of the allegations, the court awarded guardianship to Carla's mother and sister, and Carla was returned to her home. Ironically, her facilitators suggested that Carla was responsible for the false charges and stated that Carla admitted (through further facilitation) that she had lied when she made the original allegations (Heinrichs, 1992b). Although the problem was identified as originating with the facilitator, the situation was blamed on Carla.

During the first part of the 1990s, the use of FC has spread dramatically, particularly in North America, and was advocated as powerful intervention by many (e.g, Biklen, 1993). Scores of similar abuse allegations have been associated with its use. The vast majority of these allegations remain unsubstantiated, and some cases have resulted in lawsuits by people claiming that they have been falsely and maliciously or capriciously accused. The rapid growth in the use of facilitated communication slowed by the mid-1990s. and since that time, its use in North America appears to have been in decline (Beukelman & Miranda, 1998). Nevertheless, FC continues to be used by many people with autism, cerebral palsy, global cognitive deficits, and a variety of other developmental disabilities. In addition, the practice has strong and articulate advocates (e.g., Crossley, 1997).

Yet, many professional organizations have adopted policies condemning facilitated communication and recommending against its use. For example, the American Psychological Association (1994), issued a resolution pointing out that most scientific studies failed to validate FC and many have demonstrated facilitator influence or control over communication that has been inappropriately attributed to the disabled individual. The resolution points out that by wrongly attributing communications to individuals with disabilities, FC can result in a serious threat to the human rights of these individuals, in addition to those who may be wrongly accused through facilitated communication. The resolution concludes:

> THEREFORE, BE IT RESOLVED that the APA adopts the position that facilitated communication is a controversial and unproved communication procedure with no demonstrated support for its efficacy. (American Psychological Association, 1994 in Jacobson & Mulick, 1996, pp. 431-433),

As suggested by the APA resolution, the person who may be falsely accused through FC (or any other means) is harmed and often seriously harmed by the allegations. Such false allegations also hurt the individual with a severe disability who has been falsely portrayed as the source of the allegations. In addition to the loss of control over the content of their own communications, which is a significant intrusion on personal rights and sense of identity, false allegations can lead to the loss of caring and committed others, vital assets to individuals who are dependent on others for care. In addition to these harms suggested by the APA resolution, false or unsupportable allegations also do indirect but serious harm to many people who are not directly involved. All those who are truly victimized and all those who seek help for them have greater difficulty in having their allegations taken seriously as a result of cases of false and unsubstantiatable allegations.

Considering all of these problems and that the use of FC appears to be declining in frequency, a simple rejection of facilitated communication might seem in order. However, this simplistic approach also has two serious limitations.

First, there is a problem with generalizing results of research to individuals. Buekelman and Mirenda (1998), who are among the most cautious critics of FC, for example, describe several individuals who have clearly demonstrated valid use of FC. While there is no data available that allows us to know whether such genuine users of FC are a tiny minority or a somewhat larger proportion of the total number of FC users, we can be certain that some individuals have learned to communicate through FC and depend on it as their primary source of communication. Even if these individuals are only a tiny minority of FC users, should they be denied their only primary form of communication simply because many others are not using FC properly? While critics have correctly pointed out that any misrepresentation of a facilitator's message as being authored by an individual with a disability is serious violation of that individual's right to freedom of expression, denying an individual the only method of communication that he or she can use, because it has been demonstrated to be inappropriate for other people is also a major violation of that right.

Second, many of the problems attributed to FC may also be present in other forms of assisted or interpreted communication. For example, some individuals use eye gaze communication with symbols on a lap tray. In some cases, one or a few communication partners become skilled in interpreting their responses and assist others in communicating with them. In our experience, there have been some cases where these interpreters have influenced the communication to such a great extent that the interpreters have been the primary source of the communication content. This suggests that the problems attributed to FC are not unique to one form of assisted or interpreted communication and considerable caution must be used when any form of assistance or interpretation is used.

Recommendations

If better alternatives are available, avoid the use of facilitated communication and other forms of communication that depend on a third party to assist or interpret. Direct communication is typically the best for counseling.

If facilitated communication or other controversial forms of communication that involve third parties are the only alternatives available or that the client will use, it is essential to validate the use of the communication method for the individual and to determine whether and to what extent the third party may be influencing the communication. A number of excellent procedures have been developed for conducting such evaluations. While a description of these procedures go beyond the scope of this article, they generally involve determining the ability of the client to answer questions when the third party is unaware of the question or the appropriate answer. A number of such procedures for evaluating facilitated communication have been well described by researchers (e.g. Bligh & Kupperman, 1993; Cabay, 1994; Shane & Kearns. 1994; Szempuch & Jacobson, 1993) and can be easily adapted to other forms of communication.

While some counselors will be able to carry out validation procedures, it may be desirable to use other competent and independent professionals to carry out the validation procedures for two reasons. First, if skilled, experienced, and unbiased experts are available, they can often carry out the procedures more quickly and accurately. Second, evaluators must establish relationships with clients and facilitators that are very different from the role that counselors play. Evaluators must be detached and somewhat skeptical. The counselor who assumes this role at the beginning of a relationship with a client may have difficulty shifting to a more typical role of counselor. The client and facilitator may have even greater difficulty making this shift.

If FC or any other form of communication is validated for use by an individual and is the preferred or most effective form of communication use by an individual, that individual should be allowed to use it. Regardless of what form of communication is used, counselors should make on-going and continual efforts to verify that communication is free of inappropriate influence by others.

If an evaluation of an individual's communication method reveals that the individual may not be the source of the communication or is strongly influenced by a facilitator or assistant, counseling should not proceed until this issue is addressed and some other form of communication can be appropriately validated.

If a disclosure of abuse occurs through any method of communication that has not been validated, it should be treated much like an anonymous allegation. If a facilitator or other assistant influences an individual with a disability to disclose abuse, it clearly raises serious questions about the legitimacy of the allegation. However, these questions do not automatically mean that an allegation is false and dismissed without consideration. Such allegations should be investigated to determine if they can be properly substantiated through other means.

This chapter outlined communication issues and strategies pertaining to working with clients with developmental disabilities. The unique aspects of communication strategies and considerations for clients in therapy with a range of developmental and communication disabilities were examined. Some emphasis was placed on those situations where an interpreter may be used in therapy and caution was advised when considering the use of an interpreter in the therapy process. In the next chapter emphasis is placed on examining modifications of therapy techniques and the use of specific therapy components for clients with developmental disabilities who have been sexually abused.

•• 6

Individualizing Therapy: Modifications for Therapies

Many of the modifications and considerations presented for verbally oriented therapies also apply to less verbally oriented therapies, yet there are some significant differences. With the less verbally oriented therapies, the therapist will want to make some modifications, and these modifications will be more encompassing and, in varying degrees, qualitatively different from those modifications made to the more verbally oriented therapies.

Although many of the recommendations presented earlier for the more verbally oriented therapies also apply in varying degrees to clients who have difficulties with verbal communication, there will be a greater emphasis on the therapist's consultation with other professionals, flexibility, and willingness to communicate in the client's preferred mode of communication. Nonverbal therapies require a considerable amount of consultation with professionals who are well-acquainted with the client's communication style. These professionals are an important source of information about a client's communication patterns. They may be able to inform the therapist about the meaning of a client's responses or about specific behaviors he or she typically uses to communicate. For example, some therapists find it helpful to begin the initial work with the client and an additional person who is acceptable or feels safe to the client. The goal of this arrangement is to build trust and begin establishing the therapeutic relationship with the client, to carefully learn about the client's communication style, and eventually work individually with the client. This arrangement is not always necessary or appropriate, but when it seems to be a reasonable course of action, this other support person needs to be chosen carefully: For example, the person should be someone the client trusts and who is not associated with the perpetrator.

People with developmental disabilities who are described as nonverbal may have a wide array of communication abilities that can include: making eye contact, head movements, facial expressions, gesturing, and various vocalizations. It is important for the therapist to learn about the client's unique modes of communication and adapt therapy to meet his or her needs and abilities. Therapists will need to draw on both their verbal and nonverbal skills for engaging the client and be aware of particular body language cues and the variability that may exist across cultures.

Sometimes the various materials involved in the less verbally dependent forms of therapy need to be introduced slowly in order to give the therapist an opportunity to evaluate how the client responds: For example, the therapist needs to be aware that some clients with developmental disabilities have sensory integration difficulties and can have strong aversive responses to certain tactile experiences present in various media used for art or play therapies. Therapists need to be perceptive about the client's likes and dislikes and respond accordingly, particularly when introducing the less verbally oriented therapies. In family and group therapy with clients who are described as nonverbal, the therapist will need to be flexible, creative, and resourceful in order to develop the appropriate means necessary to ensure that the person with a developmental disability will be heard (Hollins, 1995). A variety of therapy approaches may be used with clients who are described as nonverbal.

LESS VERBALLY ORIENTED THERAPIES
A variety of approaches are included in the less verbally oriented therapies; however, therapists engaging in any of these approaches should receive training in play therapy techniques. When the therapeutic relationship has been established, engaging the client in these activities opens the door for communication and the acquisition of concepts: For example, play therapy can provide opportunities for the client to portray and explore feelings, inner conflicts, problems, desires, and fantasies in a concrete form. Play therapy uses a variety of different settings and materials that may include role-playing, sand tray, puppets, art, and music. The use of imagery, body movement,

sensorial processing, music, and art are less abstract, and these modes of communication represent expressive languages that are useful for clients with developmental disabilities (Seubert, 1992): For example, puppets may serve as a medium for self-expression that allows a client to safely enact or reenact scenes, roles, and conflicts. Therapeutic stories that use a storytelling format can be used to communicate salient themes and issues to clients. The use of pictorial feeling cards may help clients identify particular feelings. Art can include the following activities: drawing, painting, and sculpting, using a variety of media. When using art therapy, a variety of art media and tools, instructional sequences, and technological adaptations need to be considered: For example, clients who have difficulty with muscle control may require additional adaptations. Consultation with the client's occupational therapist can be very helpful for adapting materials to meet the client's needs. (See Anderson [1992] for a discussion describing art therapy adaptations that may be required for children with disabilities, and Caprio-Orsini [1996] for a discussion about using art with people with developmental disabilities who have been traumatized.) (A discussion detailing play therapy and the assessment process involving children with developmental disabilities is presented in Chapter 8).

Play therapy may be appropriate for both children and adults, but specific activities might be seen by both adults and adolescents as too childish. Some authors suggest that therapists need to balance the use of play therapies with adults who have developmental disabilities with normalization considerations (Prout & Strohmer, 1994a). It is important for the therapist to avoid infantilizing the client. Therapists should use approaches that will foster the client's expression, but they should be cautious when introducing play therapy materials, giving clients the opportunity to choose which materials they want to use during therapy. Providing opportunities for decision making also gives the client more control in the therapeutic relationship.

Although communication issues and adaptations represent distinctive characteristics for therapy, additional considerations that involve the identification and integration of treatment issues and the use of specific therapy components are also relevant. Many of the treatment issues that surface when providing therapy to people with developmental disabilities are similar to those that surface when providing therapy to clients without developmental disabilities; however, the impact of disability is an important issue in therapy conducted with people who have developmental disabilities. Psychoeducationally oriented approaches that are tailored to address specific issues associated with sexual abuse and developmental disabilities are presented below, and a few examples these types of approaches are provided.

SPECIFIC THERAPY COMPONENTS

When identifying the treatment issues, the therapist must consider the combined impact of sexual abuse and developmental disability. Practitioners must have realistic expectations about their clients' rate of progress because treatment issues for people with developmental disabilities may be exacerbated their disability. In addition, it is important for the therapist to consider the fact that a client's sometimes limited communication skills can result in behaviors and nonverbal language that need to be interpreted in terms of the communicative functions these may serve for the client. When providing therapy for people with developmental disabilities, therapists may find it useful to employ a variety of modalities: for example, individual, group, multimodal, and/or family therapy.

PSYCHOEDUCATIONAL APPROACHES

Certain adaptations are required to ensure the suitability of therapy for clients with developmental disabilities. Some specific therapy components will, by necessity, tend to have a psychoeducational orientation. The psychoeducational approaches presented here often possess distinct components that are intended to address issues that are, in varying degrees, particular to therapy for clients with developmental disabilities who have been sexually abused.

A psychoeducational orientation should not be interpreted as a perspective that is used to explain away the client's pain or problems. For example, when a therapist suggests that a client is not responsible for the abuse, he or she might proceed by normalizing some of the feelings associated with the abuse, which could provide an important starting point for therapy; but the normalization of some feelings does not reduce guilt as a significant issue, and it does not suggest that the client requires no further treatment. To the contrary, the client will still need to address specific treatment issues: for example, learning about specific effects; processing feelings associated with the abuse; learning alternative coping strategies and assertiveness skills; enhancing self-esteem; addressing disability related issues; and learning social, sexuality, and self-protective skills.

Specific components in therapy should take into consideration the social circumstances, heightened vulnerability to sexual abuse that people with developmental disabilities experience, and their limitations in cognitive and social skills. Therapy components that promote a client's personal safety, sense of self, and personal rights are especially important (Seubert, 1992). Distinguishing characteristics of therapy may include: the use of preparation for counseling, assessing affective vocabulary, and teaching about feelings (Ludwig & Hingsburger, 1989; Sullivan, 1993); developing social and sexuality skills (Sullivan et al., 1992); teaching about sexual abuse and self-protection skills (Rappaport, Burkhardt, & Rotatori, 1997); and addressing self-esteem (Ludwig & Hingsburger, 1993; Neal & Michalakes, 1992) and disability related issues (Hurley, 1989; Szivos & Griffiths, 1992). Inadequate sexuality and self-protection education, social isolation, and a lack of social skills contribute to the heightened vulnerability to abuse experienced by people with developmental disabilities. A psychoeducational approach might provide opportunities to address these concerns, and depending on the evaluation of the client's needs, age, and developmental level, the therapist might be able to provide appropriate education about sexuality, social relationships, assertiveness, feelings, and personal safety skills.

Preparation for Counseling
The early part of therapy is dedicated to the development and establishment of the therapeutic relationship. It is important for the therapist to talk about the purpose of meeting with the client, and it is crucial to determine if the client understands why he or she is com-

ing to therapy. Loneliness can be a very significant issue for clients with developmental disabilities, and in some cases, these clients will confuse the therapeutic relationship with friendship. The therapist needs to clarify and outline the distinctions between these two relationships. In addition, clients need to understand the limitations of the therapeutic relationship. It is important to explain what happens in therapy and to clarify the roles of the therapist and client. As part of clarifying the roles and outlining the nature of therapy, it is important for the issue of termination to be addressed earlier rather than later in therapy. Inadequate or insensitive preparation for termination can leave a client feeling abandoned, rejected, and may compound issues associated with grief or loss. The therapist needs to handle termination sensitively and be aware of the potential impact it may have on coping for a client who may have few friends, limited social skills, limited opportunities for friendships, and is socially isolated.

It is important to evaluate the client's understanding and appraisal of the abuse. The client's expressed understanding of the abuse can provide key opportunities to assess beliefs the client may have about the abuse and his or her role in it. An important aspect of the therapeutic process is making meaning of the sexual abuse experience (Friedrich, 1990), and both cognitive appraisals and emotional responses are relevant. There may be significant issues surrounding guilt, shame, and developmental disability. These beliefs might reflect an internalization of the offender's justifications for the abuse that focus on the devalued status of the person with a developmental disability and victim blaming. In addition, clients with developmental disabilities often have significant issues involving the acceptance of an identity associated with developmental disability (Hurley, 1989; Svizos & Griffiths, 1992) and self-esteem (Hingsburger, 1990b; Neal & Michalakes, 1992). In some ways, there appears to be a considerable overlap between issues associated with sexual abuse and issues associated with disability, making the healing process potentially more complicated for clients with developmental disabilities.

It is important for the therapist to assess the client's knowledge about sexuality, relationships, and affective vocabulary. Early in the therapeutic process, the therapist should spend time learning about the client's cognitive level, communicative abilities, and the nature and impact of his or her disability. These early interactions in conjunction with professional liaison will provide information about the client's specific patterns of delays and strengths in receptive and expressive communicative abilities.

Depending on the therapist's evaluation of the client's needs, it might be helpful to introduce the concept of sexual abuse and to discuss some of the possible effects as a way of normalizing the client's feelings. Some clients may have almost no sense of personal boundaries and be overly trusting or compliant, perhaps telling the therapist everything about their abuse within moments of the first session. At this point, it will be important for the therapist to model appropriate boundaries for the client. The client will need to learn that he or she may share what has happened with the therapist, but it might not be appropriate or necessary to share this information with someone who is a stranger to the client. The therapist can model appropriate boundaries and provide the client with some control and decision-making opportunities by giving the client the right to make decisions in therapy about when and how to talk about the abuse. Developing a vocabulary for feelings and learning to recognize these in self and others are central to helping clients determine when they feel safe or comfortable enough to talk about the sexual abuse. Throughout therapy, considerable time will be dedicated to learning about feelings, personal safety, and comfort. As therapy progresses, it will become possible to build in more opportunities for clients to have choices and practice making decisions. This provides not only much needed experience in these areas, but also, it allows the client to exercise some control in therapy.

When introducing fairly abstract concepts such as sexual abuse or boundaries, the use of concrete examples and repetition are beneficial. A variety of methods can be used to introduce these abstract concepts in a concrete manner. Seubert (1992), in his work on self-awareness with adults with developmental disabilities, suggests the use of Hoola Hoops as a concrete means of introducing and demonstrating the concept of personal boundaries.

Sexual Abuse

Books and videos that provide general information or tell a story about sexual abuse can be a concrete and evocative approach to therapy with clients with developmental disabilities. Hollins and Sinason's animated series on sexual abuse of people with disabilities, *Bob tells all* (Hollins & Sinason, 1993) and *Jenny speaks out* (Hollins and Sinason, 1992), are colorful and contain concrete examples that can be used for introducing the concept of sexual abuse, its effects, and therapy. Also, showing videotapes may be useful. There are a variety of animated and colorful videos on child sexual abuse, and although not many are specifically aimed at people with developmental disabilities, these materials might work well with this population. The use of books and videos that deal with sexual abuse may help clients understand what has happened to them and what they are feeling. Therapists should preview all materials before hand and consider how the client may be effected by the materials and to consider the message that clients may receive. It is key to assess the client's understanding of the materials too. In using psychoeducational approaches for introducing sexual abuse, opportunities are provided to explore the client's affective vocabulary and how the client feels he or she has been affected by the abuse. In many cases, clients will have a limited vocabulary for feelings (e.g., happy, mad, sad, bored), and it will be important to teach additional vocabulary not only for the purposes of processing feelings in therapy, but also as means of reducing risk for future sexual abuse. Using pictorial means in combination with questioning approaches that help the person attach particular kinds of events with particular feelings can be helpful. For example, if I gave you a puppy, how would you feel? etc.

Affective vocabulary

Sullivan (1993) provides an example of teaching sexually abused children with developmental disabilities how to label feelings through the use of a "feeling box." Children are encouraged to express their emotions and are given language labels that describe these feelings. Later, the children are asked to label emotions in themselves and others and put these in the "feeling box." Also, children are taught how distinguish varying levels of emotional intensity through the use of a "feeling line" (Sullivan, 1993). A variation of this approach is the use of an emotional thermometer. Using scaling techniques can also help teach clients that their feelings can change and emphasis can be placed on their ability to change how they feel. Additional ways to teach emotions may involve using pictures of people's faces from magazines or other sources that illustrate different facial expressions. Ludwig and Hingsburger (1989) have used a feeling curriculum to achieve a similar purpose. Using these approaches can provide concrete ways for clients to learn to recognize facial expressions associated with emotions. Exploring emotions is an important component not only in terms of processing trauma and grief issues, but it is crucial for learning and expressing feelings and recognizing these in others. Some social skills development groups can incorporate components that allow the use of either group member's acting out the expression or using photos of others that demonstrate different facial expressions. Exercises can be used to help group members notice how their own body feels and looks when they are showing different emotions and how to recognize emotional expressions in others. The ability to recognize personal feelings of discomfort is a key aspect in teaching people with developmental disabilities self-protection skills (Sobsey & Mansell, 1990), and teaching these self-protection skills represents a critical therapy component. Some authors suggest that in addition to teaching clients an emotional language it is important to teach the distinction between thoughts and feelings (Prout & Strohmer, 1994a).

Many of the distinctive components that comprise therapy for people with developmental disabilities who have been sexually abused can be well-suited for use in a group therapy format. Group therapy may be particularly well-suited for many of the psychoeducational therapy goals, and it has the added benefit of promoting social interactions among members.

Group Therapy
In group therapy, potential group members need to be assessed individually to determine their motivation for change, abilities for verbal expression, and the degree to which they will benefit from the group

structure (Monfils, 1985; 1989). For group therapy techniques to be successful, they must be appropriately adapted to the client's target skills, level of understanding, social adaptability, and developmental level. (A full review of group therapy with clients who have developmental disabilities is beyond the scope of this chapter. The interested reader should refer to Brown [1994] for a review of counseling approaches, techniques, and potential difficulties for group therapy.)

Duffy (1992) notes that although groups comprised of people with developmental disabilities go through the same stages as other groups the process is slower, and cohesion and group norms take longer to develop. Nevertheless, some modifications to the structure of groups can be helpful: The group should be relatively small to provide ample opportunity for input from all members; sessions should be relatively brief and more frequent; organization will be optimal if it is along developmental levels; activities that promote relaxation should be used to facilitate openness and discussion; techniques that use structure to promote expressiveness in clients with low verbal expressiveness should be used; ground rules should be presented in a concrete manner to outline clearly appropriate and inappropriate behavior during group; leaders should be flexible and use a variety of activities, including modeling, role rehearsal, relaxation techniques, biofeedback, audiotaping, videotaping, and structured games; and clients should be an integral part of the therapy process and not just passive recipients (Whitmore, 1988, cited in Brown, 1994).

Group therapy provides opportunities for clients to share and learn more specifically about their issues, and it has been applied to diverse areas: social skills, anger management, sexual relationships, grief and loss, vocational skills, and stigma associated with developmental disability. In group therapy, members can learn that others have similar problems, feelings, impulses, and goals, and they are given the opportunity to practice and learn behaviors and skills with peers. The social setting of the group also helps clients generalize what they have learned to other settings. Although generalization can be somewhat problematic for clients with developmental disabilities, the use of additional in vivo approaches may be helpful. The greatest strength of group therapy is that it reduces the feeling of isolation surrounding the abuse, and it also produces an additional source of social support and self-esteem that might not otherwise exist for clients who may be socially isolated.

Sexuality and Social Skills

The association between sexuality, abuse, and exploitation can be very strong, particularly if the client has experienced repeated sexual abuse. Frequently, clients have either no information or a bare minimum of information about their own sexuality. Most typically, sexuality education for people with developmental disabilities includes general biological information about reproduction or contraception. In some cases, sexuality education will be provided in the occasional workshop setting or on an ad hoc basis, but the impact of this education tends to be minimal as repetition and consistency are required for learning. Few programs generalize training to ensure clients transfer their learning into other settings. Many sexuality education programs have neglected more socially oriented skills such as making friends, having intimate relationships, dating, and choosing a partner. Education about sexuality, sexual practices, preferences, choices, and personal safety often are misguided or, worse, excluded completely.

Clients receiving sexuality education may require considerable preparation in order to address fears concerning sexuality and sex since many people with developmental disabilities have been punished for sexual behavior (Hingsburger, 1992b). Many group homes and agencies are segregated and have restrictive policies concerning a client's sexual behavior, and often, clients are not provided with privacy or opportunities for sexual expression. Together, these circumstances often result in an absence of normative learning about social and sexual interactions (Gorman-Smith & Matson, 1992; Hingsburger, 1990a). Appropriate sexuality education needs to be individually tailored to an individual's developmental level and should be part of an ongoing curriculum that begins young and continues throughout life. Muccigrosso (1991) identifies a few important aspects of sexuality education for people with developmental disabilities: the use of differential teaching approaches to accommodate developmental levels of individuals (e.g., role play, dramatization, plain language, and repetition); the need for inclusive education, teaching practical skills in self-protection; and the need for parental involvement in prevention and sexuality education programs. Many abuse prevention programs for people with developmental disabilities require participation and use simple, plain language and considerable repetition to promote learning (Muccigrosso, 1991). The importance of ongoing education in both sexuality and self-protection suggests how crucial it is for the therapist to gain support from both staff (Brown, 1992) and significant others in the client's various support systems.

Self-protection Skills

Training potential victims to avoid or resist abuse has been a standard approach to sexual abuse risk reduction. An unfortunate consequence of these training programs is that they place too much responsibility for sexual abuse and assault prevention on potential victims and fail to assign ultimate responsibility to offenders. It is unrealistic to expect that any program that places primary responsibility on potential victims will adequately protect them. Despite problems associated with abuse prevention training programs, there are several training approaches that appear to be useful in addressing the needs of people with disabilities.

Group formats appear to be particularly well-suited for addressing the development of sociosexual skills that promote social interaction and reduce isolation. With additional program and staff cooperation, social interaction skills can lead to more access to appropriate social and sexual relationships, and reducing isolation can reduce the risk of more abusive relationships. Learning about personal safety is crucial to reducing the risk for sexual abuse. Such training can include: the use of role plays, psychodrama, and other techniques to teach social interaction and self-protection skills. Teaching clients about their emotions early in therapy will be critical later as the therapist teaches clients to pay attention to their internal emotional cues about discomfort or feeling unsafe. Similarly, clients need to develop and refine discrimination skills to help them distinguish safe from unsafe situations. These strategies can help clients become better equipped to recognize their own discomfort and potentially dangerous situations. It should be noted that teaching discrimination skills is an area fraught with difficulties. A range of commercially available training packages is available. Many have focused on teaching about different kinds of touch (i.e., good, bad, confusing, etc.) and different types of relationships. These approaches can be appropriate for come clients, however, it is important to appreciate that there can be inherent difficulties due to the ambiguity. A recently published book focused on teaching about puberty and uses children's social reasoning to teach rules about touch (Rappaport et al., 1997). The curriculum covers teaching and reviewing these rules and uses stories and parental involvement to help reinforce these rules children in settings outside the training to promote generalization.

Clients also need to learn how to seek advice and help to prevent situations from escalating to abuse. Some emphasis should be placed on ensuring that clients understand that they need to tell someone if they are being hurt in whatever way they can and that they may need to be persistent in order to obtain help. Encouraging persistence in obtaining help, however, must be tempered with teaching clients to identify who can and cannot help. Unfortunately, encouraging people to tell others about their sexual abuse has sometimes resulted in situations where the person tells almost anyone willing to listen to their story (e.g., a stranger on a bus), which clearly has enormous possibilities for heightening their future risk for abuse.

Teaching assertiveness is also important in therapy; however, simple discussion approaches do not easily override years of socialization toward compliance. Teaching these approaches does not guarantee that the clients will be able to generalize these skills to other settings outside therapy. It can sometimes be helpful to use more concrete activities such as role playing. Role play is presented as a group strategy for developing empathy skills in children who are perpetrating against others (Sullivan, 1993). Sullivan (1993) recommends the use of in vivo generalization training toward the end of the therapy to promote the use of new skills in other settings (e.g., the group home, school).

Neal and Michalakes (1992) outline a variety of activities that can be used in group therapy to strengthen group cohesion, build self-esteem, and assertiveness skills. They recommend that clients' overall level of functioning, communication skills, and the required target skills should guide group member selection (Neal & Michalakes, 1992). Although selecting clients for group who function at similar levels appears logical, selecting people with varying levels of functioning is actually more beneficial for self-esteem groups. Participants' communication skills need to be considered only as these pertain to adapting the curriculum used in the therapy. Often, curriculum can be adapted to meet a variety of communication modalities (e.g., communication boards, sign language) (Neal & Michalakes, 1992). Client assessment is required to determine a client's specific needs in order to ensure that the group in question can appropriately meet his or her needs. It is important to consult with clients about their goals or expectations for group. Assertiveness groups may be more difficult to run than self-esteem groups due to the requirement that participants be able to recognize feelings both in themselves and others. Neal and Michalakes (1992) recommend using exercises to help members associate feeling pictures with particular emotions, and later in the therapeutic process, they suggest using games and role-play situations to further reinforce assertiveness skills.

Self-esteem and Disability
Self-esteem and the identity of a person with a developmental disability represent significant psychological issues for many clients with developmental disabilities. Increasingly, therapists are recognizing the impact of a stigmatized identity and the importance of a client's needs for a healthy self-regard. Frequently, disability related issues surface and need to be addressed in therapy. Clients with developmental disabilities often are confused about the meaning of mental retardation since cognitive deficits cannot be seen. Szivos and Griffiths (1992) note that in their group that deal with stigmatized identity many adults had difficulty recognizing their shared experience because of confusion about disability and downward comparisons occurring within the group (e.g., a person regards him- or herself as higher functioning than his or her peers and does not identify him- or

herself as having a disability or does not possess a visible physical disability and therefore does not regard him- or herself as having a developmental disability, which reduces in-group affiliation and cohesion). Hurley (1989) recommends using concrete methods to help clients gain a meaningful understanding of their disability that later is followed with ability counseling to help clients get some perspective (e.g., helping the person separate his or her disability from his or her value as a human being and focusing on his or her abilities). Szivos and Griffiths (1992) explored the experience of being labeled and rejected and the meaning of mental retardation, and they used self-assessment, ability counseling, and the use of positive language about abilities to promote greater self-acceptance.

Hingsburger (1987, 1990b) has written about the importance of promoting the development of a positive self-concept in people with developmental disabilities. He recommends that therapists use a directive approach to improve client self-concept by asking questions such as "Tell me something good about yourself." He categorizes three types of responses: 1) compliance responses, 2) likes and dislikes responses, and 3) correct responses (e.g., I am a good person). In therapy, he outlines his approach to improve answers and the client's understanding of his or her personal attributes (Hingsburger, 1987).

BEHAVIORAL CONCERNS
Clients can experience a variety of behavioral difficulties, and they might need to develop additional ways to cope with their feelings. Sometimes intensive and aversive behavior management programs have been used to control noncompliant, aggressive, sexually inappropriate, or other problem behavior of people with developmental disabilities. Unfortunately, these programs often have been used with little attention to the discovery of the cause of the inappropriate behavior. Professional unwillingness to explore the emotional reasons underlying behaviors may reflect disability related myths that suggest behavior problems are a product of the developmental disability or that people with developmental disabilities do not possess an emotional life and, therefore, only the person's behaviors need to be addressed. It is essential that attempts be made to identify the real cause

of "behavior problems" before therapists attempt to eliminate them through the intrusive use of drugs or punishment procedures (Ryan, 1992; Sobsey, 1990). Determining and investigating the cause of the behaviors will help the therapist develop an appropriately focused treatment plan that considers the influence of the client's feelings and support systems on his or her behaviors.

Working with both staff and parents in the client's various systems can help the therapist monitor specific circumstances or environmental stimuli that might be acting as possible triggers for a client's behaviors. The therapist will need to obtain the cooperation of others in these various settings in order to monitor the client's behaviors and develop appropriate interventions. Also, cooperation is required so that interventions are applied consistently across settings and that the effectiveness of the interventions can be assessed.

There are some concerns surrounding the use of behavioral approaches that take control away from the person with a developmental disability and encourage passivity and compliance. This is a particularly relevant concern in therapy with a client who has been sexually abused. Some behavioral techniques provide the client with more control than more traditional aversive approaches, and they can be used to address some of the behaviors associated with the sexual abuse experienced by people with developmental disabilities. Bicknell and Conboy-Hill (1992) note that professionals often have the tendency to respond to negative behavior through the use of withdrawal, isolation, punishment, deceit, and a general failure to acknowledge the client's feelings. These researchers point out that therapists and other professionals tend to impose control over structure and use punitive measures to eliminate behaviors instead of using rewards for behavioral development or providing attention and comfort during emotional distress. This tendency compounds the original disability, contributes to an escalation of behavioral problems (Bicknell & Conboy-Hill, 1992), and demonstrates that emotional and behavioral responses to sexual traumatization will not be tolerated. Therapists should model dignified interactions with their clients, address the possibility of emotional responses to trauma, and use humane and developmental interventions that promote respect, dignity, emotional growth, and value of the client (Bicknell & Conboy-Hill, 1992).

The considerations for individualizing therapy that have been presented thus far are often integrated in a variety of ways. The literature documents the use of individual, group, and multimodal approaches to sexual abuse treatment for people with developmental disabilities. These examples illustrate the importance of a few researchers and practitioners challenging the importance of intelligence in determining suitability for therapy by adapting existing therapeutic techniques and using more relevant indicators of a person's ability to participate in therapy. These examples point out that assessing a client's developmental level, ability to form relationships, and social adaptability provide more relevant and helpful information to the practitioner about therapy suitability than intelligence alone.

INDIVIDUAL THERAPY

Ryan (1992) reports that from a referral population of 310 people with developmental disabilities a group of 51 met the technical criteria for Post Traumatic Stress Disorder (PTSD). Almost all of the 310 persons had suffered some significant trauma or abuse, which suggests that 16.5% of people with developmental disabilities who suffer trauma develop PTSD. Ryan (1992) indicates that "trauma in this sample included sexual abuse by multiple assailants (starting in childhood), physical abuse that was commonly the cause of the person's cognitive deficits, or life threatening neglect combined with some other active abuse or trauma" (p. 8).

Ryan (1992) developed a six-point protocol based on current literature for treatment of PTSD in people without disabilities, which includes information about medication contraindications: using medications judiciously, sedation is not considered treatment; identification and treatment of concurrent medical problems; minimizing iatrogenic complications (e.g., avoiding neuroleptics that might potentially act as a dissociative trigger); and psychotherapy using the client's preferred mode of communication to process trauma and grief. Ryan (1992) also recommends habilitative changes to control dissociative triggers, stating that almost anything in a person's environment can act as a potential dissociative trigger. Ryan provides an example of a man who became terrified when his staff wore the same perfumed powder as his mother who sexually abused him. When disturbing stimuli are discovered, it becomes essential to make changes that limit or eliminate the person's contact with these triggers. Ryan also recommends providing education and support for staff. In spite of the subjects' diverse etiology, all 23 who received treatment based on the six-point protocol improved as a result of the intervention. Client's self-report of a sense of well-being, frequency and intensity of psychiatric symptoms, frequency of violence to self or others, and improved functioning in work and relationships were used as a criteria for behavior change. Ryan's adaptation of current approaches to treating PTSD combined the special considerations necessary for working with people with developmental disabilities with a recognition of the varied and complex impacts of PTSD as they affect this population (e.g., the influence of neuroleptics as dissociative triggers) (Ryan, 1993) and an evaluation of the treatment's effectiveness.

Sinason (1992) uses individual psychoanalytic treatment with people who have developmental disabilities and argues that it can be effectively applied even to those requiring the highest level of assistance. She identifies three main stages of treatment. The first stage of therapy deals with removing the abused individual's secondary psychogenic impairments to improve communication between therapist and client. Sinason (1986) suggests that these "secondary handicaps" are the apparent impairments of communication and thinking associated with mental retardation that often are partially, and sometimes entirely, the symptoms of traumatic experiences and are not the direct results of the primary disability. Through the development of trust and a communicative relationship, many of these secondary impairments can be reduced or eliminated. The second stage involves the client's experience of sorrow and deep feelings of anger or shame about his or her abuse and trauma. Once optimal communication is achieved, the client can develop a trusting relationship with the therapist that allows the individual to confront her or his feelings about being victimized. In the third stage of therapy, the client begins to establish more control over her or his own life. Support and communication between therapist and client continues to be important, but the focus of the interaction moves toward decision making and more practical issues. The therapist also must help the individual work toward her or his own independence.

GROUP THERAPY

Cruz et al. (1988) used a cotherapy approach that involves one therapist with expertise in sexual abuse and the other with expertise in developmental disability. The cotherapy approach was used in conjunction with adapted group therapy techniques such as role playing and group discussions to provide sexual abuse treatment to adults with developmental disabilities who experienced intrafamilial child sexual abuse. The level of cognitive functioning of the six women in the group ranged from mild retardation to low average with severe learning disabilities. The women who were described as "acting out" were referred from their community based programs and attended the group therapy in conjunction with individual sessions. Issues addressed in the group sessions concerned: disability, sexuality, self-esteem, social isolation, loss, and parental relationships. Cruz et al. (1988) emphasize the professional liaison inherent in the cotherapy team approach and the adaptation of a sexual abuse treatment program to ensure greater availability and appropriateness of sexual abuse treatment for people with developmental disabilities. Unfortunately, their report does not include data about the efficacy of the therapy.

Hyman (1993) recommends the use of group strategies and provides additional ideas for effective group counseling. Coleaders can be useful in many groups, especially if some members occasionally need individual support or assistance to participate. The use of coleaders allows for the inclusion of individuals with more severe disabilities and provides the opportunity for additional modeling. A different group member is encouraged to bring food to each session to encourage bonding within the group. Parallel groups for families and significant others are run to help them provide support in the home and other settings. Hyman (1993) warns against using words such as sexual abuse in early sessions because they may inhibit or otherwise influence the group members' personal perceptions of their experiences.

Fresco, Philbin, and Peters (1992) suggest that there are a variety of advantages to using a group therapy approach: learning coping and problem-solving skills; receiving acceptance and support from peers through modeling; reduced isolation; and the sharing of life experiences, information, expression of emotions, and encouragement. They present an example of a group therapy format for women with developmental disabilities who have been sexually assaulted. The therapy included eight sessions that cover several topics. Group members were introduced to the structure of the group and provided with exercises that promote self-nurturance, self-esteem, coping skills, problem-solving skills, self-protection strategies, validation, and assertiveness. The group members were assessed following therapy and continued to show significant problems when re-assessed with standardized personality tests. However, this evaluation appears to have a few methodological problems.

MULTIMODAL APPROACHES TO THERAPY
Sullivan and colleagues (1990) reviewed the literature on sexual abuse and combined it with their expertise gained from working with children with handicaps in order to adapt a sexual abuse treatment program for use with children who have developmental disabilities. Sexual abuse treatment goals include: alleviating guilt, regaining the ability to trust, treating depression, helping children express anger, teaching about sexuality and interpersonal relationships, teaching self-protection techniques, teaching an affective vocabulary to label feelings, teaching sexual preference and sexual abuse issues when appropriate, and treating secondary behavioral characteristics (Sullivan & Scanlan, 1987). Therapy techniques include: directive and nondirective counseling, play and reality therapy, psychodrama and role playing, transactional analysis, behavior therapy, didactic counseling, and generalization training (Sullivan & Scanlan, 1987).

Sullivan, Scanlan, Knutson, Brookhouser, and Schulte (1992) studied the efficacy of these therapy adaptations by using The Child Behavior Checklist (CBC) before and after therapy with a sample of 72 sexually abused children from a residential school for the deaf. The sample included 51 boys and 21 girls 12 to 16 years of age, and therapy was conducted by a therapist fluent in sign language. The study included a nontreatment control group because half of the parents refused the offer of free psychotherapy services for their children. Before therapy, both the treatment and nontreatment groups had elevated CBC scores. Children receiving therapy had significantly fewer behavior problems after therapy than children not receiving therapy. The research of Sullivan and colleagues demonstrates considerable promise in developing and determining the efficacy of adapted treatment for children with disabilities who have been sexually abused.

In this chapter, emphasis has been placed on the considerations for individualizing treatment for clients with developmental disabilities who have been sexually abused and on distinctive therapy components. In Part Four differing therapy modalities are presented. The first chapter focuses on the importance of considering the impact of systemic influences on the client and the systemic issues pertaining to providing family therapy. The remaining chapters focus on the use of play therapy and assessment of inappropriate sexual behaviors.

Part 4
Therapy Modalities

•• 7

Family Systems, Disability Issues, and Therapy

Lorraine Wilgosh & Sheila Mansell

Throughout this book emphasis has been placed on examining the distinctive features and considerations associated with providing therapy to people with a developmental disability who have been sexually abused. Emphasis has also been placed on the importance of using a systemic approach that enlists the support of, and where appropriate, engages involved caregivers and others in the treatment process. It is not the goal of this chapter to provide a comprehensive review of the family therapy literature, promote the use of a particular family therapy approach per se, or outline how to conduct family based treatment. Interested readers may refer to Becvar and Becvar (1999) for more detailed discussion of the family therapy literature.

This chapter draws from the family systems literature to provide a framework for identifying family life cycle issues and understanding the combined impact of stress, coping, and adaptation in the family with a child who has a developmental disability. The effects of sexual abuse (both incestuous and extrafamilial) on the family system are examined within the family systems context. Examples of family therapy that address developmental disability related family and sexual abuse issues are presented. As with previous discussions of treatment in this book, emphasis is placed on a therapist's need to consider the distinct coping, adaptation, and life cycle issues facing families with a member who has a developmental disability along with specific sexual abuse issues facing the person. The specific treatment considerations and accommodations for people with developmental disabilities that are outlined in Chapters 4, 5, and 6 are also relevant and applicable to systems based treatment.

FAMILY SYSTEMS CONCEPTUAL FRAMEWORK

The family is the core unit in society. With the deinstitutionalization of many people with developmental disabilities, increasing numbers of families have taken primary responsibility for raising their children. Much of the early research concerning families who have children with developmental disabilities focused on grief, problems, pathologies, and stress faced by these families. Over the years the perspectives and research concerning these families has been changing. Increasingly this body of research has been expanding and examining in greater depth the diversity, sources of strength and resiliency, and the adaptation processes and dynamics for families. The underlying premise of the family systems model is that a change in any part of the system affects the entire system and its various members.

In the 1980s, Turnbull, Summers, and Brotherson (1986) presented the family systems conceptual framework as a necessary context for viewing individual family members because the interaction of family members as a unit encompasses the behaviors and needs of individuals within the family. Turnbull et al. (1986) called for research within a family life cycle framework that focuses on dynamic, changing family characteristics as they impact on family interaction, resulting in a number of significant studies (e.g., McDonald, Kysela, Drummond, Alexander, Enns, & Chambers, 1999). Glidden, Kiphart, Willoughby, and Bush (1993) emphasized the increasing sophistication in theory and research on families in the latter part of the 20th Century, and development of complex models of family adjustment to potentially stressful events. "These new models emphasize the cognitive determinants and concomitants of coping, the macro-environment in which the family lives, and the long-term results of any potentially stressful event" (p. 184).

Within the family systems model, the resources and characteristics of the family (inputs) shape family interactions (process) and the resulting functions (outputs): "The system as a whole (input, process, and output) is in a continual state of change as the family moves through the life cycle" (Turnbull et al., 1986, p. 46). Within the family systems model, the membership of the family (e.g., single parent, child with a disability), cultural (e.g., race) and ideological style (e.g., beliefs, values, coping style) of the family, are all dimensions of family structure. Additional concepts of structure in the family systems model include hierarchy and boundaries. *Hierarchy* refers to the clear rules about who possesses the authority and decision-making power in the family. *Boundaries* refer to the rules that define the ways in which members can interact within and across particular family subsystems (e.g., parental, spousal, sibling, and individual subsystems). In 1997, Turnbull and Turnbull added empowerment through collaboration as a new concept to their family systems perspective (Turnbull & Turnbull, 1997).

For a family system to operate effectively, subsystem boundaries need to be sufficiently clear to allow problem solving to occur without other members interfering, but boundaries must also be open enough to encourage communication between the different subsystems of the family (Cobb & Gunn, 1994). *Enmeshment* occurs in a family when there are unclear boundaries between subsystems. Overinvolvement of other subsystems may produce difficulties with independent development or problem solving for individual members. In *disengagement*, subsystem boundaries are too rigid, preventing closeness between family members and impairing communication and cooperation in problem solving (Cobb & Gunn, 1994).

FAMILY LIFE CYCLE
Chapter 3 dealt briefly with life cycle and developmental issues that can affect a person with a developmental disability. As discussed earlier in this book, considering the impact of a person's systems (e.g., those involved in caregiving, educational, and social functions) and the culture in which they are embedded is critical for the therapist to understand the person's experience, context, resources and strengths, and the influence of these on treatment issues and treatment. Understanding the family life cycle provides a context for viewing family processes, dynamics, needs, and stresses that can be more comprehensive and therapeutically informative than examining individual family members' developmental milestones in isolation. Understanding this context is critical to understanding the person and the influence of their various systems.

Over time a family will experience both typical and atypical changes that alter its structure and/or its functional priorities and these also effect family interactions (Turnbull et al., 1986). There are four components that impact on the family life cycle: developmental stages, transitions, structural and functional changes, and sociohistorical changes. Changes in the family life cycle create stresses. When a member has a developmental disability, the family is in the paradoxical position of having to cope with change and cope with the chronic demands made on the family by a member with a disability: The fundamental family life cycle issue for families is learning to adjust constructively to both normative and nonnormative change, and to the chronic nature of the child's conditions (Turnbull et al., 1986). Children with disabilities and their families make indelible, lasting impressions on one another (Alper, Schloss, & Schloss, 1994).

During a family's life cycle, many stages are likely to have great significance for a family with a member who has a disability. In addition, the transitions between stages can create stress and dysfunction. For families who have a child with a developmental disability, the chronicity of the young person's dependence on the parents creates additional stresses on parents and siblings. Also, parents of older children with developmental disabilities may feel more isolated and in need of more services and supports than families with younger children. Turnbull et al. (1986) emphasized that there is little information on the impact of stage transitions on family functions when a member has a developmental disability, and they called for more research on what interventions are most supportive and effective for alleviating stress for these families.

The birth or identification of a child with developmental disabilities represents a structural change that is non-normative and creates stress and shifts in the family's interactions. A sudden change, such as sexual abuse of a child with developmental disabilities, would be a functional change in the family life cycle, creating different needs for family members and, therefore, changes in family interaction. As Turnbull et al. (1986) indicated, research is needed to examine the effective use of support systems to deal with such functional stressors, particularly because of the relative isolation in which many of these families exist. Similar concerns arise when dealing with sociohistorical changes that create stress, such as changing service delivery models and philosophies. Also, issues for both parents and siblings influence the family system and vary across the course of the family's life cycle. Therapists need to recognize that there is great diversity in how families adapt to raising a child with a disability, and this is not necessarily related to the nature or severity of the child's disability. Thus, there is no simple strategy for developing family based interventions to cope with stressors, which partly depend upon the nature of the stressor, the resources of the family, and how the family defines or interprets the stressor (e.g., McDonald et al., 1999).

PARENT AND SIBLING ISSUES ASSOCIATED WITH DISABILITY
PARENTAL ISSUES

During a family's life cycle, many stages are likely to have great significance for a family with a member who has a developmental disability. At all stages (e.g., childbearing, school age, adolescence, and young adulthood), the presence of a child with a developmental disability forces the family to modify the expectations usually held by the average family. Awareness of the developmental stages provides a basis for understanding family functioning and can serve as a guide for interventions and treatment priorities (Cobb & Gunn, 1994).

Childbearing

Childbearing is the time when the parents may learn that the child has a developmental disability. Early identification of developmental disability tends to be more common when children have more severe, multiple, or otherwise identifiable syndromes. Milder developmental disabilities in the absence of additional disabilities or a specific syndrome, are likely to be recognized in either early childhood or once entering school. Once the developmental disability is identified, however, differing issues that change over time will face families.

Powers (1993) noted that the birth or identification of a child with disabilities may cause disappointment or grief at the loss of the child that was anticipated; however, there may be relief when a disability is finally identified. Other common feelings include: shock, disorientation, and distress, which may be recurrent, greater for younger families, and dependent on the nature of the child's disability. However, families react and adapt in different ways, not predictably with grief, but typically with some amount of stress due to disability related demands. Some denial may be experienced with some parents seeking more favorable or palatable explanations of their child's slow progress and behaviors from different professionals. Even so, this stress can offer opportunities for the family to become stronger: "The experience of grief in response to the disability or health problem of a family member is a non-normative, highly individualized experience....The processing of grief has the potential to create opportunities for self-reflection and the development of strengths....Such opportunities can be highlighted and facilitated by caring friends, family members, and professionals who honor the capabilities and challenges of families and offer assistance in a manner that reflects their respect" (Powers, 1993, p. 147).

Some professionals have suggested that parents of children with disabilities go through orderly stages from grieving to acceptance. Others (Allen & Affleck, 1984; Blacher, 1984) have questioned whether parents go through these stages at all. Wilgosh (1990a) found that parents seem to go through active adjustment to increasing life demands rather than going through stages that progress from grief to final acceptance. The idea of "acceptance" appears to be too simple to explain the heterogeneity of parental adjustment; parents will have many feelings, affection as well as regret, making realistic plans once they are certain about the disability while fantasizing about other possibilities (Glendinning, 1983). There is great variability in how well parents adjust. Many previous assumptions that suggested the presence of a member with a disability resulted in greater family pathology are being more closely examined now. In many cases, rather than dwelling on how badly they feel, parents tend to make an active decision to get on with their lives (Wilgosh, 1990a). Emphasizing that all parents need some support after the birth of their child, which involves some degree of stress, Lian and Aloia (1994) noted that, when a child has a disability, the purpose of identifying parent feelings and reactions is to provide appropriate assistance.

The degree to which parents' reactions are positive or negative may be influenced by the type and severity of disability, professional comments and prognosis, as well as ethnic and cultural background. Physicians, the first contact for many of these parents, may need to refer parents to support and information services. However, research suggests that some physicians are uninformed about available resources and the outcomes of early intervention programs, and some physicians may hold negative attitudes or make inaccurate prognostic statements about children with disabilities (Lian & Aloia, 1994).

School Age
Many parents believe that their child's opportunities in life (e.g., educational and job opportunities) will be determined by the parents' initiative; consequently, their efforts to raise their child results in a sense of mission, direction, or purpose (Wilgosh, 1990a). The issues of best school programs and practices are urgent concerns for the family during this stage. This may take its toll on the family by consuming a large amount of the parents' time and energy.

Parents appreciate honest and open feedback from teachers about the education of their child with a disability, and they want to be actively involved with the school (Wilgosh, 1990a). Parents of children with disabilities realize that their children have special needs that must be considered by the schools. Foremost, these parents seek programs that include: sensitive and competent teachers who will respond to their child's needs, who will not reject the child because of the disability, and who will work in cooperation with the parents. Often, parents feel angry and frustrated because of the difficulty they experience finding good programs. Lian and Aloia (1994) noted that, as more children with disabilities are in inclusive classrooms in neighborhood schools, parents are very concerned about the acceptance of their child by teachers and non-disabled peers. During the diagnostic process parents can have significant concerns about their child being labeled by professionals and may fear that school professionals (e.g., teachers and teacher aides) will learn of their child's diagnosis and place limits on and expect less of their child. Many parents fear that school professionals will may make their child's development a lower priority and be less inclined to dedicate the necessary time, resources, and energy to helping their child develop once they know the child has a developmental disability.

Children with developmental disabilities frequently have deficits in social skills and may have great difficulty transferring or generalizing social skills to different settings or situations and initiating social contacts to make friends. Loneliness, isolation, limited social relationship experience, and poor social discrimination skills constitute significant psychological difficulties that can contribute to heightened vulnerability to abuse.

Adolescence
Families with children who have developmental disabilities tend to be more isolated from their neighbors, relatives, and friends than ordinary families. As a result, the child with a developmental disability has little opportunity to develop important social skills and friendships. Social isolation increases during adolescence (Yura, 1987). Adolescence is a developmental stage in which children with developmental disabilities and their families often need assistance. Teachers and other professionals must educate children without disabilities alongside children who have developmental disabilities so that acceptance of and friendships with children who have special needs will develop naturally. Support groups and families must assist these young people to develop hobbies and recreational interests so that they do not spend long, lonely hours watching television and in other solitary activities. Increasing social interactions provides learning and practice opportunities for children and adolescents to develop their social interaction skills and can help expand understanding of normative social relationships. Providing access to these opportunities can be important to help people develop important support networks and can serve proactive, protective functions that can reduce the risk for abuse.

Although sexuality is often a significant issue for both the adolescent and his or her parents, there can be considerable variability in responding to this issue or at least in the willingness to discuss the issue (Melberg Schwier & Hingsburger, 2000). For example, Wilgosh (1990a) reports that sexuality education and/or the topic of physical and sexual abuse rarely came up in parent interviews she conducted for her study of parents of children with disabilities. Given their other major concerns, sexuality education was probably of lesser importance to these families at this point in time. Regarding physical and sexual abuse, and perhaps sexuality as well, the parents might not have been able to discuss the issues, or the issues might not yet have touched this particular sample of parents.

Young Adulthood

For all children, the ideal future is a successful, independent life; however, for children with a developmental disability, the parents' dreams about the future may be quite different from this ideal (Wilgosh, 1990a). Parents may feel optimistic about adult independence for children with mild disabilities; but on the other hand, parents worry about the work training, community employment, and independent living opportunities for children who have moderate to severe disabilities, particularly when the parents are too old to be the primary guardians of their children. Launching in young adulthood is a time when the child with a developmental disability may be far from independent, and parents must make decisions that are different from those made for the average young person. For many parents there can be notable fears about exposing their adult children to risks and responsibilities and potential experiences of failure.

Special Concerns for Parents
Heightened awareness of vulnerability to abuse

Parents' awareness of their child's increased vulnerability to physical and sexual abuse and the fact that many incidents of abuse occur at the hands of caregivers present other special concerns for parents. Given the heightened risk for extrafamilial sexual abuse and the primary responsibility of the family for raising a child with a developmental disability, several aspects that directly impact on the vulnerability of the young person to sexual abuse must be considered. Parents have a major responsibility to screen and select educational and other caregiving services for their children. These services include provision of transportation necessary to access other services. The more dependent the child with a disability, the more vulnerable the child may be to abuse. Also, the child is less able to indicate or communicate that abuse has occurred, increasing the need for parental vigilance. Not only must parents be vigilant in screening caregivers to avoid potential offenders, they must also be aware of the signs of physical and sexual abuse in order to prevent the continuation of any such abuse and provide the necessary support to deal with the outcomes of abuse. Sullivan and Cork (1998) had explored strategies for raising awareness of professionals to issues in prevention of maltreatment for children with disabilities, with the purpose of developing programs for informing professionals. Their workshop materials have been found useful by professionals in working with families on maltreatment issues, and in investigation of maltreatment.

Sexuality education
Sexuality education is a primary responsibility of parents, yet parents may feel unprepared and uncomfortable dealing with sexuality issues (Wilgosh, 1990b). Part of their fear might stem from their belief that increased awareness of sexuality will increase sexual curiosity and interest in their child with a developmental disability, which, in turn, will increase his or her vulnerability to abuse. Therefore, part of the involvement of families in any support and therapeutic process involves dealing with issues related to sexuality and broadening the scope of sexuality education to include abuse prevention or risk reduction strategies. Hingsburger (1993) has documented parents' concerns about sexuality education: how parents and schools can teach each child about privacy and not having unconditional trust in all people; how to teach differentiation between good and bad touch; and how to prepare young people with developmental disabilities for puberty, dating, and making right and safe choices to express sexuality. The James Stanfield Publishing Company and Diverse City Press both publish a range of teaching and training sexuality and social skills related materials. Melberg Schwier and Hingsburger (2000)

recently released a book for parents that covers teaching a range of vital protective skills that include: privacy, modesty, boundaries, self-love and self-acceptance, self-esteem, values, risk reduction and assertiveness, health, homosexuality, and sexuality. Therapists are encouraged to gain access to a range of materials to determine their potential usefulness and appropriateness for their clients. Rappaport, Burkhardt, and Rotatori (1997) in their curriculum for children with developmental disabilities draw from research about children's social reasoning to teach specific rules about our bodies and include parental teaching components to promote generalizability. Consistent with parental concerns, Cole (1986) observed that "an obvious prevention measure is to encourage and assist parents and families in being comfortable with discussing sexuality and in having the skills and information necessary to provide sex education and prevention techniques" (p. 82).

The importance of social supports

Families with children who have developmental disabilities may need direct support and assistance with caregiving. They also may need emotional support from professionals and parent support groups to help them deal with personal and family stresses. Most parents with children who have disabilities want to have a parent-professional partnership that includes open discussion with knowledgeable and caring professionals who will take the time to listen to them. Parent support groups, respite care, training in coping skills, and other external supports can help parents reduce stress and increase family well-being.

Parents report that having a child with special needs has negative effects on family life because there is more stress on the family (Wilgosh, 1990a). Care demands for children with developmental disabilities differ for different disabilities, and this requires that individual support service plans must be tailored to the family's strengths and needs (e.g., McDonald et al., 1999). Mothers who have children with disabilities bear the greatest responsibility in the family for caregiving and are under greater stress than mothers with children without disabilities, but they can cope as well as other mothers when they have good support systems (e.g., Scorgie, Wilgosh, & McDonald, 1998). Because the mother is typically the primary caregiver, the father often takes a secondary role as caregiver to the child with a developmental disability; nevertheless, the family systems approach involves the participation of all family members in order to obtain an effective level of family coping. When possible, within the constraints of employment and other responsibilities, both parents should be encouraged to participate and share in caregiving and decision making with regard to the child with a disability (Murray & McDonald, 1996).

Fathers have been cast in a peripheral role, and it is only in more recent years that the father's role has been addressed in research. Lillie (1993) suggests that fathers apparently want more involvement in the family but are constrained by the "gatekeeper" roles of mothers and the structure of their children's programs. Lillie (1993) suggests that the lack of routines to foster father involvement in the lives of their children with disabilities may be a contributing factor. Murray and McDonald (1996) confirmed the absence of research on fathers' needs and ways to involve them that best meet their needs.

In addition, siblings in the family system are affected by the presence of a family member who has a disability and may require support in their roles. Parents often express regret about the effects of having a child in the family who has a disability on their other children. Even so, it seems that most families function adequately; however, there is considerable variability in the outcomes for siblings of children with disabilities, which can range from minimal effects to very involved positive or negative effects (Yura, 1987).

SIBLINGS
Powell and Ogle (1985) suggested a continuum of positive and negative outcomes for children who have a sibling with disabilities. Factors that contribute to the positive or negative outcomes for children who have a sibling with disabilities include: temperament of both siblings, parental attitudes and expectations, family size and resources, severity of the disability, and pattern of sibling interactions. While recognizing that it is not possible to generate a set of concerns for all

siblings, siblings without disabilities need respect, understanding, information, and support because the range of feelings they can experience includes: anger and joy, sadness and frustration, and jealousy and fear. The effect of a child with disabilities on his or her siblings is primarily related to the parental responses to the child.

Simeonsson and Bailey (1986) drew a number of tentative conclusions about siblings of children with disabilities. Closeness in age may lead to poorer adjustment, particularly for younger, male siblings. Younger siblings' reactions might be related to the difficulties they may have adjusting to less mature and less competent older siblings. Reactions of siblings are not always negative, but may be positive and constructive, particularly when the sibling is involved in caregiving and teaching the child with the disability. Temperament of the child with a disability and the siblings mediates the reaction of siblings, which is not necessarily related to the type or severity of disability.

Boyce and Barnett (1993), based on a review of the research on siblings of individuals with developmental disabilities, conclude that the relationships of siblings when one has a disability are very similar to the relationships that exist among siblings without disabilities. There is some limited evidence that siblings without disabilities experience mild levels of disturbance, including anxiety and depression. More research is required on gender, birth order, and spacing between siblings as well as on levels of disturbance for siblings without disabilities and siblings' impact on the child with a disability. A range of emotional issues can be present for siblings that can include: emotional neglect, resentment about competing for parental attention, jealousy, and sometimes rejection and embarrassment of the sibling with a developmental disability. Crnic and Lyons (1993) endorse the need to examine bi-directional sibling influences and to recognize that the range of effects on siblings is broad and "may only contribute to psychopathology under rather specific circumstances" (p. 268).

Gibbs (1993) recommends providing support to siblings by using a developmental perspective that incorporates the siblings' issues associated with developmental periods, the age of the sibling with a disability, and the family reaction. She reviewed the issues associated with these developmental periods and notes that certain issues take on greater importance at different points for differing time periods and that siblings' feelings will fluctuate depending on a number of factors. Wilkins (1992) presents a review of individual, family, and group therapy possibilities that might help siblings address their concerns.

Single-Parent Families
In a report on cooperative problem solving for single-parent families, Shank and Turnbull (1993) estimate that about 25% of single-parent families have a child with a disability. In this report, they identify a lack of intervention programs designed to help single parents and their children learn to work together at family problem solving. They suggest that single-parent families can be taught coping skills and family problem solving by role playing family scenarios and practicing skills as a family unit. Successful outcomes involve recognizing the roles of all family members, including the member with a disability. Shank and Turnbull (1993) emphasize that these families are not dysfunctional; rather, they have unique stresses requiring effective prevention and intervention strategies. Alper and Retish (1994) indicate that many questions remain to be answered for these families, including the role and needs of the single father, services needed by the parent and child, and existence of any significant differences in needs between such dual and single parent families.

FAMILY ISSUES
As with any family, there can be a wide variety of family dynamics and issues. For families with a child who has a disability, there may be some issues that are fairly particular: For example, the child may, depending on level of disability, require considerable care and support from family members, and there may be wide variability in the child's and parents' acceptance of the developmental disability and the various roles they have been assigned. The dysfunctional family

differs from the functional family in their ability to adapt to and cope with stress created by having a person with a disability in the family (Cobb & Gunn, 1994). In some dysfunctional circumstances, however, the child might be scapegoated, blamed, and rejected by the family members who are emotionally disengaged from the child. This disengagement may be more likely when family members are engaged in quasi-professional roles with the child (e.g., the parent who implements the physiotherapy or behavioral program at home or the sibling who is given responsibility to teach the child with a developmental disability). In other dysfunctional circumstances, the child's needs may be a significant focus of attention and energy in the family that can be used to prevent family members from confronting their own problems. Alternately, the family may deny the child's disability and fail to provide appropriate health and education services. This situation might reflect the use of denial as a coping mechanism that allows the family to maintain equilibrium. Seriously dysfunctional families may be troubled by guilt, hostility, and feelings of inadequacy and may lack both the emotional and cognitive resources to deal with the person with a disability (Cobb & Gunn, 1994). Sometimes in response to family tension and problems the person with a disability may develop behavioral symptoms that communicate their internal, emotional distress. Family homeostasis can maintain the problematic behavior and families may resist change as it may threaten their equilibrium. In such these circumstances family members may engage in a range of behaviors that interfere with treatment. Behaviors may include those that sabotage treatment (e.g., refusing to follow through on agreed upon interventions, discrediting the therapy provider, or reinforcing dependency in the person with a disability) (Cobb & Gunn, 1994). Often, children with developmental disabilities will react to their disability in the same way as do other family members. The family's reactions can have an enormous impact on the psychological well-being of the child with a developmental disability.

FAMILY COPING, ADAPTATION, AND RESILIENCY

The variability of responses in families with a member with a disability inevitably raises the question "Why do some families adjust to the stress much better than others?" (Wikler, 1986, p. 191). Part of the problem in understanding family stress and adjustment is that there is no clear notion of what constitutes successful or acceptable family functioning when coping with a family crisis and stress, and there is no clear idea about the effects over time of accommodating the needs and demands of a child with a developmental disability (Wikler, 1986). As Turnbull and Turnbull (1993) emphasized, however, "Focusing on what could help families be successful seemed to be a far more productive type of inquiry than the pathogenic emphasis that we had found in the literature" (p. 4).

Coping Strategies

The coping strategies of a family determine how the family functions (Turnbull & Turnbull, 1993). Coping strategies have been classified as internal (passive appraisal or avoidance response to problems or reframing [i.e., problem solving and identifying alterable circumstances]) or external (based on social/family supports, spiritual support, and formal community supports). Different coping strategies may apply at different points in the family life cycle. Within a family systems framework, "in the process of interaction, each member is affected and influenced by every other member and by the system as a whole" (Turnbull et al., 1986, p. 49). Key elements of family interactions include: the level of cohesion, adaptability, and the communication style of the family. Both family and individual needs must be considered and the systemic impact of any intervention on the whole family and its implications must be examined when conducting therapy with people who have a developmental disability. In addition, it is critical to for the therapist to assess the interactions among the members.

Singer, Irvin, Irvine, Hawkins, Hegreness, and Jackson (1993) have drawn three important conclusions about families with children who have disabilities: Caring for such a family member involves increased daily stress; many stresses are generated by external conditions, for example, limited school and community resources, increased financial burdens, and a sense of isolation; and most families adapt successfully to these additional life stresses. Patterson's Family Adjustment and Adaptation Response Model (FAAR; 1993) emphasizes

adaptation as the central construct rather than stress. A recent literature review by Scorgie et al. (1998) is useful in outlining the family,
parent, and child variables that influence a family's ability to cope
successfully when a child has a disability.

Effective Coping and Resiliency

A number of variables have been delineated as influencing a family's
ability to cope successfully in raising a child with a developmental
disability. A literature review by Scorgie et al. (1998) noted family
variables such as socioeconomic status, cohesion, and hardiness;
parent variables, including quality of the marital relationship and
maternal locus of control; child variables such as severity of the disability and age of the child; and external variables such as social
network support. Scorgie et al. (1996), based on a qualitative study
involving parents of children with a range of disabling conditions,
articulated the following characteristics related to stress and effective life management: being able to reframe negative thoughts and
attitudes about one's circumstances; determination to be successful;
self-confidence, self-esteem and competence; maintaining personal
control; resilience, hope and effective life management; and, sometimes, permanent transformational outcomes in self-perception, behavior, or outlook. The component of empowerment through collaboration has been added to the family systems perspective by
Turnbull and Turnbull (1997), and Dempsey (1996) has also identified family empowerment as a desirable outcome of service to such
families. Patterson (1993) called for studies of daily family process
to determine how some families are able to develop positive, adaptive meanings and beliefs, identifying the importance of the social
context to meaning making (see also Scorgie et al., [1996]). Finally,
Olsen (1999) has advocated nursing care within the context of the
whole family, to promote family hardiness, i.e., inner strengths and
durability.

Promoting family resiliency

Family resiliency is promoted by: the open expression of feelings;
family flexibility and cohesiveness in problem-solving and coping
skills; finding positive meanings in challenges; social connectedness,

particularly with other families coping with similar circumstances; and collaborative relationships with helping professionals. In order to promote resiliency, families and professionals must recognize that stress and adaptation to stress are a normal part of life. But even though stress is a normal part of life, because they bear the primary responsibility of caring for individuals with disabilities, families must be supported in their caregiving roles. Even so, Singer and Powers (1993) emphasize the need to promote family well-being and enhance the quality of life and not to focus merely on prevention and treatment. They point out that, contrary to the traditional view, most families feel that the child with a disability contributes positively to the family (Singer & Powers, 1993). Singer and Powers also feel that families make an immense impact on the well-being of a family member with a disability. The fact that the family unit affects the well-being of its members reinforces the important role of families and family therapy when a family member with or without a disability has been sexually abused.

Extrafamilial Child Sexual Abuse

The issues facing families when there has been extrafamilial sexual abuse can differ somewhat from issues associated with incest, but some similar family variables may be operating. At this time, it is unclear what preabuse family functioning is like in families who have children either with or without disabilities who experience extrafamilial sexual abuse. As indicated in Chapter 3, there may be several reasons for heightened risk for extrafamilial sexual abuse experienced by people with developmental disabilities: For example, the heightened risk may be more a product of the special service needs required by people with developmental disabilities (i.e., contact with several different service providers who may or may not be screened to ensure their safety, family and individual isolation, poor communication skills, lack of assertiveness, and devalued status). Nevertheless, studying family variables and responses to extrafamilial sexual abuse in this group constitutes an important area for future research.

In addition to the numerous parental responsibilities that require vigilance and sensitivity to reduce the child's risk of sexual abuse, sometimes the best efforts at reducing risk for abuse do not provide absolute protection. Such situations can make parents feel inadequate and powerless. Following an incident of extrafamilial sexual abuse, parents may require additional help. After sexual abuse has occurred, the need to support parents becomes critical: That is, it is necessary to assist parents to deal with their personal needs and feelings as an outcome of the abuse (e.g., fear of further abuse or guilt that they were unable to prevent the abuse). They also need intervention in order to provide support for the young person who has been abused.

In cases of extrafamilial abuse, parents may become worried and anxious about their child's vulnerability (Wilgosh, 1993). Sexual abuse may reawaken concerns parents have about their child's sexuality (Hingsburger, 1993). They may have a strong sense of powerlessness about their ability to protect their child from the abuse. Parents may experience a heightened distrust of professionals and other caregivers. Distrust may evolve into greater family involvement in caring for the person but less comfort in using disability related services and respite care, which can increase the likelihood of caregiver burnout, social isolation, and ineffective coping. This situation exemplifies the necessity for the family to be involved in any therapeutic process. Aspects of the parents' role as caregivers raise important intervention issues. A primary strategy for intervention involves providing parental support long before the occurrence of any incident of abuse.

Following incidents of extrafamilial abuse, however, a number of considerations must be made in the development of intervention plans. A primary concern lies in determining if the person was abused by a person providing care and if he or she is currently at risk. It is critical that the person is safe and not currently being abused during the treatment. Many of the issues discussed in Chapter 3 that outline crucial information about the abuse and the responses of those close the person who has been sexually abused are relevant. For example, it is critical to determine how parents, other family members, and closely

involved staff members are constructing the experience and responding to the disclosure in order to tailor interventions that build on existing sources of strength and resiliency and coping abilities. For example, in cases where a family may be coping with a person's developmental disability by using denial it can also be relevant to determine whether or not they appreciate how or why their family member was vulnerable to abuse in the first place. In cases of significant
denial, family members may be unable to understand the influence
of the person's cognitive and social delays in their vulnerability and
may provide blaming or unsupportive responses. Education can be a
critical part of the interventions that are used to help families understand their son's or daughter's experiences and to divert potentially
blaming or unsupportive responses.

In addition, where a person is unable to verbally communicate about
their sexual abuse it is important for the therapist to assess how the
family members and closely involved staff members may be interpreting and responding to the person's behavior. It is also important
to meet with the family alone and take opportunities to examine their
willingness and resistance to participate in family based therapy.

Teaching family members and involved staff about the potential effects of abuse and how these may manifest as mental health concerns
can be important to help demystify and take the power out of unusual
or disturbing behaviors. This can be especially important should a
person who has been sexually abused be demonstrating sexually inappropriate, self-injurious, aggressive, or regressive behaviors. In
order to identify specific behavioral concerns it is important that there
be assessment, diagnosis, interviews, and observation (as described
in Chapter 3) pertaining to the person's behavior and functioning.
Education and consultation with the person's system will be critical
to examine and explore interventions that may get the person's behavior difficulties under control so that he or she may actually participate in and benefit from therapy. Treatment will involve the
person's system as all will be effected by the sexual assault but interventions may involve different parts of the system interacting with
each other at different times.

Characteristics of Incestuous Families

In addition to possible disability related issues associated with families, in cases of intrafamilial abuse, it is important to consider the characteristics and dynamics of incestuous families. Alexander (1985) outlines the features of sexually abusive families that clearly have an enormous impact on the victim: poor communication; poor conflict resolution skills, which result in accumulated resentments and heightened parental isolation; parents' unresolved losses, which might include a history of abuse and family disorganization that may dominate and organize daily functioning; isolation of both individual members from each other and the family as a whole from the larger community; individual differentiation from family may be compromised, which may result in later failure to develop a mature personal identity; and there may be enmeshment among members that involves the blurring of individual boundaries and dissolution of generational boundaries.

In cases of intrafamilial abuse, often, the family will already be profoundly disrupted. Abusive families often operate at a high level of dysfunction (Friedrich, 1990) and may exhibit problems such as chaos and disruption, alcohol or substance abuse, inadequate boundaries between members, and role reversal. For intrafamilial abuse in particular, therapy primarily aims at strengthening the boundaries between the subsystems, providing more power to the parental subsystem, and addressing other family problems.

FAMILY APPROACHES TO SEXUAL ABUSE TREATMENT

Friedrich (1990) suggests that whether abuse is intrafamilial or extrafamilial family therapy may be indicated. The therapist usually begins the therapeutic process by assessing the treatment needs of an individual client, but he or she will also need to decide whether therapy should include others, such as the parent-client dyad or the entire family. Regardless of whether the abuse was perpetrated by a family member or not, in all likelihood, the family will experience considerable disruption. Since the emotional climate of the family prior to the abuse and following disclosure has a significant influence on the impact of the abuse (Ammerman & Baladerian, 1993), it is necessary for the therapist to evaluate the need for family therapy.

Kendall-Tackett, Meyers-Williams, and Finkelhor's (1993) review of studies on the symptomatology of abused children without disabilities found that the lack of maternal support at disclosure increased symptomatology. They feel that the key variable for recovery is family support, particularly maternal support.

Kitchur and Bell's (1989) literature review on group therapy for preadolescents without disabilities who had been sexually abused found that parental resistance to the group process was a major problem. In order to overcome this resistance, it was necessary to establish regular communication with the parents or parallel parent-child groups, which supports the importance of maternal/parental support for group therapy to be effective.

Berliner and Wheeler (1987) suggested a multifaceted approach to child sexual abuse therapy that includes: directive individual or group therapy; play therapy for very young children; and interventions that help educate parents about abuse effects, that help them provide support for their child, and that help them deal with their own reactions to abuse. Kolko (1987) also emphasized the need to treat both child and family and noted the emphasis of many programs on multiple therapeutic modalities: for example, individual counseling for the child, mother, and father; mother-daughter and father-daughter counseling; and marital, family, and group therapy. Kolko (1987) pointed out that "more optimistic outcomes have usually been reported by multidisciplinary programs that include family involvement" (p. 314).

Lipovsky (1991) emphasized the dilemmas faced by families, particularly mothers, when a child identifies the father as a sexual abuser. When the father denies the abuse, the mother is forced to choose between believing the father or child, and her support or rejection of the child can be significant in determining the effectiveness of treatment. Lipovsky (1991) made a strong case for involving the mother in therapy when possible in order to help her deal with her own feelings and to facilitate the mother's support and protection of the child. Mother-daughter therapy as well as individual sessions for both may be necessary, and a focus on restructuring the family is imperative. Due to the evidence that suggests a greater incidence of depression in children who have been sexually abused when there is little or no support from their mothers, Wozencraft, Wagner, and Pellegrin (1991) also supported parental involvement in the therapeutic process.

Family based dyadic therapy has been advocated by Timmons-Mitchell and Gardner (1991) for girls who have been sexually abused and their mothers, many of whom have been victims of childhood abuse. The rationale for this approach is the low self-esteem and difficulty with trust in interpersonal relationships for both mother and daughter subsequent to abuse. The loss of trust is reported in both incestuous families and extrafamilial sexual abuse. The re-establishment of trust between a mother and daughter has been identified as a primary treatment goal because the re-establishment of trust reaffirms the mother's protective parental role as advocate for the abused child.

Everson, Hunter, Runyon, Edelsohn, and Coulter (1989) stated that sexually abused children without disabilities are at risk for short- and long-term mental health problems, particularly when there has been within-family abuse because "issues of betrayal and concern about family well-being compound the trauma of sexual victimization" (p. 197). These researchers' (Everson et al., 1989) study of intrafamilial sexual abuse suggested that a mother's support tended to vary with the mother's relationship to the offender. Women were more supportive if the offender confirmed the abuse. Children who were not supported or were inconsistently supported by their mothers showed significantly higher levels of psychopathology. More attention should be paid to the importance of the mother in the child's recovery than to blaming the mother for the occurrence of abuse: "Immediate intervention aimed at supporting mothers and helping them to believe, empathize with, and offer consistent emotional support and protection to their children may be the most effective way of reducing the child's emotional stress and disruption following disclosure of incest" (Everson et al., 1989, p. 206). Family therapy should always be considered as a possible avenue for exploring issues related to disability, parenting concerns, and the impact of sexual abuse on the family.

THERAPY WITH FAMILIES WHO HAVE A MEMBER WITH A DEVELOPMENTAL DISABILITY

Although there is relatively little research on providing family therapy when a member has a developmental disability, the research that has been conducted points out that many of the central concepts and practices used in family therapy for members of the general population are applicable and relevant.

In their work providing therapy to families with adults who have developmental disabilities, Gapen and Knoll (1992) indicate that the family systems approach can be very effective with families who have had long duration, high intensity symptoms that include violence and incest. They note that these families often have their collective issues overlooked as the dually diagnosed member has most often been the focus of treatment. Also, families may have considerable experiences with treatment failure and may be sensitive about and resistant to treatment. Consideration of these treatment experiences may require more involved approaches on the part of the therapist in order to establish a therapeutic alliance. Gapen and Knoll (1992) suggest using carefully paced, respectful, nonjudgmental, nonconfrontational strategies that work with the family's defenses in order to provide support and empathy to the family. This approach is used to empower and support family members in their decision making. Gapen and Knoll also recommend that therapists attempt to make themselves more available and flexible when working with these families. They recommend working irregular hours and using outreach to engage the treatment-resistant family as a means to establish a strong therapeutic alliance. A treatment alliance that promotes the development of congruent treatment goals for therapist and family is crucial to the work of therapy. Working to engage the family, however, is balanced with the need for the therapist to maintain control by providing structure and limits in therapy (Gapen & Knoll, 1992).

Teodoru (1992) recommends the primary use of a strategic systems approach to family therapy within a broader eclectic orientation. He argues that the client's family experiences are central to the work of therapy and that it is crucial to devise therapy approaches that build upon existing cognitive behavioral approaches and place greater emphasis on emotional, affiliative, and socialization needs. Teodoru also integrates disability related issues and suggests that it is important for the therapist not to generalize his or her expectations about normal family functioning, drawn from families without a member with a disability, to the family with a member who has a disability. Instead, he recommends framing the family's situation in terms of the special challenges they do face, considering the varying issues that occur throughout the family life cycle and the various sources of natural social supports that may be available to the family (see also McDonald et al., 1999).

Anger and Hawkins (1999) describe the importance of using a brief therapy approach with families who have a member who is dually diagnosed. For brief therapy to be effective it is important for the therapist to determine exactly who in the system is invested in making a change. In many cases it is not the person who is deemed to have "the problem" who is making the referral to treatment. The problems must be defined early in the process with emphasis placed on clarifying the problem in concrete, behavioral terms and to examine the previous strategies that have been employed to address the problem. A key premise is that the strategies that clients have been using to address the problem have been maintaining it. It is also critical to have the clients prioritize their goals and help them focus on solutions that run counter to those they have already attempted (Anger & Hawkins, 1999).

Hollins, Sinason, and Thompson (1994) note the importance of assessing family functioning, strengths, patterns, and problems and engaging both the family and key professionals. The assessment of the role(s) various family members play, amount of flexibility there is for changing roles, life cycle stages, possible losses, and available coping resources are central processes in family therapy. Additional emphasis is placed on the assessment of the family's verbal and non-verbal communication, alliances, subsystems, and the therapist's own experience of being with the family (Hollins et al., 1994).

Hollins (1995) recommends the use of a family centered approach to therapy that empowers families to decide what their wishes and problems are and helps them regain some control. Issues associated with coping may concern gaining access to additional sources of care for their family member who is disabled. This decision is often a loaded issue that can evoke emotions in family members, ranging from feelings of inadequacy and discomfort to guilt and betrayal. Hollins notes that many issues for the family in relation to the family member who has a developmental disability will need to be worked through in therapy. Additional issues to those that have already been discussed in Chapters 3 and 4 may include: acceptance of difference, developing a sense of realism about dependency needs, sexuality, mortality, enhancing coping skills, improving family communication, and continuing family development (Hollins, 1995).

Many of the key considerations in providing therapy examined in chapters 3, 4, and 5 are applicable to systems oriented treatment and need to be considered within the family systems context. For example, the therapist will need to actively consider and directly involve the client's family and involved caregivers and work collaboratively with them to help them understand the client's experience, behavior, and vulnerability. In addition, it is important for the therapist to determine the person's developmental level, communication and comprehension abilities, level of behavioral and psychological functioning, and the combined influences of sexual abuse and developmental disability.

Client evaluation or assessment is a critical, ongoing process in therapy that helps guide the therapist's decision making with determining therapy interventions, accommodations, goals, and progress and requires input and support and involvement from the system. The therapist also needs to help them process their own feelings and develop their own coping strategies and ways of responding constructively to the person's behaviors, vulnerability, and emotional distress. In addition, the therapist will need to use specific therapy components that take into account the importance of implementing risk reduction or abuse prevention strategies.

Particular attention should be paid to observing how the person communicates in the familial context as there may be a number of unspoken rules about communication in the family, and it is necessary to be sensitive to subtleties in both verbal and nonverbal communication. In family therapy, when a member is described as nonverbal, the therapist will need to be flexible and resourceful in order to develop the appropriate means to have the person heard in the family (Hollins, 1995). Ensuring that the person with a developmental disability has a voice that is heard in the family can be a model for empowering the family. Therapists need to be aware of the fact that family members may be accustomed to completing sentences for the person with a developmental disability or talking for the person. Therapists should also be cognizant of how the person is perceived and responded to in the family. It will be crucial to encourage open communication between members and to promote a safe, respectful environment where everyone can have a voice.

CONCLUSION
This chapter integrated select discussions from the family systems and sexual abuse literatures. Discussion was devoted to the considerations and issues facing the family, other caregivers, and the person with a developmental disability who has been sexually abused. As part of therapy, it will be important to involve the family and other caregivers in treatment in order to address issues and explore other sources of personal support that may be available to them. Many of the previously discussed communication and comprehension considerations (noted in Chapters 4, 5, and 6) are relevant and need to be integrated with systemic treatment. It may be necessary to draw on these considerations in addition to those noted for systems based treatment so that the person with a developmental disability has a voice and can be heard and helped within the system.

The next two chapters in Part 4 follow this family systems chapter. The next chapter to follow examines the use of play therapy with people who have a   developmental disability who have been sexually abused. Part 4 concludes with closing chapter on assessing inappropriate sexual behavior in people with developmental disabilities.

•• 8

Play Therapy with People who have Developmental Disabilities

Tansel Erdem, Claire Millar, & Sheila Mansell

Thus far, the chapters in this book have covered the use of individual, group, and family therapy approaches for addressing the consequences of child sexual abuse in people with developmental disabilities. In this chapter, the emphasis is on the use of play therapy for children with developmental disabilities who have been sexually abused. A brief history of the development of play therapy and a few approaches are discussed. Although play therapy encompasses a wide variety of activities, a comprehensive review will not be provided here. The interested reader should refer to Jennings (1999), Kaduson, Cangelosi, and Schaefer (1997), Landreth (1991), McMahon (1992), O'Connor and Braverman (1997), and West (1996) for a further discussion of play therapy approaches. Although play therapy has a considerable history, there have been several attitudinal barriers that prevented the widespread use of play therapy with people with developmental disabilities. Some of these issues are covered in Chapter 1, but an important source of resistance to play therapy appears to be the debate among professionals about the cognitive, abstract-symbolic capabilities of people with developmental disabilities and, ultimately, the nature of play in children with developmental disabilities. Recent research on play and coinciding attitudinal changes toward conducting therapy with people with developmental disabilities contributed to an increased openness to the use of play therapy. This chapter includes a discussion of the issues and special considerations associated with the assessment and treatment of children with developmental disabilities who have been sexually abused and case illustrations drawn from Millar's clinical work at the Surrey Place Centre in Toronto.

PLAY

Play is the central activity of childhood. This most natural, spontaneous experience allows children to make sense of the world around them and their place in it. Children play out their cognitive, social, and interpersonal skills, and play helps children build bridges between concrete experience and abstract thought. Play creates a safe medium for children to organize their experiences, practice life tasks, and adapt to their environment (Piaget, 1962). It also provides children with an environment that allows the expression of feelings, exploration of relationships, and discovery of self (Landreth, 1982). For many reasons, it was a natural development that therapeutic modalities for children would use play as a means to understand a child's psychological world.

THE DEVELOPMENT OF PSYCHOANALYTIC PLAY THERAPY

Sigmund Freud published the first case history of psychoanalysis with a five-year-old phobic boy known as Little Hans. Freud examined the observations and conversations recorded by his parents, diagnosed the child's problem, and offered therapeutic advice to his parents (Lebo, 1982). Psychoanalytic therapy with adults relies on the client's reported dreams and transference phenomena as methods to access the unconscious; however, because children, in terms of their development and language, do not organize their experiences in this way. The principles of adult psychoanalysis were not easily applied to children, and soon it was recognized that adult psychoanalytic techniques would need to be altered for children and that the use of play should become an essential part of therapy for children (von Hug-Helmuth, 1921). Anna Freud (1929) and Melanie Klein (1927) are credited as the founders of applying psychoanalytic therapy to children. They considered the use of children's play as a therapeutic technique analogous to the use of dream analysis and free association techniques with adults. Both Freud and Klein proposed that play uncovered a child's unconscious conflicts, and they used the concepts of transference, resistance, and interpretation to help resolve these conflicts.

Psychoanalytic play therapy had a major influence on the development of several subsequent approaches. These approaches are categorized according to the emphasis they place on the therapist's responsibility for the therapeutic process and the activity during therapy. These approaches developed in two directions: directive and nondirective. An extensive review of these approaches is beyond the scope of this chapter, but a brief sampling from a few representative approaches is provided.

DIRECTIVE
Release Therapy
Release therapy or structured play therapy is a goal-oriented form of therapy, and it emerged from a psychoanalytic framework. David Levy (1939) introduced release therapy for children who had experienced a specific, traumatic, stressful situation. The cathartic value of play and the active role of the therapist in determining the direction of therapy are the key concepts of structured play therapy. With the help of selected toys, the therapist recreates a scene, and the traumatic event is played out in an environment where the child is safe and in control. The re-enactment of the traumatic event allows the child to release the pain and tension.

Cognitive-Behavioral Play Therapy
Cognitive-behavioral play therapy is a directive, goal-oriented approach that is based on cognitive/behavioral theories of emotional development and psychopathology. The therapist's role is to discover the factors that reinforce and maintain the child's problematic behaviors. This approach frequently uses self-control strategies to modify behavior and emphasizes internal thought processes and their impact on behavior. Cognitive-behavioral play therapy emphasizes the child's participation in treatment, addresses issues of control and mastery, and promotes the child's personal responsibility for behavior change. The therapist works with both the child and the family to set and achieve therapy goals. The therapist attempts to understand the child's thoughts, feelings, and fantasies to help the child identify maladaptive processes and modify them. The therapist has various intervention strategies at his or her disposal: for example, modeling, role playing, or behavioral contingencies. In addition to establishing

a positive relationship and creating a safe and trusting environment for the child, the therapist also takes on the role of an "educator" who teaches new skills to the child (Knell, 1993).

NONDIRECTIVE
Child-Centered Play Therapy

Nondirective or child-centered play therapy is based on the work of Virginia Axline (1947), and draws heavily on the work of Carl Rogers. Rogers (1961) believes that each individual possesses an innate striving toward self-actualization and growth. This innate tendency ensures that clients possess natural abilities to solve their emotional problems. Child-centered play therapy does not attempt to control or change the child's meanings; instead, it focuses on creating a therapeutic climate that may make change possible. The therapist does not guide or give direction to the child's play; instead, the therapist actively reflects the thoughts and feelings of the child and provides a secure, supportive relationship for the child. Nondirective play therapy leaves the responsibility and direction of the therapy to the child. This therapeutic relationship allows the child the opportunity to exercise free expression and a release of emotions (Moustakas, 1959). It also possesses the power to potentially activate the healing and growth of the child. The therapist genuinely tries to create a warm, empathetic therapeutic environment where the child feels accepted and protected. The child's feelings and attitudes, which can be too threatening for direct expression, may be safely projected through self-chosen toys. The process of play as it occurs in this supportive, therapeutic context is thought to heal the child (Landreth, 1992).

Jungian Play Therapy

Jungian play therapy is another form of nondirective therapy. Jungian theory is based on the concepts of the ego, the conscious mind, personal unconscious, and the collective unconscious, which contains universal archetypes. Jung (1964) believes that human personality is a self-regulating structure that can heal itself and that it communicates through dreams and creative processes such as writing, drawing, painting, and sculpting. Symbolic representation unites the conscious and the unconscious aspects of the psyche, bridges the inner and the outer world of the individual, and helps the development of the total personality. One of the techniques used by Jungian therapists is sandplay, which creates a therapeutic medium that gives the child a "free and protected space" to express inner feelings (Kalff, 1980).

The technique of sandplay originated from the work of Margaret Lowenfeld, a child psychiatrist who collected an extensive number of miniature objects that she used in therapy (Lowenfeld, 1979). Lowenfeld (1979) suggests specific dimensions for the sandtray (75cm x 50cm x 7cm) or (29.5in x 20.5in x 2.8in), a size that permit the client to view the whole tray at a glance. The limited size of the sandtray may make the client feel less overwhelmed, provide a sense of containment and boundaries for emotional issues, and increase the client's sense of safety. The sandtray and the rich collection of miniature objects invites play, imagination, and creativity. It is thought that the creations in the sandtray are a symbolic representation of the client's inner world, thoughts, and feelings (Kalff, 1980).

Clearly, there are many play therapy approaches available to therapists, and although some therapists work exclusively in either directive or nondirective approaches, many working in the area of trauma recognize the importance of using both approaches, depending on the client's needs.

THE DEBATE ABOUT THE NATURE OF PLAY

Although play therapy has a rich history, most of the literature on the use of play therapy for child sexual abuse concerns children without developmental disabilities. The lack of information about play therapy for people with developmental disabilities reflects the inadequate state of therapy services for this population. Several of the reasons for the professional pessimism and resistance toward providing any type therapy to people with developmental disabilities were discussed in Chapter 1, and most of these reasons concern myths and stereotypes about people with developmental disabilities: For example, some professionals believe that people with developmental disabilities do not feel pain or do not possess an inner psychological life.

While the pessimism about this population's ability to benefit from therapy has contributed to the poor state of therapy services, in a similar fashion, there has been professional resistance to the use of play therapy. Some of this resistance may be credited to the previously discussed issues, but some resistance appears to be related to professional debates about the cognitive, abstract-symbolic, and creative capabilities of children with developmental disabilities. Some professionals feel that deficits in abstract-symbolic abilities hinder or limit the development of play and creativity in children with developmental disabilities. Other professionals believe myths that suggest children with developmental disabilities do not play.

Until the late 1960s, it was widely believed that children with developmental disabilities do not play like their peers without developmental disabilities (McConkey, 1985). The spontaneous play behaviors of children with developmental disabilities somehow failed to live up to the expectations of what constitutes normative play. Some professionals interpreted these differences as an absence of the need or desire to play in children with developmental disabilities. Social/environmental circumstances may have contributed to this perception as playfulness was rarely tolerated, promoted, or reinforced in the busy and often unstimulating wards of institutions or during lessons in classrooms. Since many children with developmental disabilities lacked the opportunities to play, this belief turned into a self-fulfilling prophecy (McConkey, 1985). In more recent years, it has been clearly demonstrated that children with developmental disabilities do play, and research has been conducted that examines the nature and level at which these children play: For example, research has found that children with profound mental handicaps, when they are provided with the right environment and special toys, do engage in play (Murphy, Carr, & Callias, 1986).

Research on play interventions with children who have disabilities is scarce, and in many handbooks on the development of mental retardation, there is rarely any mention of play or fantasy (Hellendoorn & Hoekman, 1992). Although some researchers have started to show an interest in the play activities of children with developmental disabilities, at this time, little is known about the nature of play in children with developmental disabilities. This lack of information is due, in part, to the heterogeneity of their specific handicaps and needs (Berkson, 1993) and the difficulty associated with conducting research with this population; also, it is due to the longstanding pessimism about their abstract-symbolic capabilities. This pessimism is fueled by questions about the effect of intellectual deficiencies on the attainment of insight and whether people with mental retardation have the ability to express themselves using symbolic language (Baum, 1994). In spite of this pessimism, the play of children with developmental disabilities has become a subject of discussion and research. Since play is crucial for child development, learning about the play of children with developmental disabilities has important implications for the use and choice of play interventions.

It is known that children with developmental disabilities are unlikely to be able to play on the same symbolic level as their same-aged peers without developmental disabilities, but when developmental level is used as the criterion for comparison, children functioning in the mild to moderate range of disability play in ways that are similar to the play of young children who function at higher levels. The early play development of children with mental retardation follows approximately the same sequence as that of normally developing children, but this development occurs at a much slower rate. Similar types of play and play organization can be seen at about the same developmental level, but there can be enormous variability in abilities within the same developmental levels (Hellendoorn, 1994).

In a study of 108 children with severe mental retardation aged five to 14 years (Wing, Gould, Yeates, & Brierly, 1977), symbolic representational play did not occur in children with mental retardation with a mental age less than 20 months. This finding is similar to the expected development of symbolic play in young children without developmental disabilities. The play of children with mental retardation followed the same developmental pattern as children without developmental disabilities, but it appears to unfold on a different time schedule. A complete absence of symbolic play above the age of 20 months was found to be closely linked to the presence of early childhood autism. The children in the autistic group demonstrated stereotyped play and appeared to have a limited capacity for symbolic play. Language development was found to have a strong relationship to the presence of symbolic play.

Some studies have shown qualitative differences in the play of children with and without developmental disabilities at later developmental stages. Switzky, Ludwig, and Haywood (1979) report that children with mental retardation preferred more structured, less complex play material than their same-age counterparts without disabilities. Li (1985) used Lowenfeld's World Technique to study pretend play in children with mental retardation. Her study group was comprised of 25 children with mild mental retardation, aged five to seven years of age, and 20 children without mental retardation, four to five years of age. Li studied the elaboration of imaginative play rather than its frequency or duration. Li categorized five hierarchical levels of pretend play behaviors: nonsymbolic, object-related play, play with a scene, play with a theme, and play with a story. The results reveal that children without mental retardation had higher levels of symbolic play and that the stories created by children with mental retardation were less clear and less complex.

There are considerable differences in the results obtained across studies, and these differences may be the product of methodological differences: for example, comparing chronological age groups rather than developmental levels. Also, additional differences might be the result of the heterogeneity of developmental levels. When children with and without mental retardation are compared and matched according to mental age, the children with mental retardation will be much older chronologically and will have had more life experiences, but their play will be qualitatively different due to the reduced stimulation caused by their environment or their motor handicaps and a lack of encouragement to play (Hellendoorn & Hoekman, 1992). Hellendoorn and Hoekman (1992) also note that when there is sufficient stimulation and encouragement the same level of symbolic play found in children without developmental disabilities can be developed in children with developmental disabilities.

Hellendoorn and Hoekman (1992) also examined the play behavior of 18 kindergarten children without mental retardation and 55 children functioning at different levels of mental retardation, and they found few differences between the groups with regard to activity, types, and quality of play and play content. Although stereotyped and arranging play activity are often considered characteristics of the play of children with mental retardation, these characteristics were absent in the children who participated in Hellendoorn and Hoekman's study (1992). The higher responses achieved by the children in this study might have been evoked by the presence of an adult who provided the children with stimulating, positive interactions.

GROWING INTEREST IN PLAY THERAPY

In recent years, there has been a growing interest in the psychological needs of people with developmental disabilities, and a variety of therapists have adapted conventional therapy approaches to meet these needs. Much of this activity began in the early 1980s, and it coincided with both the growing literature dealing with the development of treatments for child sexual abuse and the growing research on therapy with people who have developmental disabilities. As a result, therapists have become more open to possibility of using play therapy. There are several reasons why play therapy may be particularly well-suited to meet the needs of the people with developmental disabilities and why this therapeutic approach has started to appeal to therapists working with people who have developmental disabilities.

Many traditional therapies rely on an average to above average level of cognitive ability in the client and are highly dependent on verbal skill, and these therapies also require a considerable vocabulary for affective states. Although many of these traditional therapies can be adapted to meet the client's cognitive and developmental levels, the high verbal demands of these therapeutic approaches (e.g., the requirement that clients express their inner experiences and feelings in fairly abstract language) appear inappropriate for clients who are described as nonverbal or who may have very poor verbal abilities. The use of less verbally oriented therapies, such as play therapy, might be a more appropriate therapeutic approach when working with some people with developmental disabilities (Caprio-Orsini, 1996).

Play therapy creates an ideal tactile, aesthetic, visual experience and activates the preverbal mode of image thinking. Play therapy has enormous possibilities for people with developmental disabilities because it is process oriented and has no age barriers. Although play therapy may be appropriate for both children and adults, specific activities might be seen by both adults and adolescents as infantilizing or childish. Care must be taken in the use of such approaches with these age groups, and it might be a more empowering and helpful strategy to provide choices about the specific materials they want to use during therapy. Nevertheless, play provides concrete opportunities for self-expression and the exploration of feelings, inner problems and conflicts, desires, and fantasies.

Play therapy uses a variety of different settings and materials and can include a wide range of activities, of which only a few will be discussed here. These activities can include: the use of play, sandtray, puppets, art, and storytelling. For example, puppets might provide a sense of safety that allows the discussion of painful issues, and therapeutic stories using a storytelling format can be used to communicate salient themes and issues to clients. Art can include diverse activities such as drawing, painting, sculpting, and the use of a variety of media. Art is commonly used to access children's experiences.

Children with developmental disabilities often have a vocabulary for feelings that is quite limited, and their feelings are sometimes inaccessible at a verbal level. Art is a visual language that may transcend verbal words (Caprio-Orsini, 1996). It can provide a safe medium for communicating and eliciting painful and frightening pictures from within (e.g., direct expressions of nightmares, fantasies, and other inner experiences) (Caprio-Orsini, 1996). Although a full discussion on the use of art falls outside the scope of this chapter, it is important for the therapist to consider a variety of art media and tools, instructional sequences, and technological adaptations. Also, consultation with an occupational therapist can provide the therapist with invaluable information about adapting various materials for use in therapy.

(See Anderson [1992] for a full discussion of adaptations in art therapy that may be required for children with disabilities and Caprio-Orsini [1996] for a full discussion about the use of art therapy with people with developmental disabilities who have been traumatized.)

Play therapy is the treatment most recommended for young victims of sexual abuse (Bagley & King, 1990; Damon, Todd, & MacFarlane, 1987; Erdem, 1994; Gil, 1991; McDonough & Love, 1987; Orenchuk-Tomiuk, Matthey, & Christenson, 1990), and it has considerable possibilities for children with developmental disabilities who have been sexually abused.

PLAY THERAPY FOR CHILDREN WITH DEVELOPMENTAL DISABILITIES

Baum (1994) integrated the use of nondirective play therapy and Jungian sandplay with people who have developmental disabilities. The presence of unconscious processes are evident in the act of dreaming, and Baum asserts that these processes exist in all human beings, regardless of cognitive abilities. Similar to dreaming, sandplay evokes inner images both at the personal and collective unconscious levels and allows archetypal images to appear on a conscious level. Resulting themes go through certain stages of development. Baum suggests that people with developmental disabilities go through the same stages of theme development in the sandtrays as people without developmental disabilities, but they appear to do so at a slower rate, which depends on the level and type of disability. In providing therapy to children with developmental disabilities, some special considerations are required for assessment and treatment.

ASSESSMENT AND TREATMENT OF CHILDREN

There are a number of issues that are unique to the psychotherapeutic treatment of children. First of all, children do not refer themselves for treatment, and therefore, they rely on the adults responsible for their care to: refer them for treatment, get them to their weekly appointments, help them to contain the anxieties that may have been generated in the therapy hour, and inform the therapist about the child's ability to cope outside the session. Doing psychotherapy with children, as opposed to adults, implies a lot of outside interaction with the child's environment. Children who have disabilities and who have been abused tend to have very complicated environmental systems. Their support systems, the nature and extent of their handicap, and their experiences of trauma all have an impact on what kind of interventions are likely to be most effective.

Once the therapist and the child have found a means of communicating and working in play therapy that is mutually acceptable, treatment proceeds in a manner similar to treatment involving children without developmental disabilities. Since therapists may encounter unfamiliar syndromes, communications disorders, dual diagnoses, and so forth when working with children who have developmental disabilities, they are faced with a major question about the assessment for treatment: How do you assess whether a child with a developmental disability can respond to psychotherapeutic interventions in ways similar to children without developmental disabilities?

Assessment

When assessing children with developmental disabilities who have been traumatized, there are two main considerations the therapist must constantly keep in mind: Is therapy indicated, and will it help the child at this time? Is the child a suitable candidate for this form of treatment?

Assessing the child in context

When the issue is sexual abuse, a child's life becomes full of confusing turmoil. The child is interviewed by parents, child protective workers, and the police. Children become confused about what people are asking of them, about what is expected of them, and about how to respond so that "they won't got in trouble" or so that "their mothers won't get mad at them." Children, in their egocentricity and omnipotence, often feel responsible for the bad events that happen to them. Not only do abusers exploit these developmentally immature weaknesses by encouraging the child to believe that the abuse is something they both wanted, but they also use threats to silence a child. These threats can be as subtle as "you'll get in trouble" or as terrifying as threats to kill both the child and his or her family if the child reveals the abuse. When entering treatment, a child may be too terrified to speak about the abuse for fear that he or she will be responsible for the death of his or her parents. Also, the child may believe that his or her fantasies of destruction, rage, and damage will destroy the therapist, and this misconception might make the child reluctant to express overwhelming feelings.

Society has yet to find definitive ways to ensure the safety of children in abusive homes. It has been slow to implement the more responsible course of removing the abuser from the home instead of the victim. Removing children from their homes following disclosures of sexual abuse can be as traumatizing and confusing to children as the trauma they may have suffered. Children in treatment who have been removed from their homes feel that this is a confirmation of their lack of self-worth or of "being bad," or they may feel that their parents have "thrown them away." Others feel they have been punished for "telling on daddy" (Perlman, Millar, & Ericson, 1993). On the other hand, there are instances when children who remain with their parents are still at risk for abuse. These issues have a profound impact on decisions regarding the assessment and treatment of abused children.

To assess whether psychotherapy for a specific child is the most appropriate and most pressing intervention following a traumatic experience, it is necessary to assess the child's environment. Can the child be considered safe in his or her present environment? Is it likely that he or she will be abused again in his or her current placement? Is the environment stable? Or is the child (justifiably) preoccupied with worries about the temporary situation of his or her home? These questions raise the issue of not only what should be done first to help the child, but also whether or not psychotherapy at this time may actually be harmful to the child. Harm can occur on two levels: the systemic level and the interpersonal level.

The systemic level
On a systemic level, child protective systems are overburdened with large numbers of at-risk children and underfunded in terms of the

number of workers and the number of foster homes available to traumatized children. Therefore, if the system perceives that the child is
being "taken care of" in treatment and as a consequence makes placement intervention a lower priority, it might be irresponsible for a
therapist to see a child for one hour a week or even one hour a day if
the child is in danger for the other twenty-three hours a day and if the
rest of the system is failing to intervene to protect the child.

The interpersonal level

On a more interpersonal level, psychotherapy can be harmful to children who are still in unsafe environments because the child might
begin to see the therapist as an idealized parent who will provide the
protection from abuse not provided by his or her parents. When a
child in treatment is re-injured outside the therapy room, the "betrayal" of yet another parent-figure failing to protect them can be
devastating:

A horrific example of this "betrayal" involved J.L., a seven-year-old
child with mild developmental disabilities who was referred for psychotherapy following two disclosures of sexual abuse. Over the course
of treatment, she disclosed abuse by three subsequent perpetrators,
all acquaintances of the child's mother. Although the investigations
by authorities corroborated the child's disclosures, she remained in
her home. The investigating workers felt it was "not the mother's
fault that her child had been abused" (regardless of her obvious inability to keep her daughter safe from harm). With each disclosure of
abuse and each accompanying failure of her environment to protect
her (including her therapist), J.L. became increasingly enraged. She
began to slip more and more into psychotic-type fantasies and began
acting out with increasingly severe suicidal gestures. In this case, the
therapist postulated that therapy had prematurely helped this child to
contain her anxiety, and it created the false hope that she would be
safe. Had therapy been delayed until she was moved to a safe environment, her prognosis might have been more hopeful.

The child's reaction to the trauma

A child's reaction to traumatic events depends on many factors: What
was the nature of the abuse? Was it brutal, sadistic, ongoing, or was

it less invasive? Who was the perpetrator? How long did the abuse continue? How did the environment respond to the child when the abuse was uncovered? Were the people in the child's environment: denying? supportive? enraged? What about the child? Did he or she: act out? become depressed? somatisize? It is necessary for the therapist to remember that not all abuse is the same, not all the consequences are the same, and not all children react in the same way.

Assessing coping skills

One of the major factors influencing the child's reaction to traumatic events involves their pre-existing repertoire of coping skills. Preverbal babies communicate distress by crying. As children mature, they develop increasingly sophisticated strategies to express their wants and fears. Young children tend to act out when they are distressed because they do not possess the verbal and cognitive skills to help them organize and communicate their experiences. Children with developmental disabilities who have suffered traumas often lack the developmental skills to help them sort out and deal with their experiences; consequently, the result is seen in the form of acting out type behaviors that are sometimes misunderstood or misdiagnosed.

Diagnostic overshadowing (Levitan & Reiss, 1983), a form of clinical bias that occurs when therapists misattribute psychological or behavioral problems to mental retardation instead of psychopathology, can present a significant problem for therapists who work with clients who have developmental disabilities. Sometimes, the signs of distress exhibited by children who have been sexually abused are misdiagnosed as Attention Deficit Hyperactivity Disorder (ADHD) or Conduct Disorders, and in some cases, children without developmental disabilities who have been sexually abused are misdiagnosed as a result of the difficulties they experience when coping with their sexual abuse. Anderson, Williams, McGee, and Silva (1987) studied children who had been sexually abused and their psychiatric diagnoses. These diagnoses included: Oppositional Defiant-Disorder, ADHD, Conduct Disorder, and Over-Anxious Disorder (American Psychiatric Association, 1987). Yet the data covered by Anderson et al. (1987) in terms of the behavioral manifestations of these diagnoses suggest that over 80% of these children were acting out. For some of these diagnoses, there appears to be a considerable overlap in some of the criteria, which can contribute to misdiagnoses, especially for children with developmental disabilities. Charlot (1998) points out that diagnostic errors occur because clinicians overlook the impact of developmental level on the presentation of clinical features in mental health disorders. The impact of developmental factors on the phenomenology of mental health disorders needs to be understood and taken into account during the diagnostic process in order to increase diagnostic accuracy.

In terms of assessment for psychotherapy, it is necessary to determine the child's current reaction to the trauma and whether one hour or two hours of psychotherapy a week is enough. A thorough psychological assessment, however, can be informative in making these determinations. Although projective techniques have not traditionally been used with people who have developmental disabilities, some reports have documented the use of the Thematic Apperception Test (Hurley & Sovner, 1985) and the Rorschach inkblot test (Hurley & Sovner, 1982) with people who have developmental disabilities. Projective tests can be used to evaluate emotional disorders and coping abilities and explore issues and treatment responses to pharmacotherapy, psychotherapy, or behavioral interventions (Hurley, 1995). Svec (1992a) has outlined the use of projective drawings and tests, free play, and sandtray to assess dually diagnosed clients. It has been traditionally believed that projective techniques can only be used with clients who are of average to above average intelligence, but Svec (1992a) asserts that these techniques can be used with dually diagnosed clients as long as the intellectual level is considered while analyzing the data and that these tools are not to be used in isolation for diagnostic decision making. Jura and Sigman (1985) suggest the importance of therapist flexibility in the administration of tests, and they recommend that the therapist consider the client's developmental level when interpreting projective assessments with clients who have developmental disabilities.

When any child presents for treatment, a therapist will always need to do a thorough assessment that includes an examination of the child's ability to cope. For example, the therapist would want to know if the child is acting out in ways that are dangerous to him- or herself and others? Can the environment cope with his or her acting out? Are other interventions necessary to help the child and the family cope?

K.M., an eleven-year-old boy with a moderate developmental disability, reacted to his abuse experience in a highly anxious way. He went into uncontrollable rages at home and at school. He woke up at four o'clock every morning and left his apartment to wander the corridors. He ran in front of cars. He removed all his clothing in public and repeatedly tried to molest other children in his class. He repeatedly put himself and others at risk. His mother, a single woman with a developmental disability, did not have the resources or the ability to contain her son's rages. In this case, it was obvious that K.M. needed much more treatment than was available on an outpatient basis and that a treatment center was indicated to help him to feel safe and to help him contain his incredible anxiety and self-destructive behaviors.

In summary, if the child is in a safe, stable, and secure environment, if the child has some ability to cope, and if the child has an environment that will help him or her through difficult periods of treatment and recovery, then it is possible to assess the child for treatment.

History
When assessing any child for treatment, it is necessary to know as much as possible about his or her early life experiences. A detailed developmental history often includes information such as: history of early development, his or her milestones (when did he or she walk, talk, become toilet trained, and so forth), his or her attachment history and history of early separations and losses, and accidents and hospitalizations (Freud, 1977; Greenspan, 1981). There are two reasons for this type of detailed assessment: 1) to get a sense of the child's normal functioning prior to the trauma and 2) to understand the nature and extent of the child's disability. For example, many children who have been abused present for treatment with problems of enuresis and encopresis. It is important for the therapist to know if the child was in such a state prior to the trauma or if this is a regres-

sive behavior in response to the abuse. This baseline information will also help the therapist gauge the child's progress in treatment. If the trauma has been ongoing, it can affect all areas of the child's functioning:

A.C. began treatment when she was five years old after disclosing that her father had "touched her birdie." She was lagging behind developmentally in all areas: gross-motor, fine-motor, language, and cognitive functioning. A.C. was also acting out violently and suffered from night-time enuresis after having been removed from her biological parents. Three years into treatment, and after heroic efforts by her foster family, A.C. had improved to the point where she was able to ride a bike and horseback ride. She was learning to read and taking a lot of pride in her accomplishments in school. Occasionally, when her foster mother went away for a few days, A.C. would revert to small acting out behaviors and would occasionally wet the bed.

A.C.'s story is not uncommon. Children who come to treatment following severe and ongoing abuse experiences and who score in the mild to borderline level of intellectual functioning on psychological tests often have improved scores once treatment has been in place. Often, it is revealed that these children are not handicapped but that their delays can be attributed to their reactions to severe trauma (Millar & Palace, 1995). It may even be the case that the impaired functioning serves as a defense in the face of ongoing abuse. The defense of "not knowing" might be the result of a reality that is too painful, threatening, and overwhelming to recognize (especially if the child still returns to an abusive home every night) (Perlman & Millar, 1991).

Understanding the child's developmental disability

When treating children who have developmental disabilities, understanding the nature and extent of their disability is an essential and often complicated aspect of assessment. Obtaining reports from previous assessments is necessary to understand the scope and complexity of the child's handicap. Useful assessment reports often include results from: genetic, neurological, psychiatric, audiological, speech-language, and psychological assessments. It is necessary for the therapist to obtain such detailed medical/developmental information so that he or she will not interpret the biological as psychological. For example, a child may present with a number of stereotypical or repetitive behaviors in the assessment room, but are these behaviors: autistic features? obsessive-compulsive features? psychiatric? Tourettic? brain injury? traumatic re-enactments? or even startle responses to loud sounds as is the standard reaction of children with William's Syndrome (Bellugi, Bihrle, Jernigan, Trainer, & Doherty, 1990).

The therapist also needs to know if the child is on any medications and what are the expected side-effects of the medication (e.g., irritability, dulling of concentration or cognitive functioning). For example, if a child has been diagnosed as having ADHD and the effects of his or her Ritalin™ are at their lowest concentration in the late afternoon, four o'clock appointments are contraindicated.

Assessing ability to communicate
Treating a child without developmental disabilities in psychotherapy involves the child's ability to somehow communicate to the therapist through play, drawings, and so forth. The therapist, deriving meaning from the child's play, tends to respond to the child verbally (by questions, interpretations, or simply by engaging in the play). Therefore, the child has to have the ability to communicate through play, hear the therapist's interpretations, and be able to understand what the therapist is saying and respond accordingly. Children with impaired cognitive abilities will often have compromised communication skills; therefore, assessing communication skills prior to engaging in treatment is of paramount importance.

Can the child hear properly? Does he or she need F. M. systems or hearing aids? This might not be as obvious as it initially appears. Hearing loss might be hard to detect without a specific audiological assessment. The loss may be intermittent, or it may only involve certain sound frequencies. Children who are developmentally handicapped are at high risk for hearing impairment. Brassem (1995) found that 50% of the children referred for mandatory audiological testing prior to speech language and psychological testing were discovered to have previously undetected hearing losses.

Can the child see properly? If the child has glasses, does he or she wear them? It is important to know that the child is physically capable of seeing what the therapist sees during psychological testing and in the play room. For example, if a child has a visual-perceptual impairment, his or her responses on the Rorschach inkblot test might be incorrectly interpreted as pathological when, in fact, the child has a distorted perceptual representation of the inkblot and cannot even see a triangle as a triangle, let alone interpret an inkblot. In the play room, any distortions a child may make should be attributable to psychological phenomena (e.g., the child sees all girl dolls as boys, all babies as monsters) and not to visual-perceptual difficulties.

How does the child communicate? What about his or her receptive language? Does he or she use precocious expressive language that exceeds his or her receptive language abilities (e.g., language used by children with Asperger syndrome)? Do the results from a speech-language assessment indicate a discrepancy between expressive and receptive language? If the therapist does not understand the child's style and level of communication, then he or she might overestimate the child's ability to comprehend and to respond to interpretations in treatment.

The ability to use play
The final stage of the assessment process involves doing an assessment of the child in the playroom. This is the most difficult part of the assessment as it is not always easy to tell if a child will be able to respond to this form of treatment. It may take four to six sessions to assess the suitability of play therapy, or it may be months into treatment before the therapist confirms his or her initial impressions about the child.

As play is the child's way of communicating in therapy as opposed to the adult's use of language, it is necessary to assess whether a child can express him- or herself through play. Is the play organized around specific themes? Can the therapist find some symbolic meaning in the child's play or in his or her drawings? These questions are designed to reveal whether the child uses toys to represent other things: For example, a child may crash two toy cars in the playroom and then comment that one of the cars is hurt and needs to go to the hospital, which indicates that the cars represent human beings. Also, puppets can be used to discover if a child can play symbolically. Do the puppets have characters, voices, or feelings? Unfortunately, the level of developmental disability may not be a good indicator of a child's ability to play symbolically. The following examples of two teenage girls who both have moderate developmental disabilities highlight the difficulty in using level of developmental disability to indicate an individual's ability to play symbolically. The first girl displayed the ability to play symbolically and did quite well in therapy. The second girl was unable to make the connections between concrete items and abstract representations, and an alternative form of treatment was implemented:

L.M. responded immediately to a family of dolls placed in front of her during an assessment. She immediately chose the smallest doll, which she named after herself. She said that this doll was bad and turned the doll's back to the rest of the play going on with the doll family. L.M., despite her moderate disability, was able to engage in therapy for a couple of years. The doll came to represent the part of L.M. that had been sexually abused by her father and that was subsequently responsible for all the acting out behavior that L.M. did outside the treatment room. Gradually, D. gave her therapist responsibility to lock up the L.M. doll and to make sure she did not get out during the week between sessions and cause trouble. The group home reported that L.M. was no longer acting out at home during this phase of treatment. When L.M. had enough in her session, she would trace the outline of her hand on a piece of paper and hold it up, signaling the therapist to "stop."

D.S., on the other hand, had great difficulty responding to the toys in the playroom. She was extremely concrete in her reaction to the toys.

For example, the dolls either had nice dresses or were messy. She enjoyed playing at the cooking stove. She would not draw, play with plasticine, and much of the time ignored the therapist. Three weeks into the assessment, D.S. placed a girl doll in a cupboard under the stairs in the doll house. In response to questioning, she said that the girl was hiding from her brother. (D.S. was referred for treatment after being raped by her brother.) The therapist then handed D.S. a boy doll. D.S. said the boy doll was looking for his sister. The therapist, attempting to engage her, used a little girl's voice and said, "Oh, no! My brother is looking for me, and I'm so afraid!" D.S. reacted in surprise, looked at the doll under the stairs, looked at the therapist, and said, "Hey! That was you!" She was unable to relate, at the most basic level, to the therapist representing the feelings of the girl under the stairs.

The child who has suffered abuse and invasion of personal boundaries has learned not to trust adults. He or she may bring a variety of behaviors that are a product of his or her relationships with the nonoffending parent and the perpetrator to his or her interactions with the therapist. These behaviors may have served important coping functions during the abuse or may reflect or represent certain issues associated with conflict and proximity. Often, children who have been abused fear the intimacy of the play room, and it may take months before they feel safe enough to reveal their inner pain to the therapist. Children may take months to begin to see the therapist as someone they can trust.

Anxiety
Understanding the nature and magnitude of the child's anxiety is an important factor in play therapy. Respecting the impact of anxiety for the child in therapy is critical (Friedrich, 1990). It is important for the therapist to determine the effects of anxiety as these pertain to treatment: For example, how does the child feel? Is there enough anxiety present to provide an opening for psychotherapeutic intervention? Or is there so much anxiety that it cannot be contained?

Since children do not refer themselves to treatment, they are at the mercy of their caregivers to seek help on their behalf: "A [child] is more likely to come into treatment when his or her symptoms are disturbing to the environment. The parents will be guided in their assessment of the seriousness of the situation by the impact of the child's neuroses on themselves" (Freud, 1945). This impetus to refer a child for therapy also exists among referrals by child protective workers of children who have been sexually abused. If the child is aggressive, destructive, or acting out, he or she is more likely to be referred as the situation will be seen as more urgent than the child who may present as withdrawn and depressed. But when assessing a child's suitability for treatment, it is necessary to determine the intensity and source of the child's pain. One way to assess this is to look at the themes and content of a child's play. Do these themes suggest feelings of anxiety, pain, suffering, damage, or deprivation? If anxiety is present, can the child contain it with help? For example, can the child respond if the therapist asks him or her to stay in the playroom? Can the child refrain from throwing toys against the one-way mirror? Or as in A.J.'s case, is the child's anxiety too much for him or her to contain in order to allow for psychotherapeutic intervention?

A.J.'s anxiety was so great that he could not be contained in the therapy room. He began exhibiting stereotypic behaviors, pacing, twirling his fingers in front of his face, and "coaching" himself verbally under his breath. Three sessions later, he was still unable to calm down and to play with toys or even to allow the therapist to close the door to the treatment room. In this case, psychotherapy was not indicated at this time. Changes had to occur at a systemic level to allow the environment to help this child to contain his extreme anxiety. Six months later he was reassessed for treatment.

Object relations
In addition to considering the effects of anxiety, it is also important for the therapist to determine if the child perceives the therapist as another person with his or her own thoughts and needs? Does the child demonstrate empathy for others (whether it is the therapist, the

receptionist in the waiting room, or a teddy bear in the playroom)? Can the child make use of the relationship with the therapist? Does the child do things in the play room that take the therapist into account? For example, the child may turn his or her back to the therapist and pretend to ignore him or her while surreptitiously glancing to make sure that the therapist is watching. Or the child may be playing alone on the other side of the room but talking very loudly for the obvious benefit of the therapist.

Some good predictors of whether the child can make use of a therapeutic relationship can be found in the child's history. Does he or she have a history of at least one good attachment figure? This may be indicative of a more hopeful prognosis for the child, but it should not be used as an exclusionary criterion for treatment.

With children who have suffered extreme abuse and deprivation and present as severely acting out, it often is useful to look at the environment's reaction to the child in order to determine whether the child can respond to the therapist during treatment: For example, despite the child's aggressive, destructive behavior, are there people in his or her life who really like him or her? Are there workers who really go out of their way to help the child and advocate for him or her? Despite all the odds, have others found something valuable in the child that they can connect with, a piece that the therapist can hope to "hold onto" for the child as an example to the child that he or she is not all bad (Perlman & Millar, 1991):

J.D. had been abused in infancy, sexually abused from ages two to five, and had been in seven foster homes in his first eight years of life. In the second assessment session, he ran wild through the treatment center, and the therapist finally cornered him in a treatment room. The child began screaming, "Fuck you! I hate you!" over and over again. J.D. was shaking with rage, and yet he was terrified by his anger and perhaps afraid that he was really out of control. The therapist quietly responded by telling J.D. that it was O.K. if he hated her, his anger would not destroy her. She repeated, "You can hate me, and I'll still like you." All of a sudden, a little voice said, "Really?"

Then he calmed down and asked the therapist if she would bring him to the waiting room and get him some milk and cookies. This pattern was repeated for several months, with the child continuously challenging the therapist by showing her how "bad" he was (hitting, punching, running out of the building and into traffic, crawling through the ceiling tiles), yet he still remained connected, and after a particularly tough session, he would hug the therapist upon leaving and happily announce that he would return the following week (news that was not always greeted with enthusiasm by the frazzled therapist).

Treatment Issues

By the time a comprehensive assessment of the child with a developmental disability and his or her environment has been completed, the therapist should be intimately familiar with the child's strengths and weaknesses. When treating children who have been abused, it is necessary to carefully outline issues of safety and confidentiality for the child. This involves letting the child know what he or she is allowed to do in the play room and what is forbidden. For instance, a child might be told, "This is your play room. You will be coming here every week at the same time, and we will have one hour together in the same room. You may play with anything you like in the room. You are not allowed to hurt yourself, to hurt me, or to hurt the toys in the room."

During the initial sessions of treatment, the issues and confines of confidentiality in the playroom must be explained repeatedly to the child. For example, the child might be told, "What you tell me in the playroom is private. I will not tell (your mother, worker, and so forth) what you have said in here except in an emergency or when I am worried about you or when I have your permission." This is especially important for children who have been abused and whose boundaries have been violated. This does not preclude consultation with the system, but the therapist must let the child know when there are consultations: "Your teacher wants to talk to me about what a tough time you have at recess when the kids tease you, so can I tell her what you said in the session today"; or "You mentioned in therapy that X....I need to talk to your mom about this as I am worried about Y."

By setting basic limits for safety, the therapist facilitates the development of a space where the child can feel safe enough to explore his or her inner world.

Themes in therapy

Once the child has established at least some feeling of relative safety, regressive behaviors may take place, and themes may start to develop in play that will be a symbolic acting out of the child's unconscious issues. The child's play may bring up issues of self-blame, control, loneliness and isolation, guilt, shame, and feelings of being bad and dirty. A child who has experienced the trauma associated with disclosure may have received several responses from family members and authorities that might have induced feelings of anxiety, confusion, betrayal, and invalidation.

Themes will arise that may or may not be directly related to the abuse; however, some play may be indicative of the child's subjective experience of the abuse and/or his or her struggles to work through conflicting emotions about the abuser. Developing play themes may be expressed in opposition to one another: for example, danger versus safety, light versus dark, dirty versus clean, victim versus aggressor, and love versus hate (Allan & Bertoia, 1992).

In incest cases, the child often feels anger toward the nonabusive parent who failed to protect him or her from harm (Perlman et al., 1993). This anger is often confounded by guilt and the knowledge that the child risks losing both parents since the mother (usually the nonoffending parent) failed to provide protection. As a result, the child may have a vested interest in protecting his or her fragile image of his or her mother as a "good mother." Knowing the extent of the abuse and the family's reaction to it will help the therapist understand the child's internal emotional struggles.

It is common to see both love and hate toward the offending parent in sexually abused children (Friedrich, 1990). The risk here is that the therapist needs to differentiate between the actual abusive parent they encounter in the waiting room and the child's representation of that parent in the play room: For example, the therapist may feel rage at the lack of empathy shown by the abusive parent for the child he or she has violated, and yet the child may represent the same parent as a loving and affectionate person through their play.

As in the example of L.M., it is important to assess whether the therapist and the child can find some meaningful way to communicate with each other. Communication can be accomplished in a number of ways: through play, through drawings, through gestures, or through a combination of all of these:

Nine-year-old A.C. was very reticent to engage in therapy. He would not play with toys, not draw, and in some sessions would say very little; however, he responded very well to Winnicott's "Squiggle game" (Winnicott, 1989). The squiggle game is a technique in which the therapist and child take turns scribbling on paper. They are then required to turn each other's squiggles into representations of something. This technique is particularly successful with children who are developmentally delayed since they often feel self-conscious about their poor fine-motor coordination and refuse to draw. Drawings that are derived from scribbles are necessarily distorted and sloppy and, therefore, less threatening.

At first, A.C.'s squiggles were of safe characters such as animals. As he engaged more in therapy, his scribbles became more elaborate: "a guy in a boat that's sinking or a boy hiking, caught in a storm, and is going to die." This nonthreatening medium allowed A.C. to move into therapy. He began to talk as he engaged in the squiggle game. He began by discussing his favorite TV shows and movies. The themes moved from trivial (names of superheroes) to profound (commenting that Oskar Schindler "should have saved all the children first, as the children are the future"). It was six months into treatment before A.C. let down his guard enough to engage with toys. His first session using toys, however, was very rich: Giant snake attacking a castle and kidnapping the baby while the king slept. The dogs in the castle sneak out, kill the snake, rescue the baby, and return him to the castle before the king awakes. The baby then falls off the tower and dies.

Changes in themes

Case studies describing children without developmental disabilities who have been sexually abused suggest that a child's play themes may change over time. Over the course of treatment, there may be an increase in the child's symbols of personal power, the central character in the child's play may be more in control, and the emotional intensity the child experiences may lessen over time. The change and movement of play themes throughout this process may enable the child to grow and heal.

Repetitive play

Freud (1920) explained repetitive play as the ego's attempt to actively repeat a traumatic event and thereby try to gain mastery over it. In some cases, children may become stuck or fixated in their play and will not progress to different themes. Such children may continually play out the same scenario, and they may not appear to reach a reasonable resolution in their play. Examples of this situation include: the development of post-traumatic play or re-enactment in children without developmental disabilities (Terr, 1990). Post-traumatic play possesses several distinctive characteristics: compulsive repetition; an unconscious link between the play and the traumatic event; literalness of play, with simple defenses only; failure to relieve anxiety; a wide age range; varying time lag prior to its development; carrying power to nontraumatized youngsters; contagion to new generations of children; danger; the use of doodling, talking, typing, and audio duplication as modes of repeated play; and the possibility of therapeutically retracing post-traumatic play to an earlier trauma (Terr, 1983, p. 309). Terr (1983) suggests, based on her work with traumatized children without developmental disabilities, that structured play therapy can be used to overcome the effects of trauma by repeating the same scenes until the child achieves some sense of mastery or resolution. Post-traumatic play, however, can become fixed and dangerous for the child (i.e., the child's play does not release his or her anxiety and reinforces feelings of powerlessness and terror) (Terr, 1990). Gil (1991) recommends using a variety of interventions to interrupt the play and help the child generate alternatives to promote the child's sense of control, expression of feelings, and future orientation.

Therapy adaptations

Psychotherapy with a child with a developmental disability essentially involves the therapist being very sensitive to the child's areas of difficulty and modifying the treatment process to exploit the child's strengths. As with any adaptation the therapist chooses to make in therapy, the changes made should represent specific adaptations of a basic set of therapeutic principles rather than a deviation from a specific technique (Sandler, Kennedy, & Tyson, 1980). That is, if the therapist makes adaptations in therapy, they should be carefully planned and should be done purposefully with a specific child in mind: For example, this might involve using a lot of visual modifications for a child who is hearing impaired, speaking very slowly and clearly for a child with auditory-processing problems, or constantly checking to make sure that the therapist understands the speech of a child with severe dysarthria. The idea is to adapt the materials available to the therapist in the playroom and adapt the therapist's skills in order to communicate with the child more effectively while remaining true to the tenets of the theoretical school the therapist normally uses to guide the treatment process. The exception to this rule involves the use of directive and nondirective processes in treatment with children who have been traumatized. The most sensitive therapist, whatever his or her orientation, uses both directive and nondirective approaches when working with children who have been abused. Essentially, it is necessary to decide when it is appropriate to use which approach.

Nondirective

In the initial stages of treatment, it is necessary to be nondirective as the therapist does not know the child's main area of anxiety or pain: For instance, does the child feel damaged by the abuse? Is the child obsessed with having been physically violated? Does the child feel guilty about disclosing the abuse and miss his or her father? Is the child preoccupied with worries about the future? Where will he or she live? Who will take care of him or her? Or does the child feel that he or she has been bad and that he or she is being punished by being banished to live in foster care? Sometimes there is a combination of many or all of the characteristics of anxiety at different times in treatment:

B.B. came into therapy and began roping all the toys in the play room to the roof of a toy car and spent the session moving from one doll house to another. He even struggled to get all the furniture onto the roof (including the kitchen set). B.B. repeated this play for months, commenting that the driver of the car never knew where he was moving to each week. Gradually, B.B. began to discuss how he had too many families. He had the therapist draw a family tree of all his foster families, and he gave it to his C.A.S. worker with the caption, "Where am I going to live next week?" It was not until two years later, when he felt secure in his foster home, that he was able to begin to explore his abusive past.

M.V. entered the playroom and began throwing all the dolls, one by one, out of the room and screaming at them, "You're bad, get out." He then sent his therapist out in the hallway to take care of all of the bad babies.

W.K. walked into the assessment room and crawled into the garbage can.

B.C.'s behavior was so sexualized (at five years old) that she began a strip-tease in front of the one-way mirror.

All of these children had histories of sexual abuse, severe deprivation, and loss. Yet they all came to treatment with different issues. To have begun treatment by exploring abuse issues would have been to deny these children their experiences.

Directive
There are two times in treatment when the therapist needs to be more directive: when specifically addressing issues of abuse and when the child is in crisis. With regard to discussing abuse issues with the child, there are times when the therapist needs to assume the role of educator. Children often harbor fantasies about the abuse and about

sex in general. These fantasies can be attributed to a combination of the child's own interpretations of his or her abuse experiences and to age-related misinformation about sexuality. Abused children need the therapist to tell them that the abuse was not their fault and to give them factual information about their bodies, normal development, and sex. Of course, the timing of such discussions has to be carefully planned and based on the child's developmental level and on the stage of treatment. Long term sexuality education that is carefully implemented can also provide some future risk reduction for sexual abuse (Sobsey & Mansell, 1990).

The other case in which the therapist needs to be more directive is when the child is in crisis. The long-term treatment of traumatized children often involves a number of very difficult stages, which can be the result of either precipitating events outside the sessions (court proceedings, retraumatization, death of a parent) or generated by the nature of the material in the treatment room:

W.W. had been repeatedly raped by her father, her two brothers, and other members of her extended family. She progressed well in treatment until she began to deal with her mother's failure to protect her. At this point, she began to "fall apart." She suffered from uncontrollable bouts of crying, recurrent flashbacks, was unable to eat, and would not leave the house.

When a child goes into crisis, when he or she starts having difficulty sorting fact from fantasy, or when he or she is unable to control extreme anxiety, nondirective therapy may be contraindicated. In such cases, the therapist needs to help the child structure his or her world and contain his or her fantasies. When a child begins to "slip" in such a way, a number of interventions outside the treatment room are usually indicated as well. Here, the therapist might want to refer the child for personality assessment to determine the strength of the child's coping capacities, to determine the sources of the anxiety, and to make specific recommendations with regard to the treatment process. If the child is unable to contain his or her anxieties and is acting out at home and in school, the therapist might want to refer the child for behavior therapy (e.g., to help the child be more contained in the classroom) or for a psychiatric evaluation to determine whether psychopharmacological intervention is indicated. Multidisciplinary consultations are often a positive and necessary adjunct to the treatment that goes on in the therapy room.

SUMMARY

In order to determine whether a child with developmental disabilities is a suitable candidate for psychotherapy, the therapist needs to carefully assess: the child's areas of strength and weakness, the nature and extent of the child's disabilities, the nature and extent of the abuse the child has suffered, and the child's and his or her environment's reaction to the abuse. With an understanding of these issues in mind, the therapist proceeds to assess the child in the playroom in order to determine if the child can use play as a means of communication. Once the child and therapist have found a mutually beneficial way to communicate, therapy can proceed.

Some issues specific to treating children with developmental disabilities who have been traumatized include: foster care and the child's loss of his or her family, issues of safety and confidentiality, the need to combine directive and nondirective approaches, and the need to consult with other professionals at certain stages throughout the assessment and treatment process.

As mentioned earlier, in some situations, therapists may be faced with dealing with children who exhibit sexualized behaviors as a result of their sexual abuse. The next chapter is dedicated to the assessment and treatment of sexualized behaviors, and it includes a discussion of various treatment issues and approaches.

•• 9

Assessment and Treatment of Individuals with Developmental Disabilities Who Have Been Sexually Victimized and Who Victimize Others: Rights in Treatment

Dave Hingsburger

In Chapter 3, the effects of sexual abuse for people with developmental disabilities were presented. This chapter deals with a significant problem that sometimes results from sexual abuse: that is, sexualized or sexually inappropriate behaviors. These behaviors present significant concerns to family, staff members, the community, and the client. It is important to remember that these behaviors run along a continuum from mild socially and sexually inappropriate behaviors to more destructive, serious sexual offending behaviors. These behaviors, however, may be caused by any number of different factors, including the sexual abuse of the individual. Evaluating the possible causes is central to the development of a treatment plan for the client who displays inappropriate sexual behavior.

This chapter discusses issues associated with the sexuality of people with developmental disabilities, outlines the therapist's evaluation process for determining the causes of the client's sexualized behaviors, and presents treatment approaches. The author provides examples drawn from his clinical work with York Central Hospital's Behaviour Management Services Sexuality Clinic in Richmond Hill, Ontario, Canada.

THE DENIAL OF SEXUALITY

"He grabbed my breast, it wasn't sexual but it still upset me." This statement, given in an interview by a young female staff member of a group home, was made during a sexual assessment of a middle-aged man with a developmental disability. The words "it wasn't sexual," while well–intentioned, demonstrate a major problem in the area of sexuality of people with developmental disabilities. For people with developmental disabilities, a sexual offense is defined as nonsexual because the performer of the act is considered nonsexual, and therefore, a sexual offense is seen as a behavior problem and treated with the same gravity as refusing to do the dishes (Hingsburger, Hillis-Ormiston, Naylor, Nethercott, & Tough, 1994). Often, offenders with disabilities perform a myriad of "small" sexual offenses, which are dismissed by their service team, and then the offenders are arrested for a "large" sexual offense by others who are less forgiving (Griffiths, Quinsey, & Hingsburger, 1989; Sgroi, 1989).

The fact that the sexuality of people with disabilities has been seen alternately as a nonissue or nonexistent (Kempton & Gochros, 1968; Monat–Haller, 1992) makes providing a solid assessment and determining a treatment plan for individuals with disabilities who act out sexually more difficult (Ward et al., 1992). As in the situation above, it is not uncommon for a therapist to be requested to work with sexualized behavior as if it were simply a "behavior problem" that can be programmed away (Hingsburger, 1990a). Until there is a clear sexual offense, often outside the bounds of the agency, the individual is seen as an immature and innocent being simply making little social skills mistakes.

This approach is unfortunate for a therapist being called to provide consultation or direct therapy. When the referral behavior is dramatic, like child molestation or rape, the response is equally dramatic. There tends to be simultaneous reactions: the jailing of the individual, which takes the form of supervision; the labeling of the person as deviant; and the punishment of the person, which is carried out by forcing the individual to enter into treatment. While supervision might be advisable and treatment a necessity, it is the labeling that will cause the most difficulty for the agency and the therapist (Demetral, 1994; Hingsburger et al., 1994). For example, when an individual with a disability performs some kind of sexualized action, such as touching a child inappropriately or forcing another adult into a sexual act, the response is often to consider the person as a paedophile (aroused by children) or as a biastophile (aroused by sexual violence) (Love, 1992; Money, 1986).

The literature on treating the sexualized behavior of people with disabilities suggests that this error of labeling is significant (Griffiths et al., 1989; Haaven, Little, & Petre-Miller, 1990; Ward et al., 1992). The tendency is to see a person with a disability as a free agent whose sexual behavior has gone out of control. Therefore, if a person with a disability sexually misbehaves, he or she is considered deviant or has deviant arousal patterns since it is assumed that they have the opportunity to behave in sexually normal and appropriate ways. Almost every piece of literature published regarding sexuality and disability states that people with disabilities are not free agents in respect to their sexuality; instead, the literature points out that their sexuality has been routinely suppressed, ignored, and punished by the systems in which they live (Fegan, Rauch, & McCarthy, 1993; Hingsburger, 1995a; Hingsburger & Griffiths, 1986; Kempton, 1993; Rowe & Savage, 1987). Even issues such as the right to privacy to express oneself sexually are still controversial and difficult to enshrine in agency policy (Brown, Carney, Cortis, Metz, & Petrie, 1994). This controversy even includes the right to privacy for behaviors as benign as masturbation (Hingsburger, 1995b; Hingsburger & Haar, 1999).

The denial of the sexuality of people with disabilities has had tragic consequences. First, it has created an environment in which people with disabilities will make serious mistakes, hurting themselves and others, that could have been avoided (Griffiths et al., 1989; Money, Wainwright, & Hingsburger, 1991). Second, when one considers the literature on the frequency of sexual victimization of people with disabilities and then looks at lists of behavioral indices of sexual victimization (Everstine & Everstine, 1989; Hingsburger, 1995a; McGuire & Grant, 1991; Sobsey, 1994; Ticoll, 1992), it is entirely possible that an individual with a disability is using sexually acting out behavior as a means of reporting and re–enacting past abuse. For example, a young teenage male returns to his group home from a parental visit. Several days later he is found in the basement of the group home forcing another male resident to perform fellatio. After weeks of supervision, punishment, and labeling (in his resident file) as a sex offender, it is discovered that he had been abused in precisely the same way and same situation in his parental home. Of course, the prior abuse does not excuse his behavior, but it does put it into perspective. As a direct result of his disability, he had not received any kind of sex education, had no language about his body, had developed no trusting relationship wherein he could ask questions about sexuality, and had been trained that anger and acting out were inappropriate at any and all times. In this circumstance, his behavior, while sexually assaultive, was also communicative. In effect, he was using his behavior as a means of communicating that "THIS HAPPENED TO ME!!!" Behavior therapists have been saying for a long time that behavior communicates. That being the case, any therapist who works with individuals with disabilities who perform sexualized behavior needs to "hear" the behavior in order to determine what is going on and how to develop a plan for treatment.

DEVELOPING A HYPOTHESIS

It is as dangerous to assume that a sexualized behavior is a result of sexual victimization as it is to assume that it is because of a deviant arousal pattern. There are a number of hypotheses that need to be investigated. The term *Counterfeit Deviance* (Hingsburger, Griffiths, & Quinsey, 1991) was coined as a means to point out that a sexual behavior is not necessarily what it seems. The following list of hypotheses provides a brief explanation of the kinds of issues that need to be investigated along the way to determining treatment. This list of hypotheses was originally published elsewhere (Hingsburger, et al. 1991), but it has been adapted for the purposes of this chapter.

STRUCTURE

Structure means that the sexual behavior is occurring directly because of the environment in which the person lives. There are two things that a therapist must investigate. First, is there a problem at all? Since many agencies have "no sex" policies, they treat any expression of sexual behavior as problematic and inappropriate. In this kind of setting, consenting sexual behavior between a man and woman is seen to be as problematic as sexual assault or rape. The therapist needs to determine what actually happened in order to proceed. Often, this is made more difficult because the individuals involved in the consenting act have been punished and lectured and have, as a result, redefined the encounter as wrong (Hingsburger, 1992a).

Second, if there is a problem with the sexual behavior, the therapist must decide the aim of therapy: Is the aim of therapy to change the individual or to change the agency? An individual who engages in public masturbation in the bushes at the park may be doing so because he or she is accorded no privacy within the agency itself. Here, the work of therapy is to change the agency's structure to accommodate healthy living strategies on the part of the person with a disability (Brown et al., 1994).

MODELING
The very nature of developmental disability means that there is often a need for some kind of professional care. The more severe the disability, the more necessary it will be to provide assistance with intimate care. This means that people with disabilities routinely have their boundaries violated in the provision of care. Individuals with disabilities become accustomed to people coming very close to them and hugging them when teaching new skills. They become accustomed to total strangers hired yesterday seeing them naked today. They become accustomed to being seen naked, being touched, lifted, wiped, washed, and dressed (Hingsburger, 1995a; Sobsey, 1994). As a result, they may have never come to understand the relationship between social relationship and social distance or to understand that certain parts of the body are more private than others. This sets them up to be perfect victims as well as to be accused of being victimizers: For example, a person who is accustomed to strangers touching them in intimate ways may not understand why the stranger in the mall is upset when being touched in precisely the same way.

PARTNER SELECTION

Many people with disabilities have learned that the only relationships that count are those with people without disabilities. In fact, the philosophy of many agencies is to actively discourage people with disabilities from socializing with others who have disabilities. The end result is that the person with a disability learns to love the kernel of normalcy inside a person without disabilities. It is not unusual to see a person with a disability try to form romantic relationships with adult women without disabilities and then receive active and loud discouragement for doing so. The individual then attempts to form relationships with teen-age women and finds that they are even less receptive than their adult peers. Finally, they approach children seeking to form relationships. In effect, this is "situational paedophilia," which is similar to the well-known phenomena of "situational homosexuality," which occurs in settings where only one gender is available for partner selection. Part of the investigation by the therapist is to determine how the individual "sees" other people with disabilities. The phrase "I don't want to date someone like that!" (where "that" refers to another person with a disability) is depressingly common.

INAPPROPRIATE COURTSHIP

Courtship skills are among the most complex social skills that people learn. Many people with disabilities have problems with social skills, and teaching social skills to people with disabilities is a well-acknowledged problem (Foxx, 1985). When a person with a disability is sexually interested in another person, they often make that sexual interest plain and concrete and communicate the desire in one of two ways: They may grab another person's genitals as a means of saying "I am interested in you sexually"; or they may expose their own genitals as a means of saying "Are you interested in me sexually?" The behavior is assaultive in both cases, but the intent of the interaction is not assault.

The problem is made even more severe given the fact that many people with disabilities lived in institutions where they developed courtship skills within the culture of the institution. One male was referred for paedophilia and exposure because he exposed himself to a child in a public washroom. Upon investigation, it was found that when living in the institution his courtship behavior was to go to the washroom, pull out his penis, and wait for a man to come in who was interested in sexual play. When he moved to the community, it was assumed that community mores and values would pop into his head on the bus ride from the facility. Once in the community, he was never taught the values of the new and predominant culture; consequently, when he was in a park and feeling aroused, he followed his courtship rituals. He went to the washroom, pulled out his penis, and waited; it was chance and not design that the first person who walked in was a child. The child ran and reported this to his mother, who called the police. The police found him still waiting in the washroom.

SEXUAL KNOWLEDGE
There are many benefits associated with sex education, chief of which is language training. A person with a disability who does not possess the language to express him- or herself sexually has to resort to other means of communication regarding abuse or assault (Hingsburger, 1994; Monat-Haller, 1987). A young woman with both a physical and developmental disability would grab staff's hands and try to make the staff touch her breasts. She would also grab at female staff's breasts and male staff's genitals. She was considered hypersexual and over-sexed according to journal notes. Once she received sex education training, she reported victimization that involved fondling and being forced to masturbate a male. Her behaviors existed as a means of communication. Therapists should seek to discover if an individual has any sexual language.

On the other hand, lack of sexual knowledge leads to increased sexual curiosity and sexually acting out. One man, arrested for assault at a bus stop, had grabbed a woman's dress and tried to pull it up. He stated that he wanted to see what women looked like "up there" and had no other means of getting that information other than by force.

LEARNING HISTORY
"Bad, bad, bad, dirty, dirty, don't touch." This phrase was the "name" that a man with a disability being assessed had for his penis. He learned

that the "thing" between his legs was bad and dirty. When given the messages that sex is wrong, your genitals are dirty, and your sexual impulses are evil, it seems logical to expect problematic behavior. Many people with disabilities have difficulty in assimilating positive information about sexuality because of this history of receiving negative and damaging information (Hingsburger 1992a; Hutchinson, 1990). This is even more true given the statistics about the relationship between abuse and disability. It is highly probable that the first sexual experience of a person with a disability is molestation or rape. Again, it is important to look at the behavioral indices of abuse, many of which, particularly those that involve sexualized behavior, are boundary violations. It is clear, then, that for many people with disabilities an abuse history is a history of boundaries being violated. Given that people with disabilities, like their peers without disabilities, learn from their environment, there is the distinct possibility that they learned abusing patterns. Also, the therapist needs to be aware of the effect of institutionalization on how people with disabilities perceive the world. Many individuals with disabilities report that when they went into the institution as children they were routinely abused by other, older people with disabilities. When they grew older, they graduated from victim to abuser. While this is horrific, it is usually presented as a cultural pattern that is accepted as a norm.

BEHAVIORAL

Some individuals with disabilities learn that they can escape demands or attract attention with sexually inappropriate behavior. These behaviors tend to be the less dramatic forms of sexually acting out: public masturbation, exposure, or rude sexual talk. While the behaviors are a concern, they are directly related to antecedent events, or they are a means of procuring some kind of specific consequence action. For example, an individual who attempts to masturbate immediately before a chore in anticipation of being given time alone in his room may successfully avoid an unwanted task. On the other hand, an individual who, when attempting to masturbate, prompts staff into offering alternative, interesting activities may be using masturbation as a means of controlling the environment rather than using it to express sexual needs.

MEDICAL

It is not necessarily an indication of a need to masturbate every time a person with a disability touches her or his groin. Some people with disabilities who have been defined as chronic masturbators have been discovered to be suffering from yeast infections, allergies, or tight underwear. It is important to ensure that the individual is physically healthy before determining that a specific behavior is sexually problematic. For example, an individual, successfully treated for paedophilia, returned to paedophilic behavior due to a developing prostate problem. He found the stimuli of children strong enough to enable him to become erect and masturbate. While the problem is paedophilic behavior, the treatment was medical in nature, along with retraining relapse prevention skills.

MEDICATION

Many people with disabilities are placed on a vast array of medications for both behavioral and physical concerns (Gabriel, 1995). It is important for the therapist to check that the medications the client is taking are not affecting his or her ability to perform sexually.

MORAL VACUUM

North America has a culturally arrogant society. The values held by North Americans are thought to be universal, and many North Americans discuss sexual values as if they are inherent in the human condition. This is patently not true. People of different cultures have vastly different sexual mores and norms that are learned through living in the culture and by being exposed to cultural materials and socializing events. People with disabilities have often not lived and participated in the larger culture, from obvious separation such as institutionalization to more subtle separation within familial homes. There has been a tendency to remove the individual from the society to which they belong. They, then, never have a natural opportunity to learn from the culture, and consequently, they may not understand (due to a lack of learning, NOT a lack of ability) social boundaries and acceptable sexual expression.

PARAPHILIA

There is a possibility that sexualized behavior can be due to deviant arousal patterns. Paraphilia presents itself in both offensive and nonoffensive forms. Arousal to deviant stimuli such as children and violence are clear concerns for the safety of the individual and members of the community. Arousal to other deviant stimuli that are involved in either fetishism or partialism are relatively typical and of much less clinical concern. People with disabilities have the right, like their peers without disabilities, to learn to express fetishistic interests in appropriate and private means. When the paraphilia is threatening to others, for example, paedophilia or biastophilia, the only way to assess this with any degree of accuracy is through the use of phallometry (Shibley-Hyde, 1990).

DEVELOPING A TREATMENT PLAN

The process of assessment is more difficult than it may seem at first glance. An individual with a disability who has sexually assaulted another person may have a deviant arousal to violence, but as is more common in the experience of the clinic, he or she may be acting out due to other more treatable reasons. A person who has sexually assaulted because of a lack of courtship skills will be easier to treat than a person who is aroused by sexual violence. Even so, despite the temptation to diminish the severity of the problem when it is determined that the behavior is due to counterfeit rather than real deviance, it is important for the therapist to ensure that everyone understands that to the victim it does not matter what the source of the behavior was: Rape is still rape. Also, while treatment is ongoing, the therapist cannot forget that the person who assaults is still at risk of reoffense until a relapse prevention program has been completed.

Once it has been determined that the individual has been engaging in sexually offensive behaviors because of past victimization, the therapist still needs to determine what kind of treatment is necessary. Having abuse as part of one's learning history often leads to sexually acting out behaviors (Everstine & Everstine, 1989; Hingsburger, 1995a; McGuire & Grant, 1991; Sobsey, 1994; Ticoll, 1992). Therapy with people who have disabilities may require one of a number of treatment plans or a combination of treatment plans in order for them to begin to express themselves in sexually healthy ways.

THE RIGHT TO COMMUNICATE—BEING HEARD

Should it be determined that the individual is using sexual behavior as a means of reporting past victimization, developing quick, effective ways for the person to talk about what has occurred is the priority. The goal here is to ensure that sexually assaulting others as a means of communication stops while the person learns new ways to say the same thing. The area of communication can be very problematic.

First, the individual may have a sexual vocabulary but not be able to use it. Learning a word for a body part is ineffective if the person finds the word as shameful as the body part and is unable to utter the word. One woman abjectly refused to use the word vagina as she felt that it was a dirty, disgusting word. She eventually agreed to use the word flower as a suitable alternative. While this may not be seen as the most age-appropriate or normative way of discussing sexual occurrences, and while it is necessary that she become desensitized to the concept of having genitals and the words associated with those genitals, it must be stated that therapy has to begin somewhere; and the best place to start might be with developing a means to communicate.

Second, the individual might have a sexual vocabulary but not be able to use it because of threats from the abuser. "Never tell" is more than a threat; it is also a command. As studies have shown, people with disabilities have learned compliance as part of their routine programming (Flynn, Reeves, Whelan, & Speak, 1985; Sobsey, 1994). It may be difficult for them to actually disclose information and answer questions. If they have used sexual behavior as a means of communication while they had the language necessary to report abuse, it may be safe to assume that the individual lacks the assertive skills necessary to use language to discuss stressful subjects and, at the same time, defy a direct command. Added to this is the probability that the person who abused the individual was in a caregiving role. If this is the case, his or her demand takes on even greater weight (Sobsey, 1994).

Third, the individual might not have a sexual vocabulary because no one ever taught one to them. In this situation, the person is going to have to learn a new language for sexual body parts. It can be stressful for a person to both have to learn a new language and to have to use that language to describe horrific acts. While the language is being taught, the therapist will need to develop more immediate ways for the person to communicate. If the individual has speech, then teaching them a new language will follow a clear pattern. If the individual does not use speech as a means of communication but uses sign language, blissymbolics, or other methods of communication, the therapist will need to be proficient in the sexual language of the alternative mode of communication (Ericson, Perlman, & Isaacs, 1994). During this process, other means of reporting can be used. Art therapy can be a very successful therapeutic approach, supplying the individual with a unique and powerful tool for communicating sexual abuse. Teaching language through art can take the focus off teaching language about sex while discussing abuse since the therapist can use art as a linguistic medium that describes both pleasurable and negative experiences (Caprio–Orsini, 1996).

In any of the above situations, the therapist needs to allow the person to tell the story until he or she feels understood. In one situation, an individual using art as the preferred medium drew the abusive situation over and over until deciding to move on to another topic. This repetitive communication can be a frustrating but necessary means for the person to ensure that you "get it."

THE RIGHT TO FEEL—APPROPRIATE EXPRESSIONS OF ANGER

If it is determined that the individual is acting out sexually and hurting others as a means of expressing anger, rage, and hurt, then the person needs to learn new ways of expressing appropriate feelings (Ludwig & Hingsburger, 1989; Hingsburger et al., 1999). The goal is to allow the abused individual to understand that while his or her feelings of anger and rage are acceptable and understandable due to past abuse there is no excuse for abusing others. Talking about the abusive situation means directly discussing emotional events. The individual may have as much difficulty talking about emotions as they do talking about abuse. People with disabilities often have learned that they are supposed to be happy and that everything is "OK." The concept of justifiable rage may be very new to a person who is accustomed to being punished or medicated for strong feelings (even appropriate ones) (Ludwig & Hingsburger, 1989). During the therapeutic process, the person should receive supportive messages, and they should be given direct and indirect messages that express the idea that what happened to him or her was wrong. The understanding of having been wronged, violated, and misused leads to anger. While this is a healing process, the individual has to have the capacity for handling the anger. It is unacceptable for a person with a disability who has never learned anger management strategies to leave a session with a therapist and immediately begin striking out at staff or others in her or his home environments.

A therapist who moves too quickly, believing that the individual with a disability has coping mechanisms, can create additional problems for the client. People with disabilities have typically learned to squash anger and deny its existence. For these individuals, opening the floodgates of emotion can be devastating. While the person is in the therapeutic relationship, the therapist needs to assess his or her capacity for handling anger. Many people without disabilities state that they are afraid of their own anger even WITH coping strategies. In this work, the therapist can offer opportunities for the person to express his or her anger through appropriate means and in a supportive environment. This kind of work needs to be done in conjunction with the home environment. Without directly discussing the content of the sessions, the staff or parents need to come to a consensus along with the individual as to what kind of strategies can be used when the person is dealing with her or his anger. Then, the therapist needs to encourage strong emotions within context of firmly developed coping skills.

THE RIGHT TO BOUNDARIES—LEARNING ABOUT SPACE

Abuse is a severe boundary violation. If it is determined that the individual has not learned appropriate boundaries or has had his or her own boundaries destroyed, then the therapeutic goal becomes the establishment of healthy boundaries. Boundaries education for people with disabilities needs to occur on two different levels: physical and social. Teaching physical boundaries involves concrete training regarding private spaces as they relate to the body and privacy as it relates to places. These concepts are simple in theory but difficult in practice as people with disabilities often live in highly public environments (Hingsburger & Harbour, 1998). Teaching that the vulva is private is acceptable only if the person lives in an environment where staff are not able to walk into a washroom or bedroom and see the individual naked. As with many goals, the therapist needs to work with both the individual and his or her support systems. Teaching the support systems to respect privacy is the first step in teaching the individual with a disability about privacy. Learning about privacy means learning an essential message: "This is my body, and no one can touch it without my permission." As a message, this both serves to build self-esteem and to prevent future abuse. It also begins to build an understanding of the individual's victimization of another. The corollary is, of course, "This is someone else's body, and YOU can't touch it without permission." For those who have sexually hurt someone else, they HAVE to understand boundaries in order to reduce the likelihood that they will offend again.

The more abstract boundary concept is the concept of social boundaries. There are many boundaries that typical members of our society understand: from boundaries of "polite topics of conversation" to "appropriate social distance when greeting." By definition, society is a network of boundaries and rules. The therapist needs to have a clear understanding about how the person perceives boundaries in order to appropriately teach this skill. If the person came too close to someone's space and scared them, spoke of sexual issues in inappropriate places, or touched someone inappropriately when greeting them, then the therapist needs to translate this abstract concept into concrete terms. An effective procedure called Video Self Monitoring (Ward et al., 1992) involves having staff make a training tape of the person engaging in the appropriate skill in the appropriate circumstance. Thus, in a counseling session, the therapist can use the video as a teaching tool so that the client can see what the therapist means. Much of our language regarding boundaries strays well into the territory of abstract concepts, and people with disabilities may not understand the nuances of the problem. Seeing him- or herself doing what is desired is not only highly reinforcing, but it gives the therapist the opportunity to develop role plays in session wherein the person can practice the skill he or she just saw him- or herself perform.

Again, it is important for the therapist to ensure that the person with the disability is having their social boundaries respected at home. It is a dangerously mixed message for a therapist to teach about social distance and social relationships when a new staff member in a group home is giving a body hug to the individual without having been introduced. The production of the video is also a sly way of teaching the client's support systems how to behave as well.

THE RIGHT TO SAY NO—ESTABLISHING SELFHOOD

If it is determined that a person has violated someone else's "No" because of a structure that teaches "No doesn't mean no," the therapeutic goal becomes teaching appropriate noncompliance skills. Teaching people about noncompliance begins with a meeting with staff or parents and establishing an appropriate way for the person to refuse and to be heard. As with situations that sometimes occur with anger management training, individuals may learn to assert themselves because of skills learned with the therapist but may be put into time-out or may receive demerit points on a program when they exercise these new behaviors. People with disabilities who are asked if they want peas and then are told that they will have to eat them even if they refuse them are learning that "No doesn't mean no." For prevention of future abuse and eventual understanding of the seriousness of abusing another, the person must know what it is to violate a very important "No!"

In a sense, through the establishment of boundaries, teaching about feelings, and teaching about the right to self-determination, the therapist is in the arena of self–esteem and selfhood (Hingsburger, 2000). Here, people with disabilities need to perceive themselves, and indeed others, as people of value. The use of reinforcement and the respect used by the therapist within the session can result in the client becoming "used" to respectful tones and respectful approaches. This may be a first for many individuals with developmental disabilities.

THE RIGHT TO TRUTH—TAKING RESPONSIBILITY

If it is determined that the individual has offended because of past victimization but that they lack an understanding of the seriousness of the abuse, then the therapeutic goal is to teach him or her the truth. What is truth? Well, in this case, the truth is that the person has sexually acted out and hurt another. It may be because of past victimization. This is no excuse. It may be because of a lack of training. This is no excuse. It may be because they misread social cues. This is no excuse. People with disabilities are in the unfortunate position of being pitied and seen as less than fully adult. This often means that they have not had to take responsibility for their own behavior in any number of areas. This must stop.

While people with developmental disabilities need to learn their rights, they also need to learn about the rights of others and the responsibilities that come along with those rights. Victim Sensitization involves learning that they violated someone else's rights. Many times, people with developmental disabilities think that what they did was wrong because staff are angry rather than because they raped a child. The person needs to be in touch with her or his own anger as a victim and use that anger to understand what he or she did to others. This is difficult work. In some circumstances, having someone come in from a rape crisis center to talk about his or her own victimization can help the client understand his or her own feelings, and then, the therapist can work from there to an understanding of what he or she did to his or her victim.

It is imperative that the therapist never get lost in this process. Yes, it is sad that people with developmental disabilities are victimized and that they live in a system that does not understand their sexual needs or protect them from victimization. Yes, this is all true, but if the therapist loses sight of the fact that the person hurt, seriously, another person, then the therapeutic goal becomes empathy, understanding, and personal healing rather than those plus learning new skills and new strategies to avoid inflicting further pain.

A WORD OF CAUTION ABOUT PROVIDING TREATMENT
The treatment plans addressed above make it clear that work with people who have developmental disabilities who have been sexually victimized and who victimize others is a combination of empathy, support, and teaching. In fact, teaching is probably the most clinical of the support provided, and its efficacy is seen in the fact that these individuals who have been treated in at the York Central Hospital's Behaviour Management Services Sexuality Clinic have never reoffended after treatment has been terminated. As such, the prognosis for treatment is excellent if the therapist does an accurate assessment as well as develops a treatment plan that correctly targets the skills and strategies that the person needs to learn. More than this, the therapist has to work in conjunction with the individual's support systems to ensure that the individual can generalize the skills learned therapeutically to the home environment.

The caution arises when realizing that the individual who has been victimized and who is victimizing others may also be clinically deviant. As such, the use of phallometric measures is recommended. Phallometry will give the therapist a good picture of what stimuli the individuals finds arousing. In most cases, the phallometric measure will show no deviance, but for those who do exhibit deviance, the therapist is faced with doing victim work, work toward arousal reduction, and developing arousal toward appropriate partners with appropriate behaviors. This subject is outside the bounds of this chapter as the focus is more on clinical deviance than past victimization (although past victimization plays a part in determining the treatment plan), but model treatment plans have been published that can give the therapist some direction.

SUMMARY

Work with people who have developmental disabilities who have been victimized and then victimize others is both rewarding and frustrating. An ethical therapist will realize that he or she has to work within systems to bring about change in these systems as well as change in the individual. In doing this, the therapist has to remember that his or her loyalty remains at any and all times with the person in therapy. Work with the agency needs to be focused, clear, and never cross the line where confidentiality will be violated. It is rewarding because one can see that one not only is working through to health, one is working with an individual who should—because of skills taught and self-esteem established—return to a state of health that is actually better than prior to the assault. Seeing a person learn to effectively assert him- or herself, draw boundaries, and express emotions is to see the birth of personhood.

References

Abramson, P. R., Parker, T., & Weisberg, S. R. (1988). Sexual expression of mentally retarded people: Educational and legal implications. *American Journal of Mental Retardation, 93*, 328-334.

Adams-Tucker, L. (1982). Proximate effects of sexual abuse in childhood: A report on 28 children. *American Journal of Psychiatry, 139*, 1252-1256.

Alexander, P. C. (1985). A systems theory conceptualization of incest. *Family Process, 24*, 79-88.

Alexander, P. C. (1992). Application of attachment theory to the study of abuse. *Journal of Consulting and Clinical Psychology, 2*, 185-195.

Allan, J. & Bertoia, J. (1992). *Written paths to healing: Education and Jungian child counselling*. Dallas, TX: Spring Publications.

Allen, D. & Affleck, G. (1984). Are we stereotyping parents? A postscript to Blacher. *Mental Retardation, 23*, 200-202.

Allen, B. & Allen, S. (1995). The process of socially constructing mental retardation: Toward value-based interaction. *Journal of the Association for Persons with Severe Handicaps. 20*, 158-160.

Alper, S. & Retish, P. (1994). Nontraditional families of children with disabilities. In S. Alper, P. Schloss, & C. Schloss (Eds.), *Families of students with disabilities: Consultation and advocacy* (pp. 123-142). Needham Heights, MA: Allyn and Bacon.

Alper, S., Schloss, P., & Schloss, C. (1994). Preface. In S. Alper, P. Schloss, & C. Schloss (Eds.), *Families of students with disabilities: Consultation and advocacy* (pp. ix-xiii). Needham Heights, MA: Allyn and Bacon.

Alvarez, A. (1992). *Live company: Psychoanalytic psychotherapy with autistic, borderline, deprived and abused children*. London: Tavistock/Routledge.

Aman, M. G. (1991). *Assessing psychopathology and behavior problems in persons with mental retardation: A review of available instruments.* Rockville, MD: U.S. Department of Health and Human Services.

Aman, M. G., Benson, B. A., Campbell, K. M., & Haas, B. A. (1999a). *Patients' rights and responsibilities: An easy-to-read guide for people taking medicine.* Columbus, OH: The Ohio State University.

Aman, M. G., Benson, B. A., Campbell, K. M., & Haas, B. A. (1999b). *Antipsychotic medicines (Neuroleptics): An easy to read guide for people who take these medicines.* Columbus, OH: The Ohio State University.

Aman, M. G., Benson, B. A., Campbell, K. M., & Haas, B. A. (1999c). *Antidepressant medicines : An easy to read guide for people who take these medicines.* Columbus, OH: The Ohio State University.

Aman, M. G., Benson, B. A., Campbell, K. M., & Griswold-Rhymer, H. M. (1999d). *Stimulant medicines: An easy to read guide for people who take these medicines.* Columbus, OH: The Ohio State University.

Aman, M. G., Benson, B. A., Campbell, K. M., & Griswold-Rhymer, H. M. (1999e). *Antimanic medicines: Medicines for people with mood problems.* Columbus, OH: The Ohio State University.

Aman, M. G., Benson, B. A., Campbell, K. M., & Griswold-Rhymer, H. M. (1999f). *Antianxiety medicines: Medicines for people with too much worry .* Columbus, OH: The Ohio State University.

Aman, M.G., Benson, B.A., Campbell, K.M., & Griswold-Rhymer, H.M. (2000). *Anticonvulsant medicines: Medicines for people with epilepsy.* Columbus, OH: The Ohio State University.

American Psychiatric Association. (1987). *Diagnostic and statistical manual of mental disorders* (3rd ed., rev.). Washington, DC: Author.

American Psychiatric Association. (1994). *Diagnostic and statistical manual of mental disorders* (4th ed.). Washington, DC: Author.

American Psychiatric Association. (1994, August 14). *Resolution on facilitated communication.* Washington, DC: Author.

Ammerman, R. T. & Baladerian, N. J. (1993). *Maltreatment of children with disabilities* (Working paper number 860). Chicago: National Committee to Prevent Child Abuse (NCPCA).

Ammerman, R. T., Van Hasselt, V. B., Hersen, M., McGonigle, J. J., & Lubetsky, M. J. (1989). Abuse and neglect in psychiatrically hospitalized multihandicapped children. *Child Abuse & Neglect, 13*, 335-343.

Anderson, F. E. (1992). *Art for all the children: Approaches to art therapy for children with disabilities.* Springfield, IL: Charles C Thomas.

Anderson, J. C., Williams, S., McGee, R., & Silva, P. A. (1987). DSM-III disorders in preadolescent children: Prevalence in a large scale sample from the population. *Archives of General Psychiatry, 44*, 69-76.

Andrew, A. K. (1989). Meeting the needs of young deaf-blind children and their parents: I. *Child Care, Health and Development, 15*, 195-206.

Anger, K. & Hawkins, J. (1999, Nov 10-13). *A brief therapy approach to working with the problems of individuals with dual diagnosis and their families.* Paper presented at the Sixteenth Annual Conference for the National Association for the Dually Diagnosed, Niagara Falls, Ontario, Canada.

Axline, V. M. (1947). *Play therapy.* New York: Churchill Livingstone.

Bagley, C. & King, K. (1990). *Child sexual abuse: The search for healing.* London: Routledge.

Baladerian, N. J. (1992). *Interviewing skills to use with abuse victims who have developmental disabilities.* Washington, DC: National Aging Resource Center on Elder Abuse.

Baladerian, N. J. (1985). *Response to: "Prosecuting cases of physical and sexual assault of the mentally retarded" issued by the California District Attorney's Association.* Culver City, CA: Author.

Baroff, G. S. (1991). *Developmental disabilities: Psychosocial aspects.* Austin, TX: Pro-ed.

Bates, R. (1992). Psychotherapy with the siblings of mentally handicapped children. In A. Waitman & S. Conboy-Hill (Eds.), *Psychotherapy and mental handicap* (pp. 81-98). London: Sage.

Baum, N. T. (1994). The phenomena of playing within the process of sandplay therapy. In N. Bouras (Ed.), *Mental health in mental retardation: Recent advances and practices* (pp. 255-272). Cambridge: Cambridge University Press.

Becvar, D. S. & Becvar, R. J. (1999). *Family Therapy: A Systemic Integration* . Needham Heights, MA: Allyn & Bacon.

Bellugi, U., Bihrle, A., Jernigan, T., Trainer, D., & Doherty, S. (1990). Neuropsychological, neurological, and neuroanatomical profiles of Williams Syndrome. *American Journal of Medical Genetics, 6*, 115-125.

Benson, B. (1995, March 8-11). *Anger management training-research and practice.* Paper presented at the International Congress II on the Dually Diagnosed, Boston, MA.

Berkson, G. (1993). *Children with handicaps: A review of behavioral research.* Hillsdale, NJ: Lawrence Erlbaum Associates.

Berliner, L. & Wheeler, J. (1987). Treating the effects of sexual abuse on children. *Journal of Interpersonal Violence, 2*, 415-434.

Best, S., Carpignano, J., Sirvis, B., & Bigge, J. (1991). Psychosocial aspects of physical disability. In J. Bigge (Ed.), *Teaching individuals with physical and multiple disabilities* (3rd ed., pp. 102-131). New York: MacMillan.

Beukelman, D.R. & Mirenda, P. (1998). *Augmentative and alternative communication: Management of severe communication disorders* (2nd Ed.). Baltimore: Paul H. Brookes.

Beutler, L. E. & Hill, C. E. (1992). Process and outcome research in the treatment of adult victims of childhood sexual abuse: Methodological issues. *Journal of Consulting and Clinical Psychology, 60*, 204-212.

Beveridge, M., Conti-Ramsden, G., & Leudar, I. (Eds.). (1989). *Language and communication in mentally handicapped people.* London: Chapman and Hall.

Bicknell, J. (1994). Psychological process: The inner world of people with mental retardation. In N. Bouras (Ed.), *Mental health in mental retardation: Recent advances and practices* (pp. 46-56). Cambridge: Cambridge University Press.

Bicknell, J. & Conboy-Hill, S. (1992). The deviancy career and people with mental handicap. In A. Waitman & S. Conboy-Hill

(Eds.), *Psychotherapy and mental handicap* (pp. 117-131). London: Sage.

Biklen, D. (1993). *Communication unbound: How facilitated communication is challenging traditional views of autism and developmental disability.* New York: Teachers College Press.

Blacher, J. (1984). Sequential stages of parent adjustment to the birth of a child with handicaps: Fact or fiction. *Mental Retardation, 22,* 55-68.

Bligh, S. & Kupperman, P. (1993). Evaluation procedure for determining the source of the communication in facilitated communication accepted in a court case. *Journal of Autism and Developmental Disorders, 23,* 553-557.

Blotzer, M. A. & Ruth, R. (Eds.) (1995). *Sometimes you just want to feel like a human being: Case studies of empowering psychotherapy with people with disabilities.* Baltimore: Paul H. Brookes

Borthwick-Duffy, S. A. (1994). Epidemiology and prevalence of psychopathology in people with mental retardation. *Journal of Consulting and Clinical Psychology, 62,* 17-27.

Bowers Andrews, A. & Veronen, L. J. (1993). Sexual assault and people with disabilities. *Journal of Social Work and Human Sexuality, 8,* 137-159.

Boyce, G. & Barnett, W. S. (1993). Siblings of persons with mental retardation: A historical perspective and recent findings. In Z. Stoneman & P. W. Berman (Eds.), *The effects of mental retardation, disability, and illness on sibling relationships: Research issues and challenges* (pp. 145-184). Baltimore: Paul H. Brookes.

Brassem, M. (1995, May 11-12). *"Would you like me to repeat the question?" Assisting hearing impaired clients.* Paper presented at Conference for Victims with Developmental Disabilities and the Law, Toronto, ON.

Briere, J. (1989). *Therapy for adults molested as children: Beyond survival.* New York: Springer.

Briere, J. (1992). *Child abuse trauma: Theory and treatment of the lasting effects.* Newbury Park, CA: Sage.

Briere, J., Evans, D., Runtz, M., & Wall, T. (1988). Symptomology in men who were molested as children: A comparison study. *American Journal of Orthopsychiatry, 58,* 457-461.

Brown, D. T. (1994). Group counseling and psychotherapy. In D. C. Strohmer & H. T. Prout (Eds.), *Counseling and psychotherapy with persons with mental retardation and borderline intelligence* (pp. 143-194). Brandon, VT: Clinical Psychology Publishing Co., Inc.

Brown, G. T., Carney, P., Cortis, J. M., Metz, L. L., & Petrie, A. M. (1994). *Human sexuality handbook: Guiding people toward positive expressions of sexuality*. Springfield, MA: The Association for Community Living.

Brown, H. (1992). Working with staff around sexuality and power. In A. Waitman & S. Conboy-Hill (Eds.), *Psychotherapy and mental handicap* (pp. 185-201). London: Sage.

Browne, A. & Finkelhor, D. (1986). Impact of child sexual abuse: A review of the research. *Psychological Bulletin, 99*, 66-77.

Brush, P. (1999, August 13). Serial rape suspect kept diary, police say: Journals say he targeted up to 20 retarded women. Wirestory: www.APBNews.com .

Burke, L. & Bedard, C. (1994). Self-injury considered in association with sexual victimization in individuals with a developmental handicap. *The Canadian Journal of Human Sexuality, 3*, 253-262.

Burke, L. & Bedard, C. (1995). A preliminary study of the association between self-injury and sexual abuse in persons with developmental handicaps. *Sexuality and Disability, 13*, 327-330.

Burleigh, M. (1994). *Death and deliverance: 'Euthanasia' in Germany 1900-1945*. Cambridge University Press.

Cabay, M. (1994). A controlled valuation of facilitated communication with four autistic children. *Journal of Autism and Developmental Disorders, 24*, 517-527.

Caprio-Orsini, C. (1996). *A thousand words: Healing through art for people with developmental disabilities*. Eastman, QUE: Diverse City Press.

Carmody, M. (1990). *Sexual assault of people with intellectual disability: Final report..* Sydney, Australia: South Wales Women's Co-ordination Unit.

Charlot, L. R. (1998). Developmental effects on mental health disorders in persons with developmental disabilities. *Mental Health Aspects of Developmental Disabilities, 1*, 29-38.

Cobb, H. C. & Gunn, W. (1994). Family interventions. In D. C. Strohmer & H. T. Prout (Eds.), *Counseling and psychotherapy with persons with mental retardation and borderline intelligence* (pp. 235-256). Brandon, VT: Clinical Psychology Publishing Co., Inc.

Cole, S. (1986). Facing the challenges of sexual abuse in persons with disabilities. *Sexuality and Disability, 7,* 71-87.

Conte, J. R. & Schuerman, J. R. (1987). Factors associated with an increased impact of child sexual abuse. *Child Abuse and Neglect, 11,* 201-211.

Corcoran, J. (1982). Affect abilities training: A competency based method for counseling persons with mental retardation. *Journal of Career Education, 8,* 301-311.

Courtois, C. (1989). *Healing the incest wound.* New York: Norton.

Cox-Lindenbaum, D. (1992, Dec. 2-5). *Caring for the caregiver: Supporting the therapist in abuse focused treatment.* Paper presented at the Ninth Annual Conference for the National Association for the Dually Diagnosed, Toronto, ON.

Cox-Lindenbaum, D. & Lindenbaum, L. (1994, Nov. 30- Dec. 3). *Group therapy-theoretical and practical application in the treatment of persons with dual diagnosis.* Paper presented at the Eleventh Annual Conference for the National Association for the Dually Diagnosed, Salt Lake City, Utah.

Crnic, K., Friedrich, W., & Greenberg, M. (1983). Adaptation of families with mentally retarded children: A model of stress, coping and family ecology. *American Journal of Mental Deficiency, 88,* 125-138.

Crnic, K. & Lyons, J. (1993). Siblings of children with dual diagnosis. In Z. Stoneman & P. W. Berman (Eds.), *The effects of mental retardation, disability, and illness on sibling relationships: Research issues and challenges* (pp. 253-271). Baltimore: Paul H. Brookes.

Crosse, S. B., Kaye, E., & Ratnofsky, A. C. (1993). *A report on the maltreatment of children of disabilities* (Contract No. 105-89-11639). Chicago: Westat Inc. National Centre on Child Abuse and Neglect.

Crossley, R. (1997). *Speechless: Facilitating communication for people without voices.* New York: Dutton Books.

Cruz, V. K., Price-Williams, D., & Andron, L. (1988). Developmentally disabled women who were molested as children. *Social Casework: The Journal of Contemporary Social Work, 69,* 411-419.

Cushna, B., Szymanski, L. S., & Tanguay, P. E. (1980). Professional roles and unmet manpower needs. In L. S. Szymanski & P. E. Tanguay (Eds.), *Emotional disorders of mentally retarded persons: Assessment, treatment and consultation* (pp. 3-17). Baltimore: University Park Press.

Damon, L., Todd., J., & MacFarlane, K. (1987). Treatment issues with sexually abused young children. *Child Welfare League of America, 66,* 125-137.

Demetral, G. (1994). A training methodology for establishing reliable self monitoring with the sex offender who is developmentally disabled. *Habilitative Mental Healthcare Newsletter, 13,* 57-60.

Dempsey, I. (1996). Facilitating empowerment in families with a member with a disability. *Developmental Disabilities Bulletin, 24*(2), 1-19.

Dimock, P. T. (1989). Adult males sexually abused as children. *Journal of Interpersonal Violence, 3,* 203-221.

Ditchfield, H. (1992). The birth of a child with a mental handicap: Coping with loss. In A. Waitman & S. Conboy-Hill (Eds.), *Psychotherapy and mental handicap* (pp. 9-23). London: Sage.

Downing, J. (1999). Teaching communication skills to students with severe disabilities. Baltimore: Paul H. Brookes.

Doucette, J. (1986). *Violent acts against disabled women.* Toronto: DAWN (DisAbled Women's Network) Canada.

Drew, C. J., Logan, D. R., & Hardman, M. L. (1992). *Mental retardation: A life cycle approach* (5th ed.). New York: Macmillan Publishing.

Duffy, T. (1992, Dec. 2-5). *Practical group counselling issues with people who are dually diagnosed.* Paper presented at the Ninth Annual Conference for the National Association for the Dually Diagnosed, Toronto, ON.

Dunne, T. P. & Power, A. (1990). Sexual abuse and mental handicap: Preliminary findings of a community-based study. *Mental Handicap Research, 3,* 111-125.

Eaton, L. & Menolascino, F. J. (1982). Psychiatric disorders in the mentally retarded: Types, problems and challenges. *American Journal of Psychiatry, 139*, 1297-1303.

Epstein, M. H., Cullinan, D., & Polloway, E. A. (1986). Patterns of maladjustment among mentally retarded children and youth. *American Journal of Mental Deficiency, 91*, 127-134.

Erdem, T. (1994, September 10-13). *Play therapy for the treatment of sexually abused children.* Paper presented at 10th International Congress on Child Abuse and Neglect. Kuala Lumpur, Malaysia.

Ericson, K., Perlman, N., & Isaac, B. (1994). Witness competency, communication issues and people with developmental disabilities. *Developmental Disabilities Bulletin, 22*, 101-109.

Eth, S. & Pynoos, R. (1985). *Post-Traumatic Stress Disorder in children.* Los Angeles, CA: American Psychiatric Association Press.

Everson, M., Hunter, W., Runyon, D., Edelsohn, G., & Coulter, M. (1989). Maternal support following disclosure of incest. *American Journal of Orthopsychiatry, 59*, 197-207.

Everstine, D. S. & Everstine, L. (1989). *Sexual trauma in children and adolescents: Dynamics and treatment.* New York: Brunner/ Mazel.

Fahs, J. (1997). *Habilitative Neuropsychiatry: Psychopharmacology (1985-1996) A Reference Guide.* Kingston, NY: The National Association for the Dually Diagnosed.

Faller, K. (1993). *Child sexual abuse: Intervention and treatment issues. The user manual series.* Chicago: U.S. Department of Health and Human Services, National Center on Child Abuse and Neglect.

Fegan, L., Rauch, A., & McCarthy, W. (1993). *Sexuality and people with intellectual disability.* Baltimore: Paul H. Brookes.

Fernald, C. D. (1995). When in London...: Differences in disability language preferences among English-speaking countries. *Mental Retardation. 33*, 99-103.

Finkelhor, D. (1988). The trauma of child sexual abuse: Two models. In G. E. Wyatt & G. J. Powell (Eds.), *Lasting effects of child sexual abuse* (pp. 61-82). Beverly Hills: Sage.

Finkelhor, D. & Baron, L. (1986). High risk children. In D. Finkelhor, S. Araji, L. Baron, A. Browne, S. Doyle Peters, & G. E. Wyatt (Eds.), *A source book on child sexual abuse* (pp. 60-89). London: Sage.

Finkelhor, D. & Browne, A. (1985). The traumatic impact of child sexual abuse: A conceptualization. *American Journal of Orthopsychiatry, 55,* 530-541.

Fletcher, R. J. & Benson, B. (1994, Nov. 30- Dec. 3) *Supportive psychotherapy for persons with mental retardation.* Paper presented at the Eleventh Annual Conference for the National Association for the Dually Diagnosed, Salt Lake City, Utah.

Flynn, M. C., Reeves, D., Whelan E., & Speak, B. (1985). The development of a measure for determining the mentally handicapped adult's tolerance of rules and recognition of rights. *Journal of Practical Approaches to Developmental Handicap, 9,* 18-24.

Foxx, R. M. (1985). Social skills training: The current status of the field. *Australia and New Zealand Journal of Developmental Disabilities, 11*(4), 9-15.

Fresco, F., Philbin, L., & Peters, K. (1992). The design and evaluation of a sexual assault support group for women with mild developmental disabilities. *Canadian Journal of Human Sexuality, 1*(4), 5-13.

Freud, A. (1929). On the theory of analysis of children. *International Journal of Psychoanalysis, 10,* 29-38.

Freud, A. (1945). Indications for child analysis. In A. Freud (Ed.), *The psychoanalytic treatment of children* (pp. 77-111). New York: Shocken.

Freud, A. (1977). Assessment of childhood disturbances. In R. Eissler, A. Freud, & A. J. Solnit (Eds.), *Psychoanalytic assessment: The diagnostic profile. An anthology of the psychoanalytic study of the child* (pp. 1-10). London: Yale University Press.

Freud, S. (1920). *Beyond the pleasure principle* (Standard Edition, Vol. 18). London: Hogarth.

Friedrich, W. N. (1990). *Psychotherapy of sexually abused children and their families.* New York: Norton.

Furey, E. M. (1994). Sexual abuse of adults with mental retardation: Who and where. *Mental Retardation, 32,* 173-180.

Gabriel, S. (1995). *The psychiatric tower of babble.* Eastman, QUE: Diverse City Press.

Gadow, K. D. & Poling, A. G. (1988). *Pharmacotherapy and mental retardation.* Boston, MA: College-Hill.

Gapen, W. R. & Knoll, F. A. (1992, Dec. 2-5). *Engaging the dysfunctional family of the dually diagnosed client.* Paper presented at the Ninth Annual Conference for the National Association for the Dually Diagnosed, Toronto, ON.

Garbarino, J., Brookhouser, P. E., & Authier, K. J. (Eds.). (1987). *Special children-special risks: The maltreatment of children with disabilities.* New York: Aldine de Gruyter.

Garmezy, N. (1983). Stressors of childhood. In N. Garmezy & M. Rutter (Eds.), *Stress, coping, and development in children* (pp. 43-84). New York: McGraw-Hill.

Gibbs, B. (1993). Providing support to sisters and brothers of children with disabilities. In G. Singer & L. Powers (Eds.), *Families, disability and empowerment: Active coping skills and strategies for family interventions* (pp. 343-363). Baltimore: Paul H. Brookes.

Gil, E. (1988). *Treatment of adult survivors of childhood abuse.* Walnut Creek, CA: Launch Press.

Gil, E. (1991). *The healing power of play: Working with abused children.* New York: Guilford Press.

Glasgow, D. V. (1993). Factors associated with learning disabilities demanding special care during sexual abuse investigations and interviews. *NAPSAC Bulletin, 4,* 3-7.

Glendinning, C. (1983). *Unshared care: Parents and their disabled children.* London: Routledge & Kegan Paul.

Glidden, L., Kiphart, M., Willoughby, J., & Bush, B. (1993). Family functioning when rearing children with developmental disabilities. In A. Turnbull, J. Patterson, S. Behr, D. Murphy, J. Marquis, & M. Blue-Banning (Eds.), *Cognitive coping, families, & disability* (pp. 183-194). Baltimore, MD: Paul H. Brookes Co., Inc.

Godschalx, S. M. (1983). Mark: Psychotherapy with a developmentally disabled adult. *Image: The Journal of Nursing Scholarship, 15,* 12-16.

Goldenberg, I. (1985). Family therapy with the dual disability client. In M. Sigman (Ed.), *Children with emotional disorders* and developmental disabilities: Assessment and treatment (pp. 315-324). Orlando, FL: Grune & Stratton, Inc.

Gorman-Smith, D. & Matson, J. L. (1992). Sexual abuse and persons with mental retardation. In W. O'Donohue & J. H. Geer (Eds.), The sexual abuse of children: Theory and research (Vol. 1., pp. 285-306). Hillsdale, NJ: Lawrence Erlbaum Associates.

Greenspan, S. (1981). The clinical interview of the child. Washington, DC: American Psychiatric Press.

Griffiths, D. (1992, Dec. 2-5). Vulnerability: What makes persons with developmental disabilities more vulnerable to abuse. Paper presented at the Ninth Annual Conference for the National Association for the Dually Diagnosed, Toronto, ON.

Griffiths, D. M., Quinsey, V. L., & Hingsburger, D. (1989). Changing inappropriate sexual behavior: A community-based approach for persons with developmental disabilities. Baltimore: Paul H. Brookes.

Grossman, H. J. (Ed.). (1983). Classification in mental retardation (3rd rev.). Washington, DC: American Association on Mental Deficiency.

Haaven, J., Little, R., & Petre-Miller, D. (1990). Treating intellectually disabled sex offenders: A model residential program. Orwell, VT: The Safer Society Press.

Hallahan, D. P. & Kauffman, J. M. (1991). Exceptional children: Introduction to special education (5th ed.). Englewood Cliffs, NJ: Prentice Hall.

Hastings, R. P. (1994). On "good" terms: Labeling people with mental retardation. Mental Retardation. 32, 363-365.

Heinrichs, P. (1992a, Feb. 16). State "tortured" family. The Sunday Age, pp. 8-9.

Heinrichs, P. (1992b, Feb. 16). "Tortured" family may call for probe on facilitated communication. The Sunday Age, pp. 8-9.

Hellendoorn, J. (1994). Imaginative play training for severely retarded children. In J. Hellendoorn, R. van der Kooij, & B. Sutton Smith (Eds.), Play and intervention (pp. 113-123). Albany, NY: State University of New York Press.

Hellendoorn, J. & Hoekman, J. (1992). Imaginative play in children with mental retardation. Mental Retardation, 30, 255-263.

Herman, J. (1992). *Trauma and recovery.* New York: Basic Books.

Herman, J., Russell, D., & Trocki, K. (1986). Long-term effects of incestuous abuse in childhood. *American Journal of Psychiatry, 143,* 1293-1296.

Highlen, P. S. & Hill, C. E. (1984). Factors affecting client change in individual counseling: Current status and theoretical speculations. In S. D. Brown & R.W. Lent (Eds.), *Handbook of counseling psychology* (pp. 334-398). New York: Wiley & Sons.

Hindle, R. (1994). Therapeutic work with children with learning disabilities who have been sexually abused. *NAPSAC Bulletin, 7,* 7-10.

Hingsburger, D. (1987). Sex counseling with the developmentally handicapped: The assessment and management of seven critical problems. *Psychiatric Aspects of Mental Retardation Reviews, 6,* 41-46.

Hingsburger, D. (1990a). *I contact: Sexuality and people with developmental disabilities.* Mountville, PA: VIDA Publishing.

Hingsburger, D. (1990b). *I to I: Self concept with people with developmental disabilities.* Mountville, PA: VIDA Publishing.

Hingsburger, D. (1992a). Erotophobic behaviour in people with developmental disabilities. *The Habilitative Mental Healthcare Newsletter, 11,* 31-34.

Hingsburger, D. (1992b). Cautions and considerations for providing sex education for people with developmental disabilities who live in group homes. *Journal on Developmental Disabilities, 1,* 42-47.

Hingsburger, D. (1993). *I openers: Parents ask questions about sexuality and children with developmental disabilities.* Vancouver, BC: Family Support Institute.

Hingsburger, D. (1994). The ring of safety: Teaching people with disabilities to be their own first line of defense. *Developmental Disabilities Bulletin, 22,* 72-79.

Hingsburger, D. (1995a). *Just say know: Understanding and reducing the risk of sexual victimization of people with developmental disabilities.* Eastman, PQ: Diverse City Press.

Hingsburger, D. (1995b). *Hand made love: A guide for teaching about male masturbation through understanding and video.* Eastman, PQ: Diverse City Press.

Hingsburger, D. & Griffiths, D. (1986). Dealing with sexuality in a community residential service. *Psychiatric Aspects of Mental Retardation Reviews, 5,* 63-67.

Hingsburger, D., Griffiths, D., & Quinsey, V. (1991). Detecting counterfeit deviance. *The Habilitative Mental Healthcare Newsletter, 10*(9), 1-4.

Hingsburger, D., Hillis-Ormiston, T., Naylor, D., Nethercott, A., & Tough, S. (1994). Community access for sex offenders with developmental disabilities: A process for dealing with trust, risk and responsibility. *Habilitative Mental Healthcare Newsletter, 13,* 98-100.

Hingsburger, D. & Haar, S. (1999) Finger Tips: Teaching about female masturbation through understanding and video, Eastman, PQ: Diverse City Press.

Hingsburger, D., Chaplin, T., Hirstwood, K, Tough, S. Nethercott, A., & Spence, D. (1999). Intervening with sexually problematic behavior in community environments In J. R. Scotti and L. H. Meyer. *Behavioral intervention: Principles, models and practices* (pp. 213-236). Baltimore: Paul H. Brookes Publishing

Hingsburger, D. & Harbour, M. (1998). *The Ethics of Touch: Establishing healthy boundaries in service to people with developmental disabilities.* Eastman, PQ: Diverse City Press.

Hingsburger, D. (2000). *Power Tools: Thoughts about power and control in service to people with developmental disabilities.* Eastman, PQ: Diverse City Press.

Hollins, S. (1995, March 8-11). *Family therapy.* Paper presented at the International Congress II on the Dually Diagnosed, Boston, MA.

Hollins, S. & Sinason, V. (1992). *Jenny speaks out.* London: The Sovereign Series, St. George's Mental Health Library.

Hollins, S. & Sinason, V. (1993). *Bob tells all.* London: The Sovereign Series, St. George's Mental Health Library.

Hollins, S., Sinason, V., & Thompson, S. (1994). Individual, group and family psychotherapy. In N. Bouras (Ed.), *Mental health in mental retardation: Recent advances and practices* (pp. 233-243). Cambridge: Cambridge University Press.

Horvath, A. O. & Greenberg, L. S. (1989). Development and validation of the Working Alliance Inventory. *Journal of Counseling Psychology, 36,* 223-233.

Horvath, A. O. & Symonds, B. D. (1991). Relation between working alliance and outcome in psychotherapy: A meta-analysis. *Journal of Counseling Psychology, 38,* 139-149.

Huber, C. H. (1979). Parents of the handicapped child: Facilitating acceptance through group counseling. *Personnel and Guidance Journal, 57,* 267-269.

Hurley, A. D. (1989). Individual psychotherapy with mentally retarded individuals: A review and call for research. *Research in Developmental Disabilities, 10,* 261-275.

Hurley, A. D. (1995, March 8-11). *Psychiatric assessment of psychological/psychiatric disorders in persons with developmental disabilities.* Paper presented at the International Congress II on the Dually Diagnosed, Boston, MA.

Hurley, A. D. & Hurley, F. J. (1987). Psychotherapy and counseling II: Establishing a therapeutic relationship. *Psychiatric Aspects of Mental Retardation Reviews, 4,* 15-20.

Hurley, A. D. & Sovner, R. (1982). Use of the Rorschach techniques in mentally retarded persons. *Psychiatric Aspects of Mental Retardation Newsletter, 1,* 5-7.

Hurley, A. D. & Sovner, R. (1985). The use of the TAT in mentally retarded persons. *Psychiatric Aspects of Mental Retardation Reviews, 4,* 9-12.

Hutchinson, M. (1990). *The anatomy of sex and power: An investigation of mind-body politics.* New York: William Morrow & Co.

Hyman, B. (1993, March 10-13). *Group therapy: A treatment model for child sexual abuse survivors with disabilities.* Paper presented at the Ninth National Symposium on Child Sexual Abuse, Huntsville, AL.

Jacobson, J. W. & Mulick, J. A. (Eds.). *Manual of diagnosis and professional practice in mental retardation.* Washington, DC: American Psychiatric Association.

James, B. (1989). *Treating traumatized children: New insights and creative interventions.* Lexington, MA: Lexington.

Jennings, S. (1999). *Introduction to developmental play therapy: Playing and health.* London: Jessica Kingsley Publishers Ltd.

Jung, C. G. (1964). *Man and his symbols.* Garden City, NY: Doubleday.

Jura, M. & Sigman, M. (1985). Evaluation of emotional disorders using projective techniques with mentally retarded children. In M. Sigman (Ed.), *Children with emotional disorders and developmental disabilities: Assessment and treatment* (pp. 229-248). Orlando, FL: Grune & Stratton, Inc.

Kaduson, H. G., Cangelosi, D., & Schaefer, C.E. (Eds.) (1997). *The playing cure: Individualized play therapy for specific childhood problems.* Northvale, NJ: Jason Aronson,.

Kalff, D. M. (1980). *Sandplay: A psychotherapeutic approach to the psyche.* California: Sigo Press.

Kang, L. & Hingsburger, D. (1990). *Counselling through an interpreter: A therapeutic case example.* Unpublished Manuscript.

Kempton, W. (1993). *Socialization and sexuality: A comprehensive training guide for professionals helping people with disabilities that hinder learning.* Haverford, PA: Kempton.

Kempton, W. & Gochros, J. S. (1968). The developmentally disabled. In H. L. Gochros, J. S. Cochros, & J. Fischer (Eds.), *Helping the sexually oppressed* (pp. 224-237). Englewood Cliffs, NJ: Prentice-Hall.

Kendall-Tackett, K. A., Williams, L. M., & Finkelhor, D. (1993). Impact of sexual abuse on children: A review and synthesis of recent empirical studies. *Psychological Bulletin, 113,* 164-180.

Kernan, K. T. & Sabsay, S. (1989). Communication in social interactions: Aspects of an ethnography of communication of mildly mentally handicapped adults. In M. Beveridge, G. Conti-Ramsden, & I. Leudar (Eds.), *Language and communication in mentally handicapped people* (pp. 229-253). London: Chapman and Hall.

Khemka, I. & Hickson, L. (2000). Decision-making by adults with mental retardation in simulated situations of abuse. *Mental Retardation, 38,* 15-26.

Kilgore, L. C. (1988). Effect of early childhood sexual abuse on self and ego development. *Social Casework, 69,* 224-230.

Kitchur, M. & Bell, R. (1989). Group psychotherapy with preadolescent sexual abuse victims: Literature review and description of an inner-city group. *International Journal of Group Psychotherapy, 39*, 285-310.

Klein, M. (1927). The psychological principles of infant analysis. *International Journal of Psychoanalysis, 8*, 25-37.

Knell, S. M. (1993). To show and not tell: Cognitive Behavioral play therapy. In T. Koffman & C. Schaeffer (Eds.), *Play therapy in action: A casebook for practitioners* (pp. 169-207). New Jersey: Jason Aronson.

Knopp, F. H. & Benson, A. R. (1996). *A primer on the complexities of traumatic memory of childhood sexual abuse: A psychobiological approach*. Brandon, VT: The Safer Society Press.

Kolko, D. (1987). Treatment of child sexual abuse: Programs, progress and prospects. *Journal of Family Violence, 2*, 303-318.

Koller, H., Richardson, S. A., Katz, M., & McLaren, J. (1982). Behavior disturbance in childhood and the early adult years in populations who were and were not mentally retarded. *Journal of Preventive Psychiatry, 1*, 453-468.

Landreth, G. L. (Ed.). (1982). *Play therapy: Dynamics of the process of counseling with children*. Springfield, IL: Charles C Thomas.

Landreth, G. L. (1991). *Play therapy: The art of the relationship*. Muncie, Indiana: Accelerated Development Inc.

Lang, R. A. & Frenzel, R. R. (1988). How sex offenders lure children. *Annals of Sex Research, 1*, 303-317.

Laterza, P. (1979). An eclectic approach to group work with the mentally retarded. *Social Work with Groups, 2*, 235-245.

Lebo, D. (1982). The development of play as a form of therapy: From Rousseau to Rogers. In G. L. Landreth (Ed.), *Play therapy: Dynamics of the process of counseling with children*. (pp. 65 -73). Springfield, IL: Charles C Thomas.

Levitan, G. W. & Reiss, S. (1983). Generality of diagnostic overshadowing across disciplines. *Applied Research in Mental Retardation, 4*, 59-69.

Levy, D. (1939). Release therapy. *American Journal of Orthopsychiatry, 9*, 713-736.

Li, A. K. F. (1985). Toward more elaborate pretend play. *Mental Retardation, 23,* 131-136.

Lian, M.G. & Aloia, G. (1994). Parental responses, roles, and responsibilities. In S. Alper, P. Schloss, & C. Schloss (Eds.), *Families of students with disabilities: Consultation and advocacy* (pp. 51-93). Needham Heights, MA: Allyn and Bacon.

Lillie, T. (1993). A harder thing than triumph: Roles of fathers of children with disabilities. *Mental Retardation, 31,* 438-443.

Lipovsky, J. (1991). Disclosure of father-child sexual abuse: Dilemmas for families and therapists. *Contemporary Family Therapy, 13,* 85-101.

Lowenfeld, M. (1979). *The world technique.* London: George Allen & Unwin.

Love, B. (1992). *Encyclopedia of unusual sex practices.* Fort Lee: Barricade Books.

Lowry, M. A. (1997). Unmasking mood disorders: Recognising and measuring symptomatic behaviours. *The Habilitative Mental Healthcare Newsletter, 16,* 1-6.

Lowry, M. A. (1998). Assessment and treatment of mood disorders in persons with developmental disabilities. *Journal of Developmental and Physical Disabilities, 10,* 387-406.

Luborsky, L., Crits-Christoph, P., Mintz, J., & Auerbach, A. (1988). *Who will benefit from psychotherapy? Predicting therapeutic outcome.* New York: Basic Books.

Luckasson, R., Coulter, D. L., Polloway, E. A., Reiss, S., Schalock, R. L., Snell, M. E., Spitalnik, D. M., & Stark, J. A. (1992). *Mental retardation: Definition, classification, and systems of supports.* Washington, DC: American Association of Mental Retardation.

Ludwig, S. & Hingsburger, D. (1989). Preparation for counseling and psychotherapy: Teaching about feelings. *Psychiatric Aspects of Mental Retardation Reviews, 8,* 1-2.

Ludwig, S. & Hingsburger, D. (1993). *Being sexual: An illustrated series on sexuality and relationships.* East York, ON: SIECCAN.

Lusk, R. & Waterman, J. (1986). Effects of sexual abuse on children. In K. Macfarlane, J. Waterman, S. Conerly, L. Damon, M.

Durfee, & S. Long (Eds.), *Sexual abuse of young children* (pp. 101-118). New York: Guilford.

MacLean, W. E. (1993). Overview. In J. L. Matson & R. P. Barrett (Eds.), *Psychopathology in the mentally retarded* (2nd ed., pp. 1-13). Boston: Allyn and Bacon.

Mansell, S. & Sobsey, D. (1993). Therapeutic issues regarding people with developmental disabilities. *Sexological Review, 1,* 139-159.

Mansell, S., Sobsey, D., & Calder, P. (1992). Sexual abuse treatment for persons with developmental disability. *Professional Psychology: Research and Practice, 23,* 404-409.

Mansell, S., Sobsey, D., & Moskal, R. (1998). Clinical findings among sexually abused children with and without developmental disabilities. *Mental Retardation, 36,* 12-22.

Martorana, G. R. (1985). Schizophreniform disorder in a mentally retarded adolescent boy following sexual victimization. *American Journal of Psychiatry, 142,* 784.

Matson, J. L. & Barrett, R. P. (Eds.). (1982). *Psychopathology in the mentally retarded.* New York: Grune & Stratton.

Mayer, M. A. & Poindexter, A. (1999, November 10-13th). *Assessment and management of anxiety and stress in persons who have developmental disabilities.* Paper presented at the Sixteenth Annual Conference for the National Association for the Dually Diagnosed, Niagara Falls, Ontario, Canada.

McBrien, J. & Candy, S. (1998). Working with organizations, or :"Why won't they follow my advice?" In E. Emerson, C. Hatton, J. Bromley, & A. Caine (Eds.), *Clinical Psychology and people with intellectual disabilities.* West Sussex, England: John Wiley & Sons.

McCabe, M. P. & Cummins, R. A. (1993). *Sexual abuse among people with intellectual disabilities: Fact or fiction?* Unpublished Manuscript, Deakin University.

McCartney, J. R. (1992). *Abuse in public residential facilities for persons with mental retardation.* Tuscaloosa, AL: The Association for Retarded Citizens of the United States and the Alabama Department of Mental Health.

McConkey, R. (1985). Changing beliefs about play and handicapped children. *Early Child Development and Care, 19,* 79-94.

McDonald, L., Kysela, G., Drummond, J., Alexander, J., Enns, R., & Chambers, J. (1999). Individual family planning using the Family Adaptation Model. *Developmental Disabilities Bulletin, 27,* 16-29.

McDonough, H. & Love, A. J. (1987). The challenge of sexual abuse: Protection and therapy in a child welfare setting. *Child Welfare League of America, 66,* 225-235.

McEnroe, P. (1999, February 7). Minnesota cases point to possible serial killer: Investigators say suspect preyed on women with mental retardation. *Minneapolis Star Tribune,* p. 1A.

McGuire, T. L. & Grant, F. E. (1991). *Understanding child sexual abuse.* Toronto: Butterworths.

McMahon, L. (1992). *The handbook of play therapy.* New York: Routledge.

Melberg Schwier, K. & Hingsburger, D. (2000). *Sexuality: Your sons and daughters with intellectual disabilities.* Baltimore: Paul H. Brookes.

Menolascino, F. J. (1989). Overview: Promising practices in caring for the mentally retarded-mentally ill. In R. J. Fletcher & F. J. Menolascino (Eds.), *Mental retardation and mental illness: Assessment, treatment, and service for the dually diagnosed* (pp. 3-14). Lexington, MA: Lexington.

Menolascino, F. J., Levitas, A., & Greiner, C. (1986). The nature and types of mental illness in the mentally retarded. *Psychopharmacological Bulletin, 22,* 1060-1071.

Millar, C. L. & Palace, L. M. (1995, May 11-12). *Developmental effects of abuse on cognition and language.* Paper presented at Conference for Victims with Developmental Disabilities and the Law , Toronto, ON.

Monat-Haller, R. K. (1987). Speech-language pathologists as counselors and sexuality educators. *Asha, 29,* 35-36.

Monat-Haller, R. K. (1992). *Understanding and expressing sexuality: Responsible choices for individuals with developmental disabilities.* Baltimore: Paul H. Brookes.

Money, J. (1986). *Lovemaps: Clinical concepts of sexual/ erotic health and pathology, paraphilia, and gender transposition in childhood, adolescence, and maturity.* New York: Irvington.

Money, J., Wainwright, G., & Hingsburger, D. (1991). *Breathless orgasm: A lovemap biography of asphixophila.* Buffalo: Prometheus Books.

Monfils, M. (1985). Theme-centered group work with the mentally retarded. *Social Casework: The Journal of Contemporary Social Work, 66,* 177-184.

Monfils, M. (1989). Group psychotherapy. In R. J. Fletcher & F. J. Menolascino (Eds.), *Mental retardation and mental illness: Assessment, treatment, and service for the dually diagnosed* (pp. 111-126). Lexington, MA: Lexington.

Monfils, M. & Menolascino, F. J. (1984). Modified individual and group treatment approaches for the mentally retarded-mentally ill. In F. J. Menolascino & J. A. Stark (Eds.), *Handbook of mental illness in the mentally retarded* (pp. 155-169). New York: Plenum Press.

Moores, D. F. (1987). *Educating the deaf: Psychology, principles, and practices* (3rd ed.). Boston, MA: Houghton Mifflin.

Morris, S. (1993). Healing for men. *NAPSAC Bulletin, 4,* 11-13.

Moskal, R. (1995). *The sexual abuse information record(SAIR): Its rationale and inception.* Unpublished Doctoral Dissertation, University of Alberta, Edmonton, Alberta.

Moustakas, C. (1959). *Psychotherapy with children: The living relationship.* New York: Harper Brothers.

Muccigrosso, L. (1991). Sexual abuse prevention strategies and programs for persons with developmental disabilities. *Sexuality and Disability, 9,* 261-271.

Mulick, J. A. & Jacobson, J. W. (1996). Introduction. In J.W. Jacobson & J.A. Mulick (Eds.), *Manual of diagnosis and professional practice in mental retardation.* (pp. 1-8). Washington, DC: American Psychiatric Association.

Mundy, P. C., Seibert, J. M., & Hogan, A. E. (1985). Communication skills in mentally retarded children. In M. Sigman (Ed.), *Children with emotional disorders and developmental disabilities: Assessment and treatment* (pp. 45-70). Orlando, FL: Grune & Stratton.

Murdock, J. & Van Ornum, W. (1989). Evaluating the dually diagnosed client. In R. J. Fletcher & F. J. Menolascino (Eds.), *Men-*

tal retardation and mental illness: Assessment, treatment, and service for the dually diagnosed (pp. 15-34). Lexington, MA: Lexington.

Murphy, G., Carr, J., & Callias, M. (1986). Increasing simple toy play in profoundly mentally handicapped children: II. Designing special toys. *Journal of Autism and Developmental Disorders, 16,* 45-58.

Murray, J. & McDonald, L. (1996). Father involvement in early intervention programs: Effectiveness, obstacles, and considerations. *Developmental Disabilities Bulletin, 24,* 46-57.

Musselwhite, C. R. & St. Louis, K. W. (1988). *Communication programming for persons with severe handicaps* (2nd ed.). Boston: Little Brown.

Myers, B. A. (1999). Psychiatric disorders mimicking psychotic disorders. *Mental Health Aspects of Developmental Disabilities, 2,* 113-121.

Nasjleti, M. (1980). Suffering in silence: The male incest victim. *Child Welfare, LIX*(5), 269-281.

Neal, S. & Michalakes, S. (1992, Dec. 2-5). *Developing self-esteem and assertiveness skills in special needs populations.* Paper presented at the Ninth Annual Conference for the National Association for the Dually Diagnosed, Toronto, ON.

Nixon, C. D. (1993). Reducing self-blame and guilt in parents of children with severe disabilities. In G. Singer & L. Powers (Eds.), *Families, disability and empowerment: Active coping skills and strategies for family interventions* (pp. 175-201). Baltimore: Paul H. Brookes.

O'Connor, K. J. & Braverman, L. M. (1997). *Play therapy theory and practice: A comparative presentation.* New York: John Wiley & Sons.

Olsen, S. (1999). Support, communication, and hardiness in families with children with disabilities. *Journal of Family Nursing, 5,* 275-291.

Orelove, F. P. & Sobsey, D. (1996). *Educating children with multiple disabilities: A transdisciplinary approach* (3rd ed.). Baltimore: Paul H. Brookes.

297 •

Orenchuk-Tomiuk, N., Matthey, G., & Christenson, C. P. (1990). The resolution model: A comprehensive treatment framework in sexual abuse. *Child Welfare League of America, 69*, 417-431.

Orlinsky, D. E. & Howard, K. I. (1986). Process and outcome in psychotherapy. In S. L. Garfield & A. E. Bergin (Eds.), *Handbook of psychotherapy and behavior change* (3rd ed., pp 311-381). New York: Wiley.

Patterson, J. (1993). The role of family meanings in adaptation to chronic illness and disability. In A. Turnbull, J. Patterson, S. Behr, D. Murphy, J. Marquis, & M. Blue-Banning (Eds.), *Cognitive coping, families, & disability* (pp. 221- 238). Baltimore, MD: Paul H. Brookes Co., Inc.

Perlman, N. B. & Millar, C. (1991, Dec. 5). *Psychotherapy with young children.* Paper presented at the Annual Convention, National Centre for Clinical Infant Programs, Washington, D. C.

Perlman, N. B., Millar, C., & Ericson, K. (1993). Therapy for sexually abused young children. *Infants and Young Children, 5*, 43-48.

Perlman, N. & Sinclair, L. (1992, Dec 2-5). *Play and psychological assessment of sexually abused child with developmental disabilities.* Paper presented at the Ninth Annual Conference for the National Association for the Dually Diagnosed, Toronto, ON.

Perry, B. D. (1994) Neurobiological sequelae of childhood trauma: PTSD in Children. In M.M. Murburg (Ed.), *Catecholamine function in posttraumatic stress disorder: Emerging concepts* (pp. 233-255). Washington, D.C.: American Psychiatric Press.

Piaget, J. (1962). *Play, dreams and imitation in childhood.* New York: Norton.

Pierce, L. H. (1987). Father-son incest: Using the literature to guide practice. *Social Casework, 68*, 67-74.

Powell, T. & Ogle, P. (1985). *Brothers & sister: A special part of exceptional families.* Baltimore: Paul H. Brookes.

Powers, L. (1993). Disability and grief: From tragedy to challenge. In G. Singer & L. Powers (Eds.), *Families, disability and empowerment: Active coping skills and strategies for family interventions* (pp. 119-149). Baltimore: Paul H. Brookes.

Price-Williams, D. (1989). Communication in therapy with emotionally disturbed mentally retarded individuals. In M. Beveridge, G. Conti-Ramsden, & I. Leudar (Eds.), *Language and communication in mentally handicapped people* (pp. 254-273). London: Chapman and Hall.

Prosser, H. & Bromley, J. (1998). Interviewing people with intellectual disabilities. In E. Emerson, C. Hatton, J. Bromley, & A. Caine (Eds.), *Clinical psychology and people with intellectual disabilities.* (pp. 99-113). West Sussex, England: John Wiley & Sons.

Prout, H. T. & Cale, R. L. (1994). Individual counseling approaches. In D. C. Strohmer & H. T. Prout (Eds.), *Counseling and psychotherapy with persons with mental retardation and borderline intelligence* (pp. 103-141). Brandon, VT: Clinical Psychology Publishing Co., Inc.

Prout, H. T. & Strohmer, D. C. (1994a). Issues in counseling and psychotherapy. In D. C. Strohmer & H. T. Prout (Eds.), *Counseling and psychotherapy with persons with mental retardation and borderline intelligence* (pp. 1-21). Brandon, VT: Clinical Psychology Publishing Co., Inc.

Prout, H. T. & Strohmer, D. C. (1994b). Assessment in counseling and psychotherapy. In D. C. Strohmer & H. T. Prout (Eds.) *Counseling and psychotherapy with persons with mental retardation and borderline intelligence* (pp. 79-102). Brandon, VT: Clinical Psychology Publishing Co., Inc.

Prout , H. T. & Nowak, K. M. (1999, Nov 10-13) The effectiveness of psychotherapy with persons with mental retardation: Status of the "research". Paper presented at the Sixteenth Annual Conference for the National Association for the Dually Diagnosed, Niagara Falls, Ontario, Canada.

Rappaport, S. R., Burkhardt, S. A., & Rotatori, A. F. (1997). *Child sexual abuse curriculum for the developmentally disabled.* Springfield, IL: Charles C Thomas.

Reichle, J., York, J., & Sigafoos, J. (1991). *Implementing augmentative and alternative communication: Strategies for learners with severe disabilities.* Baltimore: Paul H. Brookes.

Reiss, S. (1993). Assessment of psychopathology in persons with mental retardation. In J. L. Matson & R. P. Barrett (Eds.), *Psy-*

chopathology in the mentally retarded (2nd ed., pp. 17-38). Boston: Allyn and Bacon.

Reiss, S. (1994a). Psychopathology in mental retardation. In N. Bouras (Ed.), *Mental health in mental retardation: Recent advances and practices* (pp. 67-78). Cambridge: Cambridge University Press.

Reiss, S. (1994b). *Handbook of challenging behavior: Mental health aspects of mental retardation.* Worthington, OH: IDS Publishing Corporation.

Reiss, S. (1996). The concept of anxiety sensitivity: Possible implications for research on dual diagnosis. In A. Poindexter (Ed.), *Assessment and treatment of anxiety disorders in persons with mental retardation* (pp. 65-69). Kingston, NY: National Association for the Dually Diagnosed.

Reiss, S. & Aman, M. G. (Eds.). (1998). *Psychotropic Medications and Developmental Disabilities: The International Consensus Handbook.* Columbus, OH: The Ohio State University.

Reiss, S. & Aman, M. G. (1997). The international consensus process on psychopharmacology and intellectual disability. *Journal of Intellectual Disability Research, 41*, 448-455.

Reiss, S. & Benson, B. A. (1984). Awareness of negative social conditions among mentally retarded, emotionally disturbed outpatients. *American Journal of Psychiatry, 141*, 88-90.

Rindfleisch, N. & Bean, G. J. (1988). Willingness to report abuse and neglect in residential facilities. *Child Abuse and Neglect, 12*, 509-520.

Rindfleisch, N. & Rabb, J. (1984). How much of a problem is resident mistreatment in child welfare institutions? *Child Abuse and Neglect, 8*, 33-40.

Rogers, C. R. (1961). *On becoming a person.* Boston: Houghton Mifflin.

Rowe, W. S. & Savage, S. (1987). *Sexuality and the developmentally handicapped: A guidebook for health care professionals.* Queenston: Edwin Mellen Press.

Russell, D. E. H. (1983). The incidence and prevalence of intrafamilal and extrafamilial sexual abuse of female children. *Child Abuse and Neglect, 9*, 265-275.

Rutter, M. (1981). *Maternal deprivation reassessed* (2nd ed.). New York: Penguin.

Rutter, M. (1983). Stress, coping, and development: Some issues and some questions. In N. Garmezy & M. Rutter (Eds.), *Stress, coping, and development in children* (pp. 1-41). New York: MacGraw-Hill.

Rutter, M., Tizard, J., Yule, W., Graham, P., & Whitmore, K. (1976). Research report: Isle of Wight studies, 1964-1974. *Psychological Medicine, 6*, 313-332.

Ryan, R. (1992, Dec 2-5). *Post traumatic stress syndrome: Assessing and treating the aftermath of sexual assault.* Paper presented at the Ninth Annual Conference for the National Association for the Dually Diagnosed, Toronto, ON.

Ryan, R. (1993, Dec 1-4). *Medication management of post-traumatic stress disorder in persons with developmental disabilities.* Paper presented at the Tenth Annual Conference for the National Association for the Dually Diagnosed, Philadelphia, PA.

Sandieson, R. (1998). A survey on terminology that refers to people with mental retardation/ developmental disabilities. *Education & Training in Mental Retardation. 33*, 290-295.

Sandler, J., Kennedy, H., & Tyson, R. L. (1980). *The technique of child psychoanalysis: Discussions with Anna Freud.* Cambridge, MA: Harvard University Press.

Sarason, S. B. (1985). *Psychology and mental retardation: Perspectives in change.* Austin, TX: Pro-Ed.

Savage, R. D., Evans, L., & Savage, J. F. (1981). *Psychology and communication in deaf children.* Sydney: Grune & Stratton.

Scorgie, K., Wilgosh, L., & McDonald, L. (1996). A qualitative study of managing life when a child has a disability. *Developmental Disabilities Bulletin, 24*, 68-90.

Scorgie, K., Wilgosh, L., & McDonald, L. (1998). Stress and coping in families of children with disabilities: An examination of recent literature. *Developmental Disabilities Bulletin, 26*, 22-42.

Scott, C. S., Lefley, H. P., & Hicks, D. (1993). Potential risk factors for rape in three ethnic groups. *Community Mental Health Journal, 29*, 133-141.

Senn, C. (1988). *Vulnerable: Sexual abuse and people with intellectual handicap*. Downsview, ON: G. Allan Roeher Institute.

Seubert, A. (1992, Dec. 2-5). *The self coming alive: Awareness and communication training for staff and clients*. Paper presented at the Ninth Annual Conference for the National Association for the Dually Diagnosed, Toronto, ON.

Sgroi. S. M. (Ed.). (1982). *Handbook of clinical intervention in child sexual abuse*. Lexington, MA: Lexington.

Sgroi, S. M. (1989). Evaluation and treatment of sexual offense behavior in persons with mental retardation. In S. M. Sgroi (Ed.), *Vulnerable populations: Sexual abuse treatment for children, adult survivors, offenders and persons with mental retardation* (Vol. 2, pp. 245-284). New York: Lexington Books.

Shaman, E. J. (1986). Prevention programs for children with disabilities. In M. Nelson & K. Clark (Eds.), *The educator's guide to preventing child sexual abuse* (pp. 122-125). Santa Cruz: CA: Network Publications.

Shane, H. C. & Kearns. K. (1994). An examination of the role of the facilitator in "facilitated communication." *American Journal of Speech-Language Pathology, 3,* 48-54.

Shank, M. & Turnbull, A. (1993). Cooperative family problem solving: An intervention for single-parent families of children with disabilities. In G. Singer & L. Powers (Eds.), *Families, disability and empowerment: Active coping skills and strategies for family interventions* (pp. 231-254). Baltimore: Paul H. Brookes.

Shaver, D. (1992, Dec. 2-5). *Preparing for a mental health consultation: A model of interdisciplinary communication*. Paper presented at the Ninth Annual Conference for the National Association for the Dually Diagnosed, Toronto, ON.

Shibley-Hyde, J. (1990). *Understanding human sexuality*. New York: McGraw/Hill.

Silka, V. R. & Hurley, A. D. (1998). Ask the Doctor: How to get the most out of a psychiatric appointment. *Mental Health Aspects of Developmental Disabilities, 1,* 22-27.

Simeonsson, R. & Bailey, D., Jr. (1986). Siblings of handicapped children. In J. Gallagher & P. Vietze (Eds.), *Families of handi-*

capped persons: Research, programs, and policy issues (pp. 67-77). Baltimore: Paul H. Brookes.

Simonds, S. L. (1994). *Bridging the silence: Nonverbal modalities in the treatment of adult survivors of childhood sexual abuse.* New York: W. W. Norton.

Sinason, V. (1986). Secondary mental handicap and its relationship to trauma. *Psychoanalytic Psychotherapy, 2,* 131-154.

Sinason, V. (1992). *Mental handicap and the human condition: New approaches from the Tavistock.* London: Free Association Books.

Singer, G. & Irvin, L. (1991). Supporting families of persons with severe disabilities: Emerging findings, practices, and questions. In L. H. Meyer, C. A. Peck, & L. Brown (Eds.), *Critical issues in the lives of persons with severe disabilities* (pp. 271-312). Baltimore: Paul H. Brookes.

Singer, G., Irvin, L., Irvine, B., Hawkins, N., Hegreness, J., & Jackson, R. (1993). Helping families adapt positively to disability: Overcoming demoralization through community supports. In G. Singer & L. Powers (Eds.), *Families, disability and empowerment: Active coping skills and strategies for family interventions* (pp. 67-83). Baltimore: Paul H. Brookes.

Singer, G. & Powers, L. (1993). Contributing to resilience in families: An overview. In G. Singer & L. Powers (Eds.), *Families, disability and empowerment: Active coping skills and strategies for family interventions* (pp. 1-25). Baltimore: Paul H. Brookes.

Smith, J. D. (1997). Mental retardation as an educational construct: Time for a new shared view?. *Education & Training in Mental Retardation, 32,* 167-173.

Sobsey, D. & Varnhagen, C. (1989). Sexual abuse of people with disabilities. In M. Csapo & L. Gougen (Eds.), *Special education across Canada: Challenges for the 90's* (pp. 199-218). Vancouver: Centre for Human Development & Research.

Sobsey, D. (1990). Modifying the behavior of behavior modifiers: Arguments for counter control against aversive procedures. In A. Repp & N. Singh (Eds.), *Perspectives on the use of non-aversive behavior and aversive interventions for people with developmental disabilities* (pp. 421-433). Sycamore, IL: Sycamore Publishing.

Sobsey, D. (Ed.). (1994). *Violence and abuse in the lives of people with disabilities: The end of silent acceptance?* Baltimore: Paul H. Brookes.

Sobsey, D. & Doe, T. (1991). Patterns of sexual abuse and assault. *Sexuality and Disability, 9,* 243-259.

Sobsey, D., Gray, S., Wells, D., Pyper, D., & Reimer-Heck, B. (1991). *Disability, sexuality, and abuse: An annotated bibliography.* Baltimore: Paul H. Brookes.

Sobsey, D. & Mansell, S. (1990). The prevention of sexual abuse of persons with developmental disabilities. *Developmental Disabilities Bulletin, 18,* 51-65.

Sobsey, D., Wells, D., Lucardie, R., & Mansell, S. (1995). *Violence & disability: An annotated bibliography.* Baltimore: Paul H. Brookes.

Sobsey, D. & Mansell, S. (1997). *Patterns of abuse of children with developmental disabilities.* Paper presented at 121st Annual meeting of the American Association on Mental Retardation. New York, May, 1997.

Sobsey, D., Randall, W., & Parilla, R.K. (1997) Gender differences in abused children with and without disabilities. *Child Abuse & Neglect, 21,* 707-729.

Sobsey, D. & Calder, P. (1999, Oct.). *A conceptual analysis of increased risk for people with disabilities.* Irvine, CA:U.S. National Research Council's Committee on Crime and Justice Workshop on Victims with Disabilities.

Sovner, R. (1986). Limiting factors in the use of the DSM-III criteria with mentally ill/mentally retarded persons. *Psychopharmacology Bulletin, 22,* 1055-1059.

Spackman, R., Grigel, M., & MacFarlane, C. (1990). Individual counseling and therapy for the mentally handicapped. *Alberta Psychology, 19*(5), 14-18.

Stavrakaki, C. & Klein, J. (1986). Psychotherapies with the mentally retarded. *Psychiatric Clinics of North America, 9,* 733-743.

Stewart, K. (1998, August 10). Girls dream became a nightmare of instability. *Roanoke Times.* p A1.

Stimpson, L. & Best, M. C. (1991). *Courage above all: Sexual assault against women with disabilities.* Toronto, ON: DAWN (DisAbled Women's Network) Canada.

Strohmer, D. C. & Prout, H. T. (Eds.). (1994). *Counseling and psychotherapy with persons with mental retardation and borderline intelligence.* Brandon, VT: Clinical Psychology Publishing Co., Inc.

Sullivan, P. M. (1993). Sexual abuse therapy for special children. Case Conference: Mental Health Social Service Issues and Case Studies. *Journal of Child Sexual Abuse, 2,* 117-124.

Sullivan, P. & Cork, P. (1998). Maltreatment prevention programs for children with disabilities: An evaluation model. *Developmental Disabilities Bulletin, 26,* 72-80.

Sullivan, P. & Knutson, J. (in press). Maltreatment and disabilities: Population-based epidemiological study. *Child Abuse and Neglect.*

Sullivan, P. & Knutson, J. (1994). *The relationship between child abuse and neglect and disabilities: Implications for research and practice.* Omaha, NE: Boys Town National Research Hospital.

Sullivan, P. M. & Scanlan, J. M. (1990). Psychotherapy with handicapped sexually abused children. *Developmental Disabilities Bulletin, 18,* 21-34.

Sullivan, P. M. & Scanlan, J. M. (1987). Therapeutic issues. In J. Garbarino, P. E. Brookhouser, & K. J. Authier (Eds.), *Special children-special risks: The maltreatment of children with disabilities* (pp. 127-159). New York: Aldine de Gruyter.

Sullivan, P. M., Scanlan, J. M., Knutson, J. F., Brookhouser, P. E., & Schulte, L. E. (1992). The effects of psychotherapy on behavior problems of sexually abused deaf children. *Child Abuse and Neglect, 16,* 297-307.

Sullivan, P. M., Vernon, M., & Scanlan, J. M. (1987). Sexual abuse of deaf youth. *American Annals of the Deaf, 132,* 256-262.

Svec, H. J. (1992a, Dec 2-5). *Using sand trays and projective techniques for assessment and psychotherapy.* Paper presented at the Ninth Annual Conference for the National Association for the Dually Diagnosed, Toronto, ON.

Svec, H. J. (1992b, Dec 2-5). *Multiple personality or psychosis.* Paper presented at the Ninth Annual Conference for the National Association for the Dually Diagnosed, Toronto, ON.

Switzky, H. N., Ludwig, L., & Haywood, H. C. (1979). Exploration and play in retarded and nonretarded preschool children: Effects of object complexity and age. *American Journal of Mental Deficiency, 83,* 637-644.

Switzky, H. N., Haywood, H. C., & Rotatori, A. F. (1982). Who are the severely and profoundly mentally retarded? *Education and Training of the Mentally Retarded, 17,* 268-272.

Szempuch, J. & & Jacobson, J. W. (1993). Evaluation of facilitated communications of people with developmental disabilities. *Research in Developmental Disabilities, 14,* 253-264.

Szivos, S. & Griffiths, E. (1992). Coming to terms with learning difficulties: The effects of groupwork and group processes on stigmatized identity. In A Waitman & S. Conboy-Hill (Eds.), *Psychotherapy and mental handicap* (pp. 59-80). London: Sage.

Szymanski, L. S. (1980). Individual psychotherapy with retarded persons. In L. S. Szymanski & P. E. Tanguay (Eds.), *Emotional disorders of mentally retarded persons: Assessments, treatment and consultation* (pp. 131-147). Baltimore: University Park Press.

Tanguay, P. E. & Szymanski, L. S. (1980). Training of mental health professionals in mental retardation. In L. S. Szymanski & P. E. Tanguay (Eds.), *Emotional disorders of mentally retarded persons: Assessments, treatment and consultation* (pp. 19-28). Baltimore: University Park Press.

Teodoru, N. D. (1992, Dec 2-5). *Therapy workshop: Working with functional and dysfunctional dynamics in families with disabled members.* Paper presented at the Ninth Annual Conference for the National Association for the Dually Diagnosed, Toronto, ON.

Terr, L. (1983). Play therapy and psychic trauma: A preliminary report. In C. E. Schaeffer & K. J. O'Connor (Eds.), *Handbook of play therapy* (pp. 308-319). New York: Wiley & Sons.

Terr, L. (1990). *Too scared to cry: Psychic trauma in childhood.* New York: Harper & Row.

Terr, L. (1991). Childhood traumas: An outline and overview. *American Journal of Psychiatry, 148,* 10-20.

Tharinger, D., Horton, C., & Millea, S. (1990). Sexual abuse and exploitation of children and adults with mental retardation and other handicaps. *Child Abuse and Neglect, 14,* 301-312.

Ticoll, M. (1992). *No more victims: A manual to guide families and friends in preventing the sexual abuse of people with a mental handicap.* Toronto, ON: The Roeher Institute.

Timmons-Mitchell, J. & Gardner, S. (1991). Treating sexual victimization: Developing trust-based relating in the mother-daughter dyad. *Psychotherapy, 28,* 333-338.

Tomasulo, D. (1990). *Group counseling for people with mild to moderate mental retardation and developmental disabilities: An interactive-behavioral model.* New York: Young Adult Institute.

Trepper, T. S. & Barrett, M. J. (1989). *Systemic treatment of incest.* New York: Brunner/Mazel.

Turk, V. & Brown, H. (1992). *Sexual abuse of adults with learning disabilities.* Canterbury, UK: University of Kent.

Turnbull, A., Summers, J., & Brotherson, M. (1986). Family life cycle: Theoretical and empirical implications and future directions for families with mentally retarded members. In J. Gallagher & P. Vietze (Eds.), *Families of handicapped persons: Research, programs, and policy issues* (pp. 45-65). Baltimore: Paul H. Brookes.

Turnbull, A. & Turnbull III, H. (1993). Participatory research on cognitive coping: From concepts to research planning. In A. Turnbull, J. Patterson, S. Behr, D. Murphy, J. Marquis, & M. Blue-Banning (Eds.), *Cognitive coping, families, & disability* (pp. 1-14). Baltimore, MD: Paul H. Brookes Co., Inc.

Turnbull, A. & Turnbull III, H. (1997). *Families, professionals, and exceptionality: A special partnership* (3rd ed.). Upper Saddle River, NJ: Prentice-Hall, Inc.

Turner, A. (1980). Therapies with families of the mentally retarded child. *Journal of Marital and Family Therapy, 6,* 167-170.

Valenti-Hein, D. & Schwartz, L. (1994). *The sexual abuse interview for the developmentally disabled.* Santa Barbara, CA: James Stanfield Co.

van der Kolk, B. A. (1994). The body keeps score: memory and the evolving psychobiology of posttraumatic stress. *Harvard Review of Psychiatry, 1*, 253-265.

van der Kolk, B. A. & Fisler, R. E. (1993). The biologic basis of posttraumatic stress. *Primary Care Clinics of North America, 20*, 417-432.

van der Kolk, B. A. & Fisler, R. E.(1994). Childhood abuse and neglect and loss of self-regulation. *Bulletin of the Menninger Clinic, 58*, 145-168.

Vander Mey, B. J. (1988). The sexual victimization of male children: A review of previous research. *Child Abuse & Neglect, 123*, 671-672.

Varley, C. K. (1984). Schizophreniform psychoses in mentally retarded adolescent girls following sexual assault. *American Journal of Psychiatry, 141*, 593-595.

Vernikoff, S. & Dunayer, R. (1992, Dec 2-5). *Counselling and psychotherapy: Techniques of relationship building as a tool for change.* Paper presented at the Ninth Annual Conference for the National Association for the Dually Diagnosed, Toronto, ON.

Vogel, P. A. (1982). Treating lower-functioning institutionalized mentally handicapped with severe behavior problems: An emphasis on language. *Tidsskrift-for-Norsk-Psychologforening, 19*, 601-608.

von Hug-Hellmuth, H. (1921). On the technique of child analysis. *International Journal of Psychoanalysis, 2*, 287-305.

Waitman, A. & Conboy-Hill, S. (Eds.). (1992). *Psychotherapy and mental handicap.* London: Sage.

Ward, K. M., Heffern, S. J., Wilcox, D. A., McElwee, D., Dowrick, P., Brown, T. D., Jones, M. J., & Johnson, C. L. (1992). *Managing inappropriate sexual behaviors: Supporting individuals with developmental disabilities in the community.* Anchorage: ASET.

Wasserman, G. A., Lennon, M. C., Allen, R., & Shilansky, M. (1987). Contributors to attachment in normal and physically handicapped infants. *Journal of the Academy of Child and Adolescent Psychiatry, 26*, 9-15.

West, J. (1996). *Child centered play therapy* (2nd ed.). London: Arnold.

Westcott, H. (1992). *NSPCC Professionals working with disabled children: Results of an initial survey.* London, UK: NSPCC.

Westcott, H. (1993). *Abuse of children and adults with disabilities: Policy, practice, research series.* London: National Society for the Prevention of Cruelty to Children.

Whiston, S. C. & Sexton, T. L. (1993). An overview of psychotherapy research: Implications for practice. *Professional Psychology: Research and Practice, 24,* 43-51.

Whitmore, K. (1988). *Counseling and psychotherapy with the mentally retarded.* Unpublished manuscript.

Wikler, L. (1986). Family stress theory and research on families of children with mental retardation. In J. Gallagher & P. Vietze (Eds.), *Families of handicapped persons: Research, programs, and policy issues* (pp. 167-195). Baltimore: Paul H. Brookes.

Wilder, L., Wasow, M., & Hatfield, E. (1981). Chronic sorrow revisited: Parent vs. professional depiction of the adjustment of parents of mentally retarded children. *American Journal of Orthopsychiatry, 51,* 63-70.

Wilgosh, L. (1990a). Issues in education and daily living for families of children with disabilities. *Alberta Journal of Educational Research, 26,* 299-309.

Wilgosh, L. (1990b). Sexual assault and abuse of people with disabilities. *Developmental Disabilities Bulletin, 18,* 44-50.

Wilgosh, L. (1993). Sexual abuse of children with disabilities: Intervention and treatment issues for parents. *Developmental Disabilities Bulletin, 21,* 1-12.

Wilkins, R. (1992). Psychotherapy with the siblings of mentally handicapped children. In A. Waitman & S. Conboy-Hill (Eds.), *Psychotherapy and mental handicap* (pp. 24-45). London: Sage.

Wilson, C. & Brewer, N. (1992). The incidence of criminal victimization of individuals with an intellectual disability. *Australian Psychologist. 27,* 114-117.

Wing, L., Gould, J., Yeates, S., & Brierly, L. (1977). Symbolic play in mentally retarded and autistic children. *Journal of Child Psychology and Psychiatry, 18,* 167-178.

Winnicott, D. W. (1989). D.W. Winnicott (1964-68): The squiggle game. In C. Winnicott, R. Shepard, & M. Davis (Eds.), *D.*

W. Winnicott: Psycho-analytic explorations (pp. 299-317). Cambridge, MA: Harvard University Press.

Wozencraft, T., Wagner, W., & Pellegrin, A. (1991). Depression and suicidal ideation in sexually abused children. *Child Abuse and Neglect, 15*, 505-511.

Yura, M. (1987). Family subsystem functions and disabled children: Some conceptual issues. *Marriage and Family Review, 11*, 135-151.

SO-DNJ-218

THE
SUCCESSORS OF HOMER

BY

William Cranston
W. C. LAWTON

SENIOR CLASSICAL PROFESSOR IN THE ADELPHI COLLEGE, BROOKLYN

NEW YORK
COOPER SQUARE PUBLISHERS, INC.
1969

Originally Published 1898
Published by Cooper Square Publishers, Inc.
59 Fourth Avenue, New York, N. Y. 10003
Library of Congress Catalog Card No. 69-17001

Printed in the United States of America

CONTENTS.

		PAGE
PROLOGUE		1
I.	THE EPIC CYCLE	6
II.	THE WORKS AND DAYS	41
III.	THE HESIODIC THEOGONY, SHIELD OF HERACLES, ETC.	76
IV.	THE HOMERIC HYMNS	107
V.	THE HOMERIC HYMN TO APOLLO	125
VI.	THE HOMERIC HYMN TO DEMETER ...	154
VII.	HEXAMETER IN THE HANDS OF THE PHILOSOPHERS	180
EPILOGUE		198

THE SUCCESSORS OF HOMER.

PROLOGUE.

In the great panorama of literature, as of history, the chief landmarks, the brilliant epochs, stand out prominently in our memory, while the really unbroken tablelands or chains of hills between them are often unduly overlooked. Even the most general student of literature will hardly forget that, about the ninth or tenth century B.C., Homer—or the school of Homeric poets—immortalized in splendid epic verse that age of Achaian princes, which was even then passing away. Nor, again, will the trio of supreme tragic poets, who, in the fifth century B.C., so glorified their Athenian mother-city, ever become dim figures to the student of letters. But it is important also to realize that those were not merely

isolated elevations. Between Homer and Aeschylos there was probably not a single decade,
perhaps not a year, when the muse of Hellas
was silent. Two notable series of poems, in
particular, may still be traced through the
centuries that intervene, viz. the later Epic and
the early Lyric.

The drama itself, indeed, developed out of a
special form of lyric poetry (the Bacchic dithy-
ramb), and lyric—which was of course really as
old, in some form, as the Greek race itself—as
old as love and strife among men—can actually
be traced, in an unbroken succession of singers,
whose works are at least partly preserved, from
Callinos, at the beginning of the seventh century
B.C., down to its culmination in Pindar, the
contemporary of Aeschylos. We may be sure,
too, that for every name still recorded a hundred
minstrels are themselves "unhonoured and un-
sung." For centuries, before and after Callinos,
they must have been as countless as the im-
provisatori of the Tuscan valleys. No divine
festival, no harvest-home or vintage-time, no
marriage, funeral, or other hour of social joy

and grief, no victory in war or in athletic strife, lacked its crown of song.

Our present task is, however, to point out, that the staider and more formal epic impulse also lasted, and the long roll of the heroic hexameter continued in wide use, for many generations after Homer. Indeed, this verse never became unfamiliar to the classic Greek ear, epitaphs in particular recurring frequently to this oldest extant form of Hellenic rhythm. The poems we shall have occasion to discuss may be grouped under general heads thus:—

A. The Cyclic Epics, written largely to complete the Trojan myth by tales introducing, connecting, and completing the two Homeric masterpieces. Of these only meagre fragments and prose summaries have been preserved.

B. The Hesiodic Poems, representing in their present form rather a school of didactic and theological poetry, than a single great singer. We, however, probably have before us, though both mutilated and interpolated, the two poems most generally accepted as authentic, and most influential, among the later ancients.

C. The Homeric Hymns, ill-fitted by adjective or noun, since none dates from the age of the Iliad: some are rather Hesiodic in tone, while nearly all are *preludes*, in each of which the rhapsode, about to recite from the great epics, first pays his devoirs to the god at whose temple or festival he is to chant the "glories of the heroes." And—

D. The Philosophic Treatises in hexameter verse, which have their earliest suggestion, indeed, in Hesiod's Theogony. Here the three chief names, all of the sixth and fifth centuries B.C., are Xenophanes, Parmenides, and Empedocles. Each is extant only in fragments; but Lucretius' splendid De Rerum Natura — masterpiece of Latin literature and of didactic verse generally— affords us a lofty consolation for their loss; and also, by the way, a noble imitation in Latin of the Greek hexameter.

Empedocles died as late as 440 B.C., and some of the Homeric hymns are doubtless later still: so the regnant period of dactylic hexameter is one of five or more centuries; not to mention the scholarly revival of the Alexandrians, which we may call mock-archaic epic. The present volume attempts to open for the English reader this somewhat neglected page in the history of Greek literature. The space required for translations will of itself prevent much freedom of digression into the tempting fields of mythology, archaeology, and comparative religion.

I.

THE EPIC CYCLE.

THE Iliad was no doubt the culminating success in a long literary development; but it outlasted and extinguished all its predecessors. We know practically nothing of poets earlier than the author of the Iliad. In this chapter we take for granted on the reader's part a thorough familiarity with the plot of Iliad and Odyssey: such a familiarity as the Cyclic poets themselves reveal. A complete list of the lost epics may be convenient for reference in the course of the essay.

A.   (1) Theogonia.
      (2) Titanomachia.

B.   (1) Oidipodeia.
      (2) Thebais.
      (3) Epigonoi.

C. (1) Kypria.
   (2) (Iliad).
   (3) Aethiopis.
   (4) Little Iliad (Mikra Ilias).
   (5) Iliou Persis.
   (6) Nostoi.
   (7) (Odyssey).
   (8) Telegonia.

The lost epics arrange themselves into three groups, according as they deal with kosmic or world-myths, with Theban legend, and with the great tale of Troy. We pass rapidly over the first two groups of these Cyclic poems, which have less connection in plot with the Homeric story.

A. The Cyclic Theogony and Titanomachia, beginning with the wedlock of Uranos and Ge (Heaven and Earth), told the story of Creation, and of strife among immortals. Homer, by the way, makes Okeanos, not Uranos, the source of all (Il. xiv. 245, 246). Indeed we shall have occasion elsewhere to notice that Homer usually ignores, if he had heard them, the cruder tales of deadly strife, cannibalism, and mutilation among the gods. He also alludes to the Titans below, under Tartaros (Il. xiv. 274, 275), but does not tell their story (cf. infra, pp. 79 ff.). Authors, age, length, of these two Cyclic poems are unknown or disputed, though doubtless all agree they were post-Homeric. The scanty fragments deal out such trifling information as that the sun-god's steeds are two horses and two mares, or that it was the Centaur Chiron who—

" Unto Justice guided the races of mortals, and taught them
    Offerings unto the gods, and oaths, and the shapes of Olympos."

(Perhaps this Greek notion of the Centaurs as wiser than early men is a dim tradition of a horse-riding race. It will be recalled that the Homeric Greeks only drive their horses in chariots, but never mount them. The reader will remember also what amazement the Spanish riders of horses excited among the Aztecs).

This much, at any rate, we learn, even from the meagre fragments, viz. that the metre and dialect used in these Theban epics were essentially Homeric. Another single line—

"In their midst was dancing the father of men and
immortals,"

indicates that the same familiar tags and half-
lines recurred as in Homer—

"The father of men and immortals"

being a phrase which is repeated often in Iliad
and Odyssey. For the loss of these poems we are
adequately consoled by Hesiod's Theogony, which
had a much greater influence on the popular
Greek mythology of the following centuries.

B. The next three poems mentioned in the
great Cycle are concerned with the tragic story
of Thebes: the Oidipodeia, Thebais, Epigonoi.
These also deal with matters touched on by
Homer, though only incidentally. Odysseus,
e.g., saw in Hades (Odys. xi.) the ill-fated
mother, and wife as well, of Oedipus, Epicaste
(called afterwards, by the tragedians, Iocaste).
These three Theban poems together contained
twenty thousand verses, nearly twice as much
as the Odyssey. Herodotos, citing the Epigonoi,
expresses merely a passing doubt if Homer wrote
it (Herod. ix. 32). From the Oidipodeia we have

almost nothing. The first line of the Thebais
was—

"Sing, O goddess, of waterless Argos, whence the com-
    manders . . ."

From another source we have a more valuable
fragment. Athenaeus, amid his usual trivial
gossip (bk. xi. p. 465 E), has preserved a striking
passage, as to a sort of family "Luck of Eden-
hall," which Oedipus curses his sons for setting
before him.

"Yet the divinely descended hero, the fair Polyneikes,
  First at Oedipus' side made ready the beautiful table,
  Silvern, of Cadmos wise as the gods, and straightway
      upon it
  Poured for him sweet wine in a golden beautiful goblet.
  Yet when he perceived at his side that cup of his father—
  Precious, in reverence held—great woe came over his spirit.
  Instantly then upon both of his sons he uttered his curses
  Never to be escaped,—and the wrath of the gods was
      awakened—
  Wishing that they might never in amity share their
      possessions :
  Ever between them twain might strife and battle continue."

No other classical author, I believe, alludes to
this legend of the goblet: but this one passage

will suffice to show that we have lost here a large mass of valuable and independent poetic and mythologic material, in age and interest a respectable rival of the Iliad.

The story of both the Thebais and the Epigonoi is alluded to in a famous passage of the Iliad, where Agamemnon reproaches Diomedes and Sthenelos as slothful and cowardly compared with their sires, and recalls especially Tydeus, Diomedes' father, who had visited Mykenae with the banished Theban prince, Polyneikes (Il. iv. 372–410). Sthenelos (not, as is so often said, his mightier friend) answers haughtily—

" Verily we make claim to be mightier far than our fathers,
    We who captured the hold of Thebes with the sevenfold
        portals,
    Leading a lesser array beneath those bulwarks of Ares,
    Putting our trust in the aid of Zeus and the Heaven-sent
        portents :
    Whereas, they, our sires, by their own impiety perished."

The passage sounds as if Homer's audience were already familiar with the tale of Thebes, perhaps through earlier epic masters ; for this Theban legend, it is thought probable, may have been treated by poets before Homer. This is not unlikely. In this very passage, even, the poet may be speaking a bold word for his own heroes, as against the favourites of an earlier lay. Probably no one supposes any of the fragments now extant, or even any of the poems as read by the later ancients, were pre-Homeric. The exact truth as to these things, however, can no longer be descried in the "dark backward and abysm of time."

All the three great Attic tragedians have left us notable plays that draw their material from the Theban myths, and doubtless from these very epics, viz. The Seven against Thebes, of Aeschylos (sole survivor of a Theban tetralogy); the trio of noble Sophoclean plays, in all of which Antigone and Creon appear; and, lastly, Euripides' more melodramatic and over-ingenious Phoenissae. Indeed, the whole Epic Cycle was a favourite source of materials for the Attic dramatists. But we must hasten on to the Trojan epics proper.

These latter poems were, as we have said,

written for the most part, apparently, in avowed
supplementary relation to the Iliad and Odyssey. They may have drawn somewhat upon a
popular and traditional mass of myth which
Homer had not exhausted; but most students
get the impression that they are chiefly more
or less ingenious developments from incidents
or allusions in the older epics themselves. The
younger poems are known to us principally
through the prose summaries of an otherwise
untraceable Proclos—but only so far as he is
quoted in the Literary Miscellany of the
Byzantine Photios,—partly through unnamed
scholiasts upon Homer and other poets. (So
fragmentary, and at third or fourth hand, is our
knowledge of this whole Cycle, and of many
another literary epoch or artistic school!) Perhaps the chief importance of these lost epics,
now, is as evidence that the Iliad and Odyssey
had in the eighth century B.C. reached essentially
their present form and contents. Thus the in-
sults to Hector's body by Achilles in Il. xxiv.,
the meeting of Achilles and Priam, the wanderings of Telemachos in Odys. i.–iv.—that is, the

latest additions, according to modern critics, attached to Iliad and Odyssey by younger hands, —are apparently imitated in these early supplements. The manner in which the latter attach themselves to the older epics points in the same direction. This relation to Homer should be kept constantly in mind while the Cyclic poems are discussed.

The Kypria described the events preceding the story of the Iliad. It was, indeed, planned expressly to present a more adequate account of the causes and incidents leading up to the famous strife. The favourite legend made this poem also Homer's own composition, but stated that it was bestowed as a gift upon his son-in-law, the Cypriote Stasinos, who was apparently to recite it as his own. This explanation may have been an attempt to compromise between conflicting claims as to the authorship. That the poem was really of Cyprian origin is, of course, a natural conjecture, at least.

Herodotos (ii. 117) asserts confidently that the poem is "not Homer's, but some one's else; for in the Kypria it is stated that, on the third day

out from Sparta, Alexander reached Ilios with
Helen, having had a fair wind and smooth sea;
whereas the poet of the Iliad says that he
wandered about with her." Herodotos had just
quoted the allusion (Il. vi. 290–292) to the—

" Work of Sidonian women, whom Alexander the god-like
   Brought from Sidon along, as the widewayed waters he
       traversed,
   Homeward sailing to Troy with Helena, daughter of
       princes."

Herodotos shows here his usual good judgment
in literary criticism; nevertheless, in our prose
summary of the Kypria (Kinkel, Fragmenta
Epicorum, p. 18) we read: " Hera sends a storm
upon them, and Alexander, being driven to Sidon,
takes the city." This may well be a late interpolation in the Kypria itself—or merely in the
summary—suggested by the famous and trenchant
criticism of Herodotos. Doubtless, in many such
details the less illustrious poems may have been
forced into agreement with the accepted masterpieces, when the Cycle was reduced to order.
Indeed, our chief informant and summarist,
Proclos, remarks that the Cyclic epics were

preserved and studied "more for their consecutive treatment of incidents than for their intrinsic merit."

The tale of *eleven* books credited to the Kypria indicates about 5000–7000 hexameter verses : for these Alexandrian divisions into books were largely for mechanical convenience in rolling the scrolls.   The eccentric number, eleven, may have arisen when one was later trimmed away, apparently the last, which probably coincided too closely with the opening of the Iliad.

This poet probably invented, or at least first recorded, the story of the strife for the apple and the choice of Paris as umpire. From the Kypria, or at any rate under its influence, was probably interpolated into the Iliad the only allusion to those incidents, viz. the awkward and ill-placed verses, Il. xxiv. 29–30.

The opening lines of the Kypria are preserved in a somewhat corrupt form.

" Once on a time was Earth by the races of men made weary,
  Who were wandering numberless over the breadth of her
    bosom.
 Zeus with pity beheld it, and took in his wise heart
    counsel

How to relieve of her burden the Earth, life-giver to all
    things,
Fanning to flame that terrible struggle, the war upon
    Troia.
So should the burden by death be removed: and they in
    the Troad
Perished—the heroes; the counsel of Zeus was brought to
    fulfilment."

Here our informant—it is the scholiast on the
opening verses of the Iliad—suddenly breaks off.
He has given us just enough, however, to show
how skilfully the new portico was adjusted to
the old Homeric temple. The fifth line of the
Iliad also closes—

" The counsel of Zeus was brought to fulfilment,"

and he who read the Kypria first would now
understand the Iliad's opening passage to refer
back to this earlier and larger " plan of Zeus."
The scene at Aulis where the serpent devours
the sparrow and her young, alluded to in Il. i.,
was given in full in the Kypria. Such incidents,
and traits like Nestor's garrulity, seem like
elaborated cross-references, as it were, devised
between the epics.

Still, new incidents occur which hardly agree with Homer. In particular, Helen is stated, in an extant fragment, to have been the daughter of Zeus *and Nemesis*, so not mortal on either side. Polydeukes, her brother, is also immortal, whereas in Homer both he and Castor are already " covered by earth, in Lacedaemon."

Especially interesting is Achilles' desire to behold Helen, whereupon Aphrodite and Thetis bring these two glorious creatures into each other's presence. On the one hand this seems to point back toward Homer's equally bold—and dramatically better justified — conjunction of Achilles and Priam in his closing scenes. On the other side it is the first hint of the later feeling that made Achilles and Helen alike deathless, and united the two supreme types of youthful beauty in eternal wedlock.

The name and doom of Iphigenia, the tale of Philoctetes and the snake, with many another favourite tragic subject, first appear, so far as we know, in the Kypria. Just how the poem ended, and how closely it was attached to the Iliad, is not stated. Among the last incidents

noticed in the summary are the captures of
Briseis and Chryseis, as also a special "counsel
of Zeus" to withdraw Achilles from the Greek
alliance and relieve the Trojans. This repetition
of the fateful words has, even in the dry prosaic
outline, somewhat the effect of a solemn refrain.
Last of all is noted "a catalogue of the Trojans'
allies." This, of course, now stands in our Iliad
(ii. 816–877), where its authenticity has been often
attacked. It may be a late loan from the Kypria,
and its transfer may have accompanied, or caused,
the suppression of a twelfth book in the Kypria
itself.

Thus far we have depended chiefly upon
Proclos' outlines. The fragments which have
been transmitted to us give little further aid
in reconstructing the poem. One verse from the
Kypria became a very famous maxim in later
days, grimly Machiavelian though it is, reap-
pearing in Aristotle, Polybios, and others,—

"Foolish is he who, slaying the father, spareth his
     children."

Homer's praises of wine are echoed by this later

singer, who had evidently wedded his master's muse, if not his daughter—

> " Wine in truth, Menelaos, the gods for men who are mortal
> Best amid all their blessings accorded, to scatter their
> sorrows."

The largest single passage surviving describes the transformations of Nemesis when flying from the love of Zeus.   She flees—

> "Sometimes under the wave of the sea with its thunderous
> billows,
> Sometimes unto the bounds of earth and the river of Ocean,
> Sometimes over the land with its fertile meadows ; and ever
> Shapes of all earthly beasts she assumed, in the hope to
> escape him."

We certainly get the impression that this union, and the consequent divine origin of Helen, held a prominent place in the story.   It was, perhaps, the boldest addition to the Homeric tradition.

Even in this scant handful of fragments, however, the pre-eminent activity of Aphrodite, suzerain of Cyprus, fully appears.   Athenaeus, naming the flowers suitable for garlands, quotes

the verses of "Hegesias or Stasinos or whoever
the poet was "—

"Garments upon her body she put, that the Hours and the
    Graces
  Fashioned, and dipt for her in flowers that grow in the
    Springtime,
  Such as the season brings: in the crocus and hyacinth
    blossom,
  Clustering violets too, and the beautiful flowers of the
    roses—
  Sweet, unto nectar like,—and the cups of the lily ambrosial,
  With the narcissus . . . so Aphrodite
  Garments wore that with odours of every flower were
    fragrant."

Still more clearly does the queen of love
glimmer upon us in the verses,—

"Aphrodite, delighting in laughter, amid her attendants
  Out of the odorous flowers of the earth was plaiting her
    garlands."

It is but a tantalizing parting glimpse that is
accorded us, however, as she passes we know not
whither, by Nymphs and Graces attended—

"Sweetly singing adown Mount Ida abounding in fountains."

If this gleaning seems meagre, the English
reader may at least rest assured that we have

now set before him almost every scrap which has drifted to us in metrical form. The frequent allusions to the Kypria, throughout the centuries of later Hellenism, give us no material to restore the lost verses.

Even so bare an outline of the Kypria, and of the other Cyclic epics, will throw an important light on such statements as that of Aeschylos, that his dramas were "crumbs from the great banquet of Homer." Yet it is certain that the plots of the Iliad and Odyssey themselves were rarely dramatized in Athens. They would not "crumble" effectively, as Aristotle asserts. Aeschylos, if the incident be authentic at all, doubtless used the term "Homer" in the wider sense. (Nearly every prehistoric Greek poem was once popularly ascribed to the one supreme bard.) Athenaeus (277 E) expressly says of *Sophocles*, that he delighted to draw his subjects from the Epic Cycle. The general truth of this remark can still be demonstrated; but, of course, the exact extent of the dramatist's debt to this and other sources can rarely be indicated in detail. The true artist has but one rule, to

borrow wherever he finds what he needs, and
to recast no less freely, until the material seems
originally intended for the place where he sets
it. Not merely, however, as the favourite quarry
of tragic poets and other artists, but for its own
creative power and beauty, we would gladly have
restored to us this lost epic of unknown,—or at
least disputed,—authorship. Of this there is little
hope, though the Egyptian discoveries of recent
years make all things seem possible.

The Kypria, then, as we have seen, was added,
not unfittingly, as a stately portico of song,
introductory to the older epic. It was much
more evident, however, that the Iliad needed a
sequel, rather than an introduction. Readers of
the Iliad in every age must feel that the doom
of Achilles and the fall of the guilty city are
most effective subjects, yet awaiting their
minstrel. In a later age, Virgil's second book
of the Aeneid has nobly supplied the latter
scene, and the Latin poet has not failed to link
his incidents unmistakably to the earlier narrative. Such a continuation was first composed,
however, by Arctinos of Miletos, in the early

Olympiads, *i.e.* in the eighth century B.C. The ancients were quite well agreed as to this poet's name and age. That he, like the author of the Kypria, found our Iliad in its present form is pretty clearly indicated by the fact that he—or else whoever finally arranged the Cycle—even altered Homer's closing line. The Iliad ends—

> "So they made ready the grave for Hector, the tamer of horses."

The Greek scholiast on this final verse remarks:
" Some write,—

> ' So they made ready the grave for Hector : the Amazon straightway
> Came, who was daughter to Ares, the haughty destroyer of heroes.' "

This transitional passage is curiously illustrated in various works of art. For instance, the widowed Andromache, still holding her funereal urn, is seen in the group which welcomes the arrival of the Amazon queen.

About a century later still, the Lesbian poet Lesches wrote his Little Iliad, probably a rival poem to that of Arctinos, and covering essentially the same ground, viz. the whole tale from Hector's funeral to the sack of the city. But the later hand, whatever and whenever it may have been, that forced all these poems into a more perfect sequence of historical events—at the cost, as Proclos intimates, of their poetic value, seems to have culled from each lesser poem the portion which was considered most effective. Hence, in our summary, the Cycle is thus continued after (2) the Iliad.

(3) Aethiopis, by *Arctinos*, in five books, closing in the midst of Ajax' strife with Odysseus for the armour of the dead Achilles.

(4) Little Iliad of *Lesches*, in four books, beginning with Odysseus' victory, in the strife for the armour, and Ajax' suicide, ending with the reception of the wooden horse into the town.

(5) Destruction of Ilios, in two books, again by *Arctinos*, exactly joining on here (!) with the debate of the Trojans what to do with the horse, and ending with the departure of the Greeks for home, under Athene's displeasure.

Of course it is quite incredible, and indeed absurd, that Arctinos should have left any such ragged gap in his work, or between his works, to be filled by a man of alien race three generations later; nor can we believe that both his Aethiopis and the Little Iliad stopped in the midst of most absorbing crises! The explanation, which we gave beforehand, is generally accepted by students, and is made nearly certain by the extant fragments of both poems. These do not, in either case, as we shall see, confine themselves to the limits so artificially set for them in the Cycle. Let us now study the three poems in succession somewhat more closely.

The Aethiopis, whether a separate poem or, as I believe, a mere portion of Arctinos' work, was chiefly occupied with Achilles' last two exploits— the slaying of the Amazon queen, Penthesilea, and, finally, of Memnon the Ethiopian, son of Eos the Dawn-goddess. Both these gallant figures will be recalled as among the frescoes, or reliefs, on Dido's palace walls (Aen. i. 489–491). These pictures have always impressed me with a startling vividness hardly equalled elsewhere in the Aeneid. Virgil may be describing some series of panels well-known to him and to his courtly auditors.

The tragic fate and youthful beauty of Penthesilea
and Memnon made them favourite subjects for
every art. In the Aethiopis Achilles falls in love
with Penthesilea—perhaps after killing her,—and
slays Thersites for jeering at his passion. Of this
passage Schiller betrays his ignorance by a fine
verse—

" Patroclus liegt begraben, und Thersites kommt rurück ! "

The incident looks, in our summary of the
Aethiopis, like a bold embroidery on Homer's
statement that Thersites " especially railed at "
Achilles among other chieftains. The striking
adjective " Hephaistos-fashioned," applied in the
prose outline of Aethiopis to Memnon's panoply,
probably indicates a closer imitation of a familiar
Homeric passage ; and is, so far, a broad hint,
also, that the passage in question—viz. the detailed
account of Achilles' shield, generally considered a
late addition to the Iliad—was already in the text
of Homer. In the Aethiopis the slaying of
Achilles is accomplished at the Scaean gate by
Apollo and Paris, just as the dying Hector had
foretold in the Iliad. The reliance of this poem

upon motifs drawn from the Iliad is indeed especially clear and constant. *E.g.* Nestor's son Antilochos takes Patroclos' place in some degree; and Antilochos' death leads up to Memnon's, much as Patroclos' fall hastened the doom of Hector. Again, Ajax bears Achilles' body out of the fray to the ships, reminding us of the close of Il. xvii., where Patroclos' corpse is similarly rescued.

The coming of Thetis, with her sisters and the Muses, to mourn for Achilles, was needed here, and the very similar account which appears so unexpectedly in Odys. xxiv.—where Agamemnon's ghost describes to Achilles, after so many years, the latter's own funeral—may itself be borrowed, later, from this passage. This mention of the Muses' presence, also, at the funeral rites, tempts us to bring up once again the question, why Achilles in life, alone among the heroes, holds the lyre and sings "the glories of men." Is it an audacious hint by the courtly bards that the lyre is in truth as honourable as the prince's sword itself? They would hardly have dared proclaim more openly, like Clough, that—

"Hundreds of heroes fought and fell
That Homer in the end might tell!"

The only sustained passage extant from the
Aethiopis is a very curious one of eight lines,
describing two brothers, physicians, one especially
skilled in heroic surgery, the other in therapeutics
and, above all, in diagnosis—

"He was the first, indeed, to perceive the frenzy of Ajax,
Seeing his eyes that darted fire, and the gloom of his spirit."

It is very possible that the death of Achilles,
dragging Ajax, as it were, into the grave after
him, through the fatal contest for the divine
armour, formed either an important crisis in
Arctinos' work, or even the finale of a poem
complete in itself. These closing scenes in the
young Homeric hero's life have had a great power
and attraction for dramatic or epic poets in all
ages. Von Christ remarks that even Goethe has
taken his place as latest of the Homerids by his
(unfinished) Achilleis. Like his forerunners, the
German poet drew his inspiration and suggestions
chiefly from the Iliad. Some of his original
touches are demonstrably anti-Homeric, yet we
have reason to regret that the experiment was

so soon abandoned.   It is a mere fragment—left
so for half a lifetime, like Browning's projected
tragedy on Hippolytos.

A scholiast on Pindar tells us that the poet
of the Aethiopis made Ajax "slay himself at
dawn." But the death of Ajax, according to
Proclos' anatomical divisions, came not in the
Aethiopis at all, but in the Little Iliad. Still
more clearly effective in breaking down these
absurd partitions is a famous passage of Aristotle
(Poetics, xxiii. p. 1459 A), where, contrasting the
masterly simplicity of plot in the Homeric poems
with the crowded events in these supplements,
he says one or two dramas only have ever been
carved out of Iliad or Odyssey, but from the
Aethiopis many, and from the Little Iliad "more
than eight;" and in his following list are included *Sinon, Destruction of Troy,* and *The Setting
Sail,* all evident encroachments on the latter of
the two sections assigned by Proclos to Arctinos.
Indeed, one of these plays, the *Destruction of
Troy* (Iliou Persis), though drawn from Lesches'
Little Iliad, had precisely the title given to
Arctinos' closing poem ! It is also evident by

this time that the arrangement of the Cycle in
its Proclean—one is tempted to say, instead,
Procrustean—shape was a comparatively late one,
since Herodotos, the dramatists, and Aristotle
knew the several poems in their unabridged form
with all their contradictions and overlappings.
The Little Iliad really announces a larger theme
than does the elder poem. The opening couplet
may be rendered in literal prose—

" Ilios I sing, and Dardania rich in colts,
    For which the Danai, servants of Ares, much endured."

It has been remarked that the opening word
may have suggested the name "Iliad;" that it
was first applied to this poem, and only later
transferred to the greater epic. This must always
remain a mere conjecture. This exordium, quoted
for us in a life of Homer falsely attributed to
Herodotos, had probably been trimmed away
in the Proclean recension of the whole Epic
Corpus.

The longest passage from the Little Iliad now
remaining is but five lines; interesting to lovers
of Hector and his family as recording the fate
of his boy—

" Then the illustrious son of the noble-hearted Achilles
    Down to the hollowed vessels the widow of Hector conducted.
    As for the child, from the breast of the fair-tressed servant
        he tore him,
    Grasped by the feet, and hurled him down from the tower ;
        and upon him
    Crimson death as he fell laid hold—and a destiny ruthless."

The poet is, however, clearly not following any
fixed popular tradition, or other authority, but
merely attempting to work out Homer's hint at
Il. xxiv. 735, where Andromache expresses her
fear that her boy will meet some such fate
in the sack of the city. Indeed these lines of
the Little Iliad are all closely imitated from
this and various other Homeric passages (cf.
especially iii. 189; v. 26; vi. 467; i. 591, and
v. 83). The fine closing verse, in fact, occurs
thrice, without change, in the Iliad! This
passage, too, was probably trimmed away
altogether at that comparatively late period when
the Cycle was forced into continuous and consistent form. The whole story of the embarkation
was then assigned to the next poem, the Iliou
Persis.

Moreover, the Proclean synopsis of that rival

poem, the Iliou Persis, or "Sack of Troy," expressly makes Odysseus—not Neoptolemos—slay Astyanax. All such evidence strengthens our general impression, that each succeeding poet is an inventive artist, piecing his own conceptions upon the Homeric fabric, rather than merely versifying a familiar tradition. My own feeling (already voiced elsewhere) is that the Iliad, effacing the memory of the early literary attempts on the same theme, and also of the popular tradition on which they were doubtless in some degree built, remained essentially the only source of inspiration or suggestion for later minstrels.

Whether the two poems ascribed to Arctinos are but sections of an original single work, can hardly be determined with certainty. Most students are convinced that, at any rate, there was no gap consciously left between them. The Iliou Persis, however, in Proclos' summary, begins with the debate, "What shall be done with the wooden horse?" Only *one* of Laocoön's sons is slain with their father by the serpents in this, our oldest, account. This version, though not followed by Virgil, is quite reconcilable with the grouping in

the famous piece of sculpture, and is, I believe,
mentioned by Lessing in his essay "Laocoön." If
this son alone had joined in his father's warning
against the horse, his fate, and his brother's
escape, would make the deceptive portent all
the more convincing. Horrified at this event
(the summary continues), Aeneas and his following withdrew to Ida—before the sack began.
This is hardly reconcilable with the statement
quoted from the Little Iliad, that Aeneas shared
Andromache's captivity under Neoptolemos.
Indeed, these variations show once more that
the poets had usually no data before them save
the incomplete hints in Homer. Where he fails
them they disagree hopelessly. In the Iliad the
prophecy is merely that Aeneas and his posterity
shall rule "over the Trojans." Perhaps it is
merely chance that no locality is added. We
suppose Homer was flattering a race then ruling
in the Troad. Presumably in Lesches' time any
such occasion for courtly adulation had passed
away.

The general picture of the city's fall, with the
escape of Aeneas, death of Priam and Polyxena,

and more bitter fate of Cassandra, Hecabè, Andromache, and the rest, is especially familiar to every student of literature, from Virgil, from spectacular Attic tragedies like Euripides' Troades, etc. There is also a remarkably fine vase-painting, most conveniently accessible, perhaps, in Baumeister (Tafel xiv.), which may remind us how dominant an influence this myth exercised upon the plastic arts as well as in literature. These stately figures and groups, in spirit high above the humble form in which they appear, are evidently reproductions, more or less remote, after masterpieces of sculpture and painting. A comparison of this with the Tabula Iliaca (Baumeister, Tafel xiii.), will show graphically how, in the sixth century, the Sicilian poet Stesichoros (the authority cited upon the Tabula Iliaca), was already drawing Aeneas, the supposed founder of Sicilian Eryx and Segesta, into the central position which is later claimed for him as the ancestor of the Romans.

There is no hope that French excavators at Delphi will recover the greatest artistic treatment of this grim theme of Troy's downfall, viz. the

painting by Polygnotos in the Lesche, so elabo-
rately described in Pausanias.*

The last works on our list must be given even
more superficial treatment. (6) The Nostoi, or
"Return of the Heroes," is credited with five
books. It fits excellently just before (7) the
Odyssey, being, as it were, summarized Odys. i.
11, 12.

> "Then all others, as many as fled from fearful destruction,
>   Home were come, and escaped from the dangers of war and
>   the waters."

The author, Hagios, is usually assigned to
Troizene, in the Argolid. This is perhaps an
indication of late date, as the earlier epic school
is on the eastern side of the Aegean. It will be
remembered how the varying lists of Homer's
birth-places all bring him progressively west-
ward across the Archipelago. The subject ot
the Nostoi lacked unity and absorbing interest.
It seems to have many points of contact with

---

* Since these words were written, the pitiful ruins of the
Lesche have been uncovered, and our prophecy is fully
justified.

the early books of the Odyssey; but some portions of Menelaos' and Nestor's narratives, in particular, may be actually borrowed from the Nostoi into the present text of Homer. Some scholars believe that Odysseus' adventures were included too, but that seems unlikely. Rather, the intention to fit the poem into the place before the Odyssey is often indicated; for instance, by the incident, that Neoptolemos, returning home by land across Thrace, meets Odysseus at Maroneia, a place mentioned by Homer also. (Cf. Odys. ix. 40, 196.) No interesting fragments of the Nostoi have been preserved. The only complete verses transmitted to us allude to an earlier myth—the famous rejuvenation of Jason's father by Medeia:—

"Aeson straightway a lovely and vigorous stripling she
    rendered,
  Causing the marks of age by her cunning devices to vanish,
  Boiling many medicinal herbs in golden cauldrons."

(In later poetry the malicious enchantress refuses to utter the life-restoring charm.)

This statement just made, as to the lack of interesting fragments, is equally true of (8) the Telegonia, in two books, by Eugammon of Cyrene,—latest in time, last in subject, and perhaps least in poetic attractiveness, among the Trojan epics. Indeed, not a line of this poem is preserved. Beginning with the burial of the suitors, it was, without doubt, an avowed appendix to the Odyssey. We gather from the summary that Odysseus' later wanderings and loves, prophesied by Teiresias in Odys. xi., were by no means world-wide, but confined closely to Greece, and, indeed, to the neighbouring mainland. The far more impressive story of Odysseus' last voyage to the Antipodes, related by his ghost in the Dantesque Inferno, has not, I believe, been traced to any early source. The hero of the Telegonia, Telegonos, is Odysseus' son, by Circe. In his quest for his father—which, by the way, is clearly an imitation of Telemachos' wanderings—he lands in Ithaca, and unwittingly slays Odysseus. With the body he carries off, to Circe's isle, the widowed Penelope, and also Telemachos. Here the curtain falls upon a bit of melodrama, whereby both Odysseus' widows are happily consoled—for Telegonos weds

Penelope and Telemachos Circe! The rich vintage of Homeric wine is running lees indeed.

Of course, at the close of such a survey as this we return to the depressing consciousness, that a lost Cycle leaves only tantalizing fragments and insoluble problems behind it. Nevertheless, as the chief source of the plots for Attic tragedy, and doubtless in very large degree for later plastic art and painting as well, these works deserve at least passing attention. Originally built about the statelier shapes of the Iliad and Odyssey, they have crumbled away under the hand of time, like the Byzantine and Mohammedan walls which for a while disfigured the statelier outlines of the Phidian Parthenon. Such glimpses into vanished literatures tempt us to apply to authors, extant and forgotten, the lines which the poet in Thanatopsis has uttered of mankind in general—

> "All that tread
> The globe are but a handful to the tribes
> That slumber in its bosom."

NOTE.—The chief work of research on this subject is still Welcker's Der Epische Cyclus, a rather ponderous German book of the last generation. The reliefs, which with other plastic art throw important light on the Cycle, are best treated in Otto Jahn's Griechische Bilderchroniken. See also Baumeister's Denkmäler, i. pp. 317, 716, etc. A good outline of the plots, and exhaustively thorough discussion as to the age, of the Cyclic poems is found in Jevons's "History of Greek Literature," pp. 54–61 and 61–69. For the fragments themselves, the classical student will consult Kinkel, Fragmenta Epicorum Graecorum (Teubner).

II.

THE WORKS AND DAYS.

THE ancients believed that the Greek cities of
Asia Minor were colonies, founded from the little
peninsula which they regarded as the original
home of their race. Modern scholars have generally accepted this view, though Professor Curtius
dissents strongly. This tide of eastward emi-
gration began, we are told, nearly a century
after the Trojan war. Accordingly, the Homeric
poems themselves give no hint of Greek cities in
Asia in Priam's day. On the contrary, the forces
of all the East are arrayed on the Trojan side
as allies, so far as they are mentioned at all.

Professor Jebb, with many other scholars, is
confident that these colonies took with them to
Asia the Homeric poems—not, to be sure, in their

present form, but in an advanced stage of their development. This does not necessarily antagonize the prevailing ancient belief, that "Homer" was a native of Asia—Smyrna, Chios, and Colophon being, perhaps, the foremost claimants as his mother-city. The name Homer may be assigned, perhaps, to the later epic artist who gave the Iliad its present general form. Such episodes as those of Glaucos and Sarpedon are thought to show most clearly Asiatic origin and local pride. Yet the Olympian abode of gods and Muses, the birth of Achilles in Phthia, with many minor indications, certainly point to Thessaly as the earliest home of "Homeric" epic.

Colonies often have a more rapid growth to wealth and culture than the parent-land. Miletos, Smyrna, Samos, far outstripped the mother-cities of Greece. Whatever we think of Homer, certainly the later Cyclic Epic, literary lyric, and early philosophy all arose chiefly in Asia Minor.

Now, Hesiod is doubly interesting as the first Greek poet of whose localized existence we have authentic knowledge, and, further, from the fact

that he represents a back-current of Asiatic
culture, returning to the comparatively rude,
primeval, undeveloped mother-land. The personality of the Homeric poet or poets evades us
completely. Hesiod, a homely unheroic figure,
is naïvely and plainly revealed to us, dwelling
in his humble village home at Boeotian Ascra.

The ancient lives of Hesiod are for the most
part, like those of Homer, silly and contradictory
fabrications. Their few trustworthy details they
gleaned, as we may do, almost wholly from his
pastoral poem, the Works and Days (Ἔργα καὶ
Ἡμέραι), that is, "Rustic Tasks, and a Calendar
of fit and unfit days for their performance."
Hesiod's father had emigrated back to Ascra,
under Mount Helicon, from Kymè, in North-
western Asia Minor (a town doubly illustrious—
on the one hand as the especial legatee of Trojan
myth and stock, and on the other as the parent
of Cumae, oldest of Greek colonies in Italy).

> " Ascra, in Winter vile, most villainous
>   In Summer, and at no time glorious,"

the unfilial poet calls the village which was

probably his birthplace.   Strabo, to be sure, says Hesiod was born in Kymè before this return of his family.   This is, however, contradicted in our present text, at ver. 650, where the poet says he never went to sea.   We shall return to this passage (*infra*, p. 71).

Of his life as a shepherd on Helicon, where the Muses appear to him, we have a pleasing glimpse in the companion-poem, the Theogony. The nine sisters put in his hand a branch of laurel, and bid him sing the race of the gods immortal.   Though no voyager, he seems to have wandered widely by land.   In Locris, and again in Orchomenos, his tomb was shown—a curious pendant to the many claimants for Homer's birthplace.

Herodotos, in a famous chapter (bk. ii. § 53), mentions Hesiod and Homer together (putting Hesiod first), and says he judges they lived four hundred years, "and not more," before his time. Hesiod is, however, undoubtedly later than Homer, whom he often imitates; and this opinion of Herodotos, pointing to the latter half of the ninth century B.C., probably indicates somewhat

too early a date for Hesiod.   Still his metre and
dialect show that he is yet under the epic influence only.   Now, Ionian lyric arose as a literary
art early in the seventh century B.C., and one
of the earliest lyric poets, Simonides of Amorgos,
has plainly copied Hesiod.   The passage is a
proverbial one in tone, it is true, but the words
are so nearly the same that it appears to be
merely a conscious recasting of Hesiod's thought
in the new iambic metre.   Hesiod had said, in
dactyls,—

" Never a man hath won him a nobler prize than a woman—
    If she be good; but, again, there is naught else worse than
        a bad one."

And Simonides echoes—

    " Naught better than a woman one can win,
        If she be noble ; but, if bad, naught worse."

These data may fix, approximately, the poet's age.
A rather belated and second-rate epic poet of
about the eighth century B.C., then, Hesiod has
still a unique charm.   He gives us our first
glimpse of humble village life in that sequestered

Boeotian land from which Pindar and Plutarch
were also to spring in later centuries. Both his
chief poems have come down to us in unsatis-
factory condition. I shall try to give as full an
outline of them as is possible in brief space,
especially illustrating the sudden and ungraceful
transitions and gaps between the parts. In some
cases this may indicate mere rustic awkwardness.
In other passages the attempt has probably been
made, chiefly by later hands, to dovetail into the
larger frame complete independent poems, hymns,
etc., or striking fragments thereof, which may
often really belong to Hesiod or his school, but
not to their present places, where they fit—as
the Germans say—" like a fist on the eye "!

The poem commonly known as the " Works
and Days " is dedicated, or largely devoted, to
Hesiod's ungracious brother Perses, who, by
bribery of the judges, had secured the lion's
share in the family patrimony. He is, however,
again reduced by indolence and folly to utter
poverty, and has appealed for help to the more
prosperous poet. The latter had nothing to bestow on his kinsman save caustic and comfortless

advice.   The jerkiest turns of the verse are when, from time to time, it occurs to the loving brother that it is time to admonish Perses once more.

The very first ten lines may be an independent hymn, perhaps, to Zeus.   The poem opens thus—

"Muses who came from Pieria, giving renown by your
    singing,
  Come ye, and tell us of Zeus, and chant to the praise of
    the Father :
  His, who to mortal men has apportioned fame or oblivion ;
  Named or nameless are they by the will of Zeus the
    eternal " (Works and Days, vers. 1–4).

Indeed this might well find a place among the Homeric Hymns, where only one brief poem is actually dedicated to Zeus, though we are positively told, by so early and eminent authority as Pindar, that such preludes were oftenest composed in his honour.   But from—

"Zeus who thunders on high, in his lofty palace abiding "
                         (Ibid., ver. 8),

Hesiod suddenly turns away—

" Hearken and heed and behold, and righteously govern thy
    judgments,
  Thou: but I unto Perses would utter a word that is
    truthful!" (Ibid., vers. 9, 10).

Yet the admonition, when it comes, is but a
rather metaphysical discussion upon the two
sorts of strife or contention—noble Emulation
and base Jealousy. Both are personified, in true
Greek fashion, and sisters; elder and younger
daughters of Night. No trait was, indeed, more
familiar in Hellenic character than jealousy. It
is the one baser alloy constantly touched on even
in Pindar's golden songs of praise. Pindar, himself, was evidently kept awake by the rustling
laurels of Simonides. As Hesiod says presently—

" Even the potter is jealous of potter, and craftsman of
    craftsman;
  Even the beggar is grudging to beggar, and poet to poet!"
                           (Ibid., vers. 25, 26.)

This last passage is quoted by Plato, and repeatedly by Aristotle. The fraternal sermon
runs on—

"But do thou store these lessons away in thy memory,
Perses!

Let not Contention, the lover of mischief, withhold thee
from labour,

While in the market-place thou art hearkening, eager for
quarrels" (Ibid., vers. 27–29).

". . . Once we our heritage shared already. Cajoling the
rulers,

Men who were greedy for bribes, and were willing to grant
you the judgment,

You then plundered and carried away far more than your
portion.

Fools were they, unaware how the whole by a half is
exceeded,

Little they know how great is the blessing with mallow
and lentils" (Ibid., vers. 37–41).

This last is the typical food of the poor and
of rustics. Lovers of Horace will remember these
greens as his favourite food—save when invited
to Maecenas' banquets,—and Herrick is equally
sincere in his devotion to the—

"mess
Of water-cress."

But it must be confessed these dainties are here
forced rather suddenly, and awkwardly, upon the

corrupt judges.   Yet a still bolder turn is at hand.
Hesiod continues—

> "Truly the gods keep hid from mortals the means of
> existence:
> Else, in a single day, thou well might'st win by thy labour
> What would suffice for a year, although thou idle remainest.
> Ended soon were the labours of toilsome mules and of
> oxen" (Ibid., vers. 42–46).

This pessimistic and ignoble opinion of the
gods introduces, naturally enough, the tale of
Prometheus' deceitful sacrifice, and of Zeus'
consequent wrath.   The theft of fire—which had
been withheld to punish man—is merely touched
on, and the story (which is here hardly more
relevant), of Pandora, with her fatal curiosity, is
told in full detail.   That Hesiod invented the
entire story is unlikely, but this is its first appearance in extant literature.   In offering a rendering of the passage, no attempt can be made
to discuss questions of "interpolation," "double
redaction," etc.

> "Zeus, in the wrath of his heart, hath hidden the means of
> subsistence,—
> Wrathful because he once was deceived by the wily Pro-
> metheus.

The Works and Days.

Therefore it was he devised most grievous troubles for
    mortals.

Fire he hid: yet that, for men, did the gallant Prometheus

Steal, in a hollow reed, from the dwelling of Zeus the
    Adviser,

Nor was he seen by the ruler of gods, who delights in the
    thunder.

Then, in his rage at the deed, cloud-gathering Zeus did
    address him:

' Iapetionides, in cunning greater than any,

Thou in the theft of fire and deceit of me art exulting,

—Source of regret for thyself, and for men who shall be
    hereafter.

I, in the place of fire, will give them a bane, so that all
    men

May in spirit exult, and find in their misery comfort!'

Speaking thus, loud laughed he, the father of gods and of
    mortals.

Then he commanded Hephaistos, the cunning artificer,
    straightway

Mixing water and earth, with speech and force to endow it,

Making it like in face to the gods whose life is eternal.

Virginal, winning, and fair was the shape: and he ordered
    Athene

Skilful devices to teach her, the beautiful works of the
    weaver.

Then did he bid Aphrodite the golden endow her with
    beauty,

Eager desire, and passion that wasteth the bodies of
    mortals.

Hermes, guider of men, the destroyer of Argus, he ordered,

Lastly, a shameless mind to bestow, and a treacherous
nature.

So did he speak.   They obeyed lord Zeus, who is offspring
of Kronos.

Straightway, out of the earth, the renowned artificer
fashioned

One like a shame-faced maid, at the will of the ruler of
Heaven.

Girdle and ornaments added the bright-eyed goddess
Athene.

Over her body the Graces divine and noble Persuasion

Hung their golden chains; and the Hours with beautiful
tresses

Wove her garlands of flowers that bloom in the season of
springtime.

All her adornment Pallas Athene fitted upon her.

Into her bosom, Hermes the guide, the destroyer of Argus,

Falsehood, treacherous thoughts, and a thievish nature
imparted :

Such was the bidding of Zeus who heavily thunders ; and,
lastly,

Hermes, herald of gods, endowed her with speech, and the
woman

Named Pandora, because all gods who dwell in Olympos

Gave her presents, to make her a fatal bane unto mortals.

When now Zeus had finished this snare so deadly and
certain,

Famous Argus-slayer, the herald of gods, he commanded,

Leading her thence, as a gift to bestow her upon Epimetheus.

He, then, failed to remember Prometheus had bidden him never

Gifts to accept from Olympian Zeus, but still to return them

Straightway, lest some evil befall thereby unto mortals.

So he received her,—and then, when the evil befell, he remembered.

"Till that time, upon earth were dwelling the races of mortals,

Free and secure from trouble, and free from wearisome labour ;

Safe from painful diseases that bring mankind to destruction

(Since full swiftly in misery age unto mortals approacheth).

Now, with her hands, Pandora the great lid raised from the vessel,

Letting them loose : and grievous the evil for men she provided.

Hope yet lingered, alone, in the dwelling securely imprisoned,

Since she under the edge of the lid had tarried, and flew not

Forth : too soon Pandora had fastened the lid of the vessel.

Such was the will of Zeus, cloud-gatherer, lord of the aegis.

Numberless evils beside to the haunts of men had departed,

Full is the earth of ills, and full no less are the waters.

Freely diseases among mankind, by day and in darkness,

Hither and thither may pass, and bring much woe upon
  mortals :
—Voiceless, since of speech high-counselling Zeus has
  bereft them " (Ibid., vers. 47–104).

The great fame of the myth will justify such
a complete transcription from this its earliest
form. Old as the passage is, its fragmentary
and discordant details indicate that it is a crude
attempt to unite several diverse legends already
in circulation. One feature of the myth which
has doubtless puzzled us all is, Whence came
the strange jar containing all woes for men ?
Though Homer apparently knows nothing of
Pandora, he perhaps supplies an answer to this
question. It is in a famous scene of Il. xxiv.,
where Achilles, himself weary of life, is preaching
resignation to his unwelcome guest, the heart-
broken Priam. The gods make men's life bitter,
though they themselves are secure from trouble,
says Achilles ;—

" Yea, for indeed two jars in the palace of Zeus are standing,
    One of the evil gifts they bestow, and the other of
      blessings.
  He that receives them commingled, from Zeus who delights
    in the thunder,

> Chances at times upon ill, and again at times upon
>   blessings.
>
> He who receives but the troubles, him Zeus makes utterly
>   wretched."

Some have fancied Pandora was allowed to bring
this jar of ills (or, perhaps, a vessel filled from
it ?) as an unwelcome dower.

The mention of Hope, as still imprisoned, is
doubtless a peculiarly pessimistic touch. Hope,
the deluder, is herself a bane, the poet says—
or would be, if existent at all among men. For
this, and this alone, Hesiod thanks Mother
Pandora,—that she shut the lid before this
mischief could flit forth into the world. Modern
versions, down to Longfellow's "Pandora" and
Hawthorne's "Wonder-book," teach otherwise;
indeed, Aeschylos, in his Prometheus, distinctly
rejects this view of Hope; but such seems to
be Hesiod's thought. Pandora is not without
charm, as she stands forth,—

> "Garlanded by the fair-tressed Hours with the blossoms
>   of springtime;"

but so many later myth-makers and poets have
reshaped and newly adorned her, that the original

cruder conception of Hesiod is nearly hid from our imagination.   Hesiod is the earliest source to which we can trace this and many another deathless mythic fancy.   Prometheus' side of this fascinating tale is turned more fully toward us when it is retold in the Theogony.

At this point in the Works and Days any attempt at logical connection seems to be frankly abandoned.   Hesiod merely says—

" Now, if you please, I will tell you another story, in outline,
    Well and skillfully,—you, meantime, in memory hold it,—
    How from the selfsame source spring gods, and men who
    are mortal " (Works and Days, vers. 106–108).

That gods, like men, are indeed sprung from the common mother Earth, is orthodox enough, and is often repeated, notably with emphasis by Pindar (Nemean Odes, VI. i.).   The gap between the two races, gods and men, was probably chiefly caused by Prometheus' fatal championship; but here the matter is hardly touched upon.   Instead, we are told at much length of the five successive races that have dwelt upon the earth.   There is, perhaps, a certain connection, since the general thesis still is, that men, now fallen from their high estate, are doomed to unceasing and hopeless toil. The account of the successive ages is not, however, correlated duly with the tale of Pandora. It would be difficult even to bring her into it at any point. Rather is it an independent and more elaborate — though not more logical — account of man's degeneracy from a happier state. It is a sufficiently complete poem in itself, and, though comfortless and untrue in its general doctrine, abounds in fine thoughts and beautiful verses. Whether Hesiod's work at all or not, the passage is doubtless a separate composition. The episode is introduced quite abruptly, especially if, with the editors, we bracket the three lines last quoted (106–108).

"First was a golden race of men, that with language are
    gifted,
  Made by the gods immortal, who hold the Olympian
    dwellings.
  They were in Kronos' time, when he was the ruler of Heaven.
  Like to the gods they lived, and possessed their spirit
    untroubled,
  Wholly exempt from toil and misery."

                      (Ibid., vers. 109–113.)

Quite un-Homeric is the belief that the folk
of this earliest or golden age, after a long life
of hale and painless vigour, falling on death as
on a pleasant sleep, become *daemones,* (δαίμονες,)
wandering over the earth, the kindly guardians
of living men. This faith in guardian angels
reappears from time to time: strikingly in
Plato, and also in Horace (Epist. II. i. 144 and
II. ii. 187–189), where every human soul at birth
receives such a protector, his genius; but it is
especially familiar to us, of course, as a Hebrew
and Oriental, belief. Such a faith is, doubtless,
in varying forms, as extended as the dwellings
of humanity. It does not, however, appear to
have been a very wide-spread popular belief
among the Greeks. Moreover, as early as
Empedocles, the philosophers began ascribing
to the daemones those superhuman actions which
could not be defended as the deeds of virtuous and
wise gods. This, in the hands of later Christian
assailants, finally gave the word the utterly evil
significance still attaching to " demon," "demo-
niacal," etc.; while "daemon" and "daemonic"
would fain revert to the nobler connotation.

In the second, or silvern age, men had the doubtful boon of a childhood one hundred years long, spent at their mother's side, followed by briefer and troublous maturity.   This folk was finally swept away altogether by Zeus, for neglect of sacrifice.

"Still, when this race also had under the ground been
    hidden,
They, underneath our earth, though mortals, are known
    as the blessèd,
Second, indeed, yet honour to them is also accorded."

(Ibid., vers. 140–142.)

It is quite worth noting, that the nobler golden race still dwell in the goodly sunshine of our world,—a greater boon, to the Greek mind, than any unearthly Elysium, " or casual hope of being elsewhere blest." Without doubt Hesiod would have echoed Achilles' bitter word, uttered in Persephone's realm, which so shocked Plato :—

" Verily I would have chosen to live as the serf of another,
  Yea, of a needy man, who had but a scanty subsistence,
  Than to be sovran here over all who are dead and departed."

(Odys. xi.)

The third age, of bronze, took its name, partly at least, from the metal used in its utensils and arms.

> "Brazen the warlike gear they wore, and brazen their dwellings.
> Bronze it was they wrought: not yet black iron existed."
>   (Works and Days, vers. 150, 151.)

Moreover, this, as also the last and contemporary age, that of iron, corresponds exactly to what is now archaeologically established as to the development of the arts among many races. Hesiod, however, considers it all a story of constant deterioration—with one important exception.

Between the bronze and iron ages he finds place for a fourth, more just and more noble than either. These are the heroes or demigods, and he especially mentions the two great sieges in which most of them perished: about seven-gated Thebes and Priam's citadel. As they were nobler in life than their predecessors, so their after-destiny is brighter. The men of bronze, slain by each other's violent hands, passed down to Hades, leaving the bright sunlight, and—

perhaps worst of all—are *nameless* for evermore. But the later heroes are set by Zeus on the bounds of earth.

"There, by the eddying Ocean, they dwell in the Isles of the Blessed" (Ibid., ver. 171).

Whence arose this belief in the Happy Isles, where thrice a year the bounteous harvest ripens, is not easy to guess. For us they fitly typify the calm, stormless islands of Homeric poesy in which Achilles, Helen, Priam, and the rest abide in eternal majesty. No doubt Hesiod himself was more or less consciously diverted from his current of pessimistic invention by the glorifying genius of the Homeric poets, illuminating the century just before his time. The very inconsistency of the passage with its pessimistic environment seems to stamp Hesiod as a true, if reluctant, Homerid!

These four or five races Hesiod probably regarded as each a separate creation or growth, not as descended one from another. His own folk is apparently doomed to annihilation no less than the others.

" Zeus shall yet destroy this race of humanity also,
    When, from the hour of their birth, they appear gray-
        haired on the temples " (Ibid., vers. 180, 181).

Some have thought this a picturesque way of
declaring men would *never* perish from the earth.
But youthtime is, to a Greek, the flower of life,
and the degeneration from the century-long
childhood of the silver age is to be complete,
when even the new-born infant shows the marks
of exhausted vigour.   And there is quite as
much truth as poetry deeply imbedded here.
Alas for that race which crowds out the careless
merriment, the leisurely enjoyment of the passing
hour, which should characterize the early years
of life !

Hesiod becomes as stern and majestic as a
Hebrew prophet, while he tells how perjury and
treachery, insolence to parents and to gods, and
universal envy shall increase.   At last—

" Verily then will depart from the wide-wayed earth to
    Olympos,—
Wrapping about in robes of white their beautiful figures,
Leaving humankind, to abide with the race of immortals,—
Shame and Vengeance."

By the apologue of the hawk and the nightingale, Hesiod next illustrates the abhorrent doctrine that physical might makes right. The sweet-voiced bird, rather than the familiar dove, was perhaps chosen in allusion to the poet himself in the clutches of the unjust judges. This is the first appearance of the animal-fable in Hellenic literature.

In the eulogy of Justice, which next follows, she is personified as the dear daughter of Zeus, and her seat is close beside his throne. Punishing a whole race, if need be, for its ruler's sin, she bestows prosperity and abundant increase upon righteous nations. So, he adds, they have no need to voyage abroad, since the bounteous earth provides them of its crops! This notion, that foreign travel and trade are impious, occurs in Horace,—not to mention much later men!

The sermon, or admonition, has been heavily loaded with aphorisms and maxims not closely connected with each other. A nobler morality than elsewhere in the poem appears in such lines as :—

" Evil he worketh himself who worketh ill to another."
                              (Ibid., ver. 265.)

And as sloth is a form of injustice, the poem now
stoops from heavenly themes, though still not
without grace, to the need of industry, especially
for the husbandman.

". . .   But remembering still my injunction,
   Work, oh Perses, sprung from the gods, that Famine may
      ever
   Hate you, and dear may you be to Demeter, of beautiful
      garlands,
   Awesome one, and still may she fill thy garner with plenty."
                              (Ibid., vers. 298–301.)

We have now just reached the three hundredth
line, and here the poem divides into many ill-
connected verses and groups of lines, akin indeed
in general scope, as a river is divided to irrigate
many fields. The maxims strung together here
would be as helpful to Perses as to any other
rustic, no doubt.

For a score of lines the word ἔργον, *work*, is
repeated with its derivatives and synonyms in
most tedious iteration, thus :—

" Work is no disgrace, but the shame is, not to be working;
  If you but work, then he who works not will envy you
    quickly,
  Seeing your wealth increase: with wealth come honour
    and glory " (Ibid., vers. 311–313).

From such general exhortations to justice and industry we pass to more and more practical maxims.

" Summon the man who loves thee to banquet: thy enemy
    bid not.
  Summon him most of all who dwells most closely beside
    thee.
  Since, if aught that is strange or evil chance to befall thee,
  Neighbours come ungirt, but kinsmen wait to be girded."
                        (Ibid., vers. 342–345.)

" —Take your fill when the cask is broached and when it is
    failing.
  Midway spare: at the lees 'tis not worth while to be
    sparing " (Ibid., vers. 368, 369).

There is much wisdom in the advice to—

" Call, with a smile, for a witness, although 'tis your brother
    you deal with " (Ibid., ver. 371).

We know what bitter experience had taught him this. Even more gloomy is the remark a few lines later :—

"Let there be one son only, to guard the estate of his father."
(Ibid., ver. 376).

At ver. 368 the definite instructions for farmers commence :—

" When the Pleiades, the daughters of Atlas, are rising,
Then begin your harvest: the ploughing when they are
setting " (Ibid., vers. 383, 384).

From this point, in a fairly connected fashion, the tasks of the successive seasons are discussed down to ver. 617. The last three or four lines, indeed, are a mere repetition of the advice to plough when the Pleiades set. Whether these closing verses are a late addition or not, the calendar for the circling year is there completed.

These two hundred and thirty-nine lines, then, are the core of the poem, from which it takes its name. Some very general and quaint advice is given :—

" Get thee a dwelling first, and a woman, and ox for the
ploughing " (Ibid., ver. 405).

This verse is twice quoted by Aristotle, and as he took the " woman," (γυναῖκα,) for *wife*, it is thought a mischievous hand, since his day, has interpolated the strange following verse :—

" —Buy thou a woman, not wed her, that she may follow
    the oxen " (Ibid., ver. 406).

If, as often elsewhere, this last phrase here meant " guide the ploughshare," that is a fitter task for a strong mature man, and is carefully so assigned only thirty lines later :—

" After them there should follow a vigorous ploughman of
    forty,
  When he has eaten a quartern loaf, eight slices, for break-
    fast " (Ibid., vers. 441, 442).

But there are also very detailed hints, as upon the exact size of timber : three feet long for a mortar, three cubits for a pestle, seven feet for an axletree.   The advice to make the share-beam of oak, ploughtail of ilex, poles of bay or elm, may remind us of the carefully selected woods for the Deacon's " One-Hoss Shay : "—

  " The hubs of logs from the ' settler's ellum,'—
    Last of its timber,—they couldn't sell 'em.
    The panels of whitewood, that cuts like cheese,
    But lasts like iron for things like these,"

Professor Jebb calls attention to the charm often given to passages in our poem by the mention of birds, they and the stars being the commonest marks of time in the calendar of the rural year.

" Thou must be mindful, too, when the voice of the crane thou hearest
Utter its annual cry from out of the clouds above thee.
She brings signals for ploughing, and heralds the season of winter" (Ibid., vers. 448–450).

Or again :—

" This shall the remedy be, if thou art belated in ploughing.
When in the leaves of the oak is heard the voice of the cuckoo,
First, that across the unbounded earth brings pleasure to mortals,
Three days long let Zeus pour down his rain without ceasing,
So that it fills the oxhoof's print, yet not overflows it.
Then may the ploughman belated be equal with him who was timely " (Ibid., vers. 485–490).

That is, if you do put off your ploughing till spring, choose a wet week for it.

A touch that reminds us how like is human nature in Boeotia or Berkshire, may be rendered :—

" Pass by the seat at the forge, and the well-warmed tavern
    in winter.
    . . . That is the time when a man not slothful increases
    his substance " (Ibid., vers. 493–495).

The cruel doctrine of early rising has, of course,
an honoured place :—

" Shun thou seats in the shade, nor sleep *till the dawn,* in
    the season
When it is harvest-time, and your skin is parched in the
    sunshine " (Ibid., vers. 474, 475).

Honest servants seem not to have been the
unfailing rule even in these olden days. A hint
upon pilfering underlies the advice,—

" Seek thou a homeless thrall, and a serving-maid who is
    childless " (Ibid., ver. 602).

For the benefit of the tramp, sleeping by day
to plunder by night—for there is no new thing
under the sun, at least in human nature—Hesiod
advises—

    " Keep thou a sharp-toothed dog ! " *
                                (Ibid., ver. 604.)

---

* The mysterious inscription in Rudder Grange illustrates
this.

The last and pleasantest task of the circling
year is the vintage. The grapes, dried ten days
in sun and five in shade, are then to be poured
into winepresses—

> " Gifts from the bringer of joy, Dionysos."
>> (Ibid., ver. 614.)

As an indication of relative date, we may mention
that in Homer Dionysos is not yet joy-giver nor
wine-giver, nor of any apparent importance in
the daily life of man (cf. pp. 121, 122).

Here, with or without the renewed mention
of the Pleiades as the signal for ploughing, and
the blessing on the closing year, the poem might
well have ended, with a happier note of rustic
content than had filled the first section.   Instead,
the poet turns rather suddenly to the sea :—

> " But if an eager desire for storm-vext voyaging seize thee,"
>> (Ibid., vers. 618.)

This subject is discussed in sensible and fairly
connected fashion for over seventy lines.   There
are shrewd touches, like—

> " Praise thou a little vessel : bestow thy freight in a large
> one " (Ibid., vers. 643).

The only important digression is in the personal
reminiscence already mentioned (*supra*, p. 44)—

"I will the ways make known of the waters loudly resound-
ing,
Though I am nowise a master of navigation and vessels,
Since I never have traversed the wide-wayed sea upon
ship-board,
Save to Euboea across from Aulis, where the Achaians
Waited of old for winter to pass, and gathered their
forces,
Sailing from sacred Hellas to Troy with its beautiful
women.
There, to the funeral games of the wise Amphidamas faring,
Over to Chalkis I passed. The abundant prizes they
promised
Were by his valorous sons bestowed. As a victor in
music
I bore off, I declare, a tripod fitted with handles.
This to the Muses of Helicon there I in gratitude offered
Where they first had made me a master of clear-voiced
singing.
So much alone is the knowledge I have of the well-clamped
vessels ;—
Yet will I utter the thought of Zeus, who is lord of the
aegis,
Since the mysterious gift of song I received from the
Muses" (Ibid., vers. 648–662).

The passage is probably the germ of the famous

legend, that Hesiod once met and vanquished Homer in a contest of minstrelsy. The verses themselves have been doubted, however, from the days of Alexandrian scholarship until now. They are generally believed to be the utterance— whether truthful or not—of a rhapsode much later than the old poet himself. The voyage to Euboea, here mentioned, is one of *a few. rods* only, so the confession of ignorance on the very subject he is treating—navigation—is naïvely complete. But it is said the sea has in all ages, down to Barry Cornwall, been best sung by those who neither loved nor knew it: and Hesiod was under the direct inspiration and guidance of the Heliconian Muses, who could supply any gaps in his experience.

This continuous passage of advice to mariners vanishes in the midst of a sentence—

"Do not stow in the hollowed vessel the whole of thy substance,
Leave thou more behind, and carry the less for a cargo.
Hateful it is to meet with a loss on the watery billows,—
Hateful too if, loading excessive weight on a wagon,

Thou shouldst crush thine axle and so thy burden be
wasted.

Keep thou a measure due: all things have a fitting
occasion " (Ibid., vers. 689–694).

The next seventy lines are a mere string of
maxims, religious, ethical, ceremonial, and diverse
in character. Many of them open up curious
problems of folklore and superstition. Before
crossing a river, to stand gazing on its current
and to·utter a prayer is but a recognition of the
river-god's dangerous power. But why wash
the hands also? Is it an emblem of one's
innocence? "Don't pare your finger-nails at a
religious banquet" has its modern parallel.
"Don't tell lies for the sake of talking," is a
positive insult. Some yet cruder and more
elemental "Don'ts" must be passed over in
emphatic silence.

Finally, the last sixty lines of the poem are
a calendar of the lucky and unlucky days in
each month, and so may be responsible for the
latter half of the title. These precepts are, no
doubt, largely pure superstition. The fourth of
the month is the day to marry, and Proclos has

explained that this is the day sacred to Aphrodite and Hermes the guide.   Why the twentieth and tenth are fortunate days to beget a boy, and the fourteenth a girl, is not explained.   The *thirteenth* is unlucky for sowing, but proper for setting out plants—a finer distinction than our own silly fears would make.   Indeed the poet himself rebels — timidly — against such beliefs, as he makes clear in the closing strain, which is not without a quiet dignity of its own :—

" Different men praise different days : they are rare who do
    know them.
  Often a day may prove as a stepmother, often a mother :
  Blessèd and happy is he who, aware of all that concerns
    them,
  Wisely works his task, unblamed in the sight of immortals,
  Judging the omens aright, and succeeds in avoiding trans-
    gression " (Ibid., vers. 824–828).

Altogether, this poem is one which grows in interest with more careful and thoughtful perusal. The unfavourable comparison with Homer's sparkling narratives fades from our thought.   Interest of a different kind is gradually awakened.   We seem, indeed, to be learning to breathe the heavier

and more restful Boeotian air. The general relation of parts can often be felt, even where we
could hardly demonstrate an adequate logical or
artistic connection. At last we may find we are
acquiring a certain faith in, and a strong regard
for, the quaint sturdy old Ascraean farmer and
bard. At the least, he becomes a very real and
very human being.

Note.—There is a fair version of both Hesiod's chief
poems by Elton (Bohn's Classical Library), the Works in
rhymed pentameters, the Theogony in blank verse. In the
same volume of "Bohn" is a better prose version, with
many useful notes. The annotated edition of the Greek
text by the versatile F. A. Paley is one of his least satis-
factory works; but it is the only available Hesiod with
English notes. Far more learned is the Latin commentary
of Göttling. A brief but masterly (literary) critique of
Hesiod's poems is included in Professor Jebb's beautiful
volume, "Classical Greek Poetry." Symonds has also a
genial account.

III.

THE HESIODIC THEOGONY, SHIELD OF HERACLES, ETC.

WE have had occasion to mention before a famous passage in Herodotos (ii. 53), in which he declares that it was Hesiod and Homer who settled the names, the powers, the honours, and even made known the forms, of the Greek gods. Of course this does not mean that these poets used with perfect freedom their own inventive powers, but, chiefly, that the traditions and myths accepted by them gained such currency as to overpower discordant and contradictory stories. This is largely true; though it must always be kept in mind that local, tribal, or national beliefs and rites, quite irreconcilable with one another—or with any literary tradition—lived on everywhere, and may at any point still come to our knowledge through a religious monument, an inscription, or even a late piece of pottery, preserving in its decorative pictures some else-forgotten local legend. But above all this tangled thicket of contradictory polytheism and petty myth the conceptions of Homer and Hesiod do rise into something like national acceptance among the Greeks, and exercise a dominant—though not an exclusive—influence on later lyric and dramatic poets, on sculptor and painter, even, in some degree, on the tenacious local beliefs and cults themselves.

When Herodotos speaks thus of Homer, he probably thinks chiefly, but not solely, of Iliad and Odyssey. We have seen (*supra,* pp. 14, 15) that he promptly rejected the Homeric authorship of the famous and magnificent Cyprian Epic, because it disagreed with the Iliad as to the course of Paris' voyages. In regard to one, at least, of the early Theban epics, Herodotos is doubtful if it was Homeric or no. Whether he would have credited the Cyclic *Theogony* to Homer we cannot say. Probably not, for he shows more shrewdness in literary judgments than in almost anything else. At any rate, this Cyclic Theogony has utterly perished, and we can test Herodotos' statement only by the two Homeric poems proper.

Homer's gods are, on the whole, distinctly more ignoble than any of his men and women. While conceived in our human likeness, and even more subjected than we to the bodily instincts and passions, they are necessarily deprived of man's noblest attributes. They cannot risk their lives in a noble cause, for instance, since they are immortal. Xenophanes, an early philosopher, said, with savage justice, that Homer (and Hesiod too) made the gods do all the things held most shameful among men; and thereupon follows a bold enumeration of the chief crimes in the decalogue (*infra*, p. 181).

It is, perhaps, fortunate also, for our impressions as to the Homeric ideals of divinity, that the gods appear in the poems only incidentally; in the Iliad, in fact, only so far as they take an active interest in the fate of Troy. This doom of the city is, moreover, a signal example of essential justice, since treachery to the hospitality, and sin against the nuptial rights of Menelaos, bring just ruin on Paris and all his race. To be sure, Helen returns to prosperity, and is apparently assured of deathless bliss, while many innocent and noble sufferers are involved in the general calamity. But for the deepest problems of human suffering and sin, we have, perhaps, no right to demand a solution from the earliest of poets. Perhaps, again, the Helen of the Odyssey is hardly human at all.

Homer finds Zeus, so to speak, in full possession of his Olympian throne, and in fairly good control, too, of his obstreperous family. The poet had little occasion to refer to the earlier ages of elemental strife, to the legends of fatherly cannibalism and filial violence which have puzzled and shocked a hundred generations. In part, at least, Homer must have known and accepted these tales also. He knows that the Titans, the conquered uncles of imperial Zeus, sit in eternal confinement within lowest Tartarus. This was, of course, a penalty of defeat, an evidence of divine strife. Though Zeus in Homer boasts himself more than a match for all his family, yet the gentle Thetis reminds him how he had once been overpowered and cast into chains by his wife and children, and rescued only when she herself brought up to his aid the hundred-handed Briareos.

The still cruder tale of Uranos' mutilation at his children's hands, and on the instigation of his own wife, Ge, the weary Earth-mother, may have been unknown, or, again, may have been deliberately rejected, by Homer. He distinctly speaks, not of Uranos, but of Okeanos as first father of all. Here the sea-loving Ionian race may really have held firmly a creed more to their taste than the belief which afterward became the only orthodox one. For similar reasons, Poseidon the Earthshaker, who holds the world in his embrace, was long the supreme divinity of many an Ionian state. Indeed the late and reluctant compromise, which makes the sea-god a less mighty brother of Zeus', leaves him still unquestioned power in his own demesne: and he rarely takes a place at the stormy Olympian council-board at all. In early myth he is often seen unwillingly retiring before the Olympian gods proper, and his expulsion by Pallas Athene from the Athenian Acropolis, by Apollo from Delphi, was marked by open strife which was never entirely forgotten. But the assertion here to be emphasized is, that if Homer had worked out for us his full conception of Olympian ancient history and family life, it would, perhaps, shock us at least as much as does the Theogony of Hesiod.

This poem, of ten hundred and twenty-two hexameter verses, is the earliest Greek sketch of "systematic theology" we are likely ever to behold. It may well be, indeed, the first adequate attempt the Greeks had ever made to record and to reconcile the fancies, long current among them, as to the origin of the world and its divine government.

The prevailing opinion of antiquity assigned this poem also to the author of the Works and Days. (Pausanias the traveller, alone, asserts that the folk dwelling in his day about Mount Helicon accepted only the Works and Days as Hesiod's genuine work.) The general voice was probably, essentially, in the right. Some discrepancies and repetitions in the two works may be ascribed to the annoying interpolation from which both have certainly suffered. But at least, the two chief Hesiodic poems should be accredited to the same age, and to the same provincial, didactic, rather feebly inspired off-shoot of the great Homeric school. The influence of Homer is seen everywhere, in the fragments of lost works as in the extant Hesiodic poems. In particular, the marked local dialect of Boeotia, a coarse form of Aeolic Greek, has hardly coloured at all the traditional Ionic language of the epic school. Many lines and half lines are borrowed without change from Iliad or Odyssey. Occa-sionally, even, an Ionic name or usage, which must have been unintelligible in Boeotia, betrays the intrusive interpolation of a later time. But the Theogony is still, essentially, Hesiodic.

We turn to a continuous analysis of its contents, a somewhat less difficult, but also less interesting task, than in the case of the Works and Days. The first one hundred and sixteen lines are an invocation of the Muses, daughters of Zeus and Mnemosyne, or Memory. Here their

names occur, for the first time in Greek literature.
No attributes are assigned to any, though it is
said of Calliope, who was undoubtedly regarded
already as the patroness of epic poetry,—

> "She of them all is the oldest.
> She, moreover, abides in the courts of reverend monarchs."
> (Theog., vers. 79, 80.)

It should be remembered that the bards everywhere in Homer appear as courtly minstrels.
There is, indeed, a passage here almost as proud
as that haughty close of Pindar's first Olympic
ode, setting, like it, king and singer on almost
equal pedestals.　Of the ruler, Hesiod says—

> "He is supreme among his people assembled,
> Even as is among men the sacred gift of the Muses.
> Since from the Muses spring, and the mighty archer
> 　Apollo,
> Those whoso upon earth are the singers of songs, and the
> 　harpers.
> Monarchs arise from Zeus.　Yet blessèd is he whom the
> 　Muses
> Cherish: and sweet is the liquid speech from his lips that
> 　is flowing.
> Ay, though it may be a man with fresh-wrought trouble
> 　of spirit,

Bitterly vexed at heart, is pining, yet if a minstrel,
Liegeman of Muses, sing of the heroes' glories aforetime,
Or of the blessèd gods who have their abode in Olympos,
—Soon he forgets his sorrow: his cares no more are
    remembered " (Theog., vers. 92–102).

This is certainly a noble and a lofty strain,
and is all too closely imitated in one of the
Homeric Hymns (*infra*, p. 111).   Fused into
the same prologue however, indeed preceding
this appeal to the Olympian sisters nine, is a
much humbler invocation of the *Heliconian*
Muses :—

" They who Hesiod once in glorious music instructed
    While he was watching his lambs in the dales of Helicon
        sacred.
    This is the earliest word unto me by the goddesses
        uttered."

(And a very strange word it is, this first greeting
of the Muses to our race !)

" ' Shepherds that dwell in the fields, ye gluttons ignoble
    and wretched,
    Many a fiction like to the truth are we skilful to utter,
    Yet are we skilled no less to reveal, if we will, what is
        truthful ! '
    Then as a staff they gave me a branch of luxuriant laurel,

Plucking it, fair to behold : with the power of song they
    inspired me,
So I in verse could ennoble the things of the past and
    the future " (Ibid., vers. 22–32).

In truth, this long " prologue" contains certainly two, and probably half a dozen, hymns,
or preludes, each addressed to the Muses. The
announcement of the proper subject does not
even begin until ver. 105 :—

" Sing ye the sacred race of immortals ever-existing,
    Those who arose into life from the Earth and star-studded
        Heaven,
    Out of the murky Night, or else by the salt Deep
        nurtured " (Ibid., vers. 105–107).

These are alike forces and persons: for personification was not then, as with us, a device
of rhetoric, it was the resistless instinct of
childish man.

" Tell how, aforetime, gods and Earth came into existence,
    Rivers, and Deep unbounded, for ever surging and swelling,
    Stars that brightly gleam, and Heaven extended above us ;
    Then of the gods who from them sprang, the Bestowers
        of blessings ;
    Tell us how they divided their wealth, and parted the
        honours,

How they came to abide on Olympos abounding in ridges.
These things sing me, Muses who hold your Olympian
   dwellings
From the beginning:—and say what first came into
   existence " (Ibid., vers. 108–116.)

First of all, we learn, was only *Chaos*, i.e.
Yawning (space), but Earth arises. With her
appear Tartaros, *i.e.* the nether gloom, the mere
antithesis of kindly mother Earth, and Eros,
Desire or Love,

"Lord and subduer of all, who is fairest among the
   Immortals."

Such assertions about Eros are repeated constantly by later Greeks. Whether Hesiod had
any clear, or vague, insight into the cosmic law
of attraction we call gravitation, or the mystic
tie of sexual instinct on which all organic life
must depend, we may hardly dare to decide.
That Eros was the *eldest* of things created,
we find stated first by Parmenides (*infra*,
p. 187).

Earth produces out of herself overarching
Heaven to be her wedded mate. The mountains
and the woodland nymphs are her children

too. So are deep-eddying Okeanos, Hyperion,
and the other vaguely conceived brethren,
the Titans, who afterwards strive in vain
against that mightier third generation whom
Zeus leads to victory. Kronos is the youngest
and fiercest of this Titan brood. He takes the
lead in that revolting mutilation of his father
Uranos, which his mother Earth, weary of childbearing, plans and assists. Some dim figurative
meaning this legend once had, no doubt. Perhaps
Kronos is primeval man, resisting the tyranny
of the wild forces of the early world, typified
in the father Uranos.

Earth is not mother of all things. Like, if not
equal, to her, Night is sprung from Chaos, and
is also mother of a countless brood. Without
a wedded mate she bore Doom and Death,
Dreams, Nemesis, Age, and Strife,—and also the
three Fates, who are here first named : Clotho
the spinner, Lachesis, and Atropos. But strangely
enough a much later passage names the same
trio again, as daughters, not of Night at all,
but of Zeus and Themis. The commentators are
inclined to cut out the earlier passage. But,

indeed, the later philosophers, and poets also, were not quite agreed whether these rulers of destiny were themselves subject to Zeus, or older and mightier than he. Perhaps by their twofold place in the Theogony itself they typify a question which even the Christian theologian may discuss: Is a supreme but just ruling divinity himself subject to, or superior to, law and destiny ?

Night, wedded to her brother Erebos, produced also Day, and Ether, the light upper air. The Cyclic Titanomachy, we are told, made Ether the father of Uranos. Each cosmogony necessarily varied freely in such matters. But we soon weary in the attempt to extract mystic or other significance from these faint personifications and tiresome allegories. Yet even from the mere lists of names, that sometimes reach portentous length, unexpected information may be gleaned. Thus at ver. 237—

" Tethys unto Okeanos bare the eddying rivers."

The list of twenty-five streams which follows can only be a selection even from the limited geographical area known to the poet. (He says, indeed, that he could name three thousand.) Yet the very first is Neilos, which Homer knew only as "the river Aegyptos,"—so we are clearly in a later age. Next is Alpheios, and then Eridanos, probably the Po. The mention of Ister, or the Danube, shows that Greek mariners had already faced the terrors of the Black Sea. The failure of Rhone or Rhine to appear in the catalogue may perhaps indicate the Western limits of Hellenic knowledge in Hesiod's day. Simois and Scamander, the two Trojan rivers, are mentioned far apart in the list, but the epithet *divine*, applied to both, and only to them, is probably a tribute to the master's masterpiece. The name of Scamander has also a certain prominence as the closing word in the passage. A more elaborate tribute to the Poeta Sovrano was noted in the Works and Days (*supra*, pp. 60–61).

The musical harmony, even in a bare list of Greek names, may be felt in vers. 243–262, where the fifty sea-nymphs, daughters of Nereus, are all catalogued. Only a few, Amphitrite,

Achilles' mother Thetis, and Galatea who lured
the Cyclops on to make himself ridiculous, are
familiar. Yet all float, as gracefully as the
curving billows themselves, upon the bounding
dactyls of Hesiod's verse :—

" Glaukonomè, who in laughter delights, and Pontoporeia,
   Leiagorè and Euagorè and Laomedeia.
   Poulynomè and Autonoè and Lysianassa !"

Even Hesiod shrinks from enumerating the
three thousand ocean-nymphs, and we, avoiding
the strange monsters, Cerberos and Hydra,
Sphinx and Chimaera dire, may pass on rapidly
to ver. 453, the beginning of a new but still
savage age. Kronos, the unnatural son, is a yet
more cruel father. His children by Rheia are
devoured whole as fast as they are born: Hestia,
Demeter, and Herè, Hades, and Poseidon. The
sixth child is Zeus, but in his stead a great
stone, wrapt in swaddling-clothes, sated the
ostrich-like paternal voracity. Safely arrived at
maturity, Zeus rescues his brothers and sisters
from this living tomb. Moreover, his own
changeling, the stone, was itself deposited by

Zeus on earth, at Delphi, to be a memorial to mortals. Few families would set such a memorial stone on consecrated ground! Doubtless the poet Hesiod himself had seen it there, as Pausanias did many centuries later. But Xenophanes and Plato, Aeschylos and Pindar, raise a fearless cry of disbelief in all such horrors as this tale.

Less famous than Kronos is his brother-Titan Iapetos, who, wedding the ocean-nymph Clymene, begets four sons, the most familiar of whom are Atlas and Prometheus. Atlas, at Zeus' bidding, holds the sky upon his shoulders. It is, doubtless, his share in the punishment meted out to the vanquished Titans. Prometheus' story is more fully told. Why this cousin of Zeus is the champion of man is, however, not explained. Indeed, of man's creation we hear nothing at all. Neither do we learn how the human race had existed without women previous to Pandora's appearance. The tale begins abruptly (ver. 535).

"When now gods were at strife with mortal men at
    Mekonè"

Were the two races equals or companions until then? What was this strange gathering at Mekonè (Sicyon)? Even the verb (ἐκρίνοντο) is of doubtful meaning, and may signify "were deciding their dispute." At any rate, an ox is there slain, and Prometheus slily wraps the worthless bones in tempting white fat, but, on the other hand, conceals the good meat within the hide,—and offers Zeus his choice. Zeus is not deceived—so he assures us—but takes the less valuable portion knowingly, is wroth at Prometheus none the less, and in his rage refuses the gift of fire to wretched men. That they had possessed it before is not expressly said. In fact, we get no glimpse at our race's origin or previous condition. Prometheus steals the fire, and brings it to men in a hollow reed. It is later poets who explain, that he obtains it from Zeus' hearth-fire, or Hephaistos' forge, or by lighting a torch at the sun-god's chariot wheels. Singularly enough the custom among men of sacrificing to the gods, as their share, the bones of the victims wrapped in fat, and eating the rest themselves, became a permanent usage. Indeed,

the whole tale appears to be "teleological," *i.e.*
invented as an explanation for the actual Greek
habit in sacrifice, though it can hardly be accepted
as either a pious or a reassuring solution!

Pandora is now created by Zeus in his wrath,
to punish men further for Prometheus' daring.
But men and gods are apparently still dwelling
together on nearly equal terms. Probably men
were thought of by Hesiod as actually the
children of Prometheus, or as creatures that
had been fashioned out of clay and endowed
with life by him. (Both theories are found in
later writers.) Possibly the passage in which
this was explained has accidentally dropped out
of our Theogony.

It is Epimetheus (Afterthought, or the Short-
sighted One,) just as in the Works and Days, who
receives and weds Pandora, and as we hear that
" from her came the race of mortal women," he at
least, if not Prometheus, is to be regarded as our
divine ancestor. Hesiod, by the way, takes a far
more pessimistic view of the woman question in
the Theogony than in the Works. Prometheus is
bound to a column, of Zeus' hall perhaps—or, more

probably, in Tartaros.* Prometheus' liver grows miraculously every night to sate the rapacious eagle that feeds on it by day. It is Heracles who later slays the eagle, not without the approval of Zeus, who is glad to glorify his illustrious mortal son. That Zeus was prompted by any fear of Prometheus' power, or made any compromise with him, is nowhere intimated by Hesiod. In Aeschylos' great theological tragedy of Prometheus, the hero is made the son of Themis (Justice), and shares with her the knowledge of a mysterious danger threatening Zeus' throne. This gives to the sufferer the power of resistance which is almost essential to a tragic hero.

This Promethean story is for many reasons the most interesting feature of the Theogony. It is a pity that it appears there in a confused and probably in a fragmentary form. These first gropings of man's awakened intellect about those roots of primeval mystery which no human

* This column, instead of the Aeschylean rock, is seen in early pictures of the group. See, for instance, the curious black-figured vase on which Atlas and Prometheus appear together: Baumeister, p. 1411.

ingenuity can lay bare, must have a strange fascination for every thoughtful mind. We surely all share the gentle poet's faith—

> " That in even savage bosoms
> There are longings, yearnings, strivings,
> For the good they comprehend not ;
> That the feeble hands and helpless,
> Groping blindly in the darkness,
> Touch God's right hand in that darkness,
> And are lifted up and strengthened."

The great fault of our classical dictionaries and manuals of mythology is that they piece the new cloth of Lucian and Apollodorus, ay even mediæval and modern fancy, upon the tattered and faded myths of prehistoric Greece, and give us no clue to trace by themselves the crude beginnings, upon which so many generations as well as great individual poets or philosophers have made additions and alterations. Aeschylos' or Plato's Prometheus—yes, Shelley's or Lowell's—can give us much of noble suggestion ; but they do not fill out faithfully the Hesiodic sketch.

The remainder of the poem must be passed over rapidly. The most vigorous sustained passage is the war between the Titans, Zeus' uncles, on the one side, and the younger god himself with his brothers and allies on the other. Like the Trojan war on earth, this struggle lasts ten years. Tantalizing to the last, Hesiod gives us no real explanation of its origin or cause : but it is no doubt again a shadow cast upon the clouds, as it were, by man's real conflict with Nature's savage forces.

The prison-house of the vanquished Titans, as far beneath the earth as Heaven is high above, is described with a lurid splendour and vagueness in outline rather reminding us of the Miltonic imagination than of Dante's clear-cut precision. In the same general connection occurs the fine passage upon Styx. This eldest of Okeanos' daughters has rendered efficient aid to Zeus in the great war. In fact, her two sons, Kratos and Bia, Strength and Force, are indispensable supporters of the new throne, and in the opening scene of Aeschylos' play we may see how they compel the reluctant smith-god Hephaistos to spike the no less reluctant Prometheus to a crag beside the lonely Northern sea. Styx is a divinity and a mother, then, but she is at the same time a mighty river in that dark nether world, fed by a tenth part of Okeanos' own stream. For her support in danger she is rewarded by a signal honour. Zeus selects her waters as the especial safeguard against deception among the gods. She herself, indeed, never leaves her station below, by the palace of Hades and Persephone.

" There is the goddess' abode who is hated among the
　　immortals,
　Awesome Styx. She is first-born daughter to refluent
　　Ocean.
　There, far off from the gods, is set her illustrious dwelling,
　Covered above by enormous rocks : and about it on all sides,
　Firmly joined to the sky, it stands, by pillars of silver.
　Seldom thither does swift-footed Iris, the daughter of
　　Wonder,
　Fare with the message she bringeth across the sea's wide
　　ridges ;
　Only so often as strife hath arisen among the immortals.
　Whoso speaks untruth, of them that abide in Olympos,
　Iris is sent by Zeus, from afar, in her golden pitcher,
　That great oath of the gods to fetch : the water so famous.
　Coldly it trickleth down from a rock, both craggy and lofty.
　Whoso, among the immortals who dwell upon snowy
　　Olympos'
　Summits, perjures himself as he pours thereof a libation,

Breathless is destined to lie, until a year is completed.
Never to him ambrosia, the food of immortals, is proffered,
Never the nectar; but still without breathing he tarries,
   and speechless,
There on his couch outstretched; and evil the slumber
   that wraps him.
When this penalty now with the long year comes to
   completion,
Still thereafter another more grievous evil awaits him.
Nine years long is he parted from gods whose life is un-
   ending,
Never with them may he join in council, never at
   banquet,
Nine full years. In the tenth he again may mingle among
   them,
Joining in speech with immortals who hold the Olympian
   dwellings.
—Such is the oath gods swear by the deathless Stygian
   waters."

This is, perhaps, as favourable an example as
could be selected to illustrate Hesiod's loftier
style. While Zeus exacts this solemn pledge
and penalty in cases of divine perjury, there is
in Hesiod no explicit statement that oaths or
promises given by the gods under other circumstances may be lightly broken. Nevertheless,
this Hesiodic myth easily opened the way for

such an interpretation, and it was only too
widely accepted in later days.

Whether Joseph Rodman Drake was a classical
student or not, this passage must have influenced
directly or remotely some of the most delicate
fancies in the "Culprit Fay." So near do even the
latest creations of poetic art come to the Hellenic
sources of original inspiration.

It would have been better for the poem as a
work of art if it had broken off here. But the
rewards to Zeus' supporters take chiefly the form
of brides—he himself securing the leonine share,
—and the later verses return to the wearisome
genealogical lists, from which we supposed we
had escaped. Last-mentioned of creatures wholly
divine is the sorceress Medea. There is perhaps
a gap, possibly even a new work begins here, for
the Muses are invoked anew, and we now learn
of the goddesses who have borne children to
mortal fathers (ver. 963). Finally, our manuscript text ends (vers. 1021–1022) with the mere
prologue for still another catalogue now lost:—
bidding the Muses "Sing of the race of women!"
Those mortal women who had borne children to

divine fathers are undoubtedly meant. Indeed of this poem, as of others from the great Hesiodic school, many tantalizing fragments yet remain.

The great poetic fault in the Theogony is its feeble perspective and extreme lack of proportion. We have mentioned, for instance, the passage (vers. 349–361) in which fifty nymphs are swiftly catalogued by name. To pass from this to the large vague outlines of Titanic strife is like changing suddenly a microscope for a telescope. Even in the very midst of such a rapid list, we are detained, at the mention of Hecatè, while a hymn of forty lines is devoted to her alone! This may well be an interpolation, but it shares fully the interest of the rest. Indeed the value of the Theogony is not chiefly as a single work of art, nor even as literature at all. Crude, contradictory, perhaps the creation of various hands and generations, it is worthy of study as an early attempt to project our human intellect into that dark backward and abysmal mystery which still excites and baffles alike the imagination of the savage, the child, and the

philosopher. The special student of Greek literature is struck, furthermore, with the influence
exerted by the Hesiodic myths throughout the
Prometheus of Aeschylos. Indeed that great
trilogy may well have been planned in great
part as a protest against the crude and ignoble
theology of Hesiod. To this theme we may hope
to return.

We have just noticed the strange fashion in
which our manuscripts of the Hesiodic Theogony
close. The last four lines are unmistakably a
summing-up of the previous fifty verses, and an
opening invocation for a new poem—or for a
new section in a great theological corpus of
poetry :—

" These are the goddesses who, with mortal husbands
united,
Bore them children, like unto gods whose life is eternal.
—Now of the race of mortal women sing me, ye sweet-
voiced
Muses Olympian, daughters to Zeus who is lord of the
aegis " (Theog., vers. 1019–1022).

The form of these two contrasted couplets makes

the latter allusion plainly point to women who have borne children by the gods. This catalogue would, naturally, be much longer than the list of the children from goddesses by mortal mates, which had just been given. Many fragments and allusions attest the existence, and the popularity, in classical times of this Hesiodic Catalogue of Women. Indeed, learned editors like Göttling and Kinkel swell the list of these citations to more than a hundred and twenty: (though how such incidents as the union of two mortals, Telemachos and Nestor's daughter, or of the divine Thetis with human Peleus, etc., can be properly included there, I am unable to see). The truth is, that the mention of an ancestress in this list became, for many ancient families, the chief evidence of illustrious origin. This may well remind us of the royal "bar sinister," prominent in so many modern coats-of-arms.

It chances that one notable episode from the Catalogue has been preserved in full. It is the tale of Zeus' amour with Alcmene, and of Heracles' birth. The fifty-six verses were found in the fourth book of the Catalogue, as a Greek commentator positively states. The manner in which the passage is transmitted to us, however, is curious and instructive. It is now read as the opening section of a poem called the "Shield of Heracles," in 480 hexameters. To the tale of Alcmene a later rhapsode has attached, very awkwardly, an account of one among Heracles' less famous adventures, viz. the fight with Cycnus. This story is really told in 245 lines (vers. 57–140 and 320–480). But into this, again, has been thrust a description of Heracles' shield—of course an imitation of the famous passage in the Iliad on the armour of Achilles. This rather wearisome digression fills vers. 141 to 320, or much more than a third of the poem, to which it therefore, properly enough, has given its accepted name. The sutures here indicated are perfectly evident, even if we had not the positive ancient witness, who apparently still read the opening lines also in their proper place, in the Catalogue of Women. If these added portions are fair samples, then the later rhapsodes of the Hesiodic school were feeble in conception and tasteless in execution, even as compared with their own master.

Some lesser fragments from the Catalogue, *e.g.* a description of Dodona and its oracle, in ten hexameters, may be read with pleasure.

Various other titles of poems, and scanty fragments, attributed to Hesiod, still remain. A curious problem is raised by the " Eoeae," which is variously cited as identical with the Catalogue of Women, as a part of it, and as a separate poem, often in disagreement with the Catalogue ! The truth may be, that, originally poems of the same general school, but by different hands, they were united by later editors, just as the discordant Cyclic Epics were forced into a sort of harmony. The curious title is easily explained. Beginning, perhaps, with some such formula as Nestor's—

" Never have I such heroes seen, nor shall I behold them,"

each new section opened *" or such as "* ($\mathring{\eta}$ o'̈η). Several such lines still remain, among the scanty fragments quoted from either poem. In particular, the "Shield of Heracles" ("from the fourth book of the Catalogue") begins—

" *Or as,* deserting her home and the land of her father,
    Alcmene . . ."

Among the titles of lost Hesiodic works, the "Epithalamium on Peleus and Thetis," and "Theseus' Descent to Hades," are as attractive as any mythological subjects; and the former might have proved, if preserved, a welcome literary pendant for the François vase, and, perhaps, largely the source of Catullus' ideas in his largest poem. Purely didactic treatises, like one on "Astronomy," are mentioned. The "Precepts of Chiron" (the Centaur who instructed Achilles) may have been both mythic and didactic. But this, like the "Prophetic Verses," and the "Journey about the World," may well have been mere later compilations of extracts from the voluminous Hesiodic works.

Even in the sustained poems yet extant, the Works and Days, the Theogony, and the Shield of Heracles, we can hardly feel sure at any point that we have the material just as it left Hesiod's hands. The stamp set upon it is, at best, that of a school—perhaps merely the mark of any early age and of a rather rustic and crude artistic sense. Despite the inspiring Homeric examples, literature seems to be in its infancy again. Perhaps it is, rather, in the opening years of maturity, struggling vainly with philosophic thought and with a fuller personal consciousness, to which the happier singers of the morning gave little heed.

IV.

THE HOMERIC HYMNS.

WHEN Odysseus was being entertained by Nausicaa's parents (Odys. viii. 499), he asked the court minstrel Demodocos to sing the tale of the wooden horse; and the bard straightway—

"Impelled of the god began."

The Greek scholiast is in doubt whether this means "He, inspired by the god, began," or "Taking his start from the god he began." For it was their custom, he adds, to offer a prelude in the god's honour. So it is possible Homer himself contains an allusion to this custom of the poets and rhapsodes, to open their epic recital with a prelude, invoking the divinity at whose festival or shrine they were present, or under whose especial guardianship they stood.

Pindar (circa 500 B.C.), also, commences his second Pythian ode thus :—

> " As the Homeridae,
>   Minstrels of well-joined verse,
>   Begin most often with a prelude unto Zeus."

A clearer hint is given by Plutarch, in § 6 of his treatise on Music : " For first paying their devoirs to the gods, they (the rhapsodes or professional reciters) passed on quickly to the poesy of Homer and the others."

While this might well happen even at the courts of the Achaian princes in the heroic age, it seems more appropriate to the popular religious festivals, the gathering of whole nations at their common shrines, in the later more democratic days. This impression is confirmed by the passage in the great Apollo-hymn (*infra*, p. 134), describing the gathering of the Ionians on Delos. And these very verses, which are quoted by Thucydides (ii. 104, 3) unquestioningly as Homeric, probably are, as a matter of fact, among the oldest, if not the very oldest, in our collection. Yet even they are evidently much later than the royal Achaian days.

It is noticeable that Thucydides there calls the poem, not a hymn, but a prelude (*prooimion*). Preludes, then, for the most part, these *Hymni Homerici* are; all later than the great epics, and probably extending through several centuries, at least to the close of the Attic period.   In length they vary from three lines to nearly six hundred. They borrow verses and passages very freely from each other.   In particular, number twelve, only three lines long, is a tribute to Persephone's mother.   The opening verse—

"First Demeter I sing, the fair-tressed reverend goddess,"

is identical with the first hexameter in the great Eleusinian hymn (number four).   The second line—

"Her and her daughter as well, most beautiful Perse-
    phoneia,"

is, again, seemingly borrowed from ver. 493 of the larger poem, with a mere change of case. The closing strain—

"Hail, O goddess, protect this town.   And begin our
    singing,"

is no great *tour de force :* and when we find this

too, verbatim, in another hymn to Demeter—
composed by the learned Alexandrian poet,
Callimachos—we begin to question whether our
modest triplet had any separate inspiration at
all! Though an extreme, this is no isolated case.
And while the hymns borrow so freely of each
other, nearly all are more or less dependent on
the Homeric epic. One of the liveliest, in particular, the hymn to Aphrodite which describes
her love for Anchises, is largely a mere *cento*, or
patchwork, line after line being borrowed, little
or not at all changed, from Homer, but also in
some cases from Hesiod, the great Demeter-hymn,
and others.

Leaving, however, one or two of the "great"
hymns for separate discussion, we will pass in
review, in the present chapter, some typical
examples of the briefer hymns, or preludes
proper. Though Pindar speaks of such preludes as addressed oftenest to Zeus, only one,
of the briefest and weakest, in our collection,
is directed to him by name. It has but four
verses, and may be thus rendered—with some
dilution :—

"Zeus will I sing of, among all gods most mighty and
     greatest,
Wide-eyed, ruling the world, whose wishes afar are accom-
     plished,
Who, as he sits with Themis, engages in chat confidential.
Be propitious, oh wide-eyed Zeus, most famous and
     mighty!"

As a fairer type of the lesser hymns we may
render entire the twenty-fourth, which consists
of seven lines. Incidentally, the close kinship
with the prelude of Hesiod's Theogony (*supra*,
p. 83) may be noted. One poet or the other has
borrowed quite too freely.

"I with the Muses first will begin, and Zeus, and Apollo,
Since those men from the Muses come, and Apollo the
     Archer,
Whoso upon our earth are the singers of songs, and the
     harpers.
Kings are come from Zeus. Yet blest is he whom the
     Muses
Love, and sweet is the liquid speech from his lip that is
     flowing.
Greeting, children of Zeus! and grant to my minstrelsy
     honour;
I of you, and, as well, of another song, will be mindful."

Such a closing line, with its plain transition to

the epic recitation that followed, is frequently, but not invariably, found in these hymns. Indeed the question has been raised whether some may not be rather *post*-ludes, since the gods especially concerned were doubtless often invoked at the end no less than at the beginning, as our number twenty remarks :—

" Phoebos, the swan of thee sings sweetly under his feathers,
    Leaping up to the bank at the side of the eddying river,
    By the Peneios.   The minstrel, holding the clear-toned
        phorminx,
    Sweet-voiced sings of thee at the end and beginning.   Oh
        ruler,
    Be thou therefore gracious, for thee do I honour in singing."

Once, at least, in a brief hymn (No. 5) to Aphrodite, the rhapsode closes with a distinct mention of a contest ($\dot{\alpha}\gamma\dot{\omega}\nu$) about to occur, praying for victory therein.

It is not often easy to detect any especial fitness, in these rather formal invocations, to any particular section of the great epics, which the minstrel may have recited immediately thereafter.   Possibly the singer, when about to repeat, for instance, the glorious Sixth Iliad,—including

the scene where the matrons of the city, so justly
doomed, march in vain to Pallas's temple with
their suppliant gifts,—may have chosen, or even
composed, the brief but earnest prelude numbered
XI. in our collection :—

> "Pallas Athene first will I sing, the preserver of cities,
>   Terrible, who to the works of war is with Ares devoted—
>   Cities falling in ruin, the shouting, and tumult of battle.
>   She, too, saveth the host, when issuing forth or returning.
>   Greeting, oh goddess, to thee!   Prosperity grant me, and
>   fortune."

But, as a rule, we can only surmise that the
god of the festival day, or the god in whose
sacred close the minstrel stood, was thus pro-
pitiated before the epic recital itself was entered
upon.

The larger poems of the collection are no
longer mere invocations.   They contain entire
myths, usually adventures of the gods they
honour.   Some critics indeed would assign
certain poems in the group to comparatively
secular rather than religious occasions—if such
a distinction can be made at all in Hellenic life.
Thus the amour of Aphrodite and Anchises

certainly does the goddess little honour, and it has been suggested that the poem upon her was perhaps rather a courtly compliment to some prince, in the Troad or elsewhere, claiming descent from that illustrious pair. It would, in fact, be easy to drop the last two of its two hundred and ninety-four verses, wherein the singer greets the goddess, and announces that he passes from her to "another hymn." (The word *hymnos*, however, used here and often, probably had at first no especial religious connection. It seems to be derived from the verb which signifies "to weave," and may have meant a "woven song," or composition, in any key. Later it was chiefly restricted to the Apollo-cult.)

These poems are, it is thought, not only centuries apart in age, but equally diverse in local origin, each arising, as a rule, not far from the chief shrine of the god it celebrates. Yet the differences generally elude any save microscopic analysis.

Thus scholars disagree whether the delightful hymn to Pan (No. 18) betrays its Athenian origin by peculiarities of diction. If Attic, it is

probably late, as Herodotos makes Pan, when
aiding the Athenians against Xerxes, complain that
they never theretofore worshipped or honoured
him. (Lovers of Browning, or of Herodotos, will
recall the tale of Pheidippides in this connection.)
The questions of language here raised involve
such niceties as the use of nymphè (nymph) in
the sense of *daughter*, and of tithênè (nurse) for
mother. Such evidence will weigh but lightly
with those of us who know how hard it is to
ascertain whether a certain word or usage is at
the present moment limited to Old or New
England !

It is doubtless the imperial mastership of
Homer—that is, of Ionic epic—that has enforced
here, as so widely elsewhere, the outward uni-
formity of dialect and vocabulary. Yet within
and beneath these forms there is a wide diversity
in feeling, in scale, and in the point of view. In
the midst of the great Apollo hymn, even, the
centre of interest shifts so completely from Delos
to Pytho, that most scholars divide the traditional
text, and offer us two poems, each presumably of
local origin, to the Delian and the Delphic god

(see *infra*, pp. 125, ff.).   So the stately figure of the Mourning Mother, in the Eleusinian poem, is a type of maternity remote indeed from the nymph who in this very hymn to Pan, united with Hermes, bore the child—

" Goat-footed, doubly-horned, sweet-laughing, delighting in uproar,"

and, straightway, on beholding him—

" Leaped to her feet and fled, deserting her infant un-nourished."

" Probably rather late," I regret to say, is the general verdict also on the delightful hymn, Dionysos, or the Pirates, which Andrew Lang has rendered in masterly prose.   The ill-starred attack on the youthful god, with his sportive transformation of his assailants into dolphins, is often represented in works of art, notably in the Bacchic frieze of the Lysicrates Monument, the most beautiful little structure in Athens.   This building was itself a memorial of a victory gained in the Dionysiac theatre, though not in a dramatic contest.   We may, perhaps, set here a version already published.

"DIONYSOS, OR THE PIRATES.

" Glorious Semelè's child I will summon to mind, Dionysos ;
How he appeared on the brink of the sea forever unresting,
On a projecting crag, assuming the guise of a stripling
Blooming in youth ; and in beauty his dark hair floated
    about him.
Purple the cloak he was wearing across his vigorous
    shoulders.

" Presently hove in sight a band of Tyrrhenian pirates,
Borne in a well-rowed vessel along the wine-coloured
    waters.
Hither their evil destiny guided them. When they
    beheld him,
Unto each other they nodded ; then forth they darted,
    and straightway
Seized him, and haled him aboard their vessel, exultant
    in spirit,
Since they thought him a child of kings, who of Zeus are
    supported.
Then were they eager to bind him in fetters that could
    not be sundered.
Yet was he held not with bonds, for off and afar did the
    osiers
Fall from his hands and feet, and left him sitting and
    smiling
Out of his dusky eyes ! But when their pilot beheld it,
Straightway uplifting his voice, he shouted aloud to his
    comrades :

'Madmen!   Who is this god ye would seize and control
   with your fetters ?
Mighty is he!   Our well-rowed ship is unable to hold him.
Verily this is Zeus, or else it is archer Apollo,
Or, it may be, Poseidon,—for nowise perishing mortals
Does he resemble, but gods who make their home on
   Olympos.
Bring him, I pray you, again to the darksome shore, and
   release him
Straightway.   Lay not a finger upon him, lest in his
   anger
He may arouse the impetuous gusts, and the furious storm-
   wind.'

" Thus he spoke, but the captain, in words of anger, assailed
   him :
' Fellow, look to the wind, and draw at the sail of the
   vessel,
Holding the cordage in hand : we men will care for the
   captive.
He shall come, as I think, to Egypt, or may be to Cyprus,
Or to the Hyperboréans, or farther, and surely shall tell us
Finally who are his friends, and reveal to us all his pos-
   sessions,
Name us his brethren too : for a god unto us has betrayed
   him.'

" So had he spoken, and hoisted his mast and the sail of
   his vessel.
Fairly upon their sail was blowing a breeze, and the cordage

Tightened: and presently then most wondrous chances
befell them.

First of all things, wine through the black impetuous
vessel,

Fragrant and sweet to the taste, was trickling; the odour
ambrosial

Rose in the air; and terror possessed them all to behold it.

Presently near to the top of the sail a vine had extended,

Winding hither and hither, with many a cluster dependent.

Round and about their mast an ivy was duskily twining,

Rich in its blossoms, and fair was the fruit that had risen
upon it.

Every rowlock a garland wore.

                         " And when they beheld this

Instantly then to the pilot they shouted to hurry the
vessel

Near to the land; but the god appeared as a lion among
them,

Terrible, high on the bow, and loudly he roared; and
amidships

Made he appear to their eyes a shaggy-necked bear as a
portent.

Eagerly rose she erect, and high on the prow was the
lion,

Eying them grimly askance.   To the stern they darted in
terror.

There, at the side of the pilot, the man of wiser perception,

Dazed and affrighted they stood; and, suddenly leaping
   upon them,
On their captain he seized.   They, fleeing from utter
   destruction,
Into the sacred water plunged, as they saw it, together,
Turning to dolphins.   The god, for the pilot having com-
   passion,
Held him back, and gave him happiness, speaking as
   follows :
' Have no fear, oh innocent suppliant, dear to my spirit.
Semelè's offspring am I, Dionysos, the leader in revels,
Born of the daughter of Cadmos, to Zeus in wedlock
   united.'
—Greeting, oh child of the fair-faced Semelè !   Never the
   minstrel
Who is forgetful of thee may fashion a song that is
   pleasing ! "

This may be described as the longest of the
short hymns, or as the least of the " great " ones.
Though, perhaps, still too brief for independent
recitation, this tale certainly exceeds the limits
of a mere formal invocation.   Its Attic origin is
generally conceded.   May it not have been used
as a sort of " prologue in the theatre," to use the
phrase applied by Goethe to a very different
performance ?

Certainly *such* tales as this regarding Dionysos,

first sung and danced in mimicry, then elaborated into dialogues, were the earliest materials for the action in Athenian tragedy.   Indeed, the adventures of Dionysos were probably — not merely the favourite but—the only permissible subjects in early dramas.   Even in the Periclean age, the popular voice demanded that every dramatist retain, at least in the chorus of an obligatory afterpiece, the sportive satyrs, who in the Lysicratean frieze, and other versions, are seen sharing this very escapade with their master.   A curious idiom of later Attic recalls this earlier devotion of the drama to Bacchos alone.   Against any unseemly digression or dis-cursiveness, no matter where, the criticism was worded, οὐδὲν πρὸς Διόνυσον !—" That's nothing to do *with Dionysos !*"   These considerations alone might justify our recalling this earliest adequate glimpse of the merry wine-god.   The earliest, we say, for in Homer he appears only very slightly, fleeing in terror before a mortal, the Thracian king Lycurgus.   And with wine he had in Homer's mind probably no close connection.   At least, the wondrous liquor which laid Polyphemos low was a gift to Odysseus,—not from a Bacchic source at all, but from Apollo's priest.   Here again we chance upon another reminder of the un-Homeric—and post-Homeric—origin of these poems.

We have been led on to indicate the especial importance of this poem as a crosslight upon the Dionysiac drama.   But each sustained hymn in our collection is similarly a valuable original document for the history of Greek worship and myth.   In this regard they form a quarry which has hardly been duly worked.

Perhaps the most important poem in the series which has not yet been mentioned at all is the merry account of Hermes' precocious infancy and thievish pranks.   This has been freely, and delightfully, translated by the poet Shelley.   It is a pity this unique genius did not leave us a version of the Demeter hymn as well.   In some of its characteristics, such as the consciousness of marvellous life astir in all nature, and in rapturous love for flowers, it would have been especially congenial to him.   Or, perhaps, we should rather say, that Shelley's ethereally sensitive nature enabled him to reproduce some phases of Greek feeling from which most modern men, even of poetic soul, are alienated by their more artificial life. But Shelleys are rarely to be utilized as translators,—though Mr. Arnold thought it his most enduring work !

As a whole, these Hymns, with their allusions to naïve early myths, and hints of local cults, should attract greater interest, especially in our time, when so much attention is being drawn to the common elements in all earnest religious creeds.

NOTE.—This body of poetry offers the most striking illustration of the gaps and limitations in our English scholarship, to which Prof. Mahaffy calls attention so wittily and so often. There is *no* edition of these Greek poems with English notes for the student, and they are passed by in silence in the two best popular discussions on Hellenic poesy, Symonds' " Greek Poets " and Jebb's " Greek Poetry " ! Mahaffy himself discusses them in interesting but cursory fashion. The best literary translation was for centuries the free Elizabethan version in rhyme by George Chapman — the same man whose Iliad Keats has made doubly illustrious. This did not, of course, include the Demeter hymn, which was rediscovered in the eighteenth century. There is now a creditable, but little known, prose version

of all the poems, by Edgar, published in Edinburgh by
James Thin. The volume of Greek text with helpful
German notes by Gemoll (Leipsic, 1886) has not fulfilled
the editor's confident expectation of displacing Baumeister's
edition with Latin notes (1860). Both are useful. Prof.
Sterrett (Ginn, Boston) has edited the five greater hymns,
printing them so as to show clearly their heavy debt to
Homer. An important critical text has recently appeared,
and perhaps we may hope for a student's edition.

V.

THE HOMERIC HYMN TO APOLLO.

THE first among the Homeric Hymns in our
collection is a poem addressed to Apollo, in 546
hexameters. The earlier portion (vers. 1–178)
centres about Delos as the chief point of interest.
The latter section, again, has chiefly to do with
the legends of Delphi. Indeed, nearly all recent
editors have divided the hymn into two. The
exact truth as to the original form can hardly
be ascertained. The ancient allusions seem, for
the most part, to be rather to a single poem.
That some passages have been inserted where
they do not fit, is certain. Perhaps a later
attempt was made to incorporate into a single
frame nearly all the early hymn-material referring to the Apollo-group. The great antiquity of
some passages at least, and the intrinsic interest

of the subject, will justify its exposition here.
Incidentally, some of the sutures and abrupt
transitions may be indicated.

The opening passage itself has a certain
abruptness.

" I will remember and not be forgetful of archer Apollo,
  Who by the gods is dreaded within Zeus' house as he
    enters.
  Straightway all of them leap to their feet as he nearer
    approaches,
  Out of their seats, so soon as his shining weapons he
    levels " (vers. 1–4).

Then occurs a sudden change of tense which
may be merely accidental.   Possibly the poet
may himself have hesitated between a description
of Apollo's *first* appearance, and of his habitual
entrance among the immortals.

" Leto only remained, with Zeus who delights in the thunder.
  She indeed unstrung his bow and covered his quiver.
  Then with her hands she took from his stalwart shoulders
    his weapons.
  These at the side of a column she hung, in the hall of the
    father,
  Down from a golden peg.   To a chair she led him and set
    him.

Then in a golden beaker the father offered him nectar,
Pledging his well-loved son: and the other divinities
  likewise.
There they were seated together : and reverend Leto was
  joyful,
Seeing that he she had borne was a valiant god and an
  archer " (vers. 5–13).

This mention of Leto has apparently drawn
hither—perhaps at first to the margin only, and
then, by a copyist's error, into the text—what
looks like a brief separate hymn to Leto, certainly
an appeal to her directly, beginning—

" Hail, oh Leto the blessed, for glorious children thou
  barest " (ver. 14).

After these five lines (14–18) we come to an
invocation of Apollo himself, with an opening
verse which tends to justify the traditional title
of " hymns " for this whole group of poems.

" How may I hymn thee aright, who in hymns already
  aboundest ?
Everywhere, O Apollo, the pastures of song are extended:
Over the mainland, mother of cattle, and over the islands."
                                   (Vers. 19–21.)

The question which he has just asked, the poet presently answers with another—

"Shall I relate how Leto did bear thee, a joy unto mortals?
    That was in wavegirt Delos.   The darksome billows,
        around her,
    Driven along by the shrill-voiced winds, were hurrying
        landward.
    Issuing thence, thou among all mortal men art a ruler."
                                            (Vers. 25, 27–29.)

We naturally suppose the copious list of Aegean isles and seaward cities, next recorded, indicates the wide sway of Apollo.   This is indeed indirectly true, perhaps, though the long sentence ends unexpectedly with a reach backward.   The list is prevailingly Ionic, despite its beginning.

" All whoso are in Crete contained, or the people of Athens,
    In Euboea, for ships renowned, or island Aegina,—
    Or upon Thracian Athos, or Pelion's loftiest summits,
    Or in Lesbos the holy, abode of Aeolian Makar,
    Chios, that brightest of islands is set in the midst of the
        waters,
    Samos, abounding in springs, precipitous Mycale's sum-
        mits,—
    Ay, and in Naxos also, and Paros, and rocky Rheneia,

—Unto them all, ere Apollo was born, came Leto in
  travail,
If some one of the lands might offer a home to her off-
  spring.*
Greatly affrighted were they, and quaked. Not one of
  them ventured,
Even the richest, to proffer a shelter for Phoebos Apollo.
So the imperial Leto had fared, till she came unto Delos :
Then these wingèd words she uttered, and asked her the
  question :
'Delos, art thou content to become the abode of my
  offspring,
Phoebos Apollo, and rear to his honour a glorious temple ?
Never another will cleave unto thee, nor hold thee in
  honour.
Nowise rich thou'lt be, as I deem, in sheep or in cattle,
Neither abundant the vineyards, nor countless the trees
  thou producest.
Yet, if thou bearest upon thee a temple of Archer
  Apollo,
All mankind shall bring their sacred offerings hither,
Ever abundant for thee shall the odour arise of the
  victims '" (vers. 30–58).

It would seem that some prophetic knowledge
of Apollo and his character had spread through
Heaven and Earth, or at least had reached the

* Leto, it will be remembered, is persecuted by jealous
Hera.

knowledge of Delos,—whether she be the island,
or its guardian-divinity, or an inseparable fusion
of both in one.   Such imperfect knowledge of the
future is often ascribed to the Greek gods.   The
most notable case is Zeus' peril if he weds Thetis,
which is fully made known only to Prometheus,
through his mother Themis, the *seer*.   Even
Apollo the augur trips notably in this very poem
(*vide infra*, pp. 143–145).   Such strokes are
natural wherever men delineate gods in their
own likeness.   With Delos' prompt consent is
mingled one note of dread, inspired by her own
humility.

"Leto, but this word, only, affrights me, nor will I con-
ceal it.
Truly they say that Apollo will prove exceedingly haughty;
He will rule as a mighty monarch among the immortal
Gods, and mortal men who abide in the bounteous corn-
land.
Therefore greatly affrighted am I in heart and in spirit,
Lest, so soon as Apollo, thy child, shall look on the sun-
shine,
He, in contempt of the island, because I am rugged and
rocky,
Spurn with his feet and into the briny abysses may
plunge me.

He to another land will pass, which suiteth his pleasure.
So then only the dusky seals and polyps within me
Their untroubled abode will make, since men will be
    lacking" (vers. 66–78).

Leto reassures her, with the most sacred oath of gods—

"Earth be witness now, and wide-spread Heaven above us,
    Witness, Styx, with thy trickling stream, most mighty
      and holy
  Pledge to the ever-blessèd gods whose life is eternal:
  Verily here shall abide the enclosure and altar of Phoebos
  Ever, and thee shall he hold above all others in honour."

                              (Vers. 84–88.)

Leto's travail continues nine days and nights. She is consoled by the other female divinities, but the goddess whose function it should be to relieve her is detained by Hera in her jealous rage. Finally, summoned by Iris without Hera's knowledge, and bribed with a wondrous necklace of amber and gold nine cubits long, Eileithuia arrives. Apollo is the most precocious of children, thanks perhaps in part to the nectar and ambrosia which Themis straightway offers him instead of his mother's milk. Instantly bursting his swaddling-bands—doubtless a rather naïve indication of his growth in a moment to full stature — he proclaims to the admiring goddesses—

> " Dear unto me be the harp, and the curving bow and the arrows;
>   Yea, and the truthful counsel of Zeus unto men will I utter " (vers. 131, 132).

So Apollo at once announces himself as lord of music, of archery, and, above all, of prophecy to men. Delos blossomed all over with golden flowers in her joy, and felt both pride in, and affection for, her stately foster-child.

Here, again, there is a change of tense, which brings us, with hardly a breath for transition, into the poet's own day. The passage which follows is largely quoted, with slight variations, by Thucydides (circ. 400 B.C.), in his account of Delos (Thuc., ii. § 104). It is interesting to note that this earliest witness cites the verses unquestioningly as Homer's, and that the poem from which they are taken is for him (despite its length) "the prelude of Apollo." Further evidence, *e.g.* imitations by Theognis and others, strengthens the impression that this is among the oldest, if not the oldest, of all the hymns. Nevertheless, the moment we approach (as at present) any definite and realistic picture of human life, we see at once that we are in an age much later than the Homeric period proper. The change of tense we just mentioned occurs after three lines.

" Thou, oh lord of the silvern bow, Far-shooter Apollo,
   Sometimes over the slopes didst march of precipitous
      Cynthos,
   Sometimes thou didst fare to the dwellings of men and the
      temples.
   Dear all outlooks are unto thee, and the lofty mountains'
   Topmost peaks, and the rivers that down to the sea are
      descending.
   More than in all, oh Phoebos, thy heart is in Delos delighted,
   Where in their trailing robes unto thee the Ionians gather,
   They themselves, and their modest wives as well, and the
      children.
   There they do honour to thee with boxing, dancing, and
      singing " (vers. 140–149).

All manly rivalry, tending to perfect the heroic virtues, is to the Greek essentially pious. Pindar sings rapturously of the cock, who fights

for no baser motive than mere love of victory;
and a cock-fight has a prominent place among
the carvings on the high-priest's marble chair
in the Athenian theatre.

> " So they take their delight, whenever the games are
> appointed.
> One would believe them to be immortal and ageless for
> ever,
> Whoso met them, when the Ionians gather together.
> Then he the charm of them all would behold, and delight
> in their spirit,
> Seeing the men of the race, and the women gracefully
> girdled.
> Fleet are the vessels they bring as well, and many the
> treasures.
> —This is a marvel, too, whose glory never may perish,
> Even the Delian maids, attendant on Archer Apollo."
>
> (Vers. 150–157.)

This singer has evidently left far behind him
—or never knew—the haughty monarchs, the
subservient folk, of the Homeric age. Here we
have no royal and courtly ceremonial, surely.
These are the sports, this, too, is the poet, of
a free people. It is interesting that the very
next lines touch upon that same custom of the

"prelude," out of which all these poems may
have arisen.

"When they first have uttered in hymns their praise of
  Apollo,
  Next is Leto's turn, and Artemis, hurler of arrows.
  Then they remember the heroes of ancient days, and the
  women,
  Singing their hymn : and the tribes of mortal men are
  enchanted" (vers. 158–161).

That is, the invocation of the local gods must
precede the epic recital, the tales of demigods
and heroines. The use of " hymn " for the latter
poetry also, however, is a timely reminder, how
little our distinction between *secular* and *religious*
would mean to an ancient Greek, of the earlier
or the later time. Helen, the daughter of Zeus,
or Odysseus, the especial charge of Athene, was
a subject quite as fitting for the holy festival as
was the direct invocation of Pallas or her sire
which preceded it.

The next three lines are strange and curious :—

"Speech of all mankind, and even their castanets' rattle
  They can mimic, and every man would say that he heard
  them
  Speak his speech : so fairly and well is their minstrelsy
  fitted " (vers. 162–164).

Whether the "rattle of the castanets" means the musical accompaniment generally, or only the rhythm, the *tempo* of the dance and song, which might vary perceptibly from island to island, or town to town, is hard to decide. The Christian reader will be involuntarily reminded of the tongues of Pentecost.

After a single line addressed to the gods of Delos—

"Come, be thou, oh Apollo, together with Artemis, gracious "
(ver. 164),

the singer suddenly turns directly to his own special audience of Delian maidens. Why the women are his chief or sole auditors is not made plain. Thucydides' words are: "That there was a contest in music, and that they used to come to contend with each other, he (Homer) again makes clear in those verses which are from the same prelude. For, hymning the Delian chorus of women, he ended his eulogy in these lines, wherein he also mentioned himself,—

"'Greeting unto you all: and be ye of me hereafter
   Mindful, when some other of men that on earth have
      abiding

Hither may come, an outworn stranger, and ask you the
    question :
"Oh, ye maidens, and who for you is the sweetest of
    minstrels,
Whoso hither doth come, in whom ye most are delighted ? "
Then do ye all, I pray, with one voice answer and tell him,
"Blind is the man, and in Chios abounding in crags is his
    dwelling.
He it is whose songs shall all be supreme in the future." ' "

                     (Vers. 166–173.)

Here Thucydides' quotation ends, but a few
lines complete what the editors regard as the
" Delian hymn." The singer declares that he
will spread his own fame through the wide world.
The close may be rendered—

" Yet will I not cease from hymning the archer Apollo,
  Lord of the silvern bow, who is offspring of fair-tressed
    Leto " (vers. 177, 178).

This not too modest old man has, at this
moment, little in common with the elder epic
poet, who could so effectively conceal his own
identity, while unrolling before us the splendid
tapestry of Trojan story. And he who, standing
on the mound of Hissarlik, or at the extinct
crater's edge on topmost Ida, still listens to the

idle tale of Homer's blindness, must himself be
hopelessly blind—and deaf as well! Yet this
passage is the probable starting-point of two
persistent legends concerning Homer: that he
was of Chios, and that he was blind.

In turning away from Delos, we may mention
the only earlier allusion to the island.   Odysseus,
flattering Nausicaa, likens her to a graceful
young palm he had seen shooting up beside
Apollo's Delian altar: "For thither also I
came," he adds, "and much folk with me." *

Perhaps we should ask our printer to do
outward homage to the prevailing editorial
judgment, that divides the great hymn at the
point now reached—the one hundred and seventy-
eighth verse.   That the poets—or one poet—
seemed to take farewell of the song here, may
fairly be conceded.   One late author, Aristides
(ii. 558), citing this same passage, says positively,
"Talking with the Delian maids, *and closing
the Prooimion.*"   Many think, however, that

* Odyssey, bk. vi., vers. 162–164.   "Art and Humanity in
Homer," p. 221.

Aristides merely had Thucydides before him, and cited without knowledge of the hymn at first hand. (Cf. Gemoll, p. 114.)

Nevertheless, the text as it lies before us hardly makes it easy to start the new and independent Delphic hymn which we next expect. When Xenophon's Hellenic history begins, " But after that," we say, " He is continuing Thucydides," or " A leaf has been lost " — or both. Little better is the case here. The next three verses seem to form a strophe by themselves, but while neither a beginning nor a closing strain, they do equally little to bridge the transition to Delphi—

" Lycia, oh Lord, and lovely Maeonia own thy dominion ;
Over Miletos thou rulest, the sea-washed city of longing ;
Monarch art thou, as well, of Delos girt by the waters."
(Vers. 179–181.)

Next we find a passage of twenty-five lines tolerably complete in itself. Apollo, playing the lyre, and clad in fragrant robes, comes to " rocky Pytho." This mention of Delphi seems timely ; but in an instant more—

" Thence from earth to Olympos, as swift as a thought, he departed " (ver. 186).

There, in Zeus' abode, is a rather over-crowded
assemblage of the gods to whom—

" All of the Muses together, with beautiful voices, responsive
　Sang of the wondrous gifts of the gods, and the sorrows
　　of mortals :
What they endure at the hands of gods whose life is
　　eternal,
How they live in folly and feebleness, wholly unable
Safeguard against old age, or a cure for death, to discover."

(Vers. 189–193.)

Those familiar with Greek poetry of any age
will not be wholly surprised at this discordant
note of pessimism. We may suppose the theme
is an agreeable one, to divine and immortal
hearers. Amid this throng of—

" Fair-tressed Graces and fair-minded Hours " (ver. 194),

Artemis is stateliest in the dance, while the
harper Apollo is the leader of all,—

" Stepping graceful and high, and the splendour glimmers
　　about him,
Flash of the gleaming feet, and of garments cunningly
　　woven " (vers. 202, 203).

The hearts of his parents, Leto and Zeus, are
filled with pride. If the poet had set himself the

task of outdoing the earlier singer who revealed
to us the more quiet scene in Olympos at Apollo's
first arrival (*supra*, vers. 1–13), he has succeeded ;
but Delphi is quite forgotten. Indeed the later
quest of Apollo makes it clear that the allusion to
Pytho at this point is out of place.

The poem pauses and hesitates, as it were,
repeating the query already familiar—

" How may I hymn thee aright, who in hymns already
  aboundest ? " (ver. 207 = ver. 19).

Omitting the six most corrupt and hopeless
verses, in which the suggestion is feebly made that
Apollo's amours might be the best subject for
song, we accept the nobler alternative :—

" Or shall I rather relate how first, Far-shooter Apollo,
  Thou over earth didst wander, for mortals an oracle
    seeking ?
  Thou in Pieria first didst make thy descent from Olym-
    pos " (vers. 214–216).

Now, at last, the real current of the poem
begins to run, and the stately march toward the
Pythian fane may well be a far-off reminiscence
of the time when the Apollo-worship, the fairest

flower of early Greek civilization, was indeed
borne reverently on to southward, from hill to
hill, from commune to commune, till it rested for
a thousand years on rocky Pytho. Descending
through Thessaly, the route runs across Euboea
to Boeotia. The passage is by no means a bare
unpoetical catalogue. Thus the extreme antiquity
of Apollo's progress is effectively indicated when
Boeotia is reached—

> "Next thou wert come to the site of Thebè, covered by
> forests;
> None among mortal men were as yet in Thebè abiding,
> Nay, there were yet no beaten paths to be seen, nor a high-
> way
> Over the plain so rich in wheat, but only the woodland.
> Thence thou upon thy way didst fare, Far-shooter Apollo."
>
> (Vers. 225–229.)

Apollo is seeking a fit site for his temple and a
place of prophecy, and this last oft-repeated line
is doubtless an imitation of the verse which
becomes almost a refrain in the ninth book of the
Odyssey:

> "Thence did we fare on our way, exceedingly troubled in
> spirit " (Odys. ix. 62, 105, 565 ; x. 133).

The chief pause of Apollo is near "grassy Haliartos" and "many-towered Ocalea," at the spring Delphousa, or Telphousa. The resemblance of this name to Delphi probably gave a starting-point for the myth-makers, or even stimulated the invention of our poet, who has himself, as we shall see, an unpoetic penchant toward etymology. Some grass-grown prehistoric foundations without superstructure, and the overarching natural rock from which the spring appears to struggle forth, would help to explain the incident, if explanation be desired.

Apollo, then, is so charmed by the spot, that he announces to Telphousa his intention to erect there a—

> "Beautiful temple,
> Seat of an oracle for mankind,"

which will be a place of general resort from the Peloponnese, the mainland, and the islands. This is, indirectly, of course, a sketch of what Delphi has become at the time when this hymn is composed. The god actually lays the broad foundations: but now, for some reason unexplained, the

nymph's anger is aroused. She craftily suggests,
that the thronged high-road, evidently near at
hand (or destined to exist there), the noise of
teams watering their mules and horses at her
fountain, will distract men's thoughts from the
temple and oracle, which demand a less accessible
and more peaceful spot.

> " Nay, but in Crisa, beneath Parnassos' ridges erect them.
>   Never the din of the beautiful chariots there will re-echo,
>   Nor will the clatter of steeds ring round your well-built
>   altar " (vers. 269–271).

Since Apollo accepts this reasoning without
question, it is thought the verses must have been
composed before the institution, under the divine
sanction, of periodical chariot-races at Crisa itself,
which is assigned to about the year 580 B.C.

To his final abode Apollo now quickly makes
his way :—

> " Then unto Crisa, beneath snow-capt Parnassos, thou
>   camest.
>   Westward turned is the mountain's shoulder: the valley
>   below it
>   Rough and hollow extends, underneath the o'ershadowing
>   ledges " (vers. 282–284).

Announcing the glorious future of his shrine in
the very words he had already used to Telphousa,
and apparently untroubled by the grave lapse
from prophetic foresight thus so plainly exposed,—

> " Phoebos Apollo set the foundations,
> Wide and exceedingly far extended, straightway ; upon them
> Laid was a threshold of stone by Trophonios and Agamedes,
> Sons of Erginos, and dear to the gods whose life is eternal.
> Round it a temple was built by unnumbered races of mortals,
> Fashioned of shapely stones, in song to be famous for ever."
>
> (Vers. 290, 299.)

These earliest of architects, dear to Apollo and
the other immortals, are doubly famous through
the tale of their end. As the greatest of blessings,
in answer to their prayer, a painless death, while
asleep, was granted to them both ; still another
reminder that the early Greek was quite too wide-
eyed not to see the pathetic side of life, and,
especially, of old age. (As we write, the similar
death of Massachusetts' favourite son has called
forth many utterances of a sentiment closely
akin to that feeling which is implied in this and
similar Greek stories.)

It is a curious example how the accretions of

marvellous detail gather about a simpler core of legend, that in Pausanias' time the local myth at Delphi named the temple of these brother-architects, not as the first, but as the *fourth* structure in order of time. The first rude con-struction had been a hut of laurel-boughs; the second, yet more strangely, of bees' wings and wax; the third a temple of bronze. (The essayist may be permitted to refer to his own paper on these and other curious Delphic legends, *Atlantic Monthly*, p. 801, December, 1889.)

Next we have a brief mention of the fair-flowing fountain at Delphi, and of the dragon that, after slaying many men and many cattle, "working much mischief on earth," was herself destroyed by Apollo's bow, at the spring.

But from this point fifty verses (vers. 305–355) are filled with the widest digression of all. The origin of Typhaon—produced by Hera, without sire, in emulation, after Pallas' birth from her father's head—is rehearsed with much vivid but crude detail. The slight thread of connection is the assertion, that he was at birth given in

charge, " evil to the evil," to this same dragon.
Again returning to Pytho, the poet gives nearly
twenty wearisome verses (vers. 356–376) to the
death-writhings of the monster, and to the
malodorous derivation of the sanctuary's early
name from the root *pyth,* " to putrefy," in
allusion to the decaying body of the serpent.
(The rival derivation, " place of inquiry," is
pleasanter, but sins against *quantity.*)

Now the beauty of Telphousa's environment
recurs to Apollo's mind, and with it comes the
angry but tardy conviction, that it was for her
own renown, not his, she had beguiled him to seek
the lonely Parnassian dell. So he returns for a
moment to her, and hides her source under high-
piled rocks—which, I believe, still remain as wit-
nesses to the truth of the tale. He also erects
near the stream an altar, whereat offerings were
still made, at least in the singer's day, to the
Telphusian Apollo.

It next occurs to Apollo's mind, that he requires men, to celebrate his rites, and to be his
faithful servants in rocky Pytho. While ponder-
ing hereon, he descries a ship sailing the winy

deep, manned by Cretans, from Cnossos, the city of Minos. Straightway he hastens to intercept them, and in the guise of a monstrous dolphin leaps into their vessel. Remembering that the original Greek form of this fish's name is *Delphis*, we shall already guess that the poet is beginning his last and boldest assay at etymologic mythologizing. Driven by divine command about the whole Peloponnesos, the weary ship enters the Corinthian gulf, and at last, reaching the port of Crisa, she grates upon the pebbly beach.

"Then leaped forth from the vessel the lord, Far-shooter Apollo,
Like to a star at noon. Unnumbered the rays that about him
Flitted and flashed, while high to the heavens the splendour extended.
Into his shrine in the midst of his precious tripods he entered " (vers. 440–443).

There are many naïve touches in all such myths. The tripods to which the poet alludes, to which he could indeed hardly refrain from proudly alluding, were, of course, votive offerings from thankful men, bestowed *since* the activity of the oracle began. The fire now lighted in the sanctuary affrights the maids and dames of Crisa, which we had supposed till now was utterly desolate and uninhabited, no less than the Theban site mentioned before.

Once again laying aside his divine glory, this time for the figure of a goodly mortal youth, Apollo is in time to meet the bewildered Cretans at the beach, and addresses to them the Homeric inquiry, whether they sail the seas for trade and barter, or risking their lives in piracy. He calms their fears, and bids them put in to the land as is the traders' wont. Something of his divinity lingers about him, for the Cretan captain doubtingly answers—

" Stranger,—for nowise like unto mortal men is your
    semblance,
   Stature or shape, but rather to gods whose life is eternal,—
   Potent and great one, hail ! May the gods all blessings
    accord you.
   But do you tell me truly, that so I also may know it:
   Who is this folk ? What land ? What men have here
    their abiding ? " (vers. 464–468).

To their frank confession—

" Hither some one of immortals, against our wishes, has led
    us " (ver. 473),

Apollo at last responds in his own proper character—

"Strangers, ye who have dwelt in the woodland city of
    Cnossos
  Till this time, ye now shall go no longer, returning,
  Unto your lovely town, and the beautiful dwelling of each
    man,
  Nor to your faithful wives! but here my opulent temple
  Ye shall guard, that is held by men full many in honour.
  I myself am a son of Zeus, my name is Apollo.
  Over the mighty abyss of the waters I guided you hither."

(Vers. 475–481).

This tale of Cretans brought to Delphi seems to have no traceable origin, save the mere fact, generally accepted, that Minos' folk were the first, or among the first, of Greeks to wrest from their Phoenician rivals the art of navigation and the profits of commerce. At the god's bidding the wanderers now bring their ship to land, and, stepping ashore, set up on the beach an altar to Delphinian Apollo. Then, after supper and sacrifice, the final march Delphi-ward begins. Phoebos' figure reminds us of his former appearance on Olympos, as he leads the way with lyre in hand,—

" Gracefully stepping and high ; and dancing followed the
  Cretans,
Singing a paean of praise " (vers. 516, 517).

Yet, when they arrive at the temple and shrine,
some doubt arises once again, and the Cretan
captain asks—

" O thou, lord, who afar from our friends and the land of
  our fathers
  Hither hast led us—for so, it appears, it has suited thy
    pleasure—
  How may we prosper now ? For this we bid thee to
    tell us.
  This is a land not lovely nor fruitful, nor goodly its
    meadows " (vers. 526–529).

The smiling god bids them put aside all anxious
cares, all thought of grievous toil. Their only
task shall be to slay the kine, which countless
races of men will bring to them for sacrifice.

" Guard ye my temple well, and receive ye the races of
  mortals
  Hither assembling " (vers. 538, 539).

We are within eight lines of the close. The
hymn thus far seems composed in exultant
spirit, doubtless for a Delphic brotherhood which

believed itself the invincible and inviolate descendants from those Cretan guardians, who had been thus divinely led to the primeval shrine. If this is rightly guessed, and this great hymn was indeed created for such a body, then the next five lines may well be a colophon added in less happy days; or, they may even have been supplied by new lords of the sanctuary, boldly justifying, out of the divine mouth itself, their subjugation of the traditional guardians. At any rate Apollo's final speech now closes thus :—

" Yet if a foolish word shall occur hereafter, or action,
    Insolence, such as is common among mankind who are
        mortal,
    Then shall other men in that day be your commanders,
    At their hands shall you be perforce subdued, and for ever.
    Verily all is said : in your memory well be it guarded."

(Vers. 540–544.)

We are not likely ever to know what historical event was here indicated. In the Iliad, rocky Pytho is already proverbial for its wealth, which must have been bestowed as gifts from grateful pilgrims to the seat of augury. A passage of the Odyssey expressly asserts that Agamemnon sought there, beforehand, information as to the issue of the Trojan war. The oracle he obtained had all the ambiguity and vagueness so common in later days. Whatever this strange far hint of Amphictyonic victory, or other Sacred War, may mean, all is, indeed, said, save the familiar transition from prelude to epic lay, in a couplet which has, perhaps, been transferred by a later copyist hither from its place at the close of several among the briefer hymns—

" Greeting, then, unto thee, O son of Zeus and of Leto,
  I of thee and, as well, of another song will be mindful."

VI.

THE HOMERIC HYMN TO DEMETER.

PERHAPS the most pathetic and significant of all Greek myths is the tale of the daughter untimely snatched by Hades to his underworld, and of the divine mother who finds her chief consolation in administering to humanity's needs.   As Walter Pater reminds us, this myth was of very gradual growth.   From Homer it cannot be shown that Demeter and Persephone are even closely akin! Demeter appears occasionally, in the epics, but only as "the perfectly fresh and blithe goddess of the fields."   She even yields in the ploughed-land on one occasion to the embraces of a mortal lover, Iasion, from whom jealous Zeus exacts his life as a penalty for this presumption.   Perse-phone, again, stern queen of ghosts, from whose

realm the canny Odysseus flees, lest she freeze
him to stone with the Gorgon-head,—the Homeric
Persephone, I say, gives no hint of any memories
or longings for the green fields of her childhood,
if childhood she ever had.

It is once more in Hesiod's Theogony that we
must seek the first kernel of the purer and nobler
legend, the far-spreading later growth. In three
verses, only, Hesiod tells us :—

" Next was the fruitful Demeter to Zeus in wedlock united.
She gave birth to Persephone, white-armed, whom Aïdoneus
Snatched from her mother away : and Zeus the Adviser
permitted."

The original suggestion for this myth can
hardly have failed to come from the apparent
death of vegetation in Winter, and its happy
restoration to mother Nature's loving arms for
the longer season of Summer. But it is always
an error to carry such a key in hand to explain
each detail of a living legend. So Heracles and
his twelve labours may well have been, to the
first story-teller, consciously connected with the
sun and his twelve zodiacal signs ; but around
that rallying-point many a capital tale has been

invented—and others, too, which properly belonged to other heroes Hellenic and barbarian, have drifted thither—till no allegorical analysis can spoil even a tithe of them any more! Certainly into this land of marvel, where the magic narcissus blooms, we may pass only if we bring with us the unspoiled faith, the unquestioning imagination, of childhood. For our children are happily not yet born—as Hesiod has forewarned us—with "grey hair upon the temples," and they still may enter the Elysian fields of the Hellenic prime. If any reader doubts this, let him test his dullest or most practical boy by repeating to him this very tale of the lost daughter, from Hawthorne's "Wonderbook," where Persephone herself is reduced (rather boldly but daintily, and with true Hawthornesque genius) to the stature and the years of childhood.

The poem must have been inspired, probably composed, at Eleusis itself. It abounds in local allusions, and also in references, no doubt many more than we can now verify, to the noble cult of the Mother and Daughter. We can enter upon no discussion as to what the Eleusinian

mysteries really were. That the belief in an
immortal life, and even in some form of resur-
rection, was there illustrated and strengthened,
seems inevitable from the very essence of the
Persephone myth itself. The poet is, perhaps,
as early as the seventh century B.C. There is,
I believe, no distinct allusion to Athenian rule
in Eleusis, though in this the Attic poet—if such
he was—of course merely restores the conditions
of the earlier day which he is recalling. The
absence of Dionysos, and of Triptolemos as the
first teacher of agriculture, may indicate that we
have here the earliest and simplest form of the
Eleusinian myth.

Among the rather numerous classical poems
upon the same theme yet extant (all of which
Mr. Pater discusses), none approaches, on the
whole, the noble simplicity of this earliest hymn
to Demeter. Yet each adds touches, picturesque
if not always congruous, like the many hands
that piece on and piece out an historic English
country-house. Even frolicsome Ovid feels for
once in full the pathetic majesty of the theme.
He, in particular, makes Eleusinian Keleos not

a king at all, but rather a poor old man like his own Philemon ; and almost persuades us to accept this bold variation upon the imperishable tale. Many modern versions or allusions to the theme are familiar to every lover of poetry. Last of all, Tennyson, in his old age, has felt the charm of the myth, though his poem by no means displaces, or even rivals, the antique renderings of the subject.

All which may justify the selection of this Homeric hymn for a sustained experiment in hexameter translation. In order to avoid frequent interruption for comment and discussion, we may refer once for all to Mr. Pater's careful yet imaginative account of this, and of the other classical poems upon Demeter, in his precious "Greek Studies." Professor Louis Dyer gives a more analytical treatment—and also a glimpse at the archaeology of Eleusis—in his interesting and valuable book, "The Gods in Greece."

"HYMN TO DEMETER.

" First Demeter I sing, that fair-tressed reverend goddess,
  Her, and her daughter the slender-ankled, whom once
    Aïdoneus

The Homeric Hymn to Demeter. 159

> Stole—for wide-eyed Zeus, who is lord of the thunder,
> permitted.
> Quite unaware was the mother, Fruitgiver, the Bringer of
> spring-time.
> She—Persephone—played with Okeanos' deep-bosomed
> daughters,
> Plucking the blossoms—the beautiful violets, roses, and
> crocus,
> Iris, and hyacinth, too, that grew in the flowery meadow."

The names were probably applied by the poet to different plants than those which they call to our minds; but their poetic associations are essentially unchanged.

> "Earth, by command of Zeus, and to please All-welcoming
> Pluto,
> Caused narcissus to grow, as a lure for the lily-faced
> maiden.
> Wonderful was it in beauty. Amazement on all who
> beheld it
> Fell, both mortal men and gods whose life is eternal.
> Out of a single root it had grown with clusters an hundred.
> All wide Heaven above was filled with delight at the
> fragrance,
> Earth was laughing as well, and the briny swell of the
> waters.
> She, in her wonder, to pluck that beautiful plaything
> extended

Both her hands: but that moment the wide-wayed earth
  underneath her
Yawned, in the Nysian plain; and the monarch, Receiver
  of all men,
Many-named son of Kronos, arose, with his horses im-
  mortal,—
—Seized her against her will, and upon his chariot golden
Bore her lamenting away;—and the hills re-echoed her
  outcry.
Kronos' son she invoked, most mighty and noble, her
  father.
None among mortal men, nor the gods whose life is
  eternal,
Heard her voice—not even the fruitful Nymphs of the
  marsh-land.
Only Perses' daughter, the tender-hearted, had heard her,
Hecatè, she of the gleaming coronet, out of her cavern,—
Heard her on Kronides calling, her father: he from im-
  mortals
Far was sitting aloof, in a fane where many petitions
Came to him, mingled with sacrifices abundant of mortals.

" So, at the bidding of Zeus was reluctant Persephone stolen,
  Forced by her father's brother, the Many-named, offspring
    of Kronos,
  Lord and Receiver of all mankind—with his horses im-
    mortal.
  While Persephone yet could look upon star-studded heaven,
  Gaze on the earth underneath, and the swarming waters
    unresting,

Seeing the light, so long she had hope that her glorious
mother

Yet would descry her—or some from the race of the gods
ever-living.

So long hope consoled her courageous spirit in trouble.

Loudly the crests of the mountains and depths of the
water resounded

Unto her deathless voice :—and her royal mother did hear
her.

Keen was the pain at Demeter's heart, and about her
ambrosial

Tresses her tender hands were rending her beautiful wimple.

Dusky the garment was that she cast upon both her
shoulders."

(Black robes were already the sign of grief in
the Iliad. For example, they are worn in Il.
xxiv. by Thetis, of whom the younger poet borrows
many touches for his Mourning Mother. For
instance, he has just echoed the words which
announce her first appearance in Il. i., arising
out of the sea at Achilles' call—

" And his royal mother did hear him.")

" Like to a bird she darted, and over the lands and the
waters

Sped as if frenzied : but yet there was no one willing to
tell her

Truthfully, neither of gods nor of human folk who are
    mortal;
None of the birds would come unto her as a messenger
    faithful."

Mother Nature understands with equal ease the
voices of all her children; though this is a truth
which should least of all need repetition, in an
age made happy by the immortal creation of
Mowgli and his companions.

" So throughout nine days, over earth imperial Deo,
    Holding in both her hands her flaming torches, was
        roaming.
    Never ambrosia, nor ever delightsome nectar she tasted;
    Never she bathed with water her body—so bitter her
        sorrow.
    Yet when upon her there came for the tenth time glimmer-
        ing morning,
    Hecatè met her, a shining light in her hands, and addrest
        her,
    Speaking unto her thus, and bringing her news of her
        daughter:
    ' Royal Demeter, our Bountiful Lady, the Giver of Spring-
        time,
    Who among mortal men, or who of the gods ever-living,
    Brought this grief to your heart by stealing Persephone
        from you?

Truly her voice did I hear, but yet with my eyes I beheld
not

Who committed the deed. Thus all have I truthfully
told you.'

So did Hecatè speak, and in words replied not the other,

Fair-tressed Rheia's daughter, but hastily with her she
darted,

Hurrying forward, and still in her hands were the glim-
mering torches."

These torches are "still in her hands," also,
in many works of plastic art which have been
preserved. The torch played a prominent part
too in the solemn processions and figurative
ceremonies of Eleusis.

"So they to Helios came, who is watcher of gods and of
mortals.

Standing in front of his steeds, she, divine among goddesses,
asked him :

'Helios, you as a goddess should hold me in honour, if
ever

Either by word or deed I have cheered your heart and
your spirit.

I through boundless ether have heard the lament of a
maiden,

Even of her that I bore, fair blossom, of glorious beauty :

Heard her cry of distress, though not with my eyes I beheld
her.

Yet do you, who descry all earth and the billowy waters,
Out of the ether resplendent with keen glance watchfully
downward
Gazing, report to me truly, my child, if perchance you
behold her.
Tell me who among men, or of gods, whose life is unending,
Seized, and away from her mother has carried, the maiden
unwilling.'

" So did she speak; and the son of Hyperion answered her,
saying :
' Fair-tressed Rheia's daughter, our royal lady Demeter,
You shall know: for indeed I pity and greatly revere
you,
Seeing you grieved for your child, for the graceful Perse-
phone. No one
Else save cloud-wrapt Zeus is to blame among all the
immortals.
He as a blooming bride has given your daughter to Hades,
Brother to him and to you: so down to the shadowy
darkness
Hades, spite of her cries, has dragged her away with his
horses.
Yet, O goddess, abate your grief: it befits you in no wise
Thus insatiate anger to cherish. Nor yet an unworthy
Husband among the immortals is Hades, monarch of all
men,
Child of the selfsame father and mother with you: and
his honours

Fell to his share, when first amid three was the universe
  parted.
Still amid those he reigns, whose rule unto him was
  allotted.' ''

A doctrine hard indeed, yet true. Death is
verily the brother of Life, to be welcomed no
less than the other as a rightful guest among us.

"Speaking thus he aroused his steeds: and they at his
    bidding,
  Nimbly as long-winged birds with the rushing chariot
    hastened.
  Over Demeter's heart grief fiercer and keener descended.
  Then in her anger at Kronos' son, who is lord of the storm-
    cloud,
  Leaving the gathering-place of the gods and spacious
    Olympos,
  Unto the cities of men and the fertile fields she de-
    parted."

From this point the tenderest human sympathies
blend more and more with the marvellous elements
of the divine myth.

"Many a day was her form disguised: and of those who
    beheld her,
  No one, whether of men or of dames deep-girded, could
    know her.

So had she fared, till she came to the prudent Keleos'
   dwelling;
He was the ruler then of Eleusis abounding in incense."

The epithet given to Eleusis is partly antici-
patory.

" Close to the road she took her seat, sore troubled in spirit,
   Nigh to a sacred well, whence water was drawn by the
      townsfolk.
There in the shadow she sat of an olive thicket above her,
Taking upon her the form of an aged woman, who travail
Never may know, nor the gifts of garlanded Aphrodite,
Such as the ancient dames and nurses who care for the
   children,
Dwelling within the resounding halls of governing mon-
   archs.
There she was seen by the daughters of Keleos, lord of
   Eleusis.
They with their pitchers of bronze were come to the
   fountain for water,
Easily drawn, to be fetched to the pleasant abode of their
   father :
—Four, like goddesses, having the bloom of maidenly
   beauty,
Kleisidikè and Kallidikè and beautiful Demo,
Kallithoè, too, youngest and last.   They knew not
   Demeter ;
—Difficult is it in truth for the gods to be known by us,
   mortals,—

Standing close at her side with wingèd words they addrest
   her :

'Whence do you come, old dame, from the folk of a past
   generation ?

Why, thus, apart from the town do you fare, and unto the
   dwellings

Come not nigh, where dames in the shadowy halls are
   abiding—

Some as agèd as you yourself—and others are younger ?

They with words, and in deed no less, would accord you a
   welcome.'

So did they speak, and to them the imperial goddess
   responded :

'Children dear, whosoever you are among women, I greet
   you.

Yes, and your question I'll answer ; indeed it is only
   befitting,

Since you have asked me this, that I should truthfully tell
   you.'"

But the divine guest has not sworn by the
Stygian stream, and the mystic name she gives
herself is perhaps the only word not untruthful
in her reply.

"'Deo my name is : upon me my reverend mother
   bestowed it.

Over the sea's broad back from Crete I hither have
   wandered ;

Not of my own free will, but by need and compulsion,
    unwilling
Hither by pirates brought : and they at Thorikos lately
Ran their vessel ashore.   Then many a captive woman,
Many a pirate too, was fain to set foot on the mainland.
There by the stern of the ship their evening meal they
    provided.
Yet the delightful supper was nowise dear to my spirit.
Hastening forth unseen, I traversed the shadowy main-
    land,
Fleeing my insolent lords, that they, who never had
    bought me,
Might not sell me and win for themselves my value here-
    after.
So in my wanderings hither to you am I come; and I
    know not
What is the land, nor who are the people within it
    abiding.
Yet unto you may all who make their abode in Olympos
Grant you husbands, in wedlock, and make you the mothers
    of children
Such as parents crave; but do you show pity upon me,
Gentle maidens, in kindness, until I may come to the
    dwelling
Either of lady or lord, for whom I may eagerly labour,
Doing the tasks that fall to a woman as aged as I am.'
Either a new-born child I could hold in my arms, and
    could nurse him
Wisely and well, or else could keep in order the house-
    hold;

Yes, and the bed could I lay for the lords, in the well-built
    chambers,
Inner recesses—or teach their handicraft to the women.'

" Thus did the goddess speak. Straight answered the maiden
    unwedded,
  Kallidikè, who was fairest of face among Keleos' daughters :
  ' Mother, the gifts of the gods, though bitter our sorrow, we
    mortals
  Must perforce endure, since they are by far more mighty.' "

Here, as often, we catch an echo of Nausicaa's
accents.

" ' This, however, to you will I clearly explain, and will tell
    you
  As to the men who here have a larger measure of honour :
  Chiefs of our people are they, and the towering walls of
    the city
  They with their counsels hold secure, and righteous deci-
    sions.
  First Triptolemos wise in counsel, and also Dioclos,
  Polyxeinos next I name, and noble Eumolpos,
  Dolichos, too, and lastly our own illustrious father.
  —All have wedded wives, who keep in order their house-
    holds.
  No one of all these dames—not even when first she shall
    see you,

Holding you in disdain would debar you out of her dwelling.
Nay, they will welcome you :—since you are verily like the
immortals.' "

The gods, in early poetry, seem constantly in
danger of betraying their superhuman beauty or
power. The mask of humility, or age, or wretched-
ness, is always slipping aside.

" ' But if you will, here tarry until to the house of my father
We may come, and tell deep-girt Metaneira, my mother,
All that to us has befallen. It may be then she will bid
you
Into our home to come, nor seek for the dwelling of
others.
There in her well-built palace a son, most dearly-belovèd,
Late-born, prayed-for long, and eagerly welcome, is
nourished.
If you would care for him till he comes to the threshold
of manhood,
Verily every one of women who then may behold you
Not without envy may see the rewards you may win for
his rearing.'

" Such were her words. With a nod did the goddess assent,
and the maidens
Filled their shining urns with water, and bore them,
exultant.

Nimbly they came to their father's strong-built mansion,
and quickly

Told their mother of all they had seen and heard : and the
mother

Straightway bade them invite her to come, at wages unbounded.

Then did the maidens—as deer, or as calves in the season
of springtime

Gambol the meadows along, when delighted at heart with
the pasture,

—So they darted, uplifting the folds of their beautiful
garments,

Down by the hollowed way for the wagons : their tresses
about them,

Like to the crocus blossom, were floating over their
shoulders.

There, at the side of the way, they found the illustrious
goddess

Where they had left her before. Then toward the house
of their father

They led onward ; and she—distressed in spirit—behind
them

Followed along, with her face close veiled ; and her garments about her

Duskily fell in waves to the glistening feet of the goddess.

Soon to the palace of Zeus-supported Keleos came they.

Then through a porch they went their way, for the reverend
mother

There, in the well-built hall, by a pillar was sitting, and
holding

On her lap her boy, that blossom so tender.   The maidens
Ran to her side: but the goddess immovable stood at the
threshold.
Nigh to the lintel she towered, and with radiance filled was
the portal.
Shame and awe fell, then, and terror, upon Metaneira.
Out of her chair she arose, and bade the new-comer be
seated.
Yet Demeter, the Bringer of Spring, the Bestower of
bounty,
Was not willing to take her place in the glistening arm-
chair,
But with her beautiful eyes cast down, and silent, she
lingered:
Lingered at least, so long, till cunning Iambè before
her
Set her a firm-wrought chair—and a white fleece laid she
upon it.
Then Demeter was seated, and drew her veil with her
fingers.
Speechless upon her chair full long she sate, and in
sorrow.
Greeting to no one there she accorded, by word or by
gesture:
But, unsmiling, refusing to taste of food or of liquid,
Sate she, wasted away by desire for her daughter deep-
girded;
—Till at the last, with her jests full many, the cunning
Iambè,
Scoffing, diverted the holy Demeter, the reverend goddess,

The Homeric Hymn to Demeter. 173

So that she smiled, then laughed, and took on a cheerier
   spirit.
(She, too, often thereafter delighted her heart when in
   anger.) "

" The allegory," as Dante would say, " grows
thin at this point." Iambè is scoffing Jest
personified, and she had indeed a traditional
prominence amid the statelier features of the
mysteries.

" Then Metaneira proffered her honey-sweet wine, in a
   goblet,
 Filling it : yet she her head tossed back in refusal, declaring
 This was forbidden for her, to quaff of the wine : but she
   bade her
 Barley and water to give her, commingled with soft penny-
   royal.
 She made ready and offered the goddess the draught she
   had ordered.
 —Still is the gift she accepted the portion of reverend
   Deo."

And the Chthonian gods generally are austere
gods, to whom no libations of wine are welcome.
Oedipus' greeting to the " wineless goddesses "
at Colonos is as familiar a passage as any.

"Straightway among them began and spoke fair-girt
    Metaneira :
'Welcome, oh woman ! assuredly not from parents unworthy
You are sprung, but a noble race : in your eyes so clearly
Grace and modesty shine, as in those of imperial princes.'"

Is it the tradition of the Homeric school that
makes this Attic and, perhaps, democratic poet,
such a firm believer in the nobility of royal races ?

" 'Still, what the gods ordain, though bitter our sorrow, we
    mortals
Must perforce endure : to our necks their yoke has been
    fitted.
Now that to us you are come, let your share be as mine is
    in all things.
Rear for me this boy, who, late in life and unhoped-for,
Was of the gods bestowed, as an answer to many petitions.
If you would care for him, till he come to the threshold of
    manhood,
Verily every one of women, who then may behold you,
Would with envy see the rewards you may win for his
    rearing.'
Then unto her, in turn, fair-crowned Demeter responded :
'Greeting to you, too, lady; the gods all blessings accord
    you !
Gladly will I accept your child, as you have commanded,
Yes, I will rear him : nor shall he, methinks, through his
    nurse's unwisdom

Either by accident come unto harm, or by venomous poison.'

So as she spoke, in her arms immortal she took him, and clasped him

Unto her fragrant bosom: the mother was gladdened in spirit.

" So Demophoön, glorious son of the valorous Keleos,

Whom Metaneira had borne, by Demeter was reared in the palace.

Like to a god he throve, for he drew not milk from his mother,

Neither of bread did he eat, but with ambrosia Demeter

Ever anointed the child, like one that a god had begotten,

Breathing sweetly upon him, and holding him close to her bosom.

Every night in the fire like a brand she covered him over.

This his affectionate parents knew not: and greatly they marvelled,

Since so stately he grew, and like to the gods was his semblance.

She would have made him immortal as well, and ageless for ever:

But by her folly the mother, fair-robed Metaneira, prevented,

Watching by night, and peering forth from her odorous chamber.

Then upon both her thighs she smote, and shrieked in her terror,

—Such was her fear for her son,—and was utterly frenzied
in spirit.

Then she lamented aloud, and in wingèd words she addrest
him :

'Child of mine, Demophoön, surely the stranger has hid
thee

Deep in the fire, and bitterest trouble and grief she has
caused me.'

So in her sorrow aloud she spoke,—and the goddess had
heard her.

Then in her wrath at the mother, the fair-crowned goddess
Demeter

Threw to the earth from her arms immortal that infant
belovèd,

Plucking him forth from the fire, in spirit exceedingly
wrathful."

We, however, can hardly blame the mother's
fears. Though the long hymn is little more
than half rendered, this is perhaps as good a
point as any to break off: the more as in the
latter portion the text is in bad condition, while
the story follows a more conventional form of
the familiar myth. At least, there is less of the
peculiarly tender human sympathy so noticeable
in the earlier portions. Demeter, departing from
the palace in all her divine majesty, bids the

Eleusinians erect a temple in her honour. Within it she takes up her abode, refusing her presence and blessing to gods or men.

> "Many the ploughs that in vain by the oxen were drawn in the corn-land,
> Vainly into the earth white barley was cast in abundance."

After all the gods had come to plead with her, to no purpose, Zeus is forced to send and bid Pluto release Persephone. Here we have—for the first time—the familiar incident of the pomegranate seed slily divided by Pluto with the unwilling guest. It seems like an allusion to some usage by which the voluntary sharing of food by the bride under her lord's roof is to be considered as an essential consummation of wedlock. Persephone must, therefore, spend one part of the year with her husband in the nether gloom, but may tarry two parts above in the sunshine. These are, of course, the *three* seasons of the year, as the Greeks distinguish them.

The "orgies," or mysteries, (naturally in the form ever after observed at Eleusis,) are now revealed by Demeter to the chief rulers of the

land,—among whom Triptolemos is barely mentioned. The nature of the ceremonial is not
indicated, indeed the divine injunction of absolute secrecy is emphatically repeated. That
the ceremonies were peculiarly efficacious, if not
essential to salvation, may be gathered from
these earnest words :—

"Blessed is he, whosoever of men on earth may behold
     them.
He who hath entered not, nor shared in the ritual, nowise
Equally happy his doom, when dead, in the terrible
     darkness " (vers. 481–483).

At once thereafter Demeter and her daughter
take their due places in the great Olympian
council.

"There they abide at the side of Zeus, who delighteth in
     thunder ;
Holy are they, and dread.   Most happy is he whosoever
Dear to their hearts may become, among men who on
     earth have abiding.
Quickly they send him,—to dwell in his stately home at
     his hearthside,—
Plutus, who is the giver of wealth unto men that are
     mortal " (vers. 486–490).

The long hymn ends—as does the first Olympian ode of Pindar—with a note of modest consciousness that the singer deserves his reward.

> " Come, oh thou who protectest the folk of fragrant Eleusis,
>   —Rock-bound Antron, too, and Paros girt by the waters,—
> Thou and thy daughter as well, most beautiful Persephoneia,
> Kindly accord, in return for my singing, a life of contentment.
>   —Yet I of you not alone, but of other song will be mindful" (vers. 491–496).

Thus the poem closes, like so many of these Hymns or Preludes, with a transitional note. In this case, however, we can hardly accept the suggestion, and may be tempted to cancel the last verse. Surely this poem of five hundred hexameter lines is too stately, and too absorbing in interest, to have been merely a prelude to the epic recital that should follow.

VII.

HEXAMETER IN THE HANDS OF THE PHILOSOPHERS.

(XENOPHANES, PARMENIDES, EMPEDOCLES.)

AMONG the early Greek philosophers there were at least three, each of whom in succession used the hexameter verse, and epic dialect, for his poem on the origin and nature of things. At any rate, all three poems bore among later Greeks the title, Περὶ Φύσεως, of which Lucretius' caption, "De Rerum Naturâ," may be considered a translation. The earliest of the trio, Xenophanes, was a native of Colophon in Asia Minor, one of Homer's earlier birthplaces. Moreover, Xenophanes is said to have celebrated the founding of his native city, as well as the comparatively recent colonization of Elea in Italy, in brief epic poems. While Xenophanes thus shows himself a true Homerid, he will require mention elsewhere also as an elegiac poet of moderate powers. His hexameter verses still surviving make but a handful of fragments, the most famous of which is by no means in a subservient tone toward the great heads of the school :—

" Everything is ascribed to the gods by Hesiod and Homer,
  Whatsoever among mankind is shameful and wicked.
  Numberless lawless deeds of the gods by them are recorded,
  Thievishness, unchastity, ay, and deceit of each other ! "

To the whole anthropomorphic conception of the divine nature this philosopher offers fearless and scornful opposition :—

" Still men hold the belief that the gods were born and
    begotten,
  Wear such garb as themselves, and have like bodies, and
    voices, . . .
  Yet it is certain, if hands were bestowed upon oxen or
    lions,
  If with their hands they could draw, and the works of
    men should accomplish,—
  Horses like unto horses, and oxen in likeness of oxen,
  So would they draw their figures of gods, and fashion the
    bodies
  Like in every way to their own ! "

Passages are often quoted, however, from Xenophanes, as if they proved a pure monotheistic philosophy, which hardly require that interpretation. Thus, even the devout Aeschylos might apply to his own Zeus, without misgiving, such words as—

"There is a single god, amid gods most mighty, and mortals,
    Nowise like unto men in outward form, nor in spirit."

Even his own assertions, upon superhuman themes, the sage would bid us receive with a grain of agnosticism :—

" Truth itself no man hath attained, nor shall he attain it,
    Neither as to the gods, nor all whereof I am speaking.
    Yea, though what he shall utter may seem most perfect
        and finished,
    Yet he himself knows not : for opinion is ruler in all
        things."

Still, to the patient waiting student of to-day, there comes a cheery word from this far pioneer of thought—

" Nowise all was revealed by the gods at the first unto
        mortals,
    But in the course of time, by seeking, they better discover."

We have still a few reminders, also, from him,

that the stately epic verse could bend to more
familiar tones :—

" Thus it is fitting to speak, in the winter time, by the
    fireside,
  When we have eaten our fill, on a soft divan are reclining,
  Quaffing the mellow wine, and meantime munching the
    sweetmeats :
  ' Who among men art thou, and thy years how many,
    good fellow ? ' "

There could hardly be a clearer glimpse of the
unhesitating hospitality—spiced with a lively
curiosity—which, as the old Assians will all
testify, is not yet a lost virtue among Asiatic
Greeks. Most of the more familiar tones of
Xenophanes must be reserved for the later volume
in which we shall hope to treat the elegiac movement with the rest of the Greek lyric. We must
attempt, however, even here, to echo that elusive
rhythm for a single quatrain, if only to let the
hale old poet and wandering scholar answer the
question which his host just put him :—

" ' Seven and sixty years already I widely have wandered,
  Through the Hellenic land strewing the seed of my
    thought.

Twenty the years of my life ere that, and five in addition,
   If I am able to speak truthfully as to my age.' "

Lucian practically vouches for the veracity of
this tale of years, including Xenophanes among
his " Macrobioi," or long-lived folk, with a crown
of one and ninety winters. His death was probably late in the sixth century B.C.; but for a
biography of him little or no data remain.

Since Xenophanes is called the founder of the
Eleatic school of philosophy, he doubtless spent
many years, either as a colonist and citizen, or at
least as an honoured guest, in the Italian city.
Here, in Elea, also, Parmenides was born, about
500 B.C. The Platonic Socrates speaks with awe
of his venerable figure, as a far memory from his
own Athenian boyhood. Like his predecessor,
Parmenides was chiefly interested in seeking the
sources and limitations of scientific knowledge.
His great poem, or treatise in verse, was a frigid
allegory, wherein Sophia (Wisdom), entertaining
the philosopher in her rather gloomy stronghold,
delivered an interminable lecture under two chief
heads : viz. Truth ; and the false opinions of her
among men, based on the deceptive order of her

own words. We shall be quite content to tran-
scribe merely the exordium from this Johnsonian
flight of the Muse! Even the famous introduction is too confused, and too heavy, to be fully
and faithfully rendered. It seems probable that
the transcribers are to blame, in part, for the
confused clauses and the wearisome repetitions.
But Parmenides himself sags heavily in poetic
flight. *E.g.* the verb "bear" ($\phi\acute{\epsilon}\rho\omega$) occurs in
the first and fourth verses, and in the fifth line
twice!

"Steeds that bore me along, so far as my spirit might
  venture,
  Since they had carried me into the far-famed path of the
    goddess,
  Even of her who in all things guideth the wise unto
    knowledge. . . .
  There I arrived, since thither the horses of thought had
    conveyed me,
  Whirling the chariot on : and maidens guided my journey
  Unto the light, unwinding the veils that had covered their
    foreheads :
  Maidens, Helios' daughters, who came from the dwelling
    of darkness.
  There are the gates whence issue the paths of Night and
    of Daylight.

Stone their threshold, and stone is a lintel also above them.

Yet is the gateway lofty, and fitted with ponderous portals.

Justice, a mighty avenger, possesses the keys that unloose
them.

Then did the maidens beseeching with gentle voices
persuade her

Skilfully, begging that she would draw back the bolt of
the portal. . . .

Heartily there did the goddess receive me. She with her
right hand

Clasped mine own, as she spoke these words : and thus
she addrest me :

' Youth, who with charioteers immortal art come a com-
panion,

Thou who, by horses drawn, art arrived at my habitation,

Welcome ! and nowise evil the destiny hither that brings
thee.

Verily far from the tracks of men is the ˙path thou hast
followed.' "

Any eager interest we would fain feel in
Sophia's lecture is heavily drugged by her own
prompt avowal, that it matters not at what point
she may begin, since she must return perpetually
to the one essential thought. This her favourite
goal is, moreover, the most unpoetic, if philosophic, truth, that Existence and Non-existence
are absolutely diverse !

We may well imagine that the sway of hexameter was tyrannous, when such a man moulded such material into dactylic verse. In truth, he undoubtedly did so simply because he neither found prepared for him, nor was able to devise, any easier form in which to give his thought a permanent expression. Any other regular rhythm would have been yet more unfamiliar and recalcitrant: artistic prose was not yet developed.

Still, even Parmenides is a Greek, and co-heir of his Hellenic artistic inheritance. So even from his lips the rhythm is heard, unmistakably, though in monotonous and breathless fashion. The thought, too, or rather the phrase, already shaped to his hand by centuries of artists, insists upon being poetical at times, in spite of him. It is through a single verse, however, and that, too, sober enough in its intention, that Parmenides lives for poets and lovers of sentiment :—

"Eros before all other divinities first she created."

The subject of the verb was, as Plato indicates, Genesis (Creative power), or, according to another authority, Aphrodite—which in Parmenides' transparent allegory would probably mean much the same. It will be at once remembered that the atheistic Lucretius actually begins his rigidly materialistic account of creation with a splendid invocation of Venus. No doubt she, also, was but the poetic personification of creative force, yet Lucretius' irrepressible imagination, spurred apparently by national pride as well, makes the mother of Aeneas very real for us, if not for him.

To Parmenides' barren Eleatic philosophy we need not return, since it is only as a far and rather feeble disciple of the Homeric school in verse that he appears here at all.

Moreover, the last of our philosophic trio is a figure infinitely more brilliant and imposing. Indeed, among all the thronging figures of the past there are few characters more picturesque, few whom we would more gladly summon forth from the shades to respond to our eager question-ing—than Empedocles of Acragas: "Empedocles of Aetna"!

Lucretius, chief of surviving didactic and philo-sophic poets, takes occasion to refer to Empedocles (De Rerum Naturâ, i. 717 ff.) in noble and famous lines. Among all the wonders Sicily has produced, he says, " naught is more illustrious or holy, nothing more wondrous and precious, than this man. His poems moreover," Lucretius declares, "utter and expound his glorious discoveries, so that he seems hardly sprung of human stock." This characterization is evidently just. Empedocles the philosopher scarcely concerns us here, though by his discovery, if such we may call it, of the four elements, he became the father of all later ancient and even mediaeval science. But he was, above all else, as Lucretius indicates, a true poet. The four hundred and eighty hexameters which have been preserved suffice to reveal his high creative imagination, as well as the splendid march of his verse. Indeed his poem, if extant entire, would perhaps overshadow Lucretius' great work.

Empedocles' life was cast in the fifth century B.C.—the golden age of historical Greece,—and chiefly in the Sicilian city of Acragas or, as the Romans called it, Agrigentum. He evidently enjoyed hereditary wealth, as the grandfather whose name he bore won the four-horse chariot race at Olympia, probably about the time of the poet's birth, in the first decade of the fifth century.   Twenty years later, Empedocles' father, Meton, was a leader in expelling the Agrigentine tyrant Thrasidaeus.   Still later, after Meton's death, we are told, the royal power was offered to the poet, and by him refused.   Subsequently he became unpopular, went into exile, and probably died, like Dante, without ever seeing again the city of his birth.

Even so much as this we must piece together from late and often discordant statements.   The grave and haughty spirit clearly revealed in his poems would naturally bring him into conflict with the ignobler ideas of the folk: but no connected thread of biography can now be traced. The most famous incident of all is the familiar one of his death: that he secretly leaped into the crater of Aetna, in order that his disciples might believe he had been miraculously translated from earth.   The legend adds, that the volcano mocked him by throwing out one of his sandals, thus exposing the trick.   This irony of Fate doubtless betrays the romantic origin of the

legend itself, which Matthew Arnold has hardly
succeeded in vivifying.

Empedocles was without doubt a leader of
mystics, but it seems equally true—as true as
of Plato, of Swedenborg, or of Emerson—that he
was his own first and sincerest believer. In
particular, the lines in which he declares his
recollections of immortality, and of a more blest
divine existence, are as earnest as anything in
Plato or in Wordsworth.

" There is a doom of fate, an ancient decree of immortals,
　Never to be unmade, by amplest pledges attested :
　That, if a spirit divine, who shares in the life everlasting,
　Through transgression defiles his glorious body by blood-
　　　shed,
　Or if he perjure himself by swearing unto a falsehood,
　Thrice ten thousand seasons he wanders apart from the
　　　Blessèd,
　Passing from birth unto birth through every species of
　　　mortal ;
　Changing ever the paths of life, yet ever unresting :
　Even as I now roam, from gods far-wandered, an exile,
　Yielding to maddening strife."

These, as Plutarch and others testify, are the
opening lines in the Prelude of Empedocles'

great poem on Nature.   Other and briefer fragments continue the same train of thought.

> "Once already have I as a youth been born, as a maiden,
>   Bush, and wingèd bird, and silent fish in the waters. . . .
>   After what honours, and after how long and blissful
>   existence,
>   Thus am I wretchedly doomed to abide in the meadows of
>   mortals !
>   Loudly I wept and wailed at beholding the place un-
>   familiar . . .
>   . . . Joyless the place, where
>   Murder abides and Strife, with the other races of Troubles."

Indeed the belief in transmigration, which we are wont to associate especially with the Pythagorean teachings, is nowhere more earnestly and vividly expressed than by Empedocles. The conviction that man's soul is a fallen exile from a higher diviner sphere, to which he may hope to return only after long purgatorial atonement in earthly incarnations—all this has been even more magnificently elaborated in Platonic dialogues like the Phaedrus and the Phaedo; but Plato himself may well owe much of his loftiest inspiration to this Sicilian seer.

The theory of the four elements is clearly stated in a three-line fragment of the same Prelude :—

" Hearken and learn, that four, at the first, are the sources
    of all things :
Fire, and water, and earth, and lofty ether unbounded.
Thence springs all that is, that shall be, or hath been
    aforetime."

Empedocles seems to have rivalled Lucretius himself in the picturesque vividness of his similes. Here, for instance, is an attempt to illustrate how the manifold forms of the visible world might well arise from the mingling of · these few elements.

" Just as men who the painter's craft have thoroughly
    mastered
 Fashion in many a tint their picture, an offering sacred ;
 When they have taken in hand their paints of various
    colours,
 Mingling skilfully more of the one and less of another,
 Out of these they render the figures like unto all things ;
 Trees they cause to appear, and the semblance of men and
    of women,
 Beasts of the field, and birds, and fish that inhabit the
    waters,
 Even the gods whose honours are greatest, whose life is
    unending :

—Be not deceived, for such, and nowise other, the
    fountain
Whence all mortals spring, whatever their races un-
    numbered."

Incidentally we see clearly, that, while the
painter's art has made many a stride from
Homer's time to Empedocles' day, yet "Art is
still religion;" the masterpiece is (as a matter
of course) an *anathema*, an altar-piece.

Among the other fragments of the Proem is
the singular invocation of the Muse, which is
most difficult to turn into English verse, as it
demands absolute faithfulness in rendering. It
may be confessed, too, that the poetic quality
is rather disappointing. Unlike most transcen-
dental philosophers, Empedocles insists that
men—at least, other men, if not himself—must
rely simply and solely on the evidence of their
senses concerning all material things. Moreover,
despite his hatred of Strife, he has evidently just
indulged in rather strong polemic, probably
against those who profess to teach more than
man may know; for the invocation begins
thus :—

" Only do ye, oh gods, remove from my tongue their mad-
　　ness;
　Make ye to flow from a mouth that is holy a fountain
　　unsullied.
　Thou, oh white-armed Virgin, the Muse who rememberest
　　all things,
　Whatsoe'er it is lawful to utter to men that are mortal
　Bring me, from Piety driving a chariot easily-guided."

It is clear, from many such passages, that
Empedocles claimed for himself not merely a
poetic inspiration, but an absolutely superhuman
nature. It is not easy to find anywhere a more
magnificent and sublime egotism than his. The
most famous passage of this character is not from
his great work on Nature (or Creation), but is
found in the " Katharmoi " (Poems of Purifica-
tion) :—

" Oh, my friends, whoso in Acragas' beautiful city
　Have your dwelling aloft, whose hearts are set upon
　　virtue,
　Reverent harbours of guests, who have no share in dis-
　　honour,
　Greeting! But I as a god divine, no longer a mortal,
　Dwell with you, by all in reverence held, as is fitting,
　Girt with fillets about, and crowned with wreaths of re-
　　joicing.

Whatsoever the folk whose prosperous cities I enter,
There I of women and men am revered. By thousands
they follow,
Questioning where they may seek for the path that leadeth
to profit.
These are in need of prophetic words ; and others, in illness,
Since they have long been racked with the grievous pangs
of diseases,
Crave that I utter the charm whose power is sovran in all
things.
—Yet, pray, why lay stress upon this, as were it a marvel
If I surpass mankind, who are mortal and utterly
wretched ?"

The scientific discoveries of Empedocles seem
really to have been, like those of Paracelsus,
much in advance of his age. As for his attempt
to retrace the processes of creation, much in it,
of course, seems to us crude and even childish.
There are indications, however, that he saw more
clearly than his Roman pupil the great distinction
between *matter* and *force*. He would, perhaps,
hardly have thought of sound, and heat or cold,
as delicate *substances* piercing through the pores
of coarser matter—a belief Lucretius teaches and
adorns with most exquisite imagery ! Empedocles certainly did assert, however, that all

bodies actually give off "films," or thin images of themselves, which, striking the human eye, produce the effect of sight. Still, many such apparently crude statements may have been largely dictated by the tyranny of poetic diction, and the lack, as yet, of any scientific terminology.

The preservation of so considerable a mass of verse from Empedocles—and from him only— among all the early philosophers, is doubtless a tribute, even if only a half-conscious one, to his high poetic quality. That alone, or at least chiefly, not his philosophic system, concerns us here, as has already been remarked. This body of verse would, however, make an excellent subject for an English monograph by a classical scholar with scientific interests.

EPILOGUE.

THE preceding chapters have measurably covered that mass of poetry which may properly be described as "Homeric" in dialect, metre, and, perhaps, in general spirit, and which was created in the centuries from the completion of the Odyssey down to the middle of the Attic period— let us say from 800 to 400 B.C. Many other poems are mentioned, or even quoted, in later authors, which may have deserved inclusion here; but they are of uncertain date and unknown character, surviving only in the scantiest fragments. It has not been thought best to mention them at all in so general a view.

The history of the hexameter by no means ends at this point. The important revival of archaic epic in Alexandria, the bucolic school of

Theocritus, and, in general, the later developments, we may, perhaps, hope to discuss hereafter. Its prevailing use in epitaphs shows that the hexameter was always familiar and beloved, as might be expected among a people for whom Homer so long remained almost a Bible. Many Athenians, for instance, knew the whole Iliad and Odyssey by heart, and the Platonic Socrates employs a Homeric phrase or an archaic word, such as "the forceless heads of the dead," for local colour, as a modern English essayist uses "fardels," or "still-vext Bermoothes."

The body of post-Homeric verse described in the present volume never attained the same popularity; nor is the chief cause far to seek. The Iliad and Odyssey present on the whole a picture almost as remote from historic Hellas as it is from us. There may or may not have been in earlier ages such figures as Achilles and Hector, Helen and Nausicaa; but at any rate their chariots and their chivalry were as unrelated to the actual daily experience of Lysias and Isocrates as to that of Burke and Pitt. Hence their supreme charm. They make, and

they have always made, a resistless appeal to
the imagination.

" Ewig jung allein ist Phantasie."

Homer, too, sang, apparently, for the pure de-
light of singing. Any ethical impulse or meaning
is forgotten, or merged, in the delineation of truly
beautiful and heroic figures or scenes. True art
may unconsciously teach as much as you please,
but it must not consciously preach!

The mass of poetry here treated is, on the
contrary, philosophic, didactic, self-conscious, and,
in the intention at least, largely realistic. Even
the Prometheus Firebearer of Hesiod was a part
of the regular Attic belief and cult. The maxims
of the Works and Days were fitted for the
practical guidance of the peasant at his plough,
and the trader on the sea. The Hymns were
doubtless in actual use, at least locally, in oft-
recurring rituals and at stated festival-times.
Even in discussing the very early Delian hymn,
we had occasion to remark upon the local and
personal, even egotistical, tone which makes it
distinctly un-Homeric. In some cases the very

text of these works has probably suffered severely because of this very nearness to contemporary life. The Iliad we read, doubtless, essentially as Pisistratus read it. It was already an heirloom from an earlier Hellas, not to be rudely touched or added to by alien hands. But into the Works and Days, as into the corpus of Theognis' didactic poetry, almost any commonplace or maxim could be introduced.

Nevertheless, it is believed the subject-matter of this little volume has a unity, an interest, and, in particular, a close dependence on the masterpieces of Ionic epic, justifying its treatment under the title here chosen. It is less alive, less essential to the comprehension of the age in which it arose, than the Greek lyric of the same centuries. The tantalizing and, on the whole, scanty remains of that lyric, from Callinus to Simonides, would require at least another volume like the present one.

FINIS.